GUIDE TO
RURAL
WALES

Published by:
Travel Publishing Ltd
7a Apollo House, Calleva Park
Aldermaston, Berks, RG7 8TN
ISBN 1-902-00773-5
© Travel Publishing Ltd

Country Living is a registered trademark of The National
Magazine Company Limited.

First Published: *2002*

COUNTRY LIVING GUIDES:

East Anglia	The West Country
The South East of England	Wales
The South of England	

PLEASE NOTE:

All advertisements in this publication have been accepted in good faith by
Travel Publishing and they have not necessarily been endorsed by *Country
Living* Magazine.

All information is included by the publishers in good faith and is believed
to be correct at the time of going to press. No responsibility can be
accepted for errors.

Editor:	Peter Long
Printing by:	Scotprint, Haddington
Location Maps:	© Maps in Minutes ™ (2002) © Crown Copyright, Ordnance Survey 2002
Walk Maps:	Reproduced from Ordnance Survey mapping on behalf of the Controller of Her Majesty's Stationery Office, © Crown Copyright. Licence Number MC 100035812
Cover Design:	Lines & Words, Aldermaston
Cover Photo:	Nant Ffrancon Pass, Snowdon, Gwynedd: © www.britainonview.com
Text Photos:	Text photos have been kindly supplied by the Britain on View photo library and the Welsh Tourist Board photo library © www.britainonview.com © Welsh Tourist Board

Foreword

The Principality of Wales contains many gems. Best known are the Brecon Beacons and Snowdonia, but the Gower Peninsula and Pembrokeshire are also stunning - while Cardigan Bay, the Lleyn Peninsula and Anglesey are each a Mecca for birdwatchers. In Mid-Wales, the least-populated part of England and Wales, you can explore the Elan Valley, a wilderness of lakes, mountains and moors where you can walk all day without meeting a soul, surrounded by some of the most spectacular scenery imaginable.

Each month, *Country Living Magazine* celebrates the richness and diversity of our countryside with features on rural Britain and the traditions that have their roots there. So it is with great pleasure that I introduce you to the latest in our series of our *Guides to Rural Britain*.

I hope that whether you live in Wales, are already a frequent visitor or are considering crossing the border for the first time, you will find plenty to inform and entertain you in this book. Use it as a directory of places to stay, eat and drink, learn about local heritage and history, and search out regional producers of food, arts and crafts. Above all, relax and enjoy the wide open spaces and the warm welcome you will receive.

Susy Smith

Susy Smith, Editor of Country Living *Magazine*

PS To subscribe to Country Living *Magazine each month, call 01858 438844.**

Introduction

This is the third *Country Living Magazine* rural guide edited by Peter Long, an experienced travel writer who spent many years with Egon Ronay's Hotel and Restaurant Guides before joining the Travel Publishing team. As with the East Anglian and South of England editions Peter has ensured that *The Country Living Magazine Guide to Rural Wales* is packed with vivid descriptions, historical stories, amusing anecdotes and interesting facts on hundreds of places in this wonderful Celtic country which is blessed with dramatic landscapes, a rich cultural heritage and an eventful industrial past.

The coloured advertising panels within each chapter provide further information on places to see, stay, eat, drink, shop and even exercise! We have also selected a number of walks from Jarrold's Pathfinder Guides which we highly recommend if you wish to appreciate fully the beauty and charm of the varied rural landscapes of Wales.

The guide however is not simply an "armchair tour". Its prime aim is to encourage the reader to visit the places described and discover much more about the wonderful towns, villages and countryside of Wales. Whether you decide to explore this country by wheeled transport or by foot we are sure you will find it a very uplifting experience.

We are always interested in receiving comments on places covered (or not covered) in our guides so please do not hesitate to use the reader reaction form provided at the rear of this guide to give us your considered comments. This will help us refine and improve the content of the next edition. We also welcome any general comments which will help improve the overall presentation of the guides themselves.

Finally, for more information on the full range of travel guides published by Travel Publishing please refer to the details and order form at the rear of this guide or log on to our website at www.travelpublishing.co.uk

Travel Publishing

Locator Map

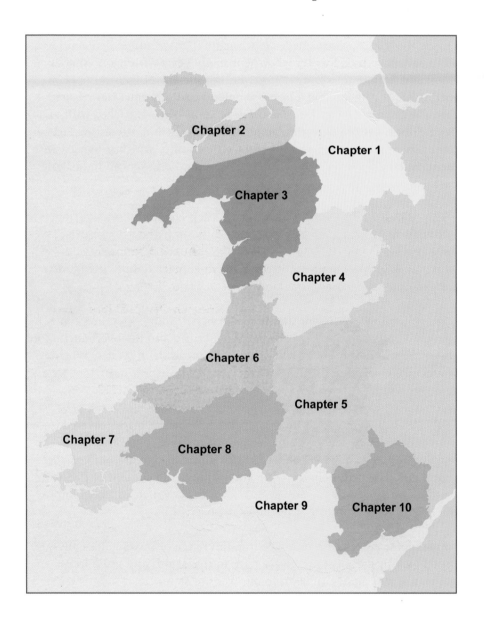

Contents

YMDDIRIEDOLAETHAU

natur CYMRU

THE WILDLIFE TRUSTS

WALES

THE WILDLIFE TRUSTS

The Wildlife Trusts in Wales are part of a UK wide movement of 47 trusts, which include all English counties plus individual bodies for the Isles of Scilly, Isle of Man, Scotland and Ulster. The Wildlife Trusts are supported by nearly 400,000 members and manage over 2300 nature reserves covering an area of 80,000 hectares. Of these 49 are National Nature Reserves.

In Wales there are 6 trusts; North Wales, Montgomeryshire, Radnorshire, Brecknock, Gwent, and South and West Wales.

The Wildlife Trusts are also core-partners in the Environment Wales Initiative.

IN WALES:

- The trusts manage 224 nature reserves of 5,440 hectares of which 2,000 hectares are Sites of Special Scientific Interest and 7 are National Nature Reserves.

- Sixty staff work with over 800 regular volunteers in various roles which leads to the protection of wildlife in town and countryside.

- Collectively the work of the Wildlife Trusts in Wales is estimated to be worth £850,000 per annum for nature conservation.

- Over 16,000 people in Wales belong to their local Wildlife Trust.

- There are 40 Watch Groups throughout Wales and more than 500 children regularly take part in activities in Wales.

WHY THE WILDLIFE TRUSTS?

Unlike other organisations the Wildlife Trusts are the only body looking after all forms of wildlife and do so by involving people at the most local level.

The Wildlife Trusts do not only concentrate on reserves. We also:

- Get involved in wider countryside issues including planning.
- Give advice to landowners and farmers on wildlife issues.
- Operate Lifelong Learning programmes for children and adults.
- Encourage local communities to care for wildlife in their area.
- Run a substantial programme of local events.

This area of Wales, the North Wales Borderlands, can easily be overlooked by visitors to the country as they speed westwards, but it is mistake not to stop and explore the towns, villages and countryside, as they are rich in history and scenic beauty. Each of the different areas has its own special character and scenery: the Clwydian Hills, a 22-mile designated Area of Outstanding Natural Beauty; the Dee estuary; the broad, gentle sweep of the Vale of Clwyd with historic towns like Ruthin, St Asaph and Denbigh; Wrexham, the largest town in North Wales, and its surrounds; The Maelor, where the Cheshire Plains transform into the Welsh Hills; Chirk and the beautiful Ceiriog Valley. The Romans certainly forayed into the area from their major town of Chester and there is also evidence of Celtic settlements.

Vale Crucis Abbey

However, it was during the 13th century that Edward I, after his successful campaign against the Welsh, set about building his ambitious Iron Ring of huge fortresses along the Dee estuary and the North Wales coast. Each was built a day's march from the last and the first stronghold was begun at Flint in 1277. Though the great fortresses are now in ruins, the remains of this massive project - the largest seen in Europe - are still very much in evidence today. The land around the Dee estuary is home to a great number of waders and wildfowl which feed on the mudflats left by the retreating tides.

Between the estuary and the Clwydian Range lie small, compact villages as well as the market towns of Mold and Holywell, a place of pilgrimage that became known as the "Lourdes of Wales". The range, a grassy line of hills above the Vale of Clwyd, offers fabulous views and exhilarating walks; it is one of the five designated Areas of Outstanding Natural Beauty in

Wales (see Anglesey, the Gower Peninsula, the Llyn Peninsula and The Wye Valley in their respective chapters).

Further south lie Llangollen and the Dee Valley. Llangollen is a delightful old town in a picturesque riverside setting which is not only a charming place to visit but is also the home of the annual International Music Eisteddfod (not the same as the National Eisteddfod). An eisteddfod was, originally, a meeting of bards where prizes were awarded for poetry reading and singing and, while local events still draw people from all over the country, the event at Llangollen has a true international flavour with such eminent figures as Luciano Pavarotti having graced its stage.

Though this northern gateway to the country is not a particularly large area, it boasts all but one of

Alwen Reservoir, Clwyd

the Seven Wonders of Wales, wonders which while not quite as spectacular as the more familiar Seven Wonders of the World are nonetheless all interesting in their own right and well worth a visit. They are listed in the famous 19th century rhyme:

> *Pistyll Rhaeadr and Wrexham Steeple,*
> *Snowdon's Mountain without its people,*
> *Overton Yew Trees, St Winefride's Well,*
> *Llangollen Bridge and Gresford Bells.*

The Borderlands offer an impressive variety of attractions, from castles and country houses to churches and museums, country parks and farm parks, lakes and canals, and leisure pursuits from walking, cycling and riding to birdwatching, golf (more than 20 courses), and superb fishing for salmon and trout on the Rivers Dee and Clwyd, sea fishing in the Dee estuary and trout or coarse fishing at numerous lake fisheries. Festivals and other special events are staged throughout the year, and visitors to the area are welcome to attend many rehearsals as well as performances by the renowned Welsh choirs - a unique and moving occasion that will long be remembered as part of the Welsh experience.

LOCATOR MAP

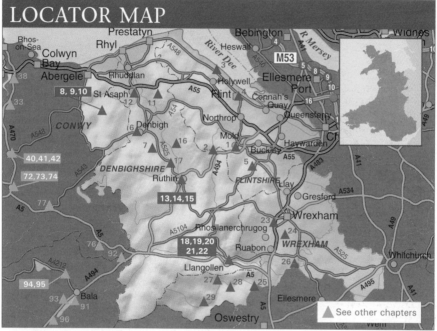

© MAPS IN MINUTES ™ 2002   © Crown Copyright, Ordnance Survey 2002

ADVERTISERS AND PLACES OF INTEREST

MOLD

The small county town of Flintshire, Mold is proud to claim the novelist and local tailor Daniel Owen as one of its own. Writing only in Welsh, it was Owen's honest accounts of ordinary life which were to not only make him one of the greatest 19th century novelists but also gained him the title the "Welsh Dickens". His statue stands outside the town library which is also the home of Mold's **Museum**, where a room is dedicated to Owen's memory. Another son of Mold was Richard Wilson, an 18th century landscape painter who spent his childhood in the town and who, after studying abroad, returned to his native Wales to concentrate on the dramatic scenes of mountainous Welsh countryside which became his trademark. Wilson's memorial can be found near the north entrance to the parish church.

Dating from the 15th century and built to celebrate Henry VII's victory at Bosworth, **St Mary's Church** has some interesting stained glass windows as well as some fine architectural ornamentation. A light and airy building, this church was constructed on the site of an earlier church whose original oak roof, carved with Tudor roses, has been retained in part. The church stands at the foot of **Bailey Hill**, the site of a Norman motte and bailey fortification which was built at this strategic point overlooking the River Alyn by Robert de Montalt. First captured by the Welsh in 1157 and then again by Llywelyn the Great in 1199, ownership of the castle passed through many hands and today, not surprisingly, little remains of the fortress; its site is now marked by a bowling green. The town owes its name to de Montalt, who

gave Mold its English name which, like the Welsh (Yr Wyddgrug), means "The Mound".

On the outskirts of Mold lies **Clwyd Theatre Cymru**, which offers a wide range of entertainment for the culturally hungry including theatre, music and frequent exhibitions of art, sculpture and photography. It has a bar, coffee shop, bookshop, free covered parking and disabled access. The composer Felix Mendelssohn was said to have been inspired by the town's surroundings when writing his opus *Rivulet* and the nearby limestone crags provide panoramic views over the surrounding countryside.

One such scenic area lies four miles from Mold on the A494 - **Loggerheads Country Park** (see below), which is

Moel Famau, Clwydian Range

situated on the edge of the Clwydian Range. Classified as an Area of Outstanding Natural Beauty, this large park is an ideal environment for all the family, especially younger members, as there are various trails which are each about one and a half miles long. The trails all start near the late-18th century mill building that used water from the River Alyn to drive a water wheel and

LOGGERHEADS COUNTRY PARK

Nr Mold, Denbighshire
Tel: 01352 810614 (call Vanessa)
websites: www.denbighshire.gov.uk or www.loggerheads.biz or www.fresh-air.info

Loggerheads Country Park is a popular visitor destination, attracting over 100,000 visitors every year. The New Countryside Centre gives visitors an insight in to the history and life within the Park and provides necessary information and an excellent learning opportunity. It is an established Rural Country Park set in a limestone

valley in the Clwydian Range Area of Outstanding Natural Beauty and encompasses a mining and tourism history. The

Park is also managed for conservation, with SSSI (Site of Special Scientific Interest) designation and rich and varied natural habitats.

The re-vamp of Loggerheads Country Park includes the design of the new Centre, described by one visitor as, "interactive, vibrant and fun and aimed at people of all ages, especially families." A new Discovery Trail gets visitors out and about in the park. They can see evidence of the history for themselves, along with abundant wildlife. Visitors also get the chance to become a Trail Detective and collect the secret symbols. New and improved bridges, signs, welcome board, and free events all year round, add to the experience, providing a fantastic day out for all the family.

two sets of stones to grind corn from the local farms.

Around 200 years ago, Loggerheads was part of the lead mining industry, which was founded in this area of ore-bearing limestone, and many relics of those days remain and can still be seen within the quiet woodland. There is a fine selection of local arts, crafts and souvenirs on display in the Craft Shop at the **Loggerheads Countryside Centre**, where there is also a tea room.

The smooth browned slopes of the **Clwydian Range** ascend from the broad and fertile planes of the Vale of Clwyd and **Moel Famau** (The Mother of Mountains), which at 1,820 feet is the range's highest peak. It is well worth the climb to the summit as not only are there the remains of a **Jubliee Tower**, started in 1810 to commemorate George III's Golden Jubilee (since blown down in a storm in 1852) but the panoramic views are breathtaking. Westwards lies the Vale of Clwyd with the river stretching down to the Irish Sea and, to the east, the land rolls gently down to the Dee estuary.

AROUND MOLD

Holywell
7 miles N of Mold on the A5026

In the town lies one of the Seven Wonders of Wales, **St Winefride's Well**, which was once a place of pilgrimage and, at one time, was referred to as "The Lourdes of Wales". According to tradition, Winefride, the niece of St Beuno, was beheaded by Prince Caradoc after refusing his advances. It is claimed that a spring gushed from the place where her head fell and that she returned to life after her head had been replaced by her uncle. Winefride (Gwenfrewi in Welsh) went on to

become an abbess at Gwytherin Convent near Llanrwst and, in 1138, her remains were given to Shrewsbury Cathedral. Caradoc was struck dead by lightning on the spot. Thought to have healing qualities, the well has been visited by pilgrims since the 7th century and still is, particularly on St Winefride's Day, the nearest Saturday to 22 June. The well, and the Vale of Clwyd, is beloved of the poet Gerard Manley Hopkins. He trained as a priest at St Beuno's College, Tremeirchion, and St Winefride's Well inspired him to write a verse tragedy, which contains many beautiful, evocative lines:

The dry dene, now no longer dry nor dumb, but moist and musical.
With the uproll and downcarol of day and night delivering water.

On Wales in general he was equally lyrical:

Lovely the woods, water, meadows, combes, vales,
All the air things wear that build this world of Wales.

St Winefride's Chapel was built by Margaret Beaufort (the mother of Henry VII) in around 1500 to enclose three sides of the well. The Victorian statue of St Winifred has a thin line round the neck showing where her head was cut off. Also here stands the **Church of St James**, the local parish church which was built in 1770 and it probably stands on the site of the original chapel which was constructed by St Beuno in the 7th century.

Linking Holywell with the ruins of Basingwerk Abbey is the **Greenfield Valley Heritage Park** (see panel opposite), a 70-acre area of pleasant woodland and lakeside walks with a wealth of monuments and agricultural and industrial history. There are animals to feed, an adventure playground and

GREENFIELD VALLEY HERITAGE PARK

Greenfield, Holywell, Flintshire CH8 7GH
Tel: 01352 714172 Fax: 01352 714791
website: www.greenfieldvalley.com

Referred to as the Borderlands best kept secret, the Greenfield Valley Heritage Park is one and a half miles of woodlands, reservoirs, ancient monuments and industrial history. The park is freely accessible year round attracting over 100,000 visitors per year. Within the Park is a Farm and Museum Complex with an attractive collection of original and reconstructed local buildings. A 16th century farmhouse, early 19th century cottage, blacksmith's forge, Victorian schoolroom and farm buildings provide an atmospheric backdrop to agricultural displays and exhibits. The museum holds events most weekends throughout the season. The whole site is a fascinating insight into times past.

There are farm animals to see and feed, an adventure playground and an indoor activity area. Facilities include a Visitor Centre, Environment Centre, free coach and car parking, toilets, cafe and gift shop. The museum and associated facilities are open from the beginning of April to the end of October.

picnic areas. In the 18th and 19th centuries this was a busy industrial area which concentrated on the newly established production processes for textiles, copper and brass. The trail through the park leads down towards the coast and to the ruins of **Basingwerk Abbey**. Built by Cistercian monks in 1132, the abbey functioned as a self-sufficient community: the Cistercians lay great emphasis upon agricultural labour. Although this was an English house, Basingwerk absorbed Welsh culture and the Welsh bard, Gutun Owain, was associated with the abbey from where he wrote *The Chronicle of Princes*, which is also known as the *Black Book of Basingwerk*.

The abbey survived until the Dissolution of the Monasteries in the 16th century by Henry VIII. In a tranquil setting that contrasts with the busy roads not far away, this magnificent ruin contains an arch which, despite weather beaten columns and faded "message of love", is a fine example of Norman ecclesiastical architecture. In one of the buildings the remains of timber beams can be seen that once supported a roof.

FLINT

5 miles N of Mold on the A5119

A small and modest town that was once the port for Chester, Flint can boast two historical firsts: it was the first

OAKENHOLT FARM COUNTRY GUEST HOUSE

Chester Road, Flint, North Wales CH6 5SD
Tel/Fax: 01352 733264 e-mail: jenny@oakenholt.freeserve.co.uk
website: www.smoothhound.co.uk

The Hulme family offer a warm and friendly welcome to **Oakenholt Farm Country Guest House**, a spacious Grade II listed farmhouse in lovely open countryside. The accommodation (all non-smoking) comprises seven en suite rooms, singles, doubles, twins or family rooms, all with central heating, tv, radio-alarm and refreshment tray. There's a large guest lounge, and an elegant dining room that overlooks the garden. The day begins with a substantial farmhouse breakfast, and evening meals are served by arrangement. Self catering is also available.

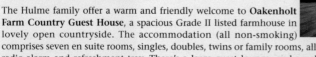

associated borough in Wales to receive a charter (in 1284) and it was also the site of the first of Edward I's Iron Ring fortresses. Dotted along the North Wales coast, a day's march apart, Edward I's ring of massive fortresses represented Europe's most ambitious and concentrated medieval building project. Started after the Treaty of Aberconwy in 1277 and completed in 1284 by James of St George, **Flint Castle**, now in ruins, stands on a low rock overlooking the coastal marshes of the Dee estuary towards the Wirral peninsula. Originally surrounded by a water-filled moat, the remains of the Great Tower, or Donjon, are an impressive sight. Set apart from the main part of the castle, this tower, which is unique among British castles, was intended as a last retreat and, to this end, it was fully self-sufficient, even having its own well.

Flint Castle featured in the downfall of Richard II, when he was lured here in 1399 from the relative safety of Conwy Castle and was captured by Henry Bolingbroke, the Duke of Lancaster and future Henry IV. The imprisonment of Richard here is remembered in Shakespeare's *Richard II*, where, in response to Bolingbroke's, "My gracious Lord, I come but for mine own," the defeated Richard replies, "Your own is yours, and I am yours, and all." At this point even the King's faithful greyhound is said to have deserted him.

During the Civil War, the town and castle remained in Royalist hands, under the leadership of Sir Roger Mostyn, until 1647, when both were taken by General Mytton, who was also responsible for dismantling the castle into the ruins we see today.

Clwyddian Hills

HALKYN
4½ miles N of Mold on the B5123

The village lies close to the long ridge of the **Halkyn Mountains**, which rise to some 964 feet at their highest point and are scarred by the remnants of ancient lead mines and quarries, some of which date back to Roman times.

RHOSESMOR
3 miles N of Mold on the B5123

Moel Y Gaer, near this small village, was considered to be a fine example of an Iron Age hill fort until archaeological digs unearthed evidence that suggested this site had been inhabited from as far back as 3500 BC.

To the west of the Rhosesmor lie the remains of a short section of **Wat's Dyke**, a much shorter dyke than Offa's which is thought to have been built by the Mercian King Aethelbald in the 8th century. Just under 40 miles long, the dyke ran southwards from the Dee estuary to Oswestry.

EWLOE
4 miles E of Mold on the B5125

Hidden in a steeply wooded glen area is the remains of **Ewloe Castle**, the

MARY JANE NEEDLEWORK STUDIO

Tri Thy, Tir y Fron Lane, Pontybodkin, Nr Mold, Flintshire CH7 4TU
Tel: 01352 771359 Fax: 01352 771881
e-mail: mary@maryjanecollection.co.uk
website: www.maryjanecollection.co.uk

Norma Restall and her daughters Mary and Jane are specialists in embroidery kits, all designed and made in-house. **Mary Jane Needlework Studio**, which Norma established in 1980, is part of a cluster of buildings on the western slopes of Hope Mountain, signposted off the A5104 12 miles southwest of Chester. Their embroidery designs, based upon country flowers and country living and inspired by the picturesque setting, include crewel work, blackwork, goldwork, cross-stitch, and stumpwork needlework accessory kits.

Their special Jubilee design, featuring the four national emblems

of Tudor rose, daffodil, thistle and shamrock, has been a great success at home and overseas, and was chosen to be included in a major mail order catalogue in the USA. In the studio shop is a vast stock of threads of all kinds, silk ribbons, charms, button embellishments and Mill Hill beads, as well as their own kits and charts. Mother and daughters all teach at the studio, running day courses and weekly sessions covering all forms of needlework and for all levels of ability. Within the courtyard of the old farm, a barn has been converted into a delightful two-bedroom cottage for self-catering accommodation.

fortification which was originally an English stronghold until it fell into the hands of the Welsh in around 1146. Owain Gwynedd set about strengthening the fortress as an ambush castle ready to surprise the soldiers of Edward I on their march through Wales when the battle of Ewloe took place in 1157. Some 150 years later, a tower, two wards protected by a curtain wall and an outer ditch were added but the castle failed to live up to expectations, particularly after the construction of nearby Flint Castle, and by the late 13th century Ewloe Castle ceased to have any military significance.

HAWARDEN

5 miles E of Mold on the A550

Mentioned in the Domesday Book, this small village close to the English border has two castles: one a ruin dating from the 13th century and another that was

once the home of the Victorian Prime Minister, William Gladstone.

Harwarden Castle, Gladstone's home for some 60 years after his marriage to the daughter of Sir Stephen Glynne in 1839, was started in 1750 and enlarged and castellated by Sir Stephen in 1809. The remains, chiefly the circular keep and the hall, of the older castle still stand in **Castle Park**.

The parish church, as well as having stained glass windows by Burne-Jones, also houses the **Gladstone Memorial Chapel**, where marble effigies of the distinguished statesman and his wife, who are buried in Westminster Abbey, can be seen. The village's connections with Gladstone continue to this day as the former Prime Minister donated his collection of books to the famous **St Deinol's Residential Library**, which lies adjacent to the church.

Continued on page 12

WALK 1

Hawarden Park

Start	Hawarden
Distance	5½ miles (8.9km)
Approximate time	2½ hours
Parking	Hawarden, Tinkersdale car park
Refreshments	Pubs at Hawarden, pub at Old Warren
Ordnance Survey maps	Landranger 117 (Chester & Wrexham), Pathfinder 773, SJ26/36 (Mold & Chester (West))

From many parts of this easy and attractive walk, close to the English border, there are fine views of Deeside and across Hawarden Park to the ruins of the medieval "Old Castle" and its successor, the "New Castle", once the home of the great Victorian statesman William Gladstone. Much of the last part of the route runs through the delightful Bilberry Wood alongside the wall of the park.

Turn right out of the car park and at a crossroads in the village centre, turn right along Glynne Way. Take the first lane on the left, Cross Tree Lane, and at a public footpath sign, turn right Ⓐ on to a path, between a wall on the right and a wire fence on the left, that runs along the edge of school grounds. Ahead are views over Deeside.

Where the fence on the left ends, keep ahead along the right edge of a field, pass through a gap, initially continue along the left edge of the next field but later bear right across it to a waymarked stile. Climb it, turn left along the left edge of a field, climb another stile and turn right along a track to a lane. Turn left and at a public footpath sign, turn right Ⓑ over a stile and walk along a hedge-lined track to climb

another stile. Keep along the right edge of a field, climb two more stiles, turn right to climb another stile in the field corner and turn left along the left edge of the next field. To the right are fine views of both the medieval Hawarden Castle and its later successor. In the frequent wars between the English and Welsh, Hawarden occupied a key position on the border and Edward I used the castle as a springboard for his invasion of Wales. Briefly captured by the Welsh under Dafydd ap Gruffyd in 1282, it was soon recovered by the English and Dafydd was killed the following year. It fell into ruin after the Civil War between Charles I and Parliament. The "New Castle" was built in 1752 and became the home of William Gladstone in 1852 after his marriage to Catherine Glynne. He lived there until his death in 1898.

Climb a stile, keep ahead, climb another one and turn right **C** along a lane to a T-junction **D**. Turn left along a road for nearly ½ mile (800m) and at a public footpath sign, turn right **E** over a stile and walk across a field to climb another one on the far side. Follow a path, waymarked with yellow-topped posts, through young conifers to a stile, climb it and continue through trees to another stile. Climb that, head downhill to cross a footbridge over a stream and keep in the same direction uphill across the next field, looking out for a stile and public footpath sign ahead after going over the brow.

Climb the stile, turn right along a tarmac track and after passing to the left of a farm and going through a metal gate, it becomes a rough track. Continue along this wide, hedge-lined track, climbing a stile, to a lane and turn right **F** through the hamlet of Old Warren. At a public footpath sign on the edge of trees, turn right **G** on to the track to Cherry Orchard Farm, climb a stile and continue along this straight track which later curves left towards Bilberry Wood. On this part of the walk are more fine views of both castles.

Climb over a stile to enter the wood and follow a well-waymarked track running through it, later keeping along its right inside edge by the boundary wall of Hawarden Park. Keep ahead, climbing three stiles and crossing a footbridge over a stream, and finally the path climbs up to emerge into the car park. ●

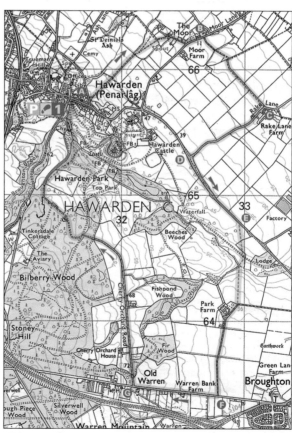

CAERGWRLE

6 miles SE of Mold on the A541

Once occupied by the Romans as an outpost station for nearby Chester, **Caergwrle Castle**, which stands on a high ridge, probably started life as a Bronze Age hill fort. It was Dafydd, brother of Llewelyn the Last, who constructed the fortification more or less in its present form and it was from here, in 1282, that Dafydd launched his last, and fatal, Welsh attack on English Edward I.

CILCAIN

3½ miles W of Mold off the A541

This charming hamlet in the heart of the Clwydian Range has a medieval church with a double nave, a hammerbeam roof and stained glass. To the south lies **Moel Famau** and a path leads from Cilcain to the summit.

CAERWYS

8½ miles NW of Mold on the B5122

Originally a Roman station, Caerwys grew to become a village of such significance that it received a charter from Henry III. Once an important market town, Caerwys is credited with being the place where, in around 1100, Gruffydd ap Cynan called the first Eisteddfod. This cultural feast was revived in the 16th century following the intervention of Elizabeth I, who gave permission for a competitive festival of Welsh music and poetry to be held here in 1568.

AFONWEN

8 miles NW of Mold on the A541

Another small village in the Clwydian Range, Afonwen is home to one of the largest craft and antique centres in north Wales. **Afonwen Craft and Antique Centre** not only has a whole host of

crafts, accessories and gifts for sale, including furniture, crystal, china and silver, but exhibitions and demonstrations are held here on a regular basis.

WHITFORD

10 miles NW of Mold off the A5026

Close to the village can be found a curious monument, **Maen Achwyfaen** (The Stone of Lamentation). This Celtic cross, sculptured in a wheel shape, is said to have been erected in about 1000 and is the tallest such cross in Britain; the person or event which it commemorates is unknown. The renowned 18th century travel writer, Thomas Pennant, is buried in the graveyard adjacent to the grand 19th century church.

DENBIGH

Recorded as a small border town in the 11th century, Denbigh, whose Welsh name "Dinbych" means little fort, grew to become a residence for Welsh princes and a leading centre of Welsh power. Today, it still retains a charm that is enhanced by buildings dating from the 16th century onwards; most of the centre is now a conservation area. The old town is concentrated around the castle that was built on the site of a Roman settlement and commands good views over the Vale of Clwyd.

Denbigh Castle was one of the biggest and most imposing fortifications in Wales and its ruins are still an impressive sight as they crown the top of a steep hill above the town. It was originally a stronghold of the Welsh prince Dafydd ap Gruffydd, brother of Llewelyn the Last, but when Henry de Lacy, Earl of Lincoln, was given the Lordship of Denbigh by Edward I during his campaigns against the Welsh, he began construction of the "new" castle in 1282, the year the town fell to Edward. De Lacy removed all traces of the older Welsh fortification and, at the same time, created a new English borough protected by town walls. Over 3,000 labourers worked on the castle and the walls. The walled town was completed by 1311 but it was subject to sporadic attacks during its occupation including, in 1402, by Owain Glyndwr, who laid siege to the town and again, during the Wars of the Roses, when the old town was burnt to the ground. In 1645, during the Civil War, Charles I stayed at the castle, which was held for him by Sir William Salusbury ("Old Blue Stockings"); it later endured a six-month siege before falling, in October 1646, to Parliament forces, after which the castle and the walls gradually fell into disrepair. But a large stretch of the **Town Walls** still exists and can be walked today, providing a splendid historic view of the town,

particularly the section that includes Countess Tower and the Goblin Tower.

Gradually Denbigh developed around its market place and town square, and by the time of the first Elizabethan era it was one of the largest and richest towns in North Wales, and also a centre of culture. Of particular interest is **Back Row**, where part of Denbigh's original medieval street pattern still exists and where several 15th century buildings, including the Golden Lion Inn, still give a flavour of those times.

Throughout the centuries Denbigh has been the home to many famous characters including the physician, musician, antiquarian and Member of Parliament, Humphrey Llwyd who, in the 16th century, made the first accurate map of Wales. He is sometimes known as the "Father of Modern Geography". Born in 1739, Thomas Edwards went on to become an actor and playwright,

under the name of Twm o'r Nant, and he was given the nickname the Welsh Shakespeare. After a full, colourful and eventful life, Edwards lived out his last days peacefully in Denbigh and he lies buried in the churchyard of the splendid 14th century St Marcella's Church. One of the few towns in Wales approved of by Dr Samuel Johnson during his travels through the Principality, Denbigh was also the birthplace of Henry Morton Stanley. He was born John Rowlands in 1841, the illegitimate son of John Rowlands and Elizabeth Parry, and grew up partly in the care of relatives and partly in the workhouse in St Asaph. In his late teens he sailed from Liverpool to New Orleans as a cabin boy. There he was befriended by a merchant, Henry Hope Stanley, whose first and last names he

NANT-Y-FELIN RESTAURANT

Pentre, Llanrhaeadr, Nr Denbigh, Denbighshire LL16 4NT
Tel: 01745 890230

Situated in the beautiful Vale of Clwyd on the A525, **Nant-y-Felin** is a restaurant of great charm, with a homely, inviting atmosphere. Proprietor Bethan Morris is also the chef, and she has established an excellent reputation with her unpretentious and enjoyable cooking. The menu is supplemented by daily specials - the fish dishes are not to be missed - and diners should leave room for one of the delicious desserts. The wine choice features a different country each month. The restaurant is open for morning coffee, lunch and dinner, bookings advisable. Closed Sunday evening and all day Monday and Tuesday. For overnight guests there are two en suite rooms above the restaurant.

LLAETH Y LLAN VILLAGE DAIRY

Llannefydd, Nr Denbigh, Conwy LL16 5DR
Tel: 01745 540256
website: www.villagedairy.com

Nestling in the tranquil Denbighshire hills between Denbigh and the coast, **Llaeth y Llan** is a historic 17th century farmstead transformed by its owners into a renowned modern dairy and visitor centre. Gareth and Falmai Roberts have turned the Village Dairy into a

prize-winning yoghurt producer making the richest, creamiest, most delicious yoghurts from the best possible ingredients. They produce two highly successful ranges - the 17-strong traditional collection and the wonderfully indulgent liqueur and fruit dessert combinations: cointreau and orange, cherry and kirsch, dark rum and raisin, limoncello and lemon, apricot and brandy, Celtic coffee.

Winner of the True Taste of Wales and many other awards, and suppliers to Waitrose, Harrods and Selfridges, Gareth and Falmai welcome visitors, but a phone call should be made first. Guided tours can be arranged of the dairy and the lovely floral farmhouse garden. New for 2002 is overnight accommodation at the dairy in three en suite bedrooms in decorated and furnished in smart country style.

took - the Morton came later. He spent the next few years as a soldier, sailor and journalist, and his several commissions for the *New York Herald* culminated in a quest to fine the explorer David Livingstone, who had set out for Africa to search for the source of the Nile. At the head of an American-financed expedition, and keeping his intentions hidden from the British, he set out from Zanzibar and struggled to Ujiji, where in 1871 he found the explorer and addressed him with the immortal words "Dr Livingstone, I presume". The two became firm friends, and Livingstone continued his quest after being restocked with provisions. He died a year later. Stanley wrote about his expedition and returned to Africa to take up the exploration where Livingstone left off. He was involved in numerous adventures and enterprises, mainly with Belgian backing, and was instrumental in paving the way for the creation of the Congo Free State. On his return to Britain, he married, spent some years as a Member of Parliament and was knighted by Queen Victoria. He died in London in 1904 and was buried in the churchyard of St Michael in Pirbright; his rough granite headstone bears the inscription "Africa".

Three miles south of Denbigh, on the A525 Ruthin road, stands the Church of St Dyfnog, whose chief treasure is a marvellous "Tree of Jesse" window (the Tree of Jesse, most often seen depicted in church windows, details the family tree of Christ down from Jesse, the father of King David). This superb window, made in 1553, was saved from destruction during the Civil War by being buried in a dug-out chest, which can also be seen in the church.

A.P.E.S. ROCKING HORSES

Ty Gwyn, Llannefydd, Denbigh LL16 5HB
Tel/Fax: 01745 540365 e-mail: macphersons@apes-rocking-horses.co.uk

Pam and Stuart MacPherson started **A.P.E.S. Rocking Horses** in 1978 and have gained a reputation for the highest quality in artistic design and workmanship. In their workshop they design, hand-build and finish new horses and undertake skilled, painstaking restoration of old horses. A.P.E.S. offers lifelike horses, hand-painted to customers' colour preference, and traditional classic English-style horses of all wooden construction, hand-carved and painted in dapple grey or to customers' specifications, with fixed or removable harness, designed and made by themselves. Award winning members of the British Toymakers Guild.

THE HAWK AND BUCKLE INN

Llannefydd, Nr Denbigh, Conwy LL16 5ED
Tel: 01745 540249 Fax: 01745 540316

The Hawk and Buckle is a fine 17th century coaching inn in a pretty village . Behind the immaculate whitewashed facade the beamed bar offers a good choice of real ales. There's a separate lounge and a games room with pool and darts. There are seats for 26 in the bar and for 30 in the restaurant, where a table for the evening lets diners enjoy a relaxed meal from a varied menu featuring prime local produce and accompanied by very good wines from Fearons of Holyhead. David Topping also provides excellent guest accommodation in 10 en suite bedrooms, seven of them on the ground floor; one with a king-size four-poster bed.

AROUND DENBIGH

BODFARI

3 miles NE of Denbigh on the B5429

Situated in the heart of the Vale of Clwyd, at the foot of the Clwydian Range, Bodfari marks the abrupt change in landscape from arable fields to heath and moorland. Thought to have been the site of a Roman station, the village is famous for **St Deifar's Holy Well**, which can be found at the inn next to the medieval St Stephen's Church.

LLANGWYFAN

5 miles E of Denbigh off the B5429

Opposite the porch of the pretty medieval Church of St Cwyfan, lies the grave of Foulk Jones who lived, remarkably, in three centuries, as he was born in 1699 and died in 1801!

TREMEIRCHION

6 miles NE of Denbigh on the B5429

This small village is home to several buildings of interest. The 13th century village church houses a 14th century tomb-niche containing the effigy of a vested priest while, in the chancel, a tablet commemorates Hester Lynch Piozzi who is better known as Dr Johnston's Mrs Trale. In 1774, Mrs Trale inherited a house in Tremeirchion she had known in her childhood and which, unfortunately, was dilapidated and in need of great repair. Following her marriage to the Italian musician, Gabriel Piozzi, the couple rebuilt the house living there happily until Piozzi's death.

In 1567, Sir Richard Clough, a wealthy merchant, built a house, Bachegraig, near the village. Though the house is now demolished, the gatehouse still stands and its unusual architectural style so shocked the local inhabitants that they thought the devil must have been the architect and had also supplied the bricks. The local story has it that the devil baked the bricks in the fires of hell and, to this day, a nearby stream is known as Nant y Cythraul or the Devil's Brook.

ST ASAPH

6 miles N of Denbigh on the A525

This small town, on a ridge between the River Clwyd and Elwy, ranks as a city because of its cathedral. Standing on a hill and constructed on the site of a Norman building, **St Asaph's Cathedral** is not only the country's smallest cathedral but it has also had to endure a particularly stormy past. It was founded in AD 560 by St Kentigern, who left his small church in 573 in the hands of his favourite pupil, Asaph, while he returned to Scotland. The cathedral was sacked by

---

BACH-Y-GRAIG COUNTRY FARMHOUSE

Tremeirchion, Nr St Asaph, North Wales LL17 0UH
Tel: 01745 730627 e-mail: anwenroberts@bachygraig.fsnet.co.uk
Fax: 01745 730971 website: www.bachygraig.co.uk

Bach-y-Graig is a working farm where owners Anwen and David Roberts offer a choice of top-grade Bed & Breakfast or self-catering accommodation in a handsome redbrick farmhouse dating back to the 16th century. There are three en suite bedrooms with tv, radio and tea/coffee-making facilities, and a lounge with log fires for B&B guests; a farmhouse breakfast starts the day. For self-catering there are three bedrooms, bathroom, oak-panelled lounge, kitchen/diner and a large shared garden with lovely views. The owners have recently opened a trail enabling guests to enjoy the wealth of animal and plant life in 40 acres of woodland.

THE GAMEKEEPER

Lower Street, St Asaph, Denbighshire LL17 0SG
Tel: 01745 583514 e-mail: ken@gamekeeperinn.co.uk
website: www.gamekeeperinn.co.uk

The **Gamekeeper** is a perfect spot to pause for a meal or to enjoy a glass of Banks's excellent brews. Brothers Ken and Robert Owen, who own this convivial hostelry, have the services of talented chef Gary Ross, who has helped make the Gamekeeper one of the most popular eating places in the region. A new conservatory has increased the capacity of the restaurant, where Gary's menus offer choices from classic Welsh and British to Oriental, game in season, and Sunday lunch should not to be missed (booking is recommended at all times). Families are welcome, and there's a safe playing area opposite the pub.

Henry III's forces in 1245 and then destroyed during Edward I's conquest of Wales just some 37 years later. Edward wished to rebuild at nearby Rhuddlan but Bishop Anian II insisted that the new cathedral remain at St Asaph and so the building still standing today was begun by Anian and completed by his two successors.

In 1402 the woodwork was burnt during Owain Glyndwr's rebellion (it was subsequently restored by Bishop Redman) and by the 17th century the matters were so desperate that many of the possessions were sold and the Bishop's Palace became a tavern! However, St Asaph's Cathedral has survived and today it holds several treasures including a first edition of the William Morgan Welsh Bible (dating from 1588) that was used at the Investiture of Charles the Prince of Wales in 1969.

Bishop of St Asaph from 1601 to 1604, William Morgan began his mammoth task of translating the Bible into Welsh while he was a rector and, during his ministry over the parish of Llanrhaeadr ym Mochnant, his congregation grew so upset with his neglect of his pastoral duties for his translation work that he had to be escorted by armed guards to the church. Not only was the finished work of importance to the Welsh churches, each one of which received a

copy, but it also set a standard for the Welsh language, which, without being codified, could have been lost forever. A special monument, the **Translator's Memorial**, commemorates and names those who, under Morgan's guidance, assisted him in translating the Bible. Major restoration work on the Cathedral was entrusted to Sir George Gilbert Scott, who also worked on the restoration of the cathedrals at Bangor and St David's as well as building many churches and houses throughout the United Kingdom. (The Scott dynasty takes a bit of sorting out: Sir George Gilbert Scott (1811-1878), the most prolific builder and restorer, had two architect sons, George Gilbert Scott Jr (1839-1897) and John Oldrid Scott (1842-1913). John Oldrid's son Sir Giles Gilbert Scott (1880-1960) was responsible for Liverpool Cathedral.)

In the centre of St Asaph is **Elwy Bridge**, which is believed to date from the 17th century although it was the fine renovation work by Joseph Turner in 1777 that allows it to carry today's heavy traffic. The River Elwy is linked with a particularly fishy tale about Bishop Asaph, after whom the town is named. One day, Queen Nest, the wife of Maelgwn Gwynedd, King of North Wales, lost a precious ring - the ancient and sacred ring of the Queens of the North - while bathing in the river. Upset and fearing her husband's anger, the Queen went to St Asaph to ask for his help in retrieving the ring. Comforting the lady, St Asaph invited the royal couple to dine with him the following evening where he told Maelgwn about the loss of the ring. The king's terrible rage could only just be contained by St Asaph and he suggested they begin their meal. As the king cut into the locally-caught salmon on his plate, lo and behold, the sacred ring fell from the flesh of the fish!

Rhuddlan Castle

RHUDDLAN
8 miles N of Denbigh on the A525

The site of an early Norman stronghold known as **Twt Hill**, which today is marked by a prominent earthen mound, Rhuddlan is now overshadowed by its impressive castle ruins. One of the Iron Ring of fortresses built by Edward I, **Rhuddlan Castle**, as one of the most massive and impenetrable of his defences, was the king's headquarters during his campaign and it was from here that Edward issued the Statute of Rhuddlan (in March 1284) that united the Principality of Wales with the Kingdom of England. He also gave the town a Royal Charter when his sovereignty was confirmed. The statute, which lasted until the Act of Union in 1536, was enacted on the site now occupied by Parliament House and there is a commemoration tablet on the wall which is said to be from the original building. Although the castle, like many, was partially destroyed during the Civil War, the town is still sometimes referred to as the "Cradle of Wales".

While the castle in its heyday was a magnificent example of medieval defensive building, the most impressive

engineering feat in the area was the canalisation of the River Clwyd to give the castle access, by ship, to the sea some three miles away. The remains of the dockgate, **Gillot's Tower**, can still be seen - this was built by James of St George, who was also responsible for the interesting concentric plan of the castle which allowed archers, stationed on both the inner and outer walls, to fire their arrows simultaneously.

DYSERTH
10 miles N of Denbigh on the A5151

Lying in the foothills of the Clwydian Range, below Craig Fawr's slopes, this village, in the scenic Vale of Clwyd, boasts a 60 foot waterfall as well as a charming parish church which dates from the 13th century.

Just to the west of the village lies **Bodrhyddan Hall**, the 17th century manor house of the Conwy family, who have had their home here since the early 15th century. As well as being the home of the Charter of Rhuddlan, visitors can also see, in the white drawing room (around the fireplaces) panels that came from the chapel of a ship of the Spanish Armada that foundered off the coast of Anglesey. Other notable items include

Hepplewhite chairs, suits of armour and ancient weapons, and a family portrait by Sir Joshua Reynolds. The **Gardens** here too are of interest, the main feature being a box-edged Victorian parterre designed by William Andrews Nesfield, father of the famous William Eden Nesfield, who remodelled the house in 1875. William E had a very varied life, being a soldier and a watercolour painter before taking up garden design when he was over 40. He worked on well over 200 estates, among the most notable being the Royal Botanic Gardens at Kew. A much older part of the garden at Bodrhyddan is centred around a well house (bearing the inscription "Inigo Jones 1612") containing a spring, St Mary's Well, that may once have had pagan significance.

BODELWYDDAN
8 miles N of Denbigh off the A55

The village church, known as the **Marble Church**, was built in 1856-60 by Lady Willoughby de Broke as a memorial to her husband. The landmark white spire is of local limestone while, inside, there is an arcade of marble, with 14 different types of marble used.

Opposite the eye-catching church stands **Bodelwyddan Castle**, a Victorian country house and estate which occupies the site of a 15th century house. The castle is the Welsh home of the National Portrait Gallery, and as well as the wonderful collection of Victorian portraits on display, visitors can also see beautiful furniture on loan from the Victorian and Albert Museum and sculptures from the Royal Academy. Anyone tiring of the glorious pieces exhibited here can relax and play one of several hands-on Victorian games and

inventions in the gallery, while outside are picnic tables, an adventure playground, maze, terrace café and secret woodland walk. A hands-on science centre is the latest attraction.

18th and 19th century landscaped parkland surrounds the castle and here, too, is an Arts and Crafts walled garden originally planted by TH Mawson, with some redesign work being undertaken by H Moggridge in 1980.

LLANARMON-YN IÂL
11 miles SE of Denbigh on the B5431

The capital of the Iâl region and found in an attractive position on the banks of the River Alun, at the southern end of the Clwydian Range, this small village has an interesting medieval church. It is one of the most notable in Denbighshire, and up until Tudor times visitors would flock to this shrine of St Garmon; today, visitors come mainly to admire the church's two naves.

RUTHIN
7 miles SE of Denbigh on the A525

This old market town lies in the Vale of Clwyd, more or less surrounded by a ring of hills, with a layout that appears to have changed little from medieval days. In fact, a description of Ruthin made in

Ruthin

Ruthin Town Centre

Elizabethan times, where it is described as "the grandest market town in all the Vale, full of inhabitants and well replenished with buildings", is as true today as it was then. **St Peter's Square** is a good place from which to view the town; it was here, in 1679, that the town's last execution took place, when a Catholic priest was hung, drawn and quartered. Situated behind a

magnificent set of 18th century wrought iron gates stands the town's splendid **St Peter's Church**. Founded in the late 13th century as a collegiate church, its notable features include an early 16th century oak roof that consists of 408 carved panels while behind the church there are some beautiful buildings in the collegiate close - 14th century cloisters, the Old Grammar School of 1284 and 16th century almshouses - that are reminiscent of Anthony Trollope's *Barchester Towers*.

St Peter's Square itself is edged with many lovely buildings, including the particularly eye-catching 15th century Myddleton Arms with its unusual Dutch style of architecture and its seven dormer windows that have been dubbed the "eyes of Ruthin". At one time there were around 60 inns and pubs in Ruthin - one for every 10 men in the town - and nine of these were to be found around the square. On the south side of St Peter's Square stands the impressive wattle and daub **Old Courthouse**, which dates from 1401 and was a temporary resting place for prisoners, who were kept in the cells below the magnificent beamed court room. On Clwyd Street, a major new attraction opened in May 2002. This is **Ruthin Gaol**, through whose gates thousands of prisoners - men, women and children, the guilty and the

innocent - passed between 1654 and 1916. Visitors (all volunteers these days!) can see how prisoners lived their daily lives: what they ate, how they worked, the punishments they suffered. The cells, including the punishment, "dark" and condemned cell, can be explored, and there are hands-on activities for children. In Castle Street can be found one the oldest town houses in North Wales. **Nant Clwyd House** is a fine example of Elizabethan architecture although the present 16th century building shows traces of an earlier house. During the reign of Elizabeth I it was the home of Dr Gabriel Goodman, an influential man who was the Dean of Westminster for 40 years. Ruthin is also renowned for **Maen Huail**, a stone that stands in the market place and which, according to legend, marks the place where Huail was beheaded by King

Ruthin Castle

Arthur because of rivalry in love.

Ruthin Castle, begun in 1277 by Edward I, was the home of Lord de Grey of Ruthin who, having proclaimed Owain Glyndwr a traitor to Henry IV,

RUTHIN CRAFT CENTRE

Park Road, Ruthin, Denbighshire LL15 1BB
Tel: 01824 704774 Fax: 01824 702060

Ruthin Craft Centre, North Wales' premier centre for the applied arts, consists of independent craft studios; two gallery exhibition spaces; a gallery retail area with contemporary craft for sale; a restaurant and a Tourist Information Centre. The main gallery is listed on the Craft Council's National List of Craft Shops & Galleries for showing the best of fine crafts by contemporary designer-makers from the British Isles. It is a modern art gallery with exhibition space and retail area under the one roof.

The regularly changing main programme runs all year round, showing the breadth of excellence in the field of applied arts and offering a stimulating and diverse view of contemporary work. The Centre also houses independent craft studios where designer craftsmen

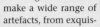

make a wide range of artefacts, from exquisite silver jewellery to wildlife sculpture. The Tourist Information Centre can help with just about anything to do with a visit to the area. Admission to the whole of the Centre is free, as is parking, and there are facilities for disabled visitors. The Centre is open in summer daily from 10 to 5.30 and in winter 10 to 5 Monday to Saturday and 12 to 5 Sunday. The Centre also offers a broads range of non-residential courses in arts and crafts.

MANORHAUS HOTEL & RESTAURANT

Well Street, Ruthin, Denbighshire LL15 1AH
Tel: 01824 704830 Fax: 01824 707333
e-mail: post@manorhaus.com website: www.manorhaus.com

Christopher Frost and Gavin Harris bought this Georgian town house in February 2002 and have quickly made their mark at the **Manorhaus**. The restaurant specialises in classic and contemporary British and European cuisine, with dishes such as vegetable tempura; guinea fowl terrine and sea bass on a crab and clam risotto. Guest accommodation comprises eight en suite bedrooms with neat, stylish decor, tv and dvd player, telephone and beverage tray. In the cellar is a new Wellbeing suite with sauna and jacuzzi. The Manorhaus is a showcase for the work of local artists, with regularly changing solo exhibitions.

was given a large area of land originally held by the Welshman. After Glyndwr crowned himself Prince of Wales, de Grey was the first to suffer when Ruthin was attacked in 1400. Though the town was all but destroyed, the castle held out and survived the onslaught. During the Civil War, the castle again came under siege, this time surviving for 11 weeks in 1646 before eventually falling to General Mytton, who had the building destroyed. Partially restored and then owned by the Cornwallis-West family, Ruthin Castle played host, before and during World War I, to many famous and influential Edwardians including the Prince of Wales (later Edward VII), the actress Mrs Patrick Campbell and Lady Randolph Churchill, the mother of Winston Churchill. Today, the castle, with its charming grounds and roaming peacocks, is a hotel that specialises in medieval banquets.

LLANFIHANGEL GLYN MYFYR

11 miles SW of Denbigh on the B5103

This sleepy village lies in the fertile vale through which the River Alwen runs. Just to the north lies the **Clocaenog Forest**, Wales' second largest commercial plantation, which covers much of the southern moorland between the vales of Clwyd and Conwy. Managed by the Forestry Commission, it has well-marked forest trails, varying in length, which lead walkers through the mixed plantation of larch, spruce, pine, beech, oak and ash.

On the edge of the forest lies **Llyn Brenig**, a massive man-made reservoir that was completed in 1976 to accompany the smaller **Llyn Alwen**,

RHYDONNEN COUNTRY FARMHOUSE

Llanychan, Nr Ruthin, Denbighshire LL15 1UG
Tel: 01824 790258
e-mail: jones@rhydonnen.co.uk website: rhydonnen.co.uk

Buddug Jones, offers en suite Bed & Breakfast accommodation in the most civilised and atmospheric of settings. **Rhydonnen** is a distinguished 15th century farmhouse with a part redbrick, part Tudor-style half-timbered facade, set in a quiet garden surrounded by beautiful countryside. Inside, the house has a wealth of oak beams and inglenook fireplaces, wattle and daub and Queen Anne panelling, and the two non-smoking guest bedrooms are both very comfortable and full of character. First-class home cooking sets the seal on a stay at Rhydonnen, an ideal base for exploring.

THE DROVERS ARMS

Rhewl, Nr Ruthin, Denbighshire LL15 2UD
Tel: 01824 703166
website: www.droversarms.co.uk

The Drovers Arms is one of the oldest public houses in the Vale of Clwyd, a pretty little white-painted building two miles north of Ruthin on the A525 road towards Denbigh. Landlord Charles Gale-Hasleham, here since 1996, has made the Drovers Arms a place of pilgrimage for lovers of good food and good beer, widely recognised in leading guides. Real ales from local breweries are promoted, and the outstanding home-cooked food ranges from bar snacks to a full restaurant menu; Sunday lunch is a high point of the week for many of the loyal locals.

which dates from the early 1900s. Close to the dam, and reached along the B4501, is a Visitor Centre which explains the local history and ecology of this tranquil Welsh valley as well as acting as a starting point for lakeside walks. By the lake, depending on the time of year, butterflies such as Orange Tip and Tortoiseshell can be seen and, along with the water sports on the lake, fishing is also available.

CERRIGYDRUDION

12½ miles SW of Denbigh on the B4501

This village's name, often misspelt as "druidion", means "Place of the Brave" and it does not have any connections with Druids. There are many tales of fairy cattle to be found in Wales, creatures that are thought to have descended from the aurochs, the wild cattle that roamed Britain in prehistoric times. Cerrigydrudion has it own cow, Y Fuwch Frech (the freckled cow), who lived on nearby Hiraethog mountain. For years she supplied the area with milk and would always fill any receptacle brought to her. One day, a witch began to milk her into a sieve and continued until the cow went insane and drowned herself in Llyn Dau Ychen.

GWAENYNOG BACH

1½ miles W of Denbigh on the A543

During the 19th century Beatrix Potter was a frequent visitor to the beautifully situated estate of Gwaenynog Hall, which was owned by her uncle. It is thought that her sketches of the kitchen garden (which has now been restored) were the basis for *The Tale of the Flopsy Bunnies* and also the working environment of the fictional Mr McGregor the gardener, who wanted to bake Peter Rabbit in a pie.

LLANGOLLEN

This busy and picturesque town draws visitors from all over the world who come here not only to enjoy Llangollen's

Llangollen

beautiful riverside position but also for the annual **International Musical Eisteddfod** which has been held here since 1947. For six days every July musicians, choirs, folk singers and dancers from all over the world, and many performing in their national costumes, converge on the town to take part in this wonderful cultural event that is centred around the **Royal International Pavilion** (see panel below). This event should not be confused with the **National Eisteddfod**, the annual Welsh language cultural festival whose venue alternates between the north and south of the country. The first recorded eisteddfod was held at Cardigan Castle in 1176, and the modern eisteddfod began

Llangollen Eisteddfod

as a competition between bards at the Owain Glyndwr hotel in Corwen in 1789; it became a truly national event at Llangollen in 1858, when thousands of people came to Llangollen from all over the country. Music, prose, drama and art are included in the festival, which

ROYAL INTERNATIONAL PAVILION

Abbey Road, Llangollen, Denbighshire LL20 8SW
Tel: 01978 860111
website: www.royal-pavilion.co.uk

HOME OF THE LLANGOLLEN INTERNATIONAL MUSICAL EISTEDDFOD

Tel: 01978 862000
website: www.international-eisteddfod.co.uk

Set in the heart of the beautiful Vale of Llangollen, nestled at the edge of the town, you will find the **Royal International Pavilion**. Each year it hosts an amazing festival - the Llangollen International Music eisteddfod - which features performers from around the world.

Competitions feature singers and dancers in national costume, who come together in a celebration of international harmony and culture. In the evenings world famous performers take to the stage - in recent years Lesley Garrett, Ladysmith Black Mambazo, and Pavarotti. The Eisteddfod is held in July, for one week, every year.

Throughout the rest of the year, the Pavilion opens its stage to shows ranging from jazz and Celtic music to world music and choirs, plus cinema, exhibitions, literary evenings and antique fairs.

culminates in the chairing and investiture of the winning poet. The venue for the National Eisteddfod alternates between the north and the south; in 2002 it was the turn of St David's (the only years when the National Eisteddfod was not held were 1914 and 1940). Throughout the rest of the year there are many other attractions in Llangollen to keep visitors satisfied. In particular, close to the river, is the **Lower Dee Exhibition Centre**, which incorporates three attractions in one place. The **Doctor Who Exhibition** is the world's largest collection of memorabilia dedicated to the cult television programme, while the **International Model Railway World** is the world's largest permanent exhibition of model railways. Finally, visitors young and old will find the **Dapol Toy Factory**, where many of the models for the other two exhibitions on the site are made, a fascinating place to wander around.

Though the above attractions give the impression that Llangollen is a relatively modern place, its history goes back to the late 6th and early 7th century when St Collen, after whom the town is named, founded a church here. The church, which is still standing, has been much restored and refurbished over the years and a local story tells of how St Collen, after fighting with a giantess in a nearby mountain pass, washed off the blood in a well, known locally as Ffynnon Collen (St Collen's Well).

BRYN HOWEL HOTEL

Llangollen, Denbighshire LL20 7UW
Tel: 01978 860331 Fax: 01978 860119

Set in the magnificent Vale of Llangollen, **Bryn Howel** was built in 1896 for the owner of the renowned Ruabon Brick Company. In 1963 it was bought by the Lloyd family, who have since that time ensured that the comfort and style of the original country house have been retained while the building has been extended and adapted to provide all the amenities expected of a modern hotel.

All 36 bedrooms have en suite bathrooms, tv, radio, direct-dial telephone and hospitality tray. They include a four-poster room, junior suites and the Maestro Suite, named in honour of Luciano Pavarotti after his stay in the hotel. Eye-catching features in the convivial bar include oak panelling, an ornate moulded ceiling and the unique "Anthem Fireplace" engraved with the first two lines of the Welsh national anthem. Equally appealing is the light, elegant restaurant, with original mullioned windows topped with terracotta angel's heads, and picture windows that provide stunning views of the Vale, with the ruins of Dinas Bran Castle in the distance and the Berwyn Mountains beyond.

Dee salmon, Welsh lamb and local game and poultry take pride of place on a regularly changing menu that is complemented by an excellent wine list. The Oak Room is available for private lunches and dinners.The Conservatory and the Glyndwr Suite cater for meetings or social events for up to 250. Residents have free use of the hotel's sauna and solarium, and can also fish for trout, salmon and grayling free of charge on a private stretch of the Dee. Bryn Howel is an ideal place to relax at any time of the year, and there's always plenty to see and do in Llangollen. The major annual event is the International Musical Eisteddfod (2003 dates are July 8-13), supported in recent years by the Llangollen Fringe Festival.

Much later, in the 19th century, Llangollen was famous as the home for 50 years of the Ladies of Llangollen: Lady Eleanor Butler and Miss Sarah Ponsonby. These two eccentric Irish women ran away from their families in Ireland and set up home together in 1780 in a cottage above the town. As well as devoting their lives to "friendship, celibacy and the knitting of blue stockings",

Plas Newydd

the ladies also undertook a great deal of improvements and alterations that turned a small, unpretentious cottage into the splendid house - **Plas Newydd** - that is seen today. The marvellous "gothicisation" of the house was completed in 1814 and some of the elaborate oak panels and the glorious stained glass windows were donated to the couple by their famous visitors, who included Sir Walter Scott, William Wordsworth, the Duke of Gloucester and the Duke of Wellington. The ladies were both buried in the churchyard of St Collen, sharing a grave with their friend and housekeeper Mary Caryll.

Although, after their deaths, some of the ladies' displays were dispersed, the work on the house was continued by another owner, General Yorke, and Plas Newydd is still well worth visiting. A small museum contains relics of the Battle of Waterloo. The **Gardens** are interesting and, while the formal layout to the front of the house was created after the ladies had died and the terraces have been altered since they lived here, they still reflect the peace and quiet the couple were seeking as well as containing more interesting curios from those early Regency days. Plas Newydd is open every day from Easter to October.

Back in the town centre and spanning the River Dee is an eye-catching **Bridge** dating from 1347 which was originally constructed by John Trevor, who went on to become the Bishop of St Asaph. One of the Seven Wonders of Wales, this

four-arched bridge has been rebuilt and widened in places over the years and is still used by today's traffic. On the northside of the river is **Llangollen Station**, home of the Llangollen Railway Society. Since taking over the disused line in 1975, the Society has restored the railway track and journeys along the banks of the River Dee can be taken on this delightful steam railway. The station houses a museum with a collection of engines, coaches

LLANGOLLEN WHARF

Llangollen,
Denbighshire LL20 8TA
Tel: 01978 860702

Since 1884, the horse-drawn pleasure boats have been a focus of tourism in Llangollen. The unique experience still attracts visitors from all over the world an experience that blends the peace of this restful mode of travel with the beauty of the unchanging yet ever changing Welsh scenery. The boat trips enable passengers to visit two of Telford's masterpieces, though the canal itself, in parts hand hewn from the rock, could count as a third.

The narrow boat *Thomas Telford* crosses that magnificent structure, the Pontcysyllte aqueduct. The country's biggest navigable aqueduct, it towers 127' above the River Dee. Refreshments, a bar on board and a live commentary add to the enjoyment of the trip. The voyage of five miles takes two hours. At the other end, a coach awaits to whisk you back to Llangollen to enjoy the rest of your day.

If you would prefer to steer yourselves on a boat, a day hire boat is available. Holding up to 10 people, this luxurious little boat is ideal for a perfect, leisurely family or corporate day out on the Llangollen Canal.

Whether you arrive by boat or on foot, there is always a welcome at the Wharf café, where home-made snacks and meals are available. From the terrace there are gorgeous views over Llangollen town, the River Dee and the green hills beyond.

Castell Dinas Bran

and rail memorabilia. Also along the banks of the Dee lies **Llangollen Wharf** (see panel above), from where pleasure cruises have started since 1884. Some trips are horse-drawn, while others cross the Pontcysylte aqueduct in the narrow boat *Thomas Telford*.

On the banks of another waterway, the **Llangollen Canal**, a branch of the Shropshire Union Canal, is the **Llangollen Canal Exhibition Centre** and just a short walk further on are the dramatic remains of **Castell Dinas Bran**. Although the remains of this Iron Age hill fort are not extensive, the climb is well worth the effort as the view over the town and the Vale of Llangollen is quite breathtaking.

The main route north out of Llangollen passes the impressive ruins of **Valle Crucis Abbey**. Situated in green

Valle Crucis Abbey

by Madog ap Gruffyd, the Prince of Powys, and was a very suitable location for the monks of this austere order. Despite a fire, the tower collapsing and the Dissolution in 1535, the ruins are in good condition and visitors can gain a real "feel" for how the monks lived and worked here. Notable surviving original features include the west front with its richly carved doorway and rose window, the east end of the abbey and the chapter house with its superb fan-vaulted roof. Also to be seen are some mutilated tombs which are thought to include that of Iolo Goch, a bard of Owain Glyndwr. Valle Crucis means "Valley of the Cross" and is named after **Eliseg's Pillar**, which stands about half a mile from the abbey and was erected in the early 9th century. The

fields and overshadowed by the surrounding steep-sided mountains, this was an ideal place for a remote ecclesiastical house, the perfect spot for the Cistercians, medieval monks who always sought out lonely, secluded places. This abbey was founded in 1201

LLANGOLLEN MOTOR MUSEUM

Pentre Felin, Llangollen LL20 8EE
Tel: 01798 860324 e-mail: llangollenmotormuseum@hotmail.com
website: www.llangollenmotormuseum.co.uk

The **Llangollen Motor Museum** is located near the town, nestling between the Llangollen Canal and the river. The building, dating back to the 1820s, was originally a slate dressing works and had many other uses before becoming a museum in 1985. The museum demonstrates in an informative , yet informal, way the charm and character of our motoring past, and the collection comprises more than 60 vehicles, from cars and motor bikes to invalid carriages and pedal cars. There is a recreation of a 1950s village garage complete with petrol pumps and the owners' living quarters. Included in the museum's collection are a Model T Ford, a splendid 1925 Vauxhall 38/93, a 1925 Citroën Boulangere from the vineyards of France and many of the cars that grandad used to drive. Among the motor bikes are great British names, including Norton, Triumph, Ariel, Sunbeam and BSA. The Museum is owned and run by the Owen family, headed by Gwylim, who was involved in the design and construction of cars at Vauxhall, his wife Ann and one of his sons, Geoffrey,

who is a car restorer. For those who like to repair and restore their own vehicles, the Museum keeps a large stock of spares for classic cars, mainly from the 1960s.

The Museum also has a small exhibition showing the history and development of the British canal network and life on the canals through models, paintings, pottery and other memorabilia. School parties are welcome, and for car clubs a private field is available for picnics or overnight camping. The Llangollen Motor Museum, which has a refreshment and souvenir shop, is open Tuesday to Sunday March to October; winter opening by arrangement.

inscription on this Christian memorial cross is now badly weatherbeaten but fortunately a record was made in 1696 of the words. It was erected in memory of Eliseg, who annexed Powys from the Saxons, by his great-grandson Concenn. The pillar was broken by Cromwell's men and not re-erected until the 18th century.

A little further northwards along this road lies the spectacular **Horseshoe Pass** which affords remarkable views of the surrounding countryside. From the top of the pass can be seen the Vale of Clwyd and the ridge of Eglwyseg Rocks where Offa's Dyke path runs.

AROUND LLANGOLLEN

JOHNSTOWN
6 miles NE of Llangollen on the B5605

On the B5605 between Johnstown and Rhosllanerchrugog lies **Stryt Las Park**, a predominantly wetland area with a large lake and three small ponds. This Site of Special Scientific Interest is home to one of Europe's largest colonies of the Great Crested Newt. The park is open daily, the visitor centre daily in summer, weekends only in winter. In Rhosllanerchrugog, the Stiwt is a forum for Welsh language choirs, stage performances and crafts.

BERSHAM
7½ miles NE of Llangollen off the A483

Lying in part of the **Clywedog Valley and Trail** that skirts around the south and west of Wrexham and includes several places of industrial interest, this village was established around 1670 and was the home of the Davis brothers. The fine workmanship of these two famous iron masters can be seen in the beautiful gates at Chirk Park and at St Giles' Church in Wrexham. The master and owner of **Bersham Ironworks** (see panel opposite) from 1762, John "Iron Mad"

Wilkinson, was himself famous for the cannons he bored for use in the American War of Independence and for the cylinders he produced at the ironworks for James Watt's steam engines. The ironworks are open in the summer, the Heritage Centre all year round. The Clywedog Trail passes through Plas Power and Nant Mill, woods that stretch along the River Clywedog between Bersham and Coedpoeth. A well-preserved section of Offa's Dyke cuts through Plas Power.

WREXHAM
9½ miles NE of Llangollen on the A483

This once small market town, which is considered to be the unofficial capital of North Wales, is now a busy place with plenty to offer the visitor. Growing and prospering around the commercial importance of its brick and tile manufacturing, brewing, steel and coal, Wrexham still holds a variety of markets today. An interesting experience for city dwellers is the cattle market held on Saturdays where farmers from the surrounding area come to socialise and oversee transactions and where visitors to the market can wander around soaking up the rural atmosphere.

For those wishing to find out more about the town and its social, industrial and local history then **Wrexham Museum**, housed in the County Buildings that were originally constructed as the militia barracks in 1857, is a very good place to start. The discovery of a skeleton nearby - it became known as Brymbo Man - traces the town's history back as far as the Bronze Age while the Romans are also known to have settled in the Wrexham area. Both Roundhead and Cavalier troops were garrisoned in the town during the Civil War and, in more peaceful times, in the late 19th century,

BERSHAM HERITAGE CENTRE & IRONWORKS

Bersham, Wrexham LL14 4HT
Tel: 01978 261529
e-mail: bershamheritggeewrexham.co.uk
website: www.wrexham.gov.uk

Hidden in the Clywedog Valley, two miles west of Wrexham can be found the real beginnings of the Industrial Revolution. Bersham's old Victorian school is now the centre for discovering the industrial heritage of Wrexham. Permanent displays feature the history behind John Wilkinson's ironworks and the later steel industry of Brymbo. Some of the most innovative ideas of the Industrial Revolution were conceived here in Bersham by John "Iron Mad" Wilkinson.

The remains of John Wilkinson's 18th century blast furnace and associated buildings can be seen at Bersham Ironworks. It is hard to believe a place so unsung in the history books could have been so important. Industry comes alive in the Heritage Centre when the working forge is used by local students and black-smiths. The centre hosts a lively prog-ramme of tempor-ary exhibitions and events to appeal to all the family.

Britain's first lager brewery was built in Wrexham in 1882. The suburb of Acton was the birthplace of Judge Jeffreys, the notoriously harsh lawman who was nicknamed "Bloody" for his lack of compassion and his belief in swift justice.

Perhaps Wrexham's best known building, and one that's a particular favourite of American tourists, is the **Church of St Giles** that dominates the town's skyline. It is famous for being the burial place of Elihu Yale, the benefactor of Yale University, who was laid to rest here on his death in 1721. Yale's tomb was restored in 1968 by members of Yale University to mark the 250th anniversary of the benefaction and it can be found in the churchyard to the west of the tower. While the churchyard certainly holds interest, the church itself is also well worth taking the time to look over; its 136 foot pinnacle tower is one of the Seven Wonders of Wales. Begun in 1506 and much restored, this Gothic tower still carries some of the original medieval carvings and, in particular, those of St Giles, which are recognisable by his attributes of an arrow and a deer.

Just to the south of Wrexham and found in a glorious 2,000-acre estate and **Country Park**, is **Erddig**, one of the most fascinating houses in Britain (see panel opposite).

Along with Erddig, which lies within the **Clywedog Valley and Trail**, is **King's Mill**, a restored mill that dates from 1769 although an older mill has been on the site since 1315.

GRESFORD

13 miles NE of Llangollen on the B5445

This former coal mining town was the site of a mine explosion in 1934 that killed 266 men. The colliery closed in 1973 but the wheel remains in memory of those who lost their lives in this terrible disaster. The town's **All Saints' Church** is one of the finest in Wales and it is also home to the famous **Gresford**

ERDDIG

Nr Wrexham LL13 0YT
Tel: 01978 355314 info line: 01978 315151

Two miles south of Wrexham, in a glorious 2,000-care estate and country park, **Erddig** is one of the most fascinating houses in Britain, not least because of the unusually close relationship that existed between the owners and their servants. This is movingly illustrated by the extraordinarily detailed exhibition of family memorabilia collected by the servants and on show to visitors. The late 17th century mansion was begun by Joshua Edisbury, the High Sheriff of Denbighshire, who subsequently fled, unable to meet his debts. The house passed into the hands of the Meller family and to their descendants until finally coming under the ownership of the National Trust. The stunning state rooms display most of their original 18th and 19th century furniture and furnishings, including some exquisite Chinese wallpaper.

The outbuildings have been restored, including kitchen, laundry, bakehouse, stables, sawmill, smithy and joiner's shop, and visitors can wander around the country park and the dairy farm. The large walled garden has been restored to its 18th century formal design and incorporates Victorian additions, notably a parterre and yew walk, as well as a canal garden and fish pool; it also contains the National Ivy Collection, and a narcissus collection. Erddig is open to the public between late March and early November except Thursday and Friday. It has a plant sales area, a shop and a licensed restaurant. Video presentations are available, and conducted tours by prior arrangement.

Bells, one of the Seven Wonders of Wales, which are still rung every Tuesday evening and on Sundays.

HOLT

15 miles NE of Llangollen on the B5102

The River Dee, which marks the boundary between Wales and England, runs through this village and its importance as a crossing point can be seen in the attractive 15th century bridge. The village of Holt was also the site of a Roman pottery and tile factory that provided material for the fort at nearby Chester.

BANGOR-IS-Y-COED

11 miles E of Llangollen on the B5069

Bangor-is-y-coed, also known as Bangor-on-Dee, is in the area known as the Maelor, where the Cheshire Plains turn into the Welsh Hills. The village is well

known to race-goers as it is home to a picturesque **Racecourse**, situated on the banks of the River Dee, that holds meetings during the National Hunt season. The village itself has a charming 17th century bridge said to have been built by Inigo Jones. There are also claims that the Romans settled here but it is more likely that they were in Holt as, at the pottery works, there is firmer evidence of their presence in the area.

Bangor was, however, the site of a Celtic monastery founded in around AD 180, which was destroyed in 607 by Ethelfrid of Northumbria in what turned out to be the last victory by the Saxons over Celtic Christianity. Apparently, 1,200 monks were laid to the sword as Ethelfrid considered praying against him was tantamount to fighting against him. Those fortunate enough to have survived are thought to have travelled to Bardsey

Island. Local legend also suggests that Owain Glyndwr married Margaret Hanmer in the hamlet of Hanmer, just four miles away.

OVERTON

10 miles E of Llangollen on the A539

This substantial border village is home to another of the Seven Wonders of Wales - the **Overton Yew Trees**, 21 trees that stand in the churchyard of the village Church of St Mary. Dating from medieval times, these tall, dark and handsome trees have a preservation order placed upon them. Within the church itself there are some interesting artefacts from the 13th century.

CEFN-MAWR

4½ miles E of Llangollen on the B5605

Towering some 126 feet above the River Dee and carrying the Llangollen branch of the Shropshire Union Canal,

Pontcysyllte Aqueduct is a magnificent construction some 1,007 feet in length. Built in 1805 by Thomas Telford, this cast iron trough supported by 18 stone pillars was much scorned by people at the time although today it is greatly admired and is still used regularly by pleasure boats.

CHIRK

5½ miles SE of Llangollen on the B5070

This attractive border town's origins lie in the 11th century castle of which, unfortunately, little remains except a small motte close to the town's 15th century church. Today, Chirk is perhaps better known for the National Trust owned **Chirk Castle** which lies a mile outside the town (see panel below).

The Myddleton family have a red hand on their coat of arms that, legend has it, appears there as a reminder of the family's past misdeeds and could not be

CHIRK CASTLE

Chirk, Wrexham LL14 5AF
Tel: 01691 777701 e-mail: gcwmsn@smtp.ntrust.org.uk

Chirk Castle, a magnificent Marcher fortress, was begun in the late 13th century on land granted by Edward I to Roger de Mortimer. Rectangular, with a massive drum tower at each corner, the Castle has been extensively rebuilt and altered from time to time down the centuries but remains a truly impressive sight. It was bought in 1595 by Sir Thomas Myddleton, Lord Mayor of London, and part of it is still lived in by the Myddleton family. Visitors can see the elegant state rooms, some fine Adam-style furniture, tapestries and portraits. By contrast, the dramatic dungeon is a reminder of the Castle's turbulent history, and that for some, life was not always so peaceful and genteel.

The estate is entered through a superb set of wrought-iron gates that were made by the famous Davis brothers of Bersham Ironworks. The Castle, whose walls are now partly covered in climbing plants, stands in an 18th century landscaped park whose layout is based on designs by William Emes.

The grounds include six acres of trees and flowering shrubs, many of them planted by Lady Margaret Myddleton. There are handsome clipped yews in the formal garden, and a fine rose garden. Among other features are an avenue of lime trees, some 19th century topiary, a rockery and an old hawk house. One mile north of Chirk village and 9 miles south of Wrexham, the Castle is open to visitors from late March to early November, closed Monday and Tuesday except Bank Holidays.

Shropshire Union Canal

the Llangollen branch of the Shropshire Union Canal, while the other one is a viaduct built in 1848 to carry the new Chester to Shrewsbury railway line over the River Ceiriog.

GLYN CEIRIOG

2½ miles S of Llangollen off the B4500

This former slate mining village is home to the **Chwarel Wynne Mine Museum** which, as well as telling the story of the slate industry that used to support the village, gives visitors a guided tour of the caverns. There is also a nature trail around the surrounding countryside. A narrow gauge tramway, the Glyn Valley Railway, once linked the Shropshire Union Canal at Gledrid with the quarries and mines at

removed until a prisoner had survived 10 years in the castle dungeons. In the centre of Chirk is a war memorial designed by Eric Gill.

Just south of the town are two splendid constructions that span the Ceiriog valley: the first, an aqueduct built in 1801 by Thomas Telford, carries

THE GARDEN HOUSE

Erbistock, Wrexham LL13 0DL
Tel: 01978 780958/781149 Fax: 01874 781144

Five miles south of Wrexham off the A528, **The Garden House** was developed from a five-acre farmland site by Simon, Joan and Susie Wingett. Joan, an enthusiastic gardener all her life, designed the garden, influenced by some of the great British garden designers, and she and Simon planted everything on the site, which they have made into one of the most beautiful and important gardens in the country. The main features include shrub

and herbaceous plantings in monochromatic, analogous and complementary colour schemes; rose pergolas; a sculpture garden; a large lily pond with a Monet-style bridge; a Victorian dovecote; a colour circle inspired by Gertrude Jekyll; and the National Collection of hydrangeas, with well over 200 species and cultivars.

Many of the rare and interesting plants grown on the site can be bought in the shop, along with fruit and vegetables from the market garden and home-produced chutneys and honey from their own hives, and Susie can provide flowers for any special occasion. A large glasshouse serves as a delightful tea room where visitors can enjoy tea, coffee and home-baked cakes while still admiring the garden. A footpath leads from the Garden House through woods and a churchyard to the banks of the Dee and the charming Boat Inn.

Glyn Ceiriog. Opened in 1873 and originally horse-drawn, it was later converted to steam and diverted through Chirk Castle estate to meet the Great Western Railway at Chirk station. It carried slate, silica, chinastone and dolerite downstream and returned with coal, flour and other commodities. It also carried passengers, and though it closed in 1935, the bed of the tramway can still be seen here and there, and the Glyn Valley Tramway Group was founded in 1974 to conserve evidence of the GVR. The Group has little museums in the Glyn Valley Hotel at Glyn Ceiriog and the former waiting room at Pontafog station, and is currently seeking funds to establish a GVR Museum and Visitor Centre in the old locomotive shed and yard at Glyn Ceiriog.

The village lies in the secluded Vale of Ceiriog and, just to the west, is the

GLYN VALLEY HOTEL

Glyn Ceiriog, Nr Llangollen, Denbighshire LL20 7EU
Tel: 01691 718896

The **Glyn Valley**, situated in the heart of the enchanting Ceiriog Valley, is an ideal choice for either a short break or a longer-stay holiday. The scenery is absolutely stunning, and guests will find all the comfort and peace they desire in the nine letting bedrooms, most of them en suite, all with tv and beverage tray. Top of the range is the honeymoon suite with a beautiful Victorian brass and cast-iron four-poster. Excellent food is served in the bars or in the spacious dining room, and the hotel, owned by local man Mike Gilchrist and managed by Sarah Davies, can cater for small conferences, functions and special occasions. An interesting feature in the hotel is a collection of memorabilia relating to the Glyn Valley Tramway.

THE GOLDEN PHEASANT COUNTRY HOTEL

Llwynmawr, Glyn Ceiriog, Nr Llangollen,
Denbighshire LL20 7BB
Tel: 01691 718281 Fax: 01691 718479
e-mail: goldenpheasant@micro-plus-web.net
website: www.goldenpheasanthotel.co.uk

Situated in one of the prettiest valleys in North Wales, the **Golden Pheasant Country Hotel** is an ideal retreat with a warm welcome for one and all - individuals, families, groups and dogs. The lovely

brick-and-stone hotel is a haven of peace, comfort and good living.

The bedrooms, 11 en suite, individually styled and centrally heated, range from cosy "inn" rooms to top-of-the-range rooms with whirlpool baths and four-poster beds.

Superior and Family rooms all have lovely views across the valley, views that are also enjoyed from the deep-cushioned comfort of the elegant lounge. Slate floors, beamed ceiling, pew seating and a log fire create an inviting period ambience in the Pheasant Bar, and guests have the choice of bar meals in the Berwyn room or the full menu in the stylish restaurant. The area is a paradise for walkers, and other outdoor activities range from pony trekking to whitewater rafting. Stays of two or more nights are preferred and champagne and flowers can be arranged for a romantic weekend.

ERW GERRIG COUNTRY COTTAGES

Tregeiriog, Glyn Ceiriog, Nr Llangollen, LL20 7HS
Tel: 01691 718596
e-mail:annekynaston@holidaymail.co.uk
website: www.northwalescottages.com

Lying amidst the dramatic landscape of the steep-sided Ceiriog Valley, these two charming cottages have been carefully converted and have received three conservation awards. Both are warm and comfortable, and retain a wealth of oak beams and stonewalls. They are perfectly placed for peace, away from the hustle of modern living. A base from which to explore Chirk Castle and the magnificent waterfalls at Llanrhaedr. There is also pony treking, walking and bird watching as the two cottages Nightingale and Kingfisher suggest.

beautiful **Ceiriog Forest** which offers surprisingly pastoral views and vistas along with forest walks and trails.

LLANARMON DYFFRYN CEIRIOG

6½ miles SW of Llangollen on the B4500

This peaceful village in the heart of the Vale of Ceiriog was the birthplace of the famous Welsh bard, Ceiriog, whose real name was John Hughes. The 14-mile Upper Ceiriog Trail for walkers, mountain bikers and horse riders passes his home, Pen-y-Bryn. In the churchyard at Llanarmon DC are two yew trees certified as over 1,000 years old.

LLANTYSILIO

1 mile W of Llangollen off the A5

Situated on the banks of the River Dee, and close to Thomas Telford's **Horseshoe Weir** which was built in 1806 to supply water to the Llangollen Canal, lies **Llantysilio Church**. A Norman building, it was here, in 1866, that Robert Browning worshipped, and a brass plaque placed by Lady Martin commemorates his visit. Lady Martin, also known as the actress Helena Faucit, lived in the house next to the church; she, too, is remembered at the church by a chapel that was built following her death in 1898.

GLYNDYFRDWY

4 miles W of Llangollen on the A5

Once the estate of Owain Glyndwr, this village lies on the historic and important A5 and between the Berwyn and Llantysilio mountains. A mound by the road, known as **Owain Glyndwr's Mound**, was once part of an impressive earthwork fortress that was later incorporated into part of the Welsh hero's manor house and estate.

Much more recently, Glyndyfrdwy has become known as the home of the "Original Butterfly" man, Eos Griffiths, who is known world-wide for creating the bright and colourful ornamental butterflies that can be seen adorning homes from Scandinavia to Australia.

CORWEN

9 miles W of Llangollen on the A5

This market town, in a pleasant setting between the Berwyn Mountains and the River Dee, has, for many years, been known as the "Crossroads of North Wales". The town's origins can be traced back to the 6th century when the Breton-Welsh saints, Mael and Sulien, founded a religious community here - Corwen's 13th century church still bears their dedication. This was also once the headquarters of Owain Glyndwr, who gathered his forces here before entering into his various campaigns. Owain Glyndwr (c1354-c1416), the self-stlyed Prince of Wales, led the last major attempt to shake off the yoke of English. His status as a national hero was reinforced with the rise of Welsh Nationalism from the 18th century onwards. Descended from the Princes of Powys, he studied law in London and served with Henry Bolingbroke, an opponent of Richard II who was later to become Henry IV. When he returned to Wales, he encouraged resentment against the oppressive English rule. In September 1400, a year after Bolingbroke had usurped the throne, Glyndwr entered into a feud with a neighbour, Reynold, Lord Grey of Ruthin, which sparked an uprising in North Wales and a national struggle for independence. Glyndwr formed an alliance with King Henry's most influential and powerful opponents and by 1404 controlled most of Wales and embarked on a series of campaigns. But by the next year he had twice been defeated by Henry IV's son Prince Henry (later Henry V), his English allies had been eliminated and even help from the French was fruitless. By 1409 Glyndwr's main strongholds were in English hands and his campaigns came to an unsuccessful conclusion. The church at Corwen has an incised dagger in a lintel of the doorway that is known as **Glyndwr's Sword**. The mark was reputedly made by Glyndwr when he threw a dagger from the hill above the church in a fit of rage against the townsfolk. However, the dagger mark actually dates from the 7th to 9th centuries and there is another such mark on a 12th century cross outside the southwest corner of the church. It was in the Owain Glyndwr Hotel in 1789 in Corwen that a local man, Thomas Jones,

organised a bardic festival that laid the foundations for the modern eisteddfod. Across the River Dee from the town lies **Caer Derwyn**, a stone rampart around a hill that dates from Roman times.

To the west of Corwen and set in pretty, landscaped grounds is the simple, stone built **Rug Chapel**. A rare example of a private chapel that has changed little over the years, Rug was founded in the 17th century by "Old Blue Stockings" Colonel William Salusbury in collaboration with Bishop William Morgan (the first translator of the Bible into Welsh) and its plain exterior gives no clues to its exquisitely decorated interior. Best described as a "painted chapel", few parts of the building have been left unadorned and, as well as the beautifully carved rood screen, the ceiling beams are painted with rose motifs. However, not all the decoration here is exuberant; there is also a sombre wall painting of a skeleton as a reminder of mortality. The architect Sir Edwin Lutyens acknowledged that his work was influenced by this beautiful chapel and evidence can be seen of this in his most elaborate commission, the Viceroy's House, New Delhi, which was completed in 1930.

Another interesting religious building can be found just to the south of Rug, in the direction of Llandrillo. **Llangar Church**, overlooking the confluence of the Rivers Dee and Alwen, is older than its near neighbour - it is medieval - and, though it was superseded in the 19th century, this small place still retains many of its original features. In particular, there are some extensive 15th century wall paintings and a minstrels' gallery. Both Rug Chapel and Llangar Church are now cared for by CADW - Welsh Historic Monuments.

LLANDRILLO

12 miles SW of Llangollen on the B4401

The road to Llandrillo, from the north, follows the Vale of Edeirion and the River Dee as it weaves its way below the northwest slopes of the **Berwyn Mountains**, another mountain range that is popular with walkers and visitors. This small village is a good starting point for walks in the Berwyns and footpaths from the village lead towards **Craig Berwyn**, whose summit is over 2,100 feet above sea level.

BRYNEGLWYS

5 miles NW of Llangollen off the A5104

Standing on the slopes of Llantysilio Mountain, the large 15th century

Church of St Tysilio, in the heart of the village is, surprisingly, connected with the family who helped to found Yale University in the United States. Close to the village lies **Plas-Yn-Yale**, the former home of the Yale family and the birthplace of Elihu Yale's father. Elihu himself was born in 1647 in Boston, Massachusetts, and went on to become a governor of India before coming to England. Known for his philanthropy, Elihu was approached by an American College who, after receiving generous help, named their new college in Newhaven after him.

In 1745, 24 years after his death, the whole establishment was named Yale University. Elihu Yale is buried in the Church of St Giles in Wrexham.

The coast of North Wales is a perennially popular stretch of British coastline that draws visitors in their thousands to its holiday resorts. This very traditional region, where Welsh is often still spoken on a daily basis, has many treasures, both man-made and natural, to discover. The coastline, from Prestatyn to Bangor was, before the coming of the railways, littered with small fishing villages. During the 19th century, as the hours of millworkers from the industrial towns of Lancashire and others working in the factories of the Midlands were reduced, the concept of an annual holiday, albeit in some cases just the odd day beside the sea, became widespread. Served by the newly built railway network, the fishing villages expanded to accommodate the visitors. Not only

Bodnant Gardens

were boarding houses and hotels built for the society visitors coming to take the sea air, but amusements and entertainment became a regular feature. Llandudno, always considered a "cut above", still retains much of its Victorian and Edwardian charm, while other resorts, such as Rhyl, have endeavoured to counter the unsettled British summer weather by the creation of indoor complexes.

This area is not without its history. Prestatyn, to the east, lies at one end of Offa's Dyke. Built more as a line of demarcation rather than a fortification, the dyke runs from the coast southwards to Chepstow. Still substantially marking the border, many sections of the ancient earthwork are visible and can be seen from the waymarked footpath that runs the length of the dyke. It was also along the coast that Edward I built his Iron Ring of castles and, while many are in ruins, two, in particular, are exceptional. Conwy Castle, now a World Heritage Site, is not only massive but was built in such a position that the surrounding land provides suitable protection from attack. Caernarfon Castle, as much a royal residence as a fortress, was the place where Edward created the first Prince of Wales when he crowned his own son. Centuries later, in 1969, it was in the grounds of the splendid castle ruins that Queen Elizabeth invested the same title on her eldest son, Prince Charles.

Caernarfon and Bangor lie at opposite ends of the Menai Strait, the channel of water that

Port Dafarch Beach, Holyhead

separates mainland Wales from the Isle of Anglesey. It was not until the 19th century that a bridge was constructed across the strait, and Thomas Telford's magnificent Menai Suspension Bridge of the 1820s was joined, some 30 years later, by Stephenson's Britannia Bridge. Two great monuments to 19th

century engineering, the bridges still carry traffic, both road and rail, today. The Isle of Anglesey, with its rolling hills, fertile farmland and miles of wild and craggy coastline, has attracted settlers from the Stone Age onward and is littered with evidence of Neolithic, Bronze Age and Iron Age people. Anglesey has its impressive castle,

Plas Newydd

Beaumaris, built by Edward I to repel invasion from its neighbours. Today's invaders are largely tourists and holidaymakers, attracted by the elegant seaside resorts, the fishing, the sailing and the walking.

LOCATOR MAP

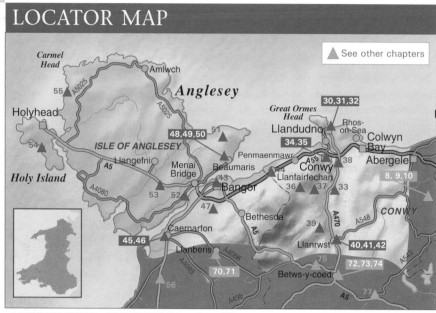

© MAPS IN MINUTES ™ 2002   © Crown Copyright, Ordnance Survey 2002

ADVERTISERS AND PLACES OF INTEREST

LLANDUDNO

Originally just a collection of fishermen's cottages, Llandudno - the largest and one of the most popular of the North Wales coast resorts - was developed in the 1850s under the watchful eye of the Liverpool surveyor, Owen Williams. A delightful place that is a wonderful example of Victorian architecture, Llandudno was planned around a pleasant layout of wide streets and, of course, the Promenade, the essential feature of a resort from that age. The **Promenade** is lined with renovated, redecorated and elegant hotels and the wide boulevard gives it an air of the French Riviera. Off the Promenade towards the Little Orme by the fields **Bodafon Farm Park** is a working farm and also home to the North Wales Bird Trust. Farm attractions include sheep shearing, ploughing, harvesting and collecting eggs. The Trust houses 1,000 birds, including eagle owls and falcons. A permanent Victorian puppet show can be watched on the promenade close to the **Pier** that, in 1914, the Suffragettes

St Tudno Hotel

The Promenade, Llandudno,
North Wales LL30 2LP
Tel: 01492 874411 Fax: 01492 860407
e-mail: sttudnohotel@btinternet.com
website: www.st-tudno.co.uk

On a prime site opposite the ornate Victorian pier, **St Tudno Hotel** is one of the most delightful seafront hotels on the coast of Britain, and the winner of numerous prestigious awards. Owners Martin and Janette Bland are the most dedicated and welcoming of hosts, and everything in their hotel speaks of care and quality. Nineteen bedrooms, ranging from singles to family rooms and suites, are individually designed and appointed, and every comfort is provided to ensure a

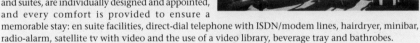

memorable stay: en suite facilities, direct-dial telephone with ISDN/modem lines, hairdryer, minibar, radio-alarm, satellite tv with video and the use of a video library, beverage tray and bathrobes.

The guest lounges overlooking the seafront are perfect places to relax, and in the air-conditioned

Garden Room Restaurant David Harding and his kitchen team produce some of the finest food in the region and have achieved 3 AA Rosettes for the ninth successive year. Classic dishes produced with considerable skill and imagination include terrine of guinea fowl and calves' sweetbreads with grapes, hotpot of scallops with basil, champagne, couscous and a medley of vegetables, and saddle of Welsh lamb with a cabbage and oatmeal cake. Desserts such as chilled orange and Cointreau soufflé with a compote of cherries keep the enjoyment level high to the end, and the fine food is complemented by a wonderful wine list with many rare and exciting bottles from around the world. The hotel has an indoor heated swimming pool, passenger lift and car park and garage. Children are welcome, and cots, high chairs and a baby listening service are available. High tea is served from 5.30 to 6.30pm.

attempted to burn down during their fight for the right of women to vote. Later, Ringo Starr, of Beatles fame, once worked on the pleasure streamers that docked at Llandudno pier, unaware that a few years later his life was to change so radically.

Llandudno

Along the seafront can also be found a statue of the **White Rabbit** from Lewis Carroll's much loved story *Alice In Wonderland*. The tribute is to the real Alice - Alice Liddell - who came here on holiday with her family; it was also at Llandudno that her parents spent their honeymoon. Among the visitors to Dean Liddell's holiday home were such notable characters of the day as William Gladstone and Matthew Arnold as well as Lewis Carroll. Though little is known today of Carroll's stay with the family, visitors can be certain that it was on the broad, sandy beaches at Llandudno that the Walrus and the Carpenter "wept like anything to see such quantities of sand" and it was the White Knight who considered "boiling it in wine" to prevent the Menai Bridge from rusting. The **Visitor Centre** at **The Rabbit Hole** presents an interesting audio-visual exhibition that is dedicated to Alice and her time in Wonderland.

Although Llandudno is very much a product of the Victorian age, it earlier played host to Bronze Age miners and the Romans and, in the 6th century, St Tudno chose Great Orme as the site of the cell from where he preached. At **Llandudno Museum** visitors are taken through the town's history, from ancient times to the present day, by a collection of interesting exhibits: a child's footprint imprinted on a tile from the Roman fort of Canovium (Caerhun), objets d'art collected from all over the world by Francis Chardon.

As well as being the home of Llandudno's roots, the massive limestone

RAVENHURST HOTEL

West Shore, Llandudno, Conwy LL30 2BB
Tel: 01492 875525 e-mail: ravenhursthotel@aol.com
website: www.ravenhurst-hotel.co.uk

The Ravenhurst Hotel is a friendly,seafront hotel run
by the Carrington family for the past 30 years. It
commands one of the finest positions in the town, with
views over the Conwy estuary and towards Snowdonia.
Ravenhurst has 25 comfortable, well-furnished rooms,
including 6 ground floor bedrooms; all have en suite
bathrooms, tv, radio and tea/coffee making facilities.
There are two lounges and a bar and dinner is served from 6 to 7 in the stylish dining room. Rooms
can be booked on a room only, B&B or dinner, B&B. Own car park and wheelchair access.

headland of **Great Orme** still dominates
the resort today and also separates the
town's two beaches. Two miles long, one
mile wide and 679 feet high, its name,
Orme, is thought to have originated
from an old Norse word for sea monster.
In what is now a country park, there are
prehistoric sites in the form of stone
circles and burial sites, the remains of
the Bronze Age mines and **St Tudno's
Church**, a 15th century building
constructed on the site of the saint's
original cell from the 6th century. The
summit can be reached by the **Great
Orme Tramway**, a magnificent
monument to Victorian engineering
constructed in 1902 that is Britain's only
cable hauled, public road tramway. The
Great Orme Copper Mine is the only
Bronze Age copper mine in the world
open to the public. Visitors can explore
the 3,500-year-old passages, see the great
opencast mine workings, peer into the
470' shaft and discover how our
ancestors turned rock into metal. The
Visitor Centre is open to non-mine
visitors, and also at the site are a tea
room serving Welsh cream teas and a
shop selling a wide variety of books,
minerals, fossils and other souvenirs.
Great Orme is home to a herd of wild
goats descended from a pair presented to
Queen Victoria by the Shah of Persia.

Just south of Llandudno lies **Deganwy**,

a once thriving fishing village that
shares the same stretch of coastline
though it has now been taken over by its
larger neighbour. Often mentioned in
Welsh history, Deganwy was a
strategically important stronghold and
its castle was the seat of Maelgwn
Gwynedd as early as the 6th century.
The first medieval castle was probably
built here by Lupus, Earl of Chester,
shortly after the Norman Conquest. The
remains seen today are, however, of a
castle built by one of the Earl's successors
in 1211. Henry II was besieged here by
the Welsh and Deganwy was finally
destroyed by Llewelyn ap Gruffyd
(Llewelyn the Last) in 1263.

AROUND LLANDUDNO

GLAN CONWY
3 miles SE of Llandudno off the A470

In Garth Road at Glan Conwy, **Felin Isaf**
has two working watermills and a
museum describing the history of the site
and the various uses and types of mills.

BODNANT
6 miles S of Llandudno off the A470

Situated above the River Conwy and
covering some 80 acres are the famous
Edwardian **Bodnant Gardens** (see panel
on page 44).

RHOS-ON-SEA
3½ miles E of Llandudno on the B5115

This very sedate North Wales coastal resort has a breakwater to shelter the pleasure boats and, along the promenade, is the small **Chapel of St Trillo**. Though the chapel's age is unknown it is said to have been built above an ancient holy well and also on the spot from where, reputedly, Owain Gwynedd set sail, in 1170, and eventually landed on the North American continent - some 322 years before Columbus made his historic voyage to the New World! The chapel is the only surviving building of an abbey that stood here in the 12th century.

Colwyn Bay

COLWYN BAY
5 miles SE of Llandudno on the A55

A more genteel place than the resorts found to the east, Colwyn Bay was built largely during the 19th century to fill the gap along the coast between Rhos-on-Sea and the village of Old Colwyn. As a result, there are many fine Victorian buildings to be seen, and the beach is served by a promenade along which most of the town's attractions can be found. Colwyn Bay includes among its famous sons ex-Monty Python Terry Jones and a former James Bond, Timothy

BODNANT GARDEN

Tal-y-Cafn, Nr Colwyn Bay, Conwy LL28 5RE
Tel: 01492 650460
e-mail: management@bodnant.co.uk

Situated above the River Conwy, with spectacular views of the Snowdonia range, the National Trust's **Bodnant Garden** is one of the finest in the Britain.

The gardens were laid out by the 2nd Lord Aberconway in 1875 and were presented to the National Trust in 1949. The rhododendrons, camellias and magnolias are a truly magnificent sight in the spring, followed by herbaceous borders, roses and water lilies in the summer and glorious colours in the autumn.

Bodnant has many other attractions, including a laburnum arch, a lily terrace and a stepped pergola; in the Dell, formed round a little tributary of the Conwy, is the tallest redwood in the country. The pretty Garden House was built in Gloucestershire in the 1730s and was later used as a Pin Mill before being brought to Bodnant in 1938. The garden has a shop (not National Trust) and a refreshment pavilion. Bodnant, which is open from mid-March to early November, is located off the A470 8 miles south of Colwyn Bay and Llandudno.

Dalton. The philosopher Bertrand Russell (1872-1970) was cremated with no ceremony at Colwyn Bay crematorium and his ashes scattered in the sea.

Although Colwyn Bay lies on the coast it is also home to the **Welsh Mountain Zoo**, a conservation centre for rare and endangered species that is best known for the Chimp Encounter, its collection of British wildlife and its feeding of the sealions. The zoo's gardens, laid out by TH Mawson at the end of the 19th century, incorporate both formal terraces and informal woodlands with paths offering superb views of Snowdonia as well as the Conwy estuary and the North Wales coast. The Tarzan Trail Adventure Playground is a surefire winner with young visitors.

ABERGELE
10½ miles SE of Llandudno on the A548

Along with **Pensarn**, its neighbour on the coast, Abergele is a joint resort which, though more modest than such places as Rhyl, Prestatyn and Colwyn Bay, is justly popular with those looking for a quieter seaside holiday. Outside the town, on Tower Hill, is a mock Norman castle, **Gwrych**, built in 1814 and formerly the seat of the Earl of Dundonald. It is now a holiday centre

and among its many attractions are medieval jousts and banquets.

Situated on higher ground behind the castle are the natural caverns of **Cefn-Yr-Ogo** where, from the summit, there are magnificent views of the surrounding coastline.

RHYL
14 miles E of Llandudno on the A548

Little more than a couple of fishermen's cottages until its development as a seaside resort from 1833, Rhyl used to be the destination for many workers and their families from the industrial towns and cities of Wales, the Midlands and the northwest of England. Though the heyday of this once elegant resort has long since passed, Rhyl still has a lot to offer the holiday maker including, not least, its three miles of sandy beaches and its bracing sea breezes.

As well as the full range of amusement arcades and seaside attractions, Rhyl is home to two large and exciting complexes: the **Sun Centre**, one of the first all-weather leisure attractions in the country, and **Sea Life**, where a thrilling journey of discovery beneath the waves is promised to all. Rhyl's parish church was built by Sir George Gilbert Scott.

To the southwest of the town lies the mouth of the River Clwyd, which is crossed by Foryd Bridge, and to the south lies Rhuddlan Marsh where, in AD 795, Caradoc was defeated by Offa of Mercia.

PRESTATYN
16½ miles E of Llandudno on the A548

With three miles or so of sandy beaches Prestatyn has proved a popular holiday destination over the years and, as expected, all types of entertainment are

Rhyl Harbour

Prestatyn

the fortification today is one stone pillar on the top of a raised mound that can be found close to Bodnant bridge.

Prestatyn lies at one end of the massive 8th century earthwork **Offa's Dyke**. Although the true origins of the dyke have been lost in the mists of time, it is thought that the construction of this border defence between England and Wales was instigated by King Offa, one of the most powerful of the early Anglo-Saxon kings; from 757 until his death in 796 he ruled Mercia, which covers roughly the area of the West Midlands. He seized power in the period of civil strife that followed the murder of his cousin King Aethelbald and, ruthlessly suppressing many of the smaller kingdoms and princedoms, created a single settled state that covered most of England south of Yorkshire. His lasting memorial is the dyke, which he had built between Mercia and the Welsh lands. With an earthwork bank of anything up to 50 feet in height and a 12ft ditch on the Welsh side, much of this massive feat of engineering is still visible today. The line of the dyke is followed by the **Offa's Dyke Path**, a long distance footpath of some 180 miles that not only crosses the English-Welsh border ten times but also takes in some extraordinarily beautiful countryside. From the Clwydian Hills through the lush plains of England and the much fought over lands of the Welsh borders, the footpath not only covers some superb terrain but also allows those walking its route to enjoy seeing a great variety of flora and fauna as well as taking in the traditional farming methods that have survived in the more remote areas of this region.

available, making the town an ideal centre for family holidays. Although the town undoubtedly expanded with the opening of the Chester to Holyhead railway line in 1848, people were flocking here 50 years before, lured by descriptions of the air being like wine and honey and with the abundant sunshine being deemed excellent in the relief of arthritic conditions and nervous disorders.

However, Prestatyn's origins go back to prehistoric times, as excavated artefacts have shown. While the Roman's 20th legion was stationed at Chester, it is thought that an auxiliary unit was based at a fort on what is now Princes Avenue. The discovery in 1984 of a Roman bath house in Melyd Avenue would certainly seem to support this assumption.

The settlement is mentioned in the Domesday Book as Prestetone, from the Anglo Saxon Preosta Tun (meaning a settlement in which two or more priests reside). It was Lord Robert Banastre who was responsible for building the Norman Prestatyn Castle; it was of a typical motte and bailey design, but all that remains of

LLANASA

20 miles E of Llandudno off the A548

Close by the village, whose church has stained glass windows taken from Basingwerk Abbey, stands **Gyrn Castle** which originates from the 1700s and was castellated in the 1820s. It now contains a large picture gallery and some pleasant woodland walks can be taken in its grounds.

TRELAWNYD

19 miles E of Llandudno on the A5151

Sometimes called Newmarket, this village is well known for its Bronze Age cairn, **Gop Hill**, which marks the place where, traditionally, Offa's Dyke begins (or ends), although the town of Prestatyn also holds this honour.

MELIDEN

17 miles E of Llandudno on the A547

Just to the south of Meliden lies **Craig Fawr**, a limestone hill that supports a wide variety of flowers and butterflies, including the Brown Argus, a rare sight in North Wales, whose larvae feed on the Common Rockrose. Nature trails have been laid around the site that not only take in the myriad of wildlife and plants but also an old quarry where the exposed limestone reveals a wealth of fossils left deposited here over 300 million years ago. The short walk to the summit is well worth the effort as there are panoramic views from the top over the Vale of Clwyd, the coastline and beyond to Snowdonia.

POINT OF AYR

21½ miles E of Llandudno off the A548

Marking the western tip of the Dee estuary and with views across the river mouth to Hilbre Island and the Wirral, this designated RSPB viewing point is an excellent place to observe the numerous birds that come to feed on the sands and mudflats left by the retreating tide.

LLANFAIR TALHAIARN

11½ miles SE of Llandudno off the A544

This village is the burial place of John Jones (1810-1869), a poet who was acclaimed as the Welsh Robert Burns.

LLANGERNYW

10½ miles SE of Llandudno on the A548

This quiet Denbighshire village was the birthplace, in 1852, of Sir Henry Jones, who became known as the cobbler philosopher. Born the son of a local shoemaker, Henry Jones left school at the age of 12 to become apprenticed to his father but, after the long working day, Henry continued his studies well into the evenings. His hard work paid off and he won a scholarship to train as a teacher and then went on to study philosophy before eventually becoming Professor of Moral Philosophy at Glasgow University. A well known and highly regarded academic and a widely acclaimed lecturer on social affairs and liberalism, Henry received his knighthood in 1912, and was made a Companion of Honour in 1922. He died in the same year. Though Sir Henry is buried in Glasgow, this village has not forgotten its local hero. In 1934, Jones' childhood home, Y Cwm, was purchased by a fund set up to honour his memory and his work. Today the recently refurbished **Sir Henry Jones Museum** takes visitors on a tour through the family house - the tiny kitchen and bedroom where the family lived and shoemaker's workshop where Henry and his father worked. Various areas of influence on the life of the young Henry are also illustrated, such as the chapel, school and life in a remote village.

The museum is not the only attraction this village has to offer as, in the

Continued on page 50

WALK 2

Elwy Valley

Start	Llanfair Talhaiarn
Distance	5 miles (8km)
Approximate time	2½ hours
Parking	Llanfair Talhaiarn
Refreshments	Pubs at Llanfair Talhaiarn
Ordnance Survey maps	Landranger 116 (Denbigh & Colwyn Bay), Pathfinder 754, SH97 (Abergele)

The walk is basically a circuit of Mynydd Bodran, the prominent hill that rises to nearly 950ft (289m) above the Elwy and Aled valleys, and provides some superb views. After a pleasant opening stretch by the River Elwy, the route contours along the side of the hill before heading over it and finally descending back into Llanfair Talhaiarn. Route-finding should present no difficulties despite the virtual absence of footpath signs, but the walk should not be attempted in misty weather as the highest part of it is across pathless, bracken-covered moorland where it is essential to be able to see certain landmarks.

The walk begins by the old bridge over the River Elwy on the edge of the pleasant village of Llanfair Talhaiarn. Turn left over the bridge and immediately turn right, at a public footpath sign, on to a riverside path. Ascend steps to climb a stile, cross a road, descend steps to climb another stile and continue along the right edge of meadows beside the river, climbing a stile and following the curve of the river to the left. Climb another stile and turn right to cross a footbridge over the Elwy. Turn left, climb a stile and ascend a steep and potentially slippery path through trees – a wire fence and handrail on the left is helpful – bending right to emerge on to a lane **Ⓐ** . Turn left along the lane, which curves right, and where it

ends by a cottage keep ahead uphill along an enclosed path to a metal gate.

Go through and continue along an undulating path – narrow and engulfed by bracken at times, but discernible – that contours along the side of Mynydd Bodran, passing through a series of gates. The views from here over the hilly and well-wooded Elwy and Aled valleys are most attractive. On meeting a track bear right along it, going through three metal gates, and after the third one you reach a T-junction **Ⓑ** . Turn right, at a fork take the right-hand upper track and go through an electric metal gate; clear operating instructions are provided. Pass between a house and outbuildings, go through a metal gate, bear right and head uphill across a field, later bearing left and making for a metal gate in the top corner. Go through, continue diagonally uphill across the next field, climb a stile and turn left through a metal gate towards Ty-canol Farm. Almost immediately turn right **C** through a metal gate, head uphill along the right edge of a field, turn right through another metal gate in the field corner and walk along the right edge of the next field. Follow the field edge to the left, go through a metal gate, continue uphill by a wire fence along the right edge of the next field and climb a waymarked stile just to the left of the corner. Now comes a difficult part of the walk as you continue across the pathless, bracken-covered slopes on the top of Mynydd Bodran. In summer the bracken can be waist-high but there are "islands" of smooth grass dotted with gorse to ease the way. Do not head up to the highest points but bear right, keeping along the edge of the bracken, descending towards a wire fence and looking out for a waymarked stile to the right of a fence

corner. Ahead are grand views of Llanfair Talhaiarn below in the valley and the outline of the Snowdonia mountains on the horizon. After locating the stile, climb it and walk along the right edge of a field, by a hedge-bank on the right. Follow the field edge to the left, continue up to go through a metal gate and keep ahead along a track, passing to the left of a cottage. The track leads down, via another metal gate, to a lane **D**. Turn right, follow the winding lane steeply downhill and turn left **E** to continue down towards Llanfair Talhaiarn. At a crossroads turn right and just before reaching Elwy Bridge, turn left through a metal kissing-gate, at a public footpath sign.

Walk along an enclosed, tree-lined, tarmac path which continues between buildings and bears left to emerge into the village square. Turn right to return to the start. ●

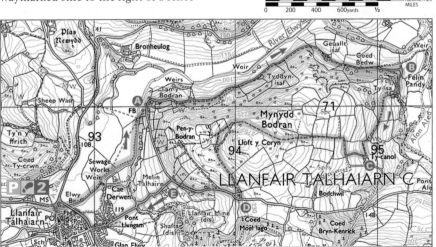

churchyard of St Digain's
Church, lies the **Llangernyw
Yew**. The oldest known tree in
Wales, and one of the oldest
living things in the world, the
yew is estimated to be over 4,000
years old.

CONWY

Situated opposite Deganwy, on
the south bank of the Conwy
estuary, Conwy has in recent
times returned to something of
its former self with the
completion of the tunnel that
carries the A5 under the estuary. No
longer harassed by heavy traffic, the
town is a delight to wander in: its small
streets steeped in history and the place
dominated by another of Edward I's
great castles. The ruins are eye-catching
and it is one of the most picturesque of
Wales' many fortresses. In superb

Conwy Castle

condition, **Conwy Castle** is situated on a
rock which overlooks the River Conwy
and its estuary, and commands
wonderful views of the whole area.
Begun in 1283, the castle's construction
was largely finished by the autumn of
1287 and, compared with other of
Edward's castles, Conwy is of a relatively

THE ROYAL CAMBRIAN ACADEMY OF ART

Crown Lane, Conwy LL32 8AN
Tel/Fax: 01492 593413
e-mail: rca@rcaconwy.org website: www.rcaconwy.org

The Royal Cambrian Academy of Art, established in 1882, is the senior
art institution in Wales. It was housed in the Elizabethan Plas Mawr in
Conwy for over 100 years but since 1993 has been based in its own modern
gallery located behind Plas Mawr. Its main aims and objectives include
the promotion of painting, engraving, sculpture, architecture and other
forms of art in Wales; and the promotion of information on art-related
subjects by lectures, discussion, correspondence with public bodies and
individuals and by the provision of reference and other libraries.

The membership of over 100 Academicians includes many of Wales'
most popular and highly respected artists. The annual exhibition
programme consists of showings by the Academy's members
and occasional guests, loan collections from national
organisations and work from other prestigious societies. At
most of the exhibitions the works are for sale. The highlight
of the Academy's year is the Summer Exhibition (2002 saw
the 120th) with work from RCA artists and selected non-
members. Among the artists to be featured towards the end
of 2002 are Isabel McWhirter, Ken Elias and Mike and Emma
Knowles. The Gallery is open 11-5 Tuesday to Saturday and
1-4.30 Sunday; closed Monday, open Bank Holidays.

simple design which relies on its position rather than anything else to provide a defence against attack. The town was walled at the same time and today the walls still encircle the vast majority of Conwy, stretching for three quarters of a mile and including 22 towers and three gateways. The Castle was also built to be a suitable royal residence and in fact was used twice by Edward I: once on his way to Caernarfon where his son, the first English Prince of Wales was born, and again in 1294, when trying to put down the rebellion of Madoc ap Llewelyn. Now a World Heritage Site, the castle not only offers visitors spectacular views from its battlements but the huge curtain walls and the eight massive round towers are still a stirring sight. In 1399, Richard II stayed at the Castle before being lured out and ambushed by the Earl of Northumberland's men on behalf of Henry Bolingbroke, the Duke of Lancaster, who later became Henry IV. Conwy was given the attention of Owain Glyndwr during his rebellion, his men burning it to the ground. As with other castles further east, Conwy was embroiled in the Civil War. A Conwy man, John Williams, became Archbishop of York and, as a Royalist, sought refuge in his home town. Repairing the crumbling fortifications at his own expense, Archbishop Williams finally changed sides after shabby treatment by

Royalist leaders and helped the Parliamentary forces lay siege to the town and castle, which eventually fell to them in late 1646.

The town developed within the shadows of its now defunct fortress, and slate and coal extracted from the surrounding area, were shipped up and down the coast from Conwy. Later, the town fathers approached Thomas Telford, who planned a causeway and bridge, as Conwy's trade and links grew with the outside world. Built in 1826, the elegant **Suspension Bridge** replaced the ferry that previously had been the only means of crossing the river so close to its estuary. The toll house has been restored and furnished as it would have been a century ago. This suspension road bridge, its design sympathetic to its surroundings, was soon followed by the construction of railways. By the side of Telford's bridge stands the Robert Stephenson designed tubular rail bridge of 1846. Both builders breached the town walls in styles that complemented the town's architecture and the two structures are still admired today.

Bridges, however, are not the only architectural gems Conwy has to offer. **Plas Mawr**, an Elizabethan town house on the High Street, is one of the best preserved buildings from that period in Britain. Built for the influential merchant Robert Wynn between 1576

CASTLE HOTEL

High Street, Conwy, North Wales LL32 8DB
Tel: 01492 582800 Fax: 01492 582300
e-mail: mail@castlewales.co.uk website: www.castlewales.co.uk

On the site of a Cistercian Abbey, the **Castle Hotel** is a famous old coaching inn whose ornate brick and granite facade makes it popular with photographers. The hotel is owned and run by Peter Lavin and his family and has many interesting features, notably a collection of paintings by Victorian artist John Dawson-Watson. In the atmospheric Shakespeare's Restaurant chef Graham Tinsley uses prime locally sourced produce, combining traditional and modern elements on a mouthwatering menu. There are 29 characterful bedrooms, all with private bathroom, tv, telephone, trouser press, hairdryer and beverage tray.

TIR-Y-COED COUNTRY HOUSE HOTEL

Rowen, Conwy, North Wales LL32 8TP
Tel/Fax: 01492 650219 e-mail: tirycoed@btinternet.com
website: www.tirycoedhotel.co.uk

Tir-y-Coed Country House Hotel is located on the edge of
Rowen, one of the most delightful villages in the Conwy Valley.
Built in the late-19th century, Tir-y-Coed was converted into a
hotel in the early 1970s but still retains the feel of a friendly
family home under resident proprietors Ken and Gwyneth
Kirkham. The hotel stands in an acre of mature landscaped gardens just inside the boundary of
Snowdonia National Park. The foothills of the Carneddau mountain range are on the doorstep, and
Tal y Fan, at around 2,000 feet, provides a stunning backdrop to Rowen nestling in the valley below.
The hotel has eight tastefully decorated and furnished guest bedrooms, most enjoying fine views over
the garden to the hills beyond. Each has either a bathroom or shower
room en suite, tv, clock radio, hairdryer and hospitality tray.

The residents' lounge is a light, airy and peaceful place to relax, to
meet the other guests and to enjoy the lovely views. Tir-y-Coed is well
known for the quality of its cuisine, and the meals served in the non-
smoking restaurant combine the best in traditional cooking with fresh,
imaginative ideas. Vegetarian and other dietary requirements can be catered
for, and the fine food is complemented by a well-chosen selection of wines.
The hotel is an excellent base for visiting the coastal resorts of North Wales
and the many attractions in the area including castles, historic houses,
narrow gauge railways and some lovely gardens. There are ample
opportunities for outdoor activity, including water sports, fishing, golf,
climbing, cycling and walking; several walks start from the hotel.

THE GROES INN

Tyn-y-Groes, Nr Conwy, North Wales LL32 8TN
Tel: 01492 650545 Fax: 01492 650855
website: www.groesinn.com

Dawn and Justin are the fourth generation of the Humphreys
family to own the historic **Groes Inn**, which has records back
to 1573. It remains a traditional refuge for travellers, a place
to seek out for its warm, inviting ambience, its homely, well-
appointed accommodation and its good wholesome food. The
14 individually styled bedrooms all have full en suite facilities, a comfortable seating area, tv, radio,
direct-dial phone, hairdryer and refreshment tray. Superior and de luxe rooms and the four-poster
room are situated at the rear of the hotel overlooking the foothills of Snowdonia and have a private
terrace or balcony; one room on the ground floor has been designed for ease of access by wheelchair
users. The day rooms are equally delightful, with beams, cosy nooks and crannies and the owners'
individualistic furnishings and decorations. The inn offers various
eating options, from light snacks and bar meals to an extensive à la
carte and a tempting daily changing table d'hote served in the lovely
conservatory restaurant. The chefs set great store by the quality and
freshness of local ingredients, including Conwy crab and plaice,
the renowned Welsh lamb and beef, and game from local estates.
Meals are a delight right from the home-baked bread to the famous
home-made ice creams with unusual varieties such as rose petal,
honey and lemon or brown bread and Baileys. The Groes is a perfect
country hideaway with its lovely gardens and glorious views, and
is also a great base for a touring or outdoor holiday.

Conwy Valley

and 1585, the house has an interesting stone facade and over 50 windows. Plas Mawr (the name means Great Hall) is particularly noted for its fine and elaborate plasterwork, seen to striking effect in the glorious decorated ceilings and friezes and in the glorious overmantel in the hall. The authentic period atmosphere is further enhanced by furnishings based on an inventory of the contents in 1665. The house came into the possession of the Mostyn family during the 18th century and in 1991 was given by Lord Mostyn to the nation. Close by is **Aberconwy House**, a delightful medieval merchant's home that dates from the 14th century. The rooms have been decorated and furnished to reflect various periods in the house's history and the property is now in the hands of the National Trust.

Occupying part of the site of a 12th century Cistercian Abbey that was moved to Maenan by Edward I, is **St Mary's Church**. This abbey church became the parish church of the borough created by Edward, and some interesting features still remain from that time though there have been many additions over the centuries.

Conwy's **Teapot Museum and Shop**, on Castle Street, is an interesting and unusual attraction where visitors can see a unique collection of antique, novelty and humorous teapots that date from the mid-1700s to the present day. Many of the pieces on show have taken their place in the annals of teapot history, including the celebrated Worcester "aesthetic" teapot of 1880, the Wedgwood cauliflower pot of 1775 and the Clarice Cliffe wigwam-shaped pot of 1930. The museum shop is also a must for tea enthusiasts' as it not only sells a wide variety of teas but also a mass of tea paraphernalia.

It is not surprising that the town and the surrounding area have strong links with the sea and Conwy also has a traditional mermaid story. Washed ashore by a violent storm in Conwy Bay, a mermaid begged the local fishermen who found her to carry her back to the

sea. The fishermen refused and, before she died, the mermaid cursed the people of the town, swearing that they would always be poor. In the 5th century, Conwy suffered a fish famine and many said that the curse was fulfilled.

St Brigid is connected to another fish famine story. Walking by the riverside carrying some rushes, she threw the rushes upon the water. A few days later the rushes had turned into fish and ever since they have been known as sparlings or, in Welsh, brwyniaid - both meaning rush-like. On the quayside the fishermen still land their catches, and from here pleasure boat trips can be taken. Nearby, in between terraced housing, can be found what is claimed to be **Britain's Smallest House**, measuring 10 feet by 6; it seems that its last tenant was a fisherman who was 6' 3" tall - he was presumably also a contortionist! Conwy was once a famous pearl fishing centre and had a thriving mussel industry, whose history is told in the **Conwy Mussel Centre**, open daily from mid-May to September.

ROWEN

4 miles S of Conwy off the B5106

From this very pretty, quiet village a track, which was once a Roman road, skirts by the foot of **Tal-y-fan**, which climbs to 2,000 feet at its peak. Roughly six miles in length, the path passes by Maen-y-Bardd, an ancient burial chamber, and eventually drops down towards the coast at Aber. Another, circular, walk of about five miles, one of several in the Conwy Valley devised by Active Snowdonia, passes many impressive cromlechs and standing stones. The route also takes in Caer Bach, where there are traces of a neolithic

settlement, the wonderfully unspoilt 14th century St Celynin's Church and the Woodlands Trust's Parc Mawr woods.

Just to the east of Rowen lies **Parc Glyn**, a traditional Welsh farm that specialises in the breeding and conservation of rare farm animals. Along with the sheep, cattle and pigs, there are peacock, guinea fowl, ducks and geese. Surrounding the animal and bird paddocks, are scenic picnic areas and pleasant mixed woodland.

TYN-Y-GROES

5 miles S of Conwy on the B5106

Before bridges were built spanning the Conwy estuary people crossed the river, by ferry, from here to Tal-y-Cafn.

TREFRIW

8 miles S of Conwy on the B5106

This village, nestling into the forested edge of Snowdonia in the beautiful Conwy valley, was once one of the homes of Llewelyn the Great; he is said to have built a church here to please his wife, who refused to climb to the nearest church, which was at Llanrhychyrn. Once the biggest inland port in Wales, the village today has two main attractions: **Trefriw Woollen Mill** and the local chalybeate springs. The

Conwy Valley, nr Tal-y-Cafn

woollen mill has been in operation since the 1830s and it is still owned by descendants of Thomas Williams, who purchased it in 1859. It is run by hydro-electric power generated from the two lakes - Crafnant and Geirionydd - which lie to the west of the village. While the source of power is modern, the tapestries and tweeds produced here from raw wool are very traditional. A footpath above the woollen mill leads to **Fairy Falls**, where in the early 19th century a forge was founded to make hammers and chisels for use in the slate quarries. It closed at the beginning of the 20th century. Sometime between AD 100 and AD 250, while prospecting for minerals in this area, the Romans opened up a cave where they found a spring rich in iron (chalybeate). Covered in later years by a landslide, it was not until the 18th century that the spring was uncovered by Lord Willoughby de Eresby, owner of nearby Gwydir Castle, who went on to built a stone bathhouse. Taking the waters became so popular that by 1874 the original bathhouse was replaced with a pumphouse and bath, and the bottled water was exported worldwide. Following a decline during much of the 20th century, interest in the natural spring waters has been rekindled. Visitors can take the waters, view the museum artefacts in the tea room and browse in the spa beauty shop. Lake Geirionydd

was the birthplace, in the 6th century, of the great bard Taliesin, to whom in 1850 Lord Willoughby erected a monument. In 1863, a local poet, Gwilym Cowlyd, being dissatisfied with the National Eisteddfod, started an arwest, a poetical and musical event that was held in the shadow of the monument every year until 1922. The monument fell down in a storm in 1976 but was restored in 1994. It lies on one of Active Snowdonia's Conwy Valley walks, which also passes Fairy Falls and old mine workings; it skirts Lake Crafnant and provides memorable views at many points along its route.

LLANRWST
10 miles S of Conwy on the A470

The market centre for the central Conwy Valley owes both its name and the dedication of its church to St Grwst (Restitutus), a 6th century missionary who was active in this area. The **Church of St Grwst** dates from 1470, though the tower and north aisle are 19th century and it replaced a thatched building from 1170 that was destroyed in the fighting of 1468.

Next to the church lies **Gwydir Chapel**, famous for its richly carved Renaissance interior. This was the private chapel of the Wynn family and among its treasures is an imposing stone sarcophagus of the Welsh prince

Llewelyn the Great. This chapel should not be confused with **Gwydir Uchaf Chapel** which lies on the opposite bank of the river Conwy and is particularly noted for its ceiling covered with paintings of angels.

Below the chapel lies **Gwydir Castle**, the Wynn family's Tudor mansion which has, in its grounds, some fine Cedars of Lebanon planted in 1625 in celebration of the marriage of Charles I to Henrietta Maria of France. Here, too, is an arch built to commemorate the end of the War of the Roses, while inside the much restored house is a secret room, once hidden by a wooden panel, which is home to the ghost of a monk said to have been trapped in the tunnel that leads the arch. A walk west from the town takes in these historic buildings, the remains of an old crushing mill and the site of the old Hafna Galena Mine.

Y DOLYDD MEADOWSWEET HOTEL

Station Road, Llanrwst, Conwy LL26 0DS
Tel/Fax: 01492 642111 e-mail: dolydd@globalnet.co.uk
website: www.users-globalnet.co.uk/~dolydd

Humphrey Hughes and his family run **Y Dolydd Meadowsweet Hotel**, which enjoys a lovely scenic location on the edge of Snowdonia National Park. The hotel has 10 bright, attractive en suite bedrooms, including doubles, twins, family rooms and a four-poster suite. The hotel restaurant has an excellent reputation for its cuisine, which features fresh local ingredients of high quality. Meals can also be taken in the bar, where a real log fire adds to the warm, inviting ambience. The area offers exhilarating walks in beautiful countryside; the world-famous Bodnant Gardens are only six miles away, and it's an easy 10-mile drive to the Aberconwy coast.

THE TANNERY

Willow Street, Llanrwst, Conwy, North Wales LL26 0ES
Tel: 01492 640172 e-mail: info@thetannerywales.com
Fax: 01492 642578 website: www.thetannerywales.com

An old tannery on the banks of the River Conwy has found an exciting new role as a showcase for visual and applied arts. **The Tannery Contemporary Craft & Design Shop** is owned and run by Geraldine Berry, daughter Tamsin and son Colin, who have renovated the premises extensively to provide light, airy showrooms and a gallery displaying work by top designer-makers from Wales and elsewhere. Many of these talented people will work to commission on a range that includes hand-built kitchens, contemporary furniture, soft furnishings, stained glass, wood carving, murals, jewellery, mosaics, framing and lifestyle photography. The Tannery also offers a full interior design service. Of

particular interest is a very special range of designer jewellery in 100% pure Welsh gold, platinum and non-conflict diamonds which attracts interest from around the world.

The gallery hosts exhibitions featuring the work of new and established designers in mixed media, while the fully licensed café - bistro is well worth a visit for its innovative, freshly prepared dishes. The cosmopolitan menu includes modern Welsh cuisine, Lavazza coffee and home-made cakes and desserts.

The balconied seating area overlooking the River Conwy is a delight on sunny days. The Tannery is open from 10 to 5 Tuesdays to Saturdays, 11 to 5 Sundays, closed Mondays. Evening meals, Fridays and Saturdays from 7.

BLAS AR FWYD/AMSER DA DELI & RESTAURANT

Heol yr Orsaf, Llanrwst, Conwy LL26 0BT
Tel/Fax: 01492 640215
e-mail: info@blasarfwyd.com website: www.blasarfwyd.com

Deiniol ap Dafydd and his partners run **Blas Ar Fwyd and Amser Da**, a

delicatessen and restaurant on opposite
sides of the road. Blas Ar Fwyd was
established in 1988 to sell fine food and
wine from Wales and across the world
and Amser Da is a café, wine bar, brasserie and restaurant where
customers can enjoy a light snack, lunch or dinner prepared from the
finest fresh ingredients and served in a friendly, relaxing Welsh
atmosphere. A comprehensive catering service is available, and orders
can be accepted by telephone or on line.

Back in town, the **Old Bridge** is
thought to have been designed by Inigo
Jones; it was built in 1636 by Sir Richard
Wynn. Next to it stands **Tu Hwnt i'r
Bont** (the House over the Bridge), a
16th century courthouse which has since
been divided into two cottages and is
now a tea room.

BETWS-Y-COED

12 miles S of Conwy on the A5

The "Gateway to Snowdonia" - see next
chapter.

CAPEL CURIG

9 miles S of Conwy on the A5

Situated at the junction of
the mountain roads to
Beddgelert, Llyn Ogwen and
Betws-y-Coed, Capel Curig is
a place popular with climbers
as well as hill walkers and
anglers who also use the
village as a base. A walk
south of the village passes by
lonely Llyn y Foel and climbs
the steep ridge of Daiar Ddu
to the top of Mount Siabod;
the reward for this
expenditure of energy is the
most spectacular panoramic
view of many of Snowdonia's

great peaks. Plas-y-Brenin, the National
Mountain Centre, provides excellent
facilities for climbing, canoeing, dry
slope skiing and orienteering.

BANGOR

A cathedral and university city, Bangor
incorporates a wide variety of
architectural styles that remind the
visitor that this is not only an interesting
and stimulating place but also one with a
long history. A monastic community
was founded here as early as AD 525 by
St Deiniol, and the town's name is
derived from the wattle fence which
surrounded the saint's primitive

Llynnau Mymbyr, Capel Curig

enclosure - "bangori" is still used in parts of Wales to describe the plaiting of twigs in a hedge. However, there were settlers in the area long before St Deiniol, including the Romans at nearby Segontium, and the **Bangor Museum and Art Gallery** is just the place to discover not only the past 2,000 years of history of this area of Wales but also to see the reconstructions of domestic life in days gone by. The art gallery exhibits a range of work by artists from all ages.

The base of the oldest bishopric in Britain, Bangor's **Cathedral** dates from the 13th century and has probably been in continuous use for longer than any other cathedral in Britain. During the Middle Ages, the Cathedral became a centre of worship for the independent principality of Gwynedd and the tomb of Owain Gwynedd, buried here after his death, became a starting point for pilgrims setting out on the arduous journey to Bardsey Island. Restored in 1866, the cathedral also contains a life-size carving of Christ dating from 1518 while, outside, there is a Biblical garden that contains plants which are associated with the Bible.

Until the slate boom of the 19th century, Bangor remained little more than a village, albeit with an impressive church. Its position on the Menai Strait made this the ideal place for nearby Penrhyn Quarry to build their docks and the town soon flourished in its new role to become a commercial centre. Its importance increased further when the **University College of North Wales** was founded here in 1884. Improvements in the roads and then the coming of the railways to the North Wales coast also saw Bangor grow in both stature and importance. The **Menai Suspension Bridge** was built by Thomas Telford between 1819 and 1826 and it was the first permanent crossing of the Menai Strait. Before its completion the crossing had been made by ferry, and cattle, on their way to and from market, would have had to swim the channel. Not surprisingly there was much opposition to the construction not only from the ferrymen but also from ship-owners worried that the structure would impede the passage of their tall ships. As a result of this concern, the road bridge stands at a height of 100 feet. The **Britannia Bridge**, a mile further southwest from Telford's bridge, is a combined road and rail crossing and was built between 1846 and 1850 by Robert Stephenson. The lions guarding the bridge are by John Thomas, who was responsible for much of the sculpture at the Houses of Parliament. Also jutting out into the Menai Strait from the town is the 1,500 foot long **Victoria Pier**, the youngest of the structures, which was built in 1896. As well as being attractive, the pier is a pleasant place from which to view Snowdonia, the coast and the busy lanes of small boats passing by, and to admire the houses, some of them magnificent, which stand beside the water. Both pleasure and fishing trips can be taken from the pierhead. Bangor is a major centre of the mussel industry.

To the west of the town and overlooking Beaumaris on the Isle of Anglesey lies **Penrhyn Castle**, a dramatic neo-Norman construction built by Thomas Hopper between 1820 and 1845, and incorporating Doll and Railway Museums (see panel on page opposite).

AROUND BANGOR

ABERGWYNGREGYN

6 miles E of Bangor off the A55

To the south of the village lie **Rhaeadr Aber Falls**, reached by taking a footpath

PENRHYN CASTLE

Bangor, Gwynedd LL57 4HN
Tel: 01248 353084 info line: 01248 371337
e-mail: ppemsn@smtp.ntrust.org.uk

On the A5122 southeast of Bangor, overlooking Beaumaris on the Isle of Anglesey, **Penrhyn Castle** is a dramatic fantasy castle built by Thomas Hopper between 1820 and 1845. He built it for the Pennant family, who had made their fortune first through their sugar estates in Jamaica and later through their nearby slate quarry. Behind a facade that is very reminiscent of Norman architecture, the Castle is decorated in a variety of styles, and filled with an eclectic assortment of fascinating treasures. Notable among these is a slate bed made for Queen Victoria that weighs a ton (literally!).

There's a spectacular Grand Staircase that took 10 years to build, hand-made wallpapers, intricate carvings, superb furniture, beautiful stained glass and one of the best collections of paintings in Wales. The extensive Victorian kitchens provide an interesting glance "below stairs", and in the grand stable block next to the house are railway museums, a dolls museum and two galleries with a programme of exhibitions throughout the season. The extensive grounds include specimen plants from around the world and a formal Victorian walled garden. Also in the grounds are a children's adventure playground and an orienteering course. The Castle and gardens, both owned by the National Trust, are open for visits between late March and early November. Audio tours are available.

through sheltered woodland, where the drop of the river is said to be among the steepest in Wales.

LLANFAIRFECHAN

8 miles E of Bangor on the A55

An excellent base for energetic walks amid stunning scenery, Llanfairfechan also has a long stretch of sandy beach and a nature reserve at Traeth Lafan.

PENMAENMAWR

10 miles E of Bangor off the A55

A tiny quarrying village before the arrival of the railway in 1848, this small holiday resort, with its sand and shingle beach, has changed little since William Gladstone holidayed here in the 19th century, and it still boasts many fine Victorian buildings. Gladstone was a frequent visitor, and there's a bust of him

RHIWIAU RIDING CENTRE

Llanfairfechan, North Wales LL33 0EH
Tel: 01248 680094

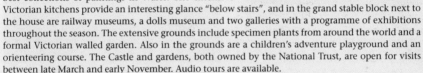

Rhiwiau Riding Centre is situated 600ft up in a secluded valley overlooking the Menai Straits and the Isle of Anglesey. Riders of all levels of ability and experience can enjoy a relaxed, informal time in the saddle. Instruction is offered on the flat and over obstacles in the two outdoor schools, and other facilities include a cross-country course, show jumping, mountain rides with no road work and lots of other equine activities. Weeks, weekends and midweek breaks are available throughout the year and comfortable accommodation (for riders and non riders) is offered in centrally heated bedrooms. Mrs Hill provides excellent home cooking, and vegetarian and special diets can be catered for with notice.

THE WELSH HIGHLAND RAILWAY
(CAERNARFON)

St Helens Road, Caernarfon
Tel: 01766 516073 Fax: 01766 516006
e-mail: info@festrail.co.uk
website: www.festrail.co.uk

The Ffestiniog Railway, the oldest independent railway company in the world, also owns and operates the Welsh Highland Railway, which runs between Caernarfon and Waunfawr; extensions are planned to Rhyd Ddu, the beginning of one of the footpaths to the summit of Snowdon, and eventually through the spectacular Aberglaslyn Pass to Porthmadog and a link with the Ffestiniog Railway. The Welsh Highland Railway (WHR) dates back to the 1870s, when work started on a narrow gauge railway between Dinas and Rhyd Ddu; the line finally reached Porthmadog in 1923.

With the growing ownership of cars and the decline in the slate trade the railway never met its full potential and closed in 1937. The revival project, led by the Ffestiniog Railway, has brought back this splendid little system, linking places of beauty and providing fun and nostalgia. WHR trains first steamed out of Caernarfon on the re-opened line in October 1997, and Millennium Year saw the line extended along the track bed for the first time in 60 years from Dinas to Waunfawr, one of the gateways into Snowdonia National Park.

Starting beneath the shadow of Caernarfon Castle, the line climbs away from the harbour into pastureland with views of the Menai Strait and the mountains of Snowdonia, then into woodland beyond Dinas to Waunfawr. Many trains are steam-hauled, and the Pullman car *Bodysgallen* is attached to some trains. Caernarfon is the main terminus, with a booking office and souvenir shop. As with the Ffestiniog Railway, support is always welcome either by assisting on the railway or by joining the WHR Society.

on a granite obelisk in Paradise Road. Penmaenmawr has a small industrial heritage park, Parc Plas Mawr.

In the town's steep mountain-backed hinterland can be found many prehistoric sites including one of Wales' best known Bronze Age stone circles, **Cefn Coch**. An urn was uncovered here containing the remains of a child as well as a bronze dagger said to be evidence of a ritual sacrifice that once took place here.

CAERNARFON CASTLE

Caernarfon, Gwynedd LL55 2AY
Tel: 01286 677617

Mighty Caernarfon is possibly the most famous of Wales' many castles. Its sheer scale and commanding presence easily set it apart from the rest and, to this day, still trumpet in no uncertain terms the intentions of its builder, Edward 1. Begun in 1283 as the definitive chapter in his conquest of Wales, Caernarfon was constructed not only as a military stronghold but also as a seat of government and royal palace.

The castle's majestic persona is no architectural accident: it was designed to echo the walls of Constantinople, the imperial power of Rome and the dream castle, "the fairest that ever man saw", of Welsh myth and legend. After all these years, Caernarfon's immense strength remains undimmed. Standing at the mouth ot the Seiont river, the fortress (with its unique polygonal towers, intimidating battlements and colour banded masonry) dominates the walled town also founded by Edward. Caernarfon's symbolic status was emphasized when Edward made sure that his son, the first English Prince of Wales, was born here in 1284. In 1969, the castle gained worldwide fame as the setting for the investiture of Prince Charles as Prince of Wales.

History comes alive at Caernarfon in so many ways along the lofty wall walks, beneath the towered gatehouse and within imaginative exhibitions located within the towers.

CAERNARFON

Situated on the right bank of the River Seiont, near the southwest end of the Menai Strait, Caernarfon (the name means "fort on the shore") is a town steeped in history as well as a bastion of the Welsh language and of national pride. The history of Caernarfon goes back to Roman times and **Segontium Roman Fort**, half a mile from the town centre on the road towards Beddgelert, is the only place in Wales where it is possible to see something of the internal layout of an auxiliary station. Built to defend the Roman Empire against attack from rebellious tribes, the fort dates back to AD 77, when the Roman conquest was finally completed following the capture of Anglesey. Certainly this was one of the most important garrisons on the edge of the Roman Empire and, during

its life, it was not only a military but also an administrative centre for northwest Wales. It is believed that Constantine the Great was born at the fort. Excavations of the site have revealed coins which show that the fort was garrisoned at least until AD 394 and this long occupation can be explained by its strategic position controlling the fertile lands and mineral rights of Anglesey and providing a defence against Irish pirates. The well-preserved site is managed by CADW and the **Museum**, which is run by the National Museum and Galleries of Wales, displays many items, including coins, pottery and weapons which have been uncovered during excavation work.

However, it is another great construction and symbol of military power - the impressive **Caernarfon Castle** (see panel above) - that still dominates the town today. The most famous of Wales' numerous great fortresses, the Castle was begun in 1283 by Henry de Elreton, who was also building Beaumaris Castle, under the orders of Edward I; it took some 40 years to complete. Built not only as a defence but as a royal palace and a seat of government, the Castle's majestic appearance was no accident as it was designed to be Wales' dream castle and is based around two oval-shaped courts divided by a wall. The outer defences are strengthened at intervals by towers and are, in places, up to 15 feet thick! Many attempts were made by the Welsh, over the years, to destroy the castle but their failure is confirmed by the presence of this magnificent building today. It was here that, in 1284, Edward I crowned his son the first English Prince of Wales and the castle was once again used for such an investiture when, in 1969, the Queen crowned Prince Charles Prince of Wales.

Also at the Castle, and housed in the Queen's Tower, is the **Museum of the Royal Welsh Fusiliers**, the country's oldest regiment.

The castle sits where the River Seiont meets the Menai Strait, the expanse of water that separates mainland Wales from the Isle of Anglesey. Close by, the old Slate Quay, from where slate was once shipped, is now the place from where fishing trips and pleasure cruises depart up the Strait to Beaumaris. Castle Square, on the landward side of the castle, holds markets and here, too, can be found statues of two famous Welshmen: the gesticulating, urging David Lloyd-George, once a member of Parliament for the area, and Sir Hugh Owen, the founder of Further Education in Wales.

The Anglesey Hotel and the **Hanging Tower** stand by the Castle walls and were

Ty Mawr Farm-Bed & Breakfast, Self Catering Cottages

Llanddeiniolen, Caernarfon, Gwynedd LL55 3AD
Tel/Fax: 01248 670417 Mobile: 07989621987
e-mail: jane@tymawrfarm.freeserve.co.uk
website: www.tymawrfarm.co.uk

Ty Mawr, is a working farm dating back to the 1620s, offering bed and breakfast and optional evening dinner. There are three rooms all twins or doubles with bath/shower en-suite, two lounges with woodburning stoves and panelled dining room with separate dining tables. A stone-built granary has been converted into two luxury cottages standing in their own grounds with a garden and ample parking space. Hafod and Hendre are both full of character, with inglenooks and exposed beams. The entrance to Hafod is by the original stone and slate enclosed stairway. On the first floor are a fully-equipped kitchen-diner and comfortable lounge areas; the kitchen has a microwave, full-sized oven, fridge, gas hob and double ceramic sink. An ornate spiral staircase leads down to the Stag furnished bedroom with a bath/shower en suite, and a door from the bedroom leads out on to a patio in the courtyard.

Two-bedroom Hendre is similarly appointed and equally delightful; its kitchen-diner and hallway have splendid slate flag floors. Both cottages have gas central heating, and hot water is on tap 24 hours a day. Guests have the use of a gas barbecue, and there's a play area with swings and a slide. Jane Llewellyn-Pierce's 100-acre farm rears suckler cows and a flock of the famous Welsh Badger Faced sheep. It lies five miles from Caernarfon and commands magnificent views of the Snowdonia mountain range just four miles away. An ideal base for touring North Wales.

a customs house until 1822. The last hanging to take place in the tower was in 1911 when an Irishman named Murphy was executed for murdering a maid. It is said that when he died the bell clapper in **St Mary's Church** fell off. The church itself was founded in 1307 and, though much of it has since been reconstructed, the arcades of the eastern and southern walls are part of the original 14th century building.

Northgate Street is called, in Welsh, Stryd Pedwar a Chewch - meaning four and six street. Apparently it originates from the time when sailors flocked to this part of town looking for lodgings: four pence for a hammock and six pence for a bed!

From the town, walkers can enjoy a scenic footpath, the **Lôn Las Menai**, which follows the coastline along the Menai Strait towards the village of Y Felinheli and from which there are views across the water to the Isle of Anglesey.

To the southwest of Caernarfon and overlooking Caernarfon Bay is **Caernarfon Air World**, located on the site of an RAF station that was built in 1940 and which is also the home of the first RAF mountain rescue team. As well as offering pleasure flights to visitors, there is the **Aviation Museum**, housed in one of the great hangars which not only displays over 400 model aircraft but has various planes and helicopters on show and also provides visitors with the opportunity to take the controls in a flight trainer.

Y FELINHELI
4 miles NE of Caernarfon off the A487

Situated on the other side of the main road from this village is **The Greenwood Centre**, a forest heritage and adventure park that will delight and inform all the family. Opened in the early 1990s, this centre concentrates on exploring and explaining man's relationship with trees and how, using conservation techniques, the loss of species of trees from the countryside can be halted whether in the equatorial rain forests or ancient temperate forests of Europe. The skills of ancient carpenters and joiners are also on show, particularly in the Great Hall, a building that was constructed entirely using medieval skills and knowledge and is held together by 500 oak pegs!

A couple of miles further east off the A487, bordering the Menai Strait, is a National Trust property, Glan Faenol, that includes parkland and farmland around Vaynol Hall, once one of the largest estates in North Wales. This is an important habitat for wildlife, and a pleasant walk leads to the sea and two viewing platforms. The estate has tracts of ancient woodland and several follies, including one built to rival the Marquess' Column on Anglesey. The views of Snowdonia and across the strait are memorably depicted in one of Rex Whistler's murals at Plas Newydd.

BETHESDA
9 miles E of Caernarfon on the A5

This old quarry town takes its name from the Nonconformist chapel that was built here and served many of the 2,300 men (and their families) who worked in the quarry at its peak in 1875. The gouged rock of the **Penrhyn Slate Quarries** forms a huge hillside amphitheatre; it was the largest open cast slate mine in the world and still produces high-quality slate 250 years after it was first worked.

From the town, the main road travels through the beautiful **Nant Ffrancon Pass**, which runs straight through and up the valley of the River Ogwen and into the Snowdonia National Park. Five miles south of Bethesda on the A5, Llyn Idwal is one of several lakes on the National Trust's Carneddau estate. In

1954 it was declared the first National Nature Reserve in Wales.

MENAI BRIDGE

Acting as a gateway to Anglesey, this largely Victorian town grew and developed after the construction of Thomas Telford's **Menai Suspension Bridge**, which connects the island to mainland Wales. The waterfront is a popular place for anglers and for those wishing to view the annual Regatta on the Menai Strait held every August, and the promenade, known as the Belgian Promenade because it was built by refugees from Belgium who sought shelter here during The First World War.

Menai Straits Bridge

On **Church Island**, reached by a causeway from the town, there is a small 14th century church built on the site of a foundation by St Tysilio in AD 630. The site is thought to have been visited by Archbishop Baldwin and Giraldus when they may have landed here in 1188.

For a place with a difference, **Pili Palas** (**Butterfly Palace**) is an interesting and unusual attraction that will delight everyone. The vast collection of exotic butterflies and birds, from all over the world, can be seen in tropical environments, where visitors can not only marvel at the colourful creatures but also see the wonderful tropical plants. There is also a Tropical Hide, an amazing Ant Avenue and a Snake House and while adults relax in Pili Palas' café children can let off steam in the adventure play area.

AROUND MENAI BRIDGE

PENTRAETH
4 miles N of Menai Bridge on the A5025

Before land reclamation this sleepy village stood on the edge of Red Wharf Bay, where, at low tide, the almost 15 square miles of sand supported a flourishing cockling industry. Nowadays, this is a popular place for a holiday even though it is not ideal for swimming due to the strong tidal currents experienced around this part of the Anglesey coast.

Close to **Plas Gwyn**, an 18th century Georgian mansion, is the **Three Leaps** - three stones that commemorate a contest between two rivals for the hand of the same girl. The contest was won by the man who could leap the further, in this case, by a champion named Hywel, jumping in about AD 580 for the hand of the grand-daughter of the warrior

Geraint. The stones mark his efforts, in possibly what we now know as the triple jump; the loser is said to have died of a broken heart.

BENLLECH
6½ miles N of Menai Bridge on the A5025

With its excellent beach to attract holidaymakers, Benllech is probably the most popular resort on Anglesey, but those coming here should take care as there are strong tidal currents and the sands can be treacherous. This resort has another claim to fame, as the birthplace of the poet Goronwy Owen.

Traces of a hill fort, **Castell Mawr**, can be found on the west side of Red Wharf Bay, near Benllech, and on the evidence of coins found here, the site could once have been occupied by the Romans.

MOELFRE
9 miles N of Menai Bridge on the A5108

This is a charming coastal village with a sheltered, pebbled beach, attractive cottages and sandy beaches to both the north and the south. Fame, however, came to Moelfre in an unfortunate and bizarre way via its lifeboat which, over the years, has been involved in many rescues but there are two which are worthy of mention. Returning to Liverpool from Australia in October 1859, laden with cargo and passengers, including gold prospectors coming home after making their fortunes in the Australian Gold Rush, *The Royal Charter* sank. A rigged iron vessel and the pride of the merchant fleet, the ship was all set to make the long passage in record time but, while sheltering from a hurricane in Moelfre Bay, she foundered with the loss of 450 passengers and crew. Only 39 passengers and crew survived and many believe that the gold still lies with the wreck out in the bay. Efforts have been made to recover the lost fortune with

varying but not overwhelming degrees of success and it has been said that the larger houses around Moelfre were paid for with gold washed ashore from the wreck. This is despite Customs Officers swamping the village in an attempt to ensure that any salvaged gold ended in the Exchequer rather than in the hands of the locals. Charles Dickens visited the site on New Year's Eve, 1859, and apparently based a story on the disaster in *The Uncommercial Traveller*.

One hundred years later, almost to the day, in October 1959, the coaster *Hindlea*, struggling in foul weather, had eight crew members rescued by the Moelfre Lifeboat. The rescue earned Richard Evans, the lifeboat's coxswain, his second RNLI gold medal for gallantry.

Beyond the station is a small outcrop of rocks, **Ynys Moelfre**, a favourite spot for seabirds and, occasionally, porpoises can also be seen in the bay. About a mile inland from the village, off the narrow road, is the impressive **Lligwy Burial Chamber**, a Bronze Age tomb which has a huge capstone supported by stone uprights, which lies half hidden in a pit dug out of the rock. Close by is **Din Lligwy Village**, the remains of a Romano British settlement that covers over half an acre. Certainly occupied around the 4th century AD, after the Roman garrison on Anglesey had been vacated, some of the stone walls of the buildings can still be seen and excavations of the site have unearthed pottery, coins and evidence of metal working from that period. Nearby are the ruins of the 14th century **Capel Lligwy**.

PENMON
7 miles NE of Menai Bridge off the B5109

On the eastern tip of Anglesey, this is a beauty spot whose lovely views across the Menai Strait go some way to explaining why it was chosen, centuries earlier, as a religious site. **Penmon Priory** was established by St Seiriol in the 6th century and in 1237 Llywelyn the Great gave the monastery and its estates to the prior of Puffin Island. **St Seiriol's Church**, now the parish church, was rebuilt in the 12th century and contains wonderful examples of Norman architecture and a carved cross, recently moved to the church from the fields nearby, that shows influences from both Scandinavia and Ireland. The ruins of the priory's domestic buildings include a 13th century wing with a refectory on the ground floor where traces of the seat used by the monk who read aloud during meals can still be seen.

A nearby **Dovecote**, built in around 1600 by Sir Richard Bulkeley, contains nearly 1,000 nesting places. A path, beginning across the road, leads up to **St Seiriol's Well**, which was probably the site of the original 6th century priory. Although the upper part of the building covering the well appears to date from the 18th century, the lower portion is much older and could indeed incorporate something from the priory's original chapel.

An abandoned quarry close to the village once provided stone for Beaumaris Castle as well as the Telford and Stephenson bridges which link the island and the Welsh mainland.

PUFFIN ISLAND
8½ miles NE of Menai Bridge off the B5109

Once known as Priestholm and now often called **Ynys Seiriol**, this island is the home of the remains of St Seiriol's sanctuary and is thought once to have been connected to the mainland as St Seiriol was said to have a chapel across the bay in Penmaenmawr and ancient records tell of journeys between the two. The remains of monastic buildings that

date back to the 6th century can still be seen here.

The island was so named because of the large puffin colonies that nested here. However, the numbers of the nesting birds declined in the 19th century partly due to rats on the island and also because the young birds were considered a delicacy when pickled.

LLANGOED
6 miles NE of Menai Bridge on the B5109

In Edwardian times, this historic village was a popular resort with the lower middle classes who came here to relax in boarding houses by the sea. Llangoed's seaside charm is enhanced by its pastoral setting where a walk downstream, alongside the river, leads to **Castell Aberlleiniog**, found in the midst of some trees. This was originally a timber castle, built in around 1090 by Hugh Lupus, Earl of Chester, who, along with Hugh the Proud, Earl of Shrewsbury, exacted great cruelty on the Welsh. Lupus was later killed during an attack on the castle by Magnus, King of Norway, when he was struck in the eye by an arrow. The ruins of the bailey, which was constructed later, are still visible. Close by is the site of a battle where, in 809, the Saxons were, albeit briefly, victorious over the defending Welsh. Haulfre Stables is a small equestrian museum housed in a historic stable block and containing a collection of Victorian harnesses and saddlery, carts and carriages. Visits by appointment, Tel: 01248 490709/724444.

LLANFAES
5 miles NE of Menai Bridge off the B5109

Now a quiet and sedate place, Llanfaes was a busy commercial village long before the establishment of Beaumaris as one of the island's major centres, and travellers from the mainland arrived here after crossing the Menai Strait from Aber and the Lavan Sands.

In 1237, Llywelyn the Great founded a monastery in the village over the tomb of Joan, his wife and the daughter of King John. The tomb can now be seen in St Mary's Church, Beaumaris, where it was moved at the time of the Dissolution. In 1295 Edward I moved the inhabitants of Llanfaes to Newborough so that he could use the stone in the town to built Beaumaris Castle. During World War Two, flying boats were built at the factory by the village.

Beaumaris Castle

BEAUMARIS
4 miles NE of Menai Bridge of the A545

An attractive and elegant town, Beaumaris was granted a charter by Edward I in 1294 and it adopted the Norman name "beau marais" which translates as "beautiful marsh". The lawned seafront, now with its elegant Georgian and Victorian terraces, was once a marsh that protected the approaches to **Beaumaris Castle**. Often cited as the most technically perfect medieval castle in Britain, Beaumaris Castle was the last of Edward I's Iron Ring of fortresses built to stamp his authority on the Welsh. Begun in 1295 and designed by the king's military architect, James of St George, this was to be his largest and most ambitious project. Regarded as a pinnacle of military architecture of the time, with a concentric defence rather than the traditional keep and bailey, the outer walls contained 16 towers while the inner walls were 43 feet high and up to 16 feet thick in places. It was never

MUSEUM OF CHILDHOOD MEMORIES

1 Castle Street, Beaumaris, Isle of Anglesey LL58 8AP
Tel: 01248 810448

One of Britain's leading and oldest established toy and doll museums is Bob Brown's **"Museum of Childhood Memories"** on the Isle of Anglesey in North Wales. At the age of 82 Bob is still very active and running the museum, which he founded 26 years ago with the help of his wife Joan.

The museum was originally situated in the hamlet of Menai Bridge where the famous suspension bridge carried road traffic across the waters of the Menai Strait from Bangor.

The Museum was officially opened in 1973 by the Marquess of Anglesey, and moved in 1985 to larger premises further along the Anglesey coast. It is now to be found in historic premises in Beaumaris, almost opposite the ruins of the 13th century moated Beaumaris Castle. Visitors can arrive on Anglesey via the Suspension Bridge at Bangor, or by following the A51 over the Britannia Bridge.

BISHOPSGATE HOUSE HOTEL

Castle Street, Beaumaris, Isle of Anglesey LL58 8BB
Tel: 01248 810302 Fax: 01248 810166

The nine guest bedrooms at Hazel Johnson-Ollier's **Bishopsgate House Hotel** provide very comfortable and elegant accommodation in the centre of historic Beaumaris. The 18th century town house has been splendidly adapted for use as a small hotel, and each of the en suite rooms has its own character. Modern amenities blend harmoniously with antique beds, and the two four-poster rooms are perfect for special occasions. The residents' lounge, which retains its original wall panelling, offers a very agreeable, relaxed ambience for enjoying a drink and meeting the other guests, and the hallways and landings are graced with many items of antique furniture and fine glass and china.

Perhaps the most important original feature of the house is the "Chinese Chippendale" staircase, considered one of the finest of its kind in the country. Food is an important part of a stay at Bishopsgate

House, and the chef sets great store by local produce, which he prepares and presents with skill and flair. Typical dishes on an ever-changing menu run from starters such as garlic mushrooms or king prawn brochette with a mango salsa to fillet of cod topped with Snowdonia cheddar cheese, roast duck with a red wine jus and T-bone steak served on a bed of onions, mushrooms and tomatoes. Vegetarian and other special dietary requests can be met with prior notice. All in all, this is a fine, civilised base either for sitting back and relaxing or for exploring the many delights of Anglesey and Snowdonia.

SARAH'S DELICATESSEN

11 Church Street, Beaumaris, Isle of Anglesey LL58 8AB
Tel/Fax: 01248 811534
e-mail: sarahs-deli@yahoo.co.uk

Sarah Walczak has been putting her years of catering experience to excellent use since opening her first retail outlet in 1999. Sarah's Delicatessen, in the centre of town on the corner of Church Street and Margaret Street, occupies the ground floor of a redbrick building. Superbly fitted in light wood, with shelves on three sides and a vast central chilled display, it is a paradise for food-lovers, attracting not only the discriminating citizens of Beaumaris but many devotees from further afield.

The selection of Welsh, English and Continental cheeses can run to an impressive 200, and other specialities include olives and oils, pickles and preserves, cakes, coffees, teas, wines and liqueurs, handmade Belgian chocolates, Anglesey sea salt, Forest Products and Linda & Hartley ice creams. To order or take away there are cheese boards, cold meat platters, salad pots, home-made soup and quiche, baked potatoes, picnic bags and hampers made up to customers' specifications. **Sarah's Delicatessen** is open from 9 to 5 Monday to Saturday, and Saturday browsers are treated to a cup of freshly ground coffee.

actually completed, as the money ran out before the fortifications reached their full planned height. Perhaps a measure of the castle's success was that, unlike other castles built by Edward I, it never experienced military action. Now a World Heritage listed site and in the hands of CADW (Welsh Historic Monuments), Beaumaris Castle is still virtually surrounded by its original moat; there was also a tidal dock here for ships coming in through a channel in the marshes - an iron ring where vessels of up to 40 tons once docked still hangs from the wall.

Although Beaumarais saw little or no military action, the town briefly enjoyed notoriety as a haven for pirates, as well as being a busy trading port. With the advent of steam ships and paddle boats, the resort developed during Victorian times as visitors from Liverpool and elsewhere took the sea trip down to Beaumaris. The town is now a popular place with the yachting fraternity due to its facilities and involvement in the annual **Menai Strait Regatta**.

While having connections with both sea trade and developing as a holiday resort, Beaumaris was at one time also an administrative and legal centre for the island. The **Courthouse**, dating from 1614, is open to the public during the summer and, although it was renovated in the 19th century, much of its original Jacobean interior remains. It was here, in 1773, that Mary Hughes stood in the dock and was sentenced to transportation for seven years after she had been found guilty of stealing a bed gown valued at six pence!

Close by is **Beaumaris Gaol**, which was designed as a model prison by Hansom in 1829. In this monument to Victorian law and order, the last man to hang was Richard Rowlands, who cursed the church clock opposite as he climbed to the scaffold in 1862. Today's visitors can relive those days of harsh punishment as well as view the cells and the treadwheel and follow the route taken by the condemned men to their rendezvous with the hangman.

An equally interesting place for all the family to visit is the **Museum of Childhood Memories** (see panel on page 67), a treasure house of nostalgia with a collection of over 2,000 items. In nine different rooms, each with its own theme, such as entertainment, pottery and glass and clockwork tin plate toys, visitors can wander around and see the amazing variety of toys which illustrate the changing habits of the nation over the last 150 years.

PLAS NEWYDD

2 miles SW of Menai Bridge off the A4080

Bryn Celli Ddu, a wonderful example of a Bronze Age passage grave, lies up a narrow country road close to Plas Newydd, which is situated on the banks of the Menai Strait.

The splendid mansion house (see panel on page 71) is surrounded by gardens and parkland laid out in the 18th century by Humphrey Repton. Not only are there fabulous views over the water to Snowdonia from the lawns but there is a woodland walk, an Australian arboretum and a formal Italian style garden terrace. Two miles away, at Llanfair PG, stands the Marquess of Anglesey's Column (see under Llanfair PG on page 73).

BRYNSIENCYN

5 miles SW of Menai Bridge on the A4080

Close to this village there was once an important centre of Druid worship, but no signs remain of the temple that stood at **Tre-Drwy**. There are, however, several other interesting remains in the area.

Wern Y Wylan Court

Llanddona, Nr Beaumaris,
Isle of Anglesey LL58 8TR
Tel/Fax: 01248 810964

Robert Macaulay, entrepreneur, farmer and gentleman, offers unique holiday accommodation in an attractive rural setting overlooking Llanddona beach and Red Wharf Bay. Wern Y Wylan Court comprises a 1930s former hotel, now a private residence, and seven self-catering holiday units to the rear of the main house overlooking the grounds and paddock. Fitted and equipped to a very high standard, the units provide a range of accommodation sleeping from 3 to 8 guests.

Each has a full inventory of furniture, fittings and effects, including fitted kitchens with microwave, cooker and fridge; three also have dishwashers, and one has a washer/dryer. "Oak" (sleeps 5), "Honeysuckle" (6/8), "Ivy" (5 - all on the ground floor) and "Hawthorn" (4) have independent access from the main entrance hall of the former hotel, while "Sycamore" (4), "Holly" (4) and "Birch" (3 - all on the ground floor) have their own independent entrances. Parking space is provided by each unit, and common amenities include a payphone, launderette and barbecue area.

Plas Newydd

Llanfairpwll, Anglesey LL61 6DQ
Tel: 01248 714795
Fax: 01248 713673
e-mail: ppmsn@smtp.ntrust.org.uk

Two miles south of Llanfairpwll, on the banks of the Menai Strait, Plas Newydd is an elegant 18th century country house designed by James Wyatt. Once the home of the Marquis of Anglesey, it is now in the care of the National Trust and is open to the public from late March to early November. The artist Rex Whistler was a regular visitor to the house, and his largest painting, commissioned by the 6th Marquis in the 1930s, hangs in the dining room; there is also a permanent exhibition of his work. Also housed here is a military museum with relics of the Battle of Waterloo, including some that belonged to the 1st Marquis, who commanded the cavalry at the battle in 1815. Of particular interest here are a boot and a pair of mutilated trousers worn by the 1st Marquis, who, in the heat of the battle, had this famous exchange with the Duke of Wellington:

"By God Sir, I've lost my leg."

"By God, so you have."

The house is surrounded by gardens and parkland laid out by Humphry Repton. These include woodland and marine walks, an Italianate terrace with views of Snowdon, an arboretum with understudy of shrubs and wild flowers, a picnic area and a playground. A superb rhododendron garden, located some distance from the house, is a wonderful sight, especially in the spring. Historical cruises on the Menai Strait can be arranged, weather and tides permitting, and the house has a shop and licensed tea room.

Just to the west of the village lies **Caer Leb**, an Iron Age earthwork consisting of a pentagonal enclosure 200 feet by 160 feet encircled by banks and ditches, while, just a short distance away is **Bodowyr Burial Chamber**, a massive stone that is, seemingly, delicately perched upon three upright stones. To the south of the burial chamber, and just a mile west of Brynsiencyn, are the earthwork remains of **Castell Bryn Gwyn**, a site which has been excavated and shows traces of having been used from as far back as the New Stone Age through to the time of the Roman occupation of Britain.

Back in the village and found down the small road leading to the shore lies **Foel Farm Park**, a real working farm which offers visitors the opportunity to bottle feed lambs and baby calves, cuddle rabbits, see and help with milking and

enjoy the home-made ice cream. There are also covered areas for rainy days which include an adventure play den and an indoor picnic room.

Also overlooking the Menai Strait is the **Anglesey Sea Zoo**, an award winning attraction that takes visitors beneath the waves and into the underwater world of a wide variety of sea creatures. The imaginative and innovative displays allow visitors a unique view of these interesting beasts, which include sea horses, oysters, conger eels and rays.

Dwyran

8 miles SW of Menai Bridge off the A4080

Just outside the village lies **Bird World**, a wonderful family attraction set in extensive parkland, with views over to the Snowdonia mountain range, where visitors can admire the wide variety of birds on display as well as picnic in the beautiful surroundings of the lake. There is also a small animal farm and pet area for the children along with a huge indoor play barn.

NEWBOROUGH

9 miles SW of Menai Bridge on the A4080

Founded in 1303 by the former inhabitants of Llanfaes, who had been moved here by Edward I, the village stands on the edge of a National Nature Reserve that covers 1,566 acres of dunes, coast and forest. Among the many footpaths through the reserve, there are several forest trails that show how the Forestry Commission is constantly trying to stabilise the dunes. **Newborough Warren** is so called because, before myxomatosis, about 80,000 rabbits were trapped here annually. There is a route through the warren to **Abermenai Point**, but the way can be dangerous and advice concerning tidal conditions should be sought before considering the walk.

Llanddwyn Island is also accessible on foot but again tidal conditions should be carefully studied before setting out. Until the 1920s, marram grass, which has been grown for conservation purposes from Elizabethan times, was also a mainstay of the area, helping to sustain a cottage industry in the production of ropes, baskets, matting and thatching materials. A high embankment was built here in the 18th century by Thomas Telford to stop the sea, which had previously almost cut the island into two.

Charles Tunnicliffe, the renowned wildlife artist, had a studio on the island for over 30 years and Anglesey Council

Llanddwyn Island

has purchased a collection of his marvellous work which can be seen at the Oriel Ynys Môn in Llangefni. On the A4080 signposted from Newborough, Newborough Forest is a pine forest with rides, glades and miles of walks.

Situated between Newborough and Dwyran lies **Anglesey Model Village and Gardens**, a delightful place where visitors can wander through the attractive landscaped gardens and see many of the island's many landmarks - all built to one twelfth scale. There is a children's ride-on train, as well as the garden railway, and the gardens themselves are particularly beautiful, with many water features and a good collection of plants and trees.

LLANGADWALADR

10½ miles W of Menai Bridge on the A4080

Around the time that Aberffraw was the capital of Gwynedd, this small village was said to have been the burial place of the Welsh princes. True or not, the church here has a memorial stone to Cadfan, King of Gwynedd, and the village is dedicated to Cadwaladr, Cadfan's grandson, who is thought to have been the last Briton to wear the crown before the invasion of the Saxons.

ABERFFRAW

12½ miles W of Menai Bridge on the A4080

Though this was once the capital of Gwynedd, between the 7th and 13th centuries, there remains little trace of those times, although a Norman arch, set into St Beuno's Church, is said to be from the palace of the ruling princes. However, the **Llys Llywelyn Museum**, although modest, has exhibitions recounting the area's fascinating history.

Inland, the **Din Dryfol Burial Chamber** provides further evidence of Iron Age life on the island while, to the north of Aberffraw, on the cliff tops above Porth Trecastell, is the **Barclodiad y Gawres Burial Chamber**. Considered to be one of the finest of its kind, this burial chamber, along with Bryn Celli Ddu, contains some notable murals.

LLANFAIR PG

1 mile W of Menai Bridge off the A5

Llanfairpwllgwyngyll, often called Llanfair PG, is better known as the village with the world's longest place name. The full, tongue-twisting name is: Llanfairpwllgwyngyllgogerychwyrndrobwyllllantysiliogogogh - and the translation is even longer - St Mary's Church in a hollow of white hazel near to a rapid whirlpool and St Tysilio's Church near the red cave. The name is said to have been invented, in humorous reference to the burgeoning tourist trade, by a local man. Whether this is true or not, it has certainly done the trick, as many visitors stop by initially out of curiosity in the name.

The village, overlooking the Menai Strait, is where the Britannia Bridge crosses to the mainland. The **Marquess of Anglesey Column** looks out from here over to Snowdonia and the quite splendid views from the top of the column are available to anyone wishing to negotiate the spiral staircase of some 115 steps. The column was finished two years after the battle of Waterloo, and the statue on top of the column was added, in 1860, after the death of Henry Paget, Earl of Uxbridge and 1st Marquess of Anglesey, whom it commemorates. Paget fought alongside the Duke of Wellington at Waterloo, where he lost a leg to one of the last shots of the battle. He lived to be 85, having twice been Lord-Lieutenant of Ireland after his military career (see also under Plas Newydd on page 71).

The last public toll house, designed by Thomas Telford when he was working on the London-Holyhead road in the 1820s, stands in the village; it still displays the tolls charged in 1895, the year the toll house closed. Next door is the modest building where, in 1915, the Women's Institute was founded.

However, the most famous building in Llanfair PG is undoubtedly its railway station - the often filmed station whose platform has the longest station sign and where the longest platform ticket in Britain was purchased. Today, visitors can see a replica of the Victorian ticket

Llanfair PG Railway Station

HOLLAND ARMS GARDEN CENTRE

Gaerwen, Isle of Anglesey LL60 6LA
Tel: 01248 421655 Fax: 01248 421896
e-mail: sue@hollandarms.co.uk
website: www.hollandarms.co.uk

What started as a modest stone-built private house has expanded over the years into the large and successful **Holland Arms Garden Centre**. It was started 50 years ago by the parents of Susan Knock, who is now one of three partners in the business. All that a good garden centre should be, Holland Arms offers real inspiration for garden and home, and the range of the stock makes it the foremost garden centre in North Wales. Visitors will find a tremendous variety of plants, house plants, trees and shrubs, plus garden furniture, barbecues, water gardens, ponds, fountains, tools, candles, chocolates and gifts of all kinds. There's also a wide choice of garden ornaments, silk flowers, jewellery and sundries.

A delight at any time of the year, the Centre really excels itself on the run-up to Christmas, with literally thousands of decorations and gifts and lots of seasonal special events. There's parking for over 100 cars, and in the Gardener's Café delicious home baking, breakfasts, light lunches and snacks are served, accompanied by tea, coffee, beer or wine. Visitors should allow plenty of time to explore everything the Holland Arms has to offer. Open seven days a week, it lies on the A5 at Gaerwen, a short drive west of the Menai Bridge.

office, examine some rare miniature steam trains and wander around the numerous craft and souvenir shops that can now be found here.

LLANGEFNI
6 miles NW of Menai Bridge on the B5420

The island's main market and administrative centre, Llangefni is also the home of **Oriel Ynys Môn** (the **Anglesey Heritage Centre**), an attractive art gallery and heritage centre, built in 1991, which gives an insight into the history of Anglesey. From prehistoric times to the present day, the permanent exhibition covers a series of themes including Stone Age Hunters, Druids, Medieval Society and Legends.

Llyn Cefni Reservoir to the northwest of the town is an important wildlife habitat and nature reserve overlooked by a hide; it is also provides a pleasant picnic area. On the northwest edge of

town by the River Cefni, **The Dingle** is a local nature reserve with footpaths through mature woodland. The A5114, which connects Llangefni to the A5, is the shortest A road in the British Isles.

LLANDDYFNAN
5 miles NW of Menai Bridge on the B5109

To the west of the village lies **Stone Science**, a most unusual attraction that tells the story of the earth from its beginning to the present - a journey spanning 650 million years. The museum illustrates the science with displays of fossils, crystals and artefacts, and there are numerous and varied items for sale in the Stone Science shop.

HOLYHEAD

Holyhead Mountain (Mynydd Twr) rises to 720 feet behind this town, which is the largest on Anglesey and is itself on an island - Holy Island. A busy rail and ferry terminal, especially for travellers to and from Ireland, Holyhead has all the facilities needed to cater for visitors passing through although it is also, despite being something of an industrial and commercial centre, a seaside resort. Its origins lie back in the times of the Romans and the early Celtic Christians. Parts of **St Cybi's Parish Church** date from the 14th to the 17th century and it is situated within the partially surviving walls of the small Roman fort, Caer Gybi (the source of Holyhead's Welsh name) and on the site of a 6th century chapel. Close to the church is a smaller church, **Egylwys Bedd**, which reputedly contains the tomb of Seregri, an Irish warrior who was repelled by the Welsh chief, Caswallon Lawhir. The town's triumphal arches, built in 1821, commemorate George IV's visit here as well as the end of the A5, the major road from London.

The interesting **Canolfan Ucheldre Centre**, housed in an old convent chapel, is a complete arts centre for northwest Wales and, opened in 1991, it presents both film, music and drama events as well as holding all manner of art and craft exhibitions and workshops. **Salt Island** (Ynys Halen), close to the

town centre, is virtually self-explanatory: a factory was built here to extract salt from the seawater. Rock salt was added to improve its quality and inevitably an excise duty was charged and smuggling flourished, particularly between Four Mile Bridge and the Isle of Man, where salt was duty free.

While the town itself is not without interest, it is the immediate surrounding area that draws most visitors to Holyhead. **Breakwater Quarry Country Park**, just northwest of the town, incorporates Britain's largest breakwater. Designed by James Meadow and started in 1845, the structure, which shields an area of 667 acres, took 28 years to construct. From the country park there are many walks along the coast, including a route to **South Stack**. This is a reserve of cliffs and heath teeming with birdlife, including puffins, guillemots, razorbills. The RSPB visitor centre is open daily, the café daily in summer, and the lighthouse is open daily in summer for guided tours. The lighthouse, one of the most impressive in Wales, was built in 1809 and stands on a beautiful but dangerous site reached by a steep stone stairway of over 400 steps. Above the harbour and breakwater, is a memorial in tribute to Captain Skinner, who drowned when his packet boat, *Escape*, was lost in 1832.

At the summit of Holyhead Mountain, from where, on a clear day, Snowdonia, the Isle of Man and the Mourne Mountains in Ireland can be seen, there is evidence of an ancient settlement. The remains of **Caer y Twr**, a hill fort, are visible and, close by, is **Cytiau'r Gwyddelod**, a hut settlement from the 2nd century.

Trearddur Bay

Between South Stack and North Stack lies **Gogarth Bay**, where the RSPB sea bird centre includes a cavern, known as Parliament House Cave, which is used by a profusion of sea birds such as puffins, guillemots and even falcons. Visitors here can also watch the thousands of cliff nesting birds via live television pictures and enjoy the beautiful cliff top walks. **Ellin's Tower**, in the centre, is another spot favoured by ornithologists.

Aqua diving, windsurfing, water skiing and fishing are some of the many attractions of **Trearddur Bay**, a popular part of Anglesey's extensive coastline that lies just to the southwest of Holyhead. With large sandy beaches, clear water and safe bathing, it is obviously popular; the Georgian house, Towyn Lodge, on the south side of the bay, played host to Thomas Telford while

he was working on what is now the A5 road in the 19th century. The Trearddur Bay Hotel is host to the Anglesey Oyster and Shellfish Festival from the 11th to the 13th October 2002.

AROUND HOLYHEAD

LLANFAIRYNGHORNWY
7 miles NE of Holyhead off the A5025

This village, on the approach to **Carmel Head**, has two claims to fame. It was here, in the 19th century, that Frances Williams founded the Anglesey Association for the Preservation of Life from Shipwreck. Along with her husband, who was the local rector, Frances raised funds for lifeboats on the island and, through her efforts, the first lifeboat station in the area was established.

THE WATERFRONT RESTAURANT
Lon Isalit, Trearddur Bay, Isle of Anglesey LL65 2UW
Tel: 01407 860006

A modern building right on the seafront at Trearddur Bay is now home to the **Waterfront Restaurant**, one of the most exciting new restaurant openings on Anglesey in recent times. Owner-chef Wayne Roberts runs the 120-cover restaurant in partnership with Simon Dale, front of house, and Tom Carpenter of Carreglwyd, in charge of marketing and promotion. Local produce features prominently on the frequently changing menu, because, as Wayne says, "it is as good as it gets". Opened in June 2002, the restaurant is just 20 metres from the sea, so fresh seafood naturally appears regularly on the menu, along with locally sourced lamb, beef, pork, fruit and vegetables.

The produce may be predominantly local, but Wayne and his brigade take their inspiration from both local and worldwide cuisines: stir-fried squid with chilli and soy; salmon with crushed garden peas, pepper coulis and herb oil; slow-cooked pork with fennel, pears and sage; chicken, tomato and mushroom lasagne; braised lamb with baby onions and white beans. Local raw materials, notably soft fruits from Carreglwyd, feature among the mouthwatering desserts. Wayne has been a member of the Welsh National Culinary Association for a number of years and his CV includes stints at the head of the stoves at Penmaenuchaf Hall in Dolgellau and the Celtic Manor Hotel in Caernarfon. To find the Waterfront Restaurant follow the B4545 off the A5 into Trearddur Bay.

Llanfairynghornwy's other claim to fame is as the centre of the "bonesetters of Anglesey", one of whom improved the splint.

Lying two miles offshore from the point at Carmel Head are **The Skerries**, a group of windswept islets whose Welsh name, Ynysoedd y Moelrhoniaid, means Island of Porpoises. On the islets stands the last **Lighthouse** to be privately owned (ships had to pay a toll as they passed); it now has a beam of light which is capable of throwing out a four million candle power light. When braziers stood there during the 18th century they burnt approximately 100 tons of coal a night!

CEMAES
11 miles NE of Holyhead off the A5025

Boasting two glorious, safe, sandy beaches, **Cemaes Bay** is a popular place on the island that was also once a favourite with smugglers. However, today, Cemaes is a quiet and picturesque fishing village, with a small tidal harbour with much to offer holidaymakers: wonderful walks, abundant wildlife, fishing, hotels, shops, pubs and also the opportunity to learn a little of the Welsh language. **Ogof y March Glas** - the cave of the blue horse - on Cemaes Bay was named after an incident that took place over 200 years ago. Following a family dispute, a young man furiously galloped away from his house near the bay on his dappled grey horse. Blinded by rage, he galloped headlong over the cliff; only his hat was ever seen again, although the carcass of his horse was found washed up in the cave.

Around the headland at the western edge of the bay lies **Wylfa Nuclear Power Station**; its Visitor Centre is the starting point for a guided tour of the station and also contains a mass of information about the nature trail surrounding the plant. The stretch of coast west from Cemaes to Clegir is designated a Heritage Coast. Cemlyn Bay, home to thousands of terns between April and July, is managed as a nature reserve by the North Wales Wildlife Trust; Mynachdy contains old settlement sites and the remains of some long disused copper mines.

AMLWCH
14 miles NE of Holyhead on the A5025

South of this seaside town lies the pock-marked **Parys Mountain**, which has provided copper for prospectors from as early as Roman times. In 1768 a copper boom helped make Anglesey the copper centre of the world but, by 1820, the rush was over as prices fell and the mineral deposits became exhausted. Amlwch had fed off this wealth and the harbour, which was built during more prosperous times, is now used mainly by pleasure craft. In its heyday Amlwch had 6,000 inhabitants and 1,000 ale houses.

DULAS
15 miles NE of Holyhead off the A5025

A once thriving village, Dulas was, in the early 19th century, home to both a brickworks and a shipbuilding industry. Standing at the head of the Dulas River, which runs into the bay, the village overlooks **Ynys Dulas**, a small island which lies a mile or so offshore and is the haunt of grey seals. On the island itself is a 19th century tower built as a beacon and a refuge for sailors; the lady of Llysdulas manor house once had food left there for stranded mariners.

LLANERCHYMEDD
11 miles E of Holyhead on the B5112

To the north of the village lies **Llyn Alaw**, Anglesey's largest lake, well known for its fine trout fishing as well as the abundant wildlife found around its

CARREGLWYD LTD

Carreglwyd, Nr Holyhead, Isle of Anglesey
Tel: 01407 730208/730098   Fax: 01407 730088
e-mail: tomcarpenter@carreglwyd.co.uk
website: www.carreglwyd.co.uk

Tom and Ninni Carpenter continue a family
connection going back to the 18th century at
Carreglwyd, a fine Grade II listed estate on the
northwest coast of the Isle of Anglesey. The manor,
a fine Georgian house filled with antiques and
family portraits, can be let throughout the year, with
accommodation for up to 12 guests; ideal for family
reunuions, either self-catering or fully serviced. The
house has seven bedrooms on the first floor and two single staff rooms on the second floor. The rooms
vary greatly in style and mood: two have four-posters, and one is a teenager's room with a double
water bed. Two rooms have bathrooms en suite, the rest share another two bathrooms. On the ground
floor are a hall with open fire, sofa and chairs; a superb sitting room with open fire, tv and stereo; an
office/library with desk, bookshelves and fax machine; an elegant dining room with a table that can
seat up to 18; a splendidly equipped kitchen/breakfast room; a large utility room with freezer, washer
and dryer; a children's play room and an Edwardian guest cloakroom.

The house is fully centrally heated, and outside in the
impressive grounds, there is a walled kitchen garden, garden
furniture, a play area with swings, a lake with a boathouse and
rowing boat and woodland walks leading down to a lovely sandy
beach. Domestic help three mornings a week is included in the
tariff, and a local dinner party cook is available on request. The
owners are very keen to raise the profile of the Isle of Anglesey in
terms of food and restaurants, and the estate produces a range of
foods which are supplied to a number of outlets, including some
of the top restaurants on the island.

shores. Covering some 770 acres, the
lake is actually man-made, from the
flooding of marshland, and it supplies
most of the island's industrial and
domestic needs.

LLANDDEUSANT

6½ miles E of Holyhead off the A5025

This village is home to Anglesey's only
stone tower working windmill, built in
1775-76 at a total cost of £529-11-0. Four
storeys high, with a boat-shaped cap, it
ceased milling by wind power in 1924,
but was restored and opened to the
public in 1984. **Llynnon Mill** not only
mills stoneground flour for sale (wind
and conditions willing) but also has an
attractive craftshop and a popular tea
room for visitors to enjoy.

Tradition has it that the green mound,
Bedd Branwen, near the River Alaw, is
the grave of Branwen, the heroine of the
Welsh epic, *Mabinogion*. Opened in 1813,
it later revealed a rough baked clay urn
containing fragments of burnt bone and
ashes. Since the discovery of more
funeral urns in 1967, the site has become
even more significant.

VALLEY

3½ miles SE of Holyhead on the A5

Valley was thought to have gained its
name while Thomas Telford was cutting
his road through the small hill here.
Centuries earlier this was the home of
Iron Age man whose weapons and horse
trappings found in the area are now on
display in the National Museum of Wales.

However, Valley is perhaps better known today for the nearby airfield established here during World War II as a fighter pilot base. In 1943, the American Air Force expanded the base's capability for use as an Atlantic terminal and now the RAF uses it for training flights and for Air/Sea rescue. Opposite the barracks is **Llyn Penrhyn**, a complex of reed-fringed lakes with lots of wildfowl and dragonflies. Before the bridges to Holyhead were built, during the construction of the A5, the crossing to the town was made via **Pont Rhyd Bont**, which is now called **Four Mile Bridge**.

Rhosneigr
7½ miles SE of Holyhead on the A4080

This small resort is situated in a quiet spot, close to the sandy beaches and rocky outcrops of **Cymyran Bay**. The River Crigyll, which runs into the sea by the town, was the haunt, in the 18th century, of the "Wreckers of Crigyll", who were famous for luring ships on to the rocks. Tried at Beaumaris in 1741, where the group of desperate men were found guilty and hanged, the wreckers became the subject of a ballad, *The Hanging of the Thieves of Crigyll*.

The 1,400 acres of gorse and dunes at **Tywyn Trewan Common** is a paradise for botanists and ornithologists.

Rhoscolyn
4½ miles S of Holyhead off the B4545

With a wide sandy beach that is excellent for swimming and fishing, this village was once home to a thriving oyster industry that is now, sadly, in decline. China clay was also once quarried here, while the local marble was used in the construction of Worcester, Bristol and Peterborough Cathedrals.

St Gwenfaen founded a church here in the 6th century and her **Well**, on **Rhoscolyn Head**, was said to have properties that cured, in particular, mental illness. The headland is a superb place for cliff walking and there are splendid views northwards over Trearddur Bay and, southwards, over Cymyran Bay. At **Bwa Gwyn** (White Arch) is a memorial to Tyger, a remarkable dog who, in 1817, led to safety the four-man crew from a sinking ketch. After dragging the cabin boy ashore and returning for the ship's captain, the dog collapsed and died from exhaustion.

3 SNOWDONIA: COAST AND INLAND

To the south of Anglesey lies the Llyn Peninsula, which forms the great curve of Caernarfon Bay. This is one of the most secluded and most beautiful parts of Wales, and over 100 miles of its shoreline is designated an Area of Outstanding Natural Beauty. During the Middle Ages, Bardsey Island, lying off the western tip of the peninsula, was a place of pilgrimage, and the ancient route to Aberdaron, from where the pilgrims sailed to their destination, can still in parts be followed. Reminders of the area's early Christian past can be found throughout Llyn, along with more ancient monuments such as hill forts. This region, like the northern coast and the Isle of Anglesey, has been a favourite holiday destination since the coming of the railways in the mid-19th century.

Sunrise from Snowdon

The attractive Victorian resorts along the southern shore of the peninsula are sheltered and provide plenty of scope for sailing, swimming and fishing. The

Continued Page 82

ADVERTISERS AND PLACES OF INTEREST

LOCATOR MAP

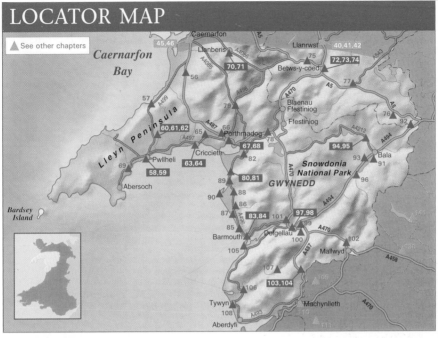

▲ See other chapters

Caernarfon
Bay

Caernarfon
45,46
Llanberis
70,71
56
Llanrwst
40,41,42
75
Betws-y-coed
72,73,74
77

57
79
Blaenau
Ffestiniog
76

Lleyn Peninsula
60,61,62
65
66
Porthmadog
78
Ffestiniog
92

Pwllheli
63,64
Criccieth
67,68
82
94,95
93
Bala
91

69
58,59
89
80,81
Snowdonia
National Park
96

Abersoch
88
GWYNEDD

90
86

Bardsey
Island
87
83,84
101
97,98
99
85
100

Barmouth
Dolgellau
102

Mallwyd

105
107
103,104
106

Tywyn
108
Machynlleth

Aberdyfi

birthplace of one of the country's greatest statesmen, David Lloyd George, is a popular place to visit, but the whole region is filled with splendid attractions to see and exciting things to do. Perhaps the most visited of all is the fantasy village of Portmeirion, built from the 1920s to the 1970s by Sir Clough Williams-Ellis.

There are three National Parks in Wales, and Snowdonia, at some 840 square miles, is the largest and certainly the most dramatic scenically. Set up in 1951, and embracing a number of mountain and hill ranges, Snowdonia also extends southwards into the heart of Wales and incorporates stretches of the coastline and Cadair Idris. There are several routes up to the summit of Snowdon beginning at

Llynnau Cregennan, Dolgellau

various points around its base. Some call for more energy than others, but the least arduous ascent is by the Snowdon Mountain Railway that runs from Llanberis. At, and around, nearby Betws-y-Coed, the walking is gentler and includes surviving tracts of the vast forests that once covered much of Wales. From the earliest times, this region was mined for its minerals. Gold was known here long before the Romans arrived, and as recently as the 19th century there were mini-gold rushes in a belt that stretched from Bontddu along the line of the River

Llyn Gwnant, Snowdonia

Mawddach. Copper, lead and slate were also mined up until the start of the 20th century, and the scars left by those industries can still be seen today. Several of the mines have found new roles as visitor attractions, along with the little railways that once carried the minerals from the mines and quarries to the coast. In the middle of the 19th century, the coastal villages and towns, many of them obscure, quiet fishing communities, were put on the map and changed radically in character with the arrival of the main railway network. As the fashion for sea air grew and communications were made easier, they became popular seaside resorts, and today many of them still retain Victorian and Edwardian buildings constructed to cater for holidaymakers. The scenery throughout the region is truly inspirational, and few would disagree with the verdict of the 19th century traveller and writer George Borrow:

"Perhaps in all the world there is no region more picturesquely beautiful."

THE LLYN PENINSULA

DINAS DINLLE
3 miles S of Caernarfon off the A499

A seaside village at the mouth of the Menai Strait. With a shingle beach and cliffs overlooking Caernarfon Bay, there are many pleasant spots to picnic and enjoy the views down the Llyn Peninsula or across the bay to Anglesey. At the beach's northerly tip lies **Fort Belan**, which was built in the 18th century along with neighbouring **Fort Williamsburg**. Constructed by the 1st Lord Newborough, who felt concern over the threat of invasion by Napoleon, the lord also raised and equipped his own private army, The Royal Caernarfonshire Grenadiers, which, by the time of his death in 1807, had cost him a quarter of his fortune.

LLANDWROG
4 miles S of Caernarfon off the A499

Originally an estate village built by Lord Newborough for Glynllifon Park, the village is associated with an interesting though gruesome tale. One night, a midwife of Llandwrog was called out by a mysterious stranger, who carried her on horseback to a wonderful underground castle so that she could help a beautiful queen with her labour. After the birth, the stranger gave the midwife some ointment to anoint the baby's head but warned her not to touch her own eyes with the cream. Unfortunately, the midwife accidentally did so and the scene before her changed dramatically: the castle became a cave and the queen turned into her former serving maid. Some weeks later, the midwife saw the stranger in Caernarfon and asked after the health of the new mother. After replying that all was well, the stranger asked the midwife which eye she saw him with. When she answered, he took a rush and poked the eye out!

CLYNNOG FAWR
10 miles SW of Caernarfon on the A499

This typical Llyn Peninsula village on the Heritage Coast is famous for its remarkably large and beautiful church - **St Beuno's Church** - which stands on the site of the chapel founded by the Saint around AD 616. One of the son's of the royal family of Morgannwg, St Beuno had great influence in North Wales and he built his chapel on land which was presented to him by Cadwallon, King of Gwynedd. St Beuno's burial place and his shrine can be seen in this early 16th century building, which lies on the Pilgrims'

Route to Bardsey Island. For many years, his tomb was thought to have curative powers.

Nearby is **St Beuno's Well**, whose waters were also thought to cure all manner of illness and conditions, especially if the sufferer had first visited the church. Close by, and virtually on the seafront, stands the capstone and three uprights of **Bachwen**, a neolithic burial chamber.

Yr Eifl, Llyn Peninsula

TAI'N LÔN

2 miles E of Clynnog Fawr off the A487

Beside the River Descach lies the **Museum of Old Welsh Life**, which features a variety of bygone themes and which is itself housed in a 17th century water mill.

TREFOR

3½ miles SW of Clynnog Fawr off the A499

This coastal village is dominated by **Yr Eifl** (The Forks), which lies to the southwest and which, from its 1,850 foot summit, affords stunning views out over

---

BRYN EISTEDDFOD COUNTRY HOUSE HOTEL

AA 4 Diamonds - WTB 3 star

Clynnog Fawr, Caernarfon, Wales LL54 5DA
Tel: 01286 660431 e-mail: bryn.eisteddfod@virgin.net
website: www.bryneisteddfod.com

Bryn Eisteddfod Country House Hotel is a charming Victorian property in peaceful and tranquil country surroundings. Situated approximately nine miles south of Caernarfon, Bryn Eisteddfod stands close by the landmark 13th century St Beuno's Church near the village of Clynnog Fawr. The hotel enjoys breathtaking sea and mountain outlooks and the surrounding area is designated as one of "Outstanding Natural Beauty."

Bryn Eisteddfod is set in 1½ acres of landscaped grounds and enjoys 360° panoramic views - the Eifl Mountains (the Rivals), Caernarfon Bay, the foothills of Snowdonia and, to the north, Ynys Mon (the Isle of Anglesey). The hotel is ideally situated for exploring the magic of North Wales – historic castles; sites of ancient mystery and legend; the beaches, coves and spectacular scenery of the Lleyn Peninsula and Anglesey; endless opportunities for hiking and walking; myriad challenging golf courses; and, of course, the all year round wonders of Snowdonia.

The comfortable, ensuite, spacious and well-equipped double, twin or family rooms all have

stunning views over the surrounding sea or hills (or both). Enjoy homecooking (including vegetarian) and good wine in the elegant dining room, a drink in the light and airy conservatory or relax in the tranquil lounge. Roaring log fires keep you cosy in winter, and the welcome is warm all year round.

Join hosts Carol and Andrew Croxton and experience for yourself the comfort, personal service, good food and warm friendly atmosphere of this fully licensed, non-smoking country house. "Arrive as welcome guests – leave as friends".

Caernarfon Bay to Anglesey and across the Llyn Peninsula. On the southeastern slopes of the hill is **Tre'r Ceiri** (Town of Giants), one of the finest Iron Age forts in the country. A stone wall surrounds this once heavily populated circle of 150 huts.

The road between here and Clynnog Fawr passes by the ancient looking **Gurn Ddu** and **Bwlch Mawr** hills which sweep down towards the sandy beach.

Porth Dinllaen, Nefyn

NEFYN

9 miles SW of Clynnog Fawr on the A497

Once a fishing village, this resort was granted a charter in 1355, along with Pwllheli, by the Black Prince. It was here in 1284 that Edward I celebrated his conquest over Wales. Housed in St Mary's church, whose tower supports a sailing ship weathervane, is the **Llyn**

Historical and Maritime Museum, an excellent place to visit to find out more about this interesting and beautiful part of Wales.

PWLLHELI

Pwllheli is the chief town of the peninsula and, like Nefyn, was granted a

GWYNFRYN FARM HOLIDAYS

Pwllheli, Gwynedd LL53 5UF
Tel/Fax: 01758 612536
e-mail: sharon@gwynfryn.freeserve.co.uk
website: www.gwynfrynfarm.co.uk

Guests of all ages are welcome at **Gwynfryn Farm Holidays** on a 100-acre organic dairy farm a mile from Pwllheli. Alwyn and Sharon Ellis have masterminded the imaginative transformation of barns into 11 luxurious self-catering cottages sleeping from two to eight guests. All are equipped to a very high standard, with a modern kitchen, dishwasher, fridge-freezer, microwave, tv and video, radio-cassette-CD player and hairdryer. A laundrette with free washing machine and dryer is in the quadrangle, and optional services include freshly cooked meals, a daily cleaner and local produce for sale. Baby sitting is free from September to April.

The farm is an ideal base for exploring the beautiful coast and countryside of the Llyn Peninsula, but there are plenty of attractions on the farm. Guests can watch the cows being milked and help to feed the calves, lambs, pigs and hens and collect eggs - children might even be lucky enough to have a ride on Penny, the Welsh mountain pony. The games room offers table football, table tennis, pool and darts and there's a heated swimming pool, sauna and jacuzzi. Children can have the time of their lives in the adventure play area, bouncing on the trampoline and saying hello to Dot the Jack Russell and the farm cats.

ORIEL PWLLDEFAID

46 High Street, Pwllheli, Gwynedd
Tel/Fax: 01758 721433
e-mail: indi@pwlldefaid.freeserve.co.uk

A handsome three-storey building on Pwllheli's main street contains a range of craftware that is probably unsurpassed in the whole country. **Oriel Pwlldefaid** (Oriel is the Welsh for Gallery) is run by young, enthusiastic Bethan Roberts and Eirian Williams. Bethan produces and sells original Welsh pottery; and Eirian designs and makes her own range of clothing for children and adults. Their flair and imagination are evident in the choice and variety of the stock.

Largely, though not exclusively sourced in Wales, the dazzling display includes items large and small, from cards and trinkets to unique pieces of furniture and also porcelain, pottery, jewellery, original pictures, mobiles, fabrics and garments.

charter in 1355; this was a gift by the Black Prince to Nigel de Loryng, who had helped the Prince win the Battle of Poitiers. A popular holiday resort with all the usual amusements, this is also still a market town, though its once busy port, where wine was imported from the Continent, is now home to pleasure craft, with a 420-berth marina and an annual sailing regatta. As well as being an ancient town, Pwllheli has played its part in the more recent history of Wales. During the National Eisteddfod in 1925, three members of the Army of Welsh Home Rulers met with three members of the Welsh Movement at the town's Temperance Hotel and joined forces to form the political party, Plaid Cymru.

Just to the east of the town, lies **Penarth Fawr**, an interesting 15th century manor house.

Chwilog

4½ miles NE of Pwllheli on the B4354

Close to the village lies **Talhenbont Hall**, an early 17th century manor house that was once the home of William Vaughan. A place of history with its fair share of ghosts, the hall was used, during the Civil War, as a garrison for Parliamentary soldiers. However, what attracts most visitors to the hall are its magical grounds, through which the River Dwyfach flows in a series of waterfalls, and, as well as the nature and river trails, there is a quackery and an adventure playground.

Llangybi

5 miles NE of Pwllheli off the B4354

Just to the north of the village is **St Cybi's Well** and, behind it, the Iron Age fort of **Garn Pentyrch**. The well was

Glasfryn Parc

Pencaenewydd, Pwllheli, Gwynedd LL53 6RE
Tel: 01766 810202 Fax: 01766 810707
e-mail: ema@glasfryn.co.uk website: www.glasfryn.co.uk
Glasfryn Parc, located on the A499 four miles North of Pwllheli, is a fully certified activity provider and a Wales Tourist Board approved attraction. In an area of Outstanding Natural Beauty on the shoulder of the Llyn Peninsula, it is perfect for the activities available:Senior and Junior go karting, quad bike trekking, coarse fishing and archery. Karting takes place on a 600-metre track that has proved a big hit with both karting enthusiasts and day visitors. For the senior hour-long guided quad trek around the farm and estate for 12 year olds and over. Booking is advisable. Also on site there is a cafe-diner selling home-made food, and a farm shop well stocked with Welsh-sourced products.

Glasfryn Holiday Cottages

Mrs Helen Williams-Ellis
Glasfryn, Pencaenewydd, Pwllheli,Gwynedd LL53 6RE Tel: 01766 810688
e-mail: helenwe@enterprise.net website: www.glasfryn.co.uk

Three cottages are also available for self-catering. A top quality five star detached cottage in beautiful unspoilt surroundings. A 16th century stone cottage which sleeps 4/5 and a 17th century farmhouse which sleeps up to 10. All have beamed ceilings, log fires and all mod cons. They are ideal for family celebrations, get-togethers or romantic weekends. There are beautiful gardens, woodlands and lakes, a BBQ and picnic tables. Contact Helen on either 01766 810688 or by the Activity Park. Book early to avoid disappointment.

PATHFINDER - SNOWDONIA MOUNTAIN, RIVER & LAKE ACTIVITIES

The Coach House, Pencaenewydd, Pwllheli, Gwynedd LL53 6RD
Tel: 07781 121820 or 01766 810909
e-mail: bob@pathfindersnowdonia.co.uk
website: www.pathfindersnowdonia.co.uk

Owner Bob Postings and his hand-picked team of instructors offer
excitement and adventure in the special atmosphere of the
breathtakingly beautiful Snowdonia National
Park. Mountaineering, hill walking, rock
climbing, abseiling, gorge scrambling, navigation training, orienteering,
kayaking and Canadian canoeing are guaranteed to test the nerve, skill and
stamina of participants, who could be any number from individuals with a
personal guide to groups of 100 or more needing many instructors.

The instructors are all experienced, qualified professionals, and **Pathfinder**
is a holder of the hard-earned licence of the AALA (Adventure Activities
Licensing Authority) to take young people on adventurous activities. Among
the most popular offerings is the Lake and
River Day involving canoes, kayaks, raft
building and racing and crossing a river by
rope. Perhaps the most challenging is the

Mountain Adventure Day, where strength, courage and a real sense of
adventure are needed and success brings a terrific sense of achievement.
For all-inclusive holidays Pathfinder has a variety of accommodation,
from camp sites and bunk houses to a 50-bed mountain centre, country
cottages, village B&Bs and five-star hotels.

THE CHAPEL OF ART • CAPEL CELFYDDYD

8 Marine Crescent, Criccieth, Gwynedd LL52 0EA
Tel: 01766 523570   e-mail: postbox@the-coa.org.uk
website: www.the-coa.org.uk

Nestled below Criccieth Castle, The **Chapel of Art** is a delightful little gallery,
housed in a tastefully restored 19th century chapel with splendid leaded glass
windows. Regular exhibitions of contemporary, fine and decorative art by carefully
selected local, national and international artists and makers. Specialists in ceramics,
the eclectic collection is reflected in the unique *International Potters Path* at the
entrance. An intimate venue for concerts and events, especially the annual *Criccieth Festival*, this is
well worth a visit. Easter to October: Tues. to Sun. 10.00 to 18.00 hrs. Closed Mondays (except Bank
Holidays) and 'hanging days'. Limited winter opening: Thurs. to Sun. 10:30 to 16:30 hrs.

SIOP GREFFTAU

27 High Street, Criccieth, Gwynedd LL52 0BS
Tel: 01766 523390

Siop Grefftau is a cooperative venture run by a group of six local artists,
craftworkers and designers who work from their homes and sell their
work in their shop on Criccieth's main street. The six are Helen Brodt-
Savage (stained glass, jewellery, hand-made soaps); Iris Crick (quilting,
patchwork, cards); Mike Crick (wood-turning, lampstands, bowls, dishes); Lyndsey Jennings (hand-
painted silks - scarves, pictures, etc); Peter Jennings (gold and silver jewellery); and Megan Mentzoni
(designer knitwear - jackets, hats, shirts, cushions, etc). They undertake commissions and offer a mail
order service and the shop also stocks the work of other locally-based artists and artisans.

established in the 6th century when St Cybi was in the process of setting up religious cells and a monastery in Holyhead. Sheltered by an unusual building with beehive vaulting, which is thought to be unique in Wales, the well had a reputation for curing blindness and warts among many ailments.

LLANYSTUMDWY
6½ miles E of Pwllheli on the A497

This small coastal village is best known as being the home of David Lloyd George, the Member of Parliament for Caernarfon for 55 years and the Prime Minister who, at the beginning of the 20th century, was responsible for social reform as well as seeing the country through the Armistice at the end of World War I. Lloyd George's childhood home, **Highgate**, is now just as it would have been when the great statesman lived here, and the **Lloyd George Museum** features a Victorian schoolroom and an exhibition of the life of this reforming Liberal politician. When he died in 1945, he won this tribute in Parliament from Winston Churchill: "As a man of action, resource and creative energy he stood, when at his zenith, without a rival. His name is a household word throughout our Commonwealth of Nations. He was the greatest Welshman which that unconquerable race has produced since the age of the Tudors. Much of his work abides, some of it will grow greatly in the future, and those who come after us will find the pillars of his life's toil upstanding, massive and indestructible." The Museum is open Easter to October, and at other times by appointment. David Lloyd

George, 1st Earl Lloyd-George of Dwyfor, is buried in the village church, in a tomb designed by Clough Williams-Ellis, architect of Portmeirion. Opposite his grave is a set of **Memorial Gates** presented to the village by Pwllheli in 1952. They feature an elephant and a castle - elephants are part of the town's coat of arms.

CRICCIETH
8 miles E of Pwllheli on the A497

This small family resort lies near the northeast corner of Cardigan Bay and enjoys fine views down the Llyn coastline and northeastwards to Snowdonia. Unlike many of the other resorts on the peninsula, Criccieth is more reminiscent of a south coast seaside town rather than one set in North Wales.

An attractive Victorian town, Criccieth is dominated by **Criccieth Castle**, which stands on a rocky outcrop with commanding views over the sea. Built in the early 13th century by Llywelyn the Great as a stronghold of the native Welsh princes, it was captured, in 1283, and extended by Edward I but the core of the structure - the powerful twin towered gatehouse - still exists from the original

Criccieth Castle

GLAN-Y-WERN

Pentrefelin, Criccieth, Gwynedd LL52 0PT
Tel: 01766 522432
e-mail: derek.jones3@tesco.net
website: www.smoothHound.co.uk/hotels/glanywern

Glen-y-Wern is a modern property in a rural setting on the
southern edge of Pentrefelin. Patricia and Derek Jones provide
excellent bed and breakfast accommodation in two superbly
furnished bedrooms with private en suite bathrooms, central

heating, tv, clock radio and tea/coffee making facilities. An iron,
ironing board and hairdryer can be provided on request, and
the owners keep a large selection of books, maps and local
information. The bedrooms enjoy
fine views of the beautiful
countryside. The dining room, where
a hearty breakfast is served, looks out
on to a picturesque hillside.

An evening meal can be provided
on Sunday by prior arrangement.
The number of guests in the house is limited to four (no children), so personal
attention is assured. The pleasant resort town of Criccieth is just a mile away
along the A497, while Porthmadog is three miles in the other direction.
Among the numerous local attractions are sandy beaches, hill and woodland
walks, golf, fishing, several castles and the wonderful Ffestiniog Railway.
Glan-y-Wern is a non-smoking house.

fortification. Despite Edward's
strengthening of the defences, in 1404
the castle was taken by Owain Glyndwr
and burnt and the castle walls still bear
the scorch marks. One of the best
preserved of the 13th century castles that
litter the North Wales countryside, the
romantic ruins of Criccieth Castle have
inspired many artists down the centuries
including JMW Turner, who used it as
the backdrop for a famous painting of
storm wrecked sailors. The annual
Criccieth Festival is renowned for its
traditional Celtic music and song.
Criccieth won the "Wales in Bloom"
large village section in 2001.

GOLAN

9 miles NE of Pwllheli on the A487

Between the entrances to two wonderful
valleys, Cwm Pennant and Cwm
Ystradllyn, and a mile off the A487
Porthmadog-Caernarfon road, lies

Brynkir Woollen Mill. Originally a
corn mill, it was converted over 150
years ago for woollen cloth production
and, though now modernised (the River
Henwy is used to generate electricity
although the waterwheel still turns),
visitors can still see the various
machines that are used in the
production process: Tenterhook Willey,
carders, spinning mules, doubling and
hanking machines, cheese and bobbin
winder, warping mill and looms. A wide
variety of woollen products made at the
mill can be bought. The mill is open
Monday to Friday; admission is free,
and there's ample parking.

TREMADOG

12 miles E of Pwllheli on the A487

This village, developed, like its close
neighbour Porthmadog, by William
Alexander Madocks, is a wonderful
example of early 19th century town

GOLDEN FLEECE INN & BISTRO

Tremadog, Gwynedd LL49 9RB
Tel: 01766 512421 Fax: 01766 513421

Stewart and Gareth are the owners of the **Golden Fleece**, a famous old coaching inn on the village square of Tremadog. The inn has long been renowned for its hospitality, its ales and its food. There's a cosy, inviting atmosphere in the bar with its arched brick ceiling, and the choice of fine ales (15 and guests) is equalled by a well-chosen selection of wines. Home cooking spans bar snacks and full restaurant meals, with local produce featuring in many of the dishes. The bistro, situated beyond the courtyard in converted stables, is a delightful setting for a candlelit supper. The Golden Fleece also has three guest bedrooms (one twin-bedded, two double-bedded) with en suite shower rooms, tv and tea/coffee-making facilities.

planning and contains many fine Regency buildings. Madocks, who was the MP for Boston in Lincolnshire, bought the land in 1798 and built Tremadog on the reclaimed land in classical style, with broad streets and a handsome market square with a backdrop of cliffs. He hoped that the town would be a key point on the intended main route from the south of England to Ireland, but his rivals in Parliament preferred the North Wales route, with Holyhead becoming the principal port for Ireland. The little town of Tremadog, with its well-planned streets and fine buildings, remains as a memorial to Madocks, who died in Paris in 1828; he is buried in the Père Lachaise cemetery (see also Porthmadog). The soldier and author TE Lawrence (of Arabia) was born in Tremadog in 1888 and the poet Shelley is known to have visited on several occasions.

PORTMEIRION

13½ miles E of Pwllheli off the A487

This very special village, in a wonderful setting on a wooded peninsula overlooking Traeth Bay, was conceived and created by the Welsh architect Sir Clough Williams-Ellis between 1925 and 1972. An inveterate campaigner against the spoiling of Britain's landscape, he set out to illustrate that building in a beautiful location did not mean spoiling

the environment. In looks this is the least Welsh place in Wales: the 50 or so buildings, some of which consist only of a façade, were inspired by a visit Williams-Ellis made to Sorrento and Portofino in Italy and they are mainly either part of the hotel or pastel cottages. There are eccentric, humorous and flamboyant touches at every turn: butterflies stuck on the entrance arch, a Buddha figure in a roadside shrine, a

Portmeirion

FFESTINIOG RAILWAY

Harbour Station, Porthmadog,
Gwynedd LL49 9NF
Tel: 01766 516073 Fax: 01766 516006
e-mail: info@festrail.co.uk
website: www.festrail.co.uk

The world-famous Ffestiniog Railway was
originally built to transport slate from the
mines to Porthmadog, where it was
transferred to ships for export and use
throughout the world. Like many other
little railways, its original role has been
superseded, but this one has found fame as
one of the country's leading attractions. The
world's oldest narrow-gauge passenger-
carrying railway, it runs behind steam locomotives on the 13½-mile journey from Porthmadog to
Blaenau Ffestiniog; the route climbs 700 feet into Snowdonia National Park through pastures and
forests, by lakes and waterfalls, round horseshoe bends and at one point turning back on itself in a
complete spiral.

Calling en route at Minffordd, Penrhyn
and Tan-y-Bwlch, the trip takes just over an
hour. Trains can be hired for private functions,
anniversaries or fine dining evenings, and the
year brings many special events, including
trips on vintage trains using rolling stock
dating from as far back as 1860. The Ffestiniog
found itself at the cutting edge of railway
technology in the 1870s: pivoted wheels, or
bogie, which gave a superior ride and allowed
coaches to take curves more smoothly, had
appeared in North America in 1873 and it was
on the Ffestiniog that it first came to the UK.

There are shops selling gifts and souvenirs
at the termini and Tan-y-Bwlch. Porthmadog
has a café serving anything from sandwiches and snacks to three-course meals, and the café at Tan-y-
Bwlch is open while the trains run. Most trains have corridor coaches where refreshments are sold.

The railway may be little, but it provides a big
experience with a variety of driving programmes,
starting with the more easily handled Penrhyn
Lady class locomotives *Linda* and *Blanche* or the
new *Taliesin*, leading up to the ultimate challenge
of one of the famous Double Fairlies hauling
10carriages. Drivers will enjoy one-to-one personal
tuition and work an eight hour shift, with 14 miles
driving and 14 miles firing. Another course
involves operating one of the oldest steam engines
in the sidings at Minffordd, shunting a rake of slate
wagons.

The Ffestiniog Railway is operated and
maintained by volunteers, and help is always
welcome, either working with the railway or joining
the Ffestiniog Railway Society.

concrete ship moored to the harbour wall. In the central Piazza of this seaside village, theatre productions are occasionally staged during the summer months, and the occasional firework displays are spectacular. The village also has shops selling the famous **Portmeirion Pottery**. The hotel burnt down in 1981, but has been restored to its former glory. The cult television series *The Prisoner* was made at Portmeirion and wandering around the village, the delightful woodlands and the secluded beaches, those familiar with the programme will recognise the locations. The site also includes a castle, a lighthouse, campanile and grottoes, and is surrounded by the lovely Gwyllt woodland gardens, which contain many rare and exotic plants. Williams-Ellis' ancestral home, **Plas Brondanw**, lies some five miles away, up the A4085 northeast of **Garreg**, and the marvellous gardens here make the extra journey well worth while. Designed to please the eye, and also provide some fabulous views over the mountain scenery, there are, among the splendid plants, charming statues and elegant topiary terraces. Sir Clough continued working up until his death at the age of 94 in 1978.

PORTHMADOG
12½ miles E of Pwllheli on the A487

This is a busy town that can become quite packed as holidaymakers take advantage of its many amenities, which include a cinema, the Porthmadog Pottery and galleries. Out of the town, towards Tremadog and across The Cob, the scenery to the left is magical and, at low tide, cattle graze alongside herons and other seabirds and waders.

Seeing Porthmadog today it is hard to believe that this was once the busiest slate port in North Wales and, in fact, the town would never have existed had

it not been for William Madocks, also responsible for neighbouring Tremadog. Member of Parliament for Boston, Lincolnshire, and a great entrepreneur, Madocks drained the mud flats that made up this estuary to create land for grazing cattle in the early 19th century. The embankment, built to keep the tides at bay, enclosed some 7,000 acres of land and re-routed the River Glaslyn to produce a deep water channel that was ideal for the docks. Naming Porthmadog after himself (nearby Tremadog was named after his brother), he saw the beginning of the blossoming of the town in the 1820s. The history of the town and its waterfront is described in the **Maritime Museum** where, too, the importance of the trade in slate and Porthmadog's shipbuilding industry is told.

Porthmadog is also home to both the **Ffestiniog Railway** (see panel opposite), the world's oldest narrow track passenger

Porthmadog

TYDDYN LLWYN HOTEL

Black Rock (Morfa Bychan) Road, Porthmadog,
Gwynedd LL49 9UR
Tel: 01766 513903 e-mail: admin@tyddynllwyn.com
Fax: 01766 515091 website: www.tyddynllwyn.com

Set in the idyllic surroundings of the rolling Welsh countryside,
the **Tyddyn Llwyn Hotel** is the perfect choice for a relaxing break
and is also an ideal base for seeing the sights and scenery of this
marvellous part of the country. The Wright family's hotel has 10
non-smoking bedrooms, all with bath or shower en suite, including
a family room that can sleep five in comfort. Each has a tv and tea/
coffee-making facilities. The
hotel is modern, but is imbued

with an unmistakable Welshness, assisted by the use of oak beams
and quarried slate.

 The Tudor Bar serves a full range of beers, guest real ales, wines
and spirits, and lunches and dinners are served in the restaurant.
The residents' lounge is a comfortable spot to unwind, and the
hotel has a fully licensed function room with seats for up to 100.
Tyddyn Llwyn is situated less than a mile from the centre of
Porthmadog, whose attractions include a bustling, picturesque
harbour, museums and the wonderful narrow-gauge Ffestiniog
railways. There are several golf courses in easy reach, and for
anglers the fishing harbour of Borth Y Gest is just a few minutes'
drive away.

PLAS GLYN-Y-WEDDW GALLERY & ARTS CENTRE

Llanbedrog, Pwllheli, Gwynedd LL53 7TT
Tel: 01758 740763 Fax: 01758 740232
e-mail: enquiry@oriel.org.uk
website: www.oriel-org.uk

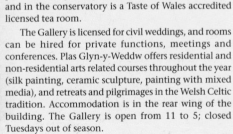

Oriel Plas Glyn-y-Weddw is one of the oldest art
galleries in Wales and is located in a Grade II* listed
Victorian Gothic mansion with views of Cardigan Bay
and the mountains of Snowdonia. Contemporary
Welsh paintings form the core of the works in the
Gallery, which has a varied programme of art
exhibitions throughout the year and also has a
permanent exhibition of Swansea and Nantgarw porcelain. Pictures, prints, jewellery, local crafts,
postcards and greetings cards are for sale in the gift shop,
and in the conservatory is a Taste of Wales accredited
licensed tea room.

 The Gallery is licensed for civil weddings, and rooms
can be hired for private functions, meetings and
conferences. Plas Glyn-y-Weddw offers residential and
non-residential arts related courses throughout the year
(silk painting, ceramic sculpture, painting with mixed
media), and retreats and pilgrimages in the Welsh Celtic
tradition. Accommodation is in the rear wing of the
building. The Gallery is open from 11 to 5; closed
Tuesdays out of season.

carrying railway, and the **Welsh Highland Railway** (see panel on page 60) which, in 1922, was the longest narrow gauge railway in Wales. Maintaining the theme of transport, the **Madog Car and Motorcycle Museum** displays a gleaming collection of vintage British vehicles.

LLANBEDROG
3½ miles SW of Pwllheli on the A499

Named after the 6th century St Pedrog, Llanbedrog lies on the other side of **Myndd Tir y Cwmwd** from Abersoch. The views from the summit are stunning, and another attraction is the **Tin Man**, a modern sculpture made of beachcombed material. In Llanbedrog itself is **Plas Glyn y Weddw**, a neo-Gothic mansion which houses a collection of Welsh furniture and holds various Welsh art exhibitions.

ABERSOCH
6 miles SW of Pwllheli on the A499

A popular family resort with safe beaches, Abersoch lies on each side of the estuary of the River Soch. Its sheltered harbour attracts a wide variety of pleasure craft and just off the coast lie **St Tudwal's Islands** - so called because the saint founded a religious cell there in the 6th century. Both islands are now privately owned and are the home of bird sanctuaries.

The site of the 17th century mansion, **Castellmarch**, was said to be the home of March Amheirchion, one of King Arthur's Knights. Reputed to have the ears of a horse, March (the name is Welsh for horse) kept them hidden and killed anyone who saw them - burying the bodies in a nearby reed bed.

RHIW
11 miles SW of Pwllheli off the B4413

This hamlet lies on a miniature pass and overlooks **Porth Neigwl** (Hell's Mouth),

a four mile sweep of beach so called because of its reputation for strong currents; it is a favourite spot for surfing.

Sheltered from strong gales by Mynydd Rhiw, **Plas yn Rhiw** is a small, part medieval, part Tudor, part Georgian manor house which was given to the National Trust in 1952 by the unconventional Keating sisters from Nottingham. The three spinsters, Eileen, Lorna and Honora, purchased the property in 1938 and lovingly restored it after the house had lain neglected for some 20 years. This they did with the help of their friend Sir Clough Williams-Ellis, the architect of Portmeirion. The house is surrounded by glorious grounds, which were also restored by the sisters, providing fabulous views over Porth Neigwl. Visitors can wander through ornamental gardens and, in the spring, the bluebell and snowdrop woodlands. At one time the poet RS Thomas lived in one of the estate cottages, where he wrote some of his finest poetry.

ABERDARON
13½ miles SW of Pwllheli on the B4413

A small and delightful village which is often busy in the height of summer. It was here, in 1405, that the Tripartite Indenture - the agreement to divide Britain with Wales becoming independent under the rule of Glyndwr - was signed. However, these plans were subsequently ruined by Henry IV and Henry V. Close to the sea and originally dating from the 6th century, **St Hywyn's Church** is thought to have sheltered the 12th century Prince of Wales, Gryffydd ap Rhys, from marauding Saxons and, during the Civil War, the church once again proved a place of sanctuary as Cromwell's soldiers also sought refuge here. One of Aberdaron's most famous natives was Richard Robert Jones, the son of a local carpenter. A strange vagabond, known as Dic Aberdaron, this self-educated linguist is said to have spoken 35 languages and is renowned for having compiled dictionaries in Welsh, Greek and Hebrew. The great poet RS Thomas (1913-2000) also hailed from Aberdaron. He wrote many inspired lines about his beloved country, summed up in this extract:

Every mountain and stream, every farm and little lane announces to the world that landscape is something different in Wales.

A mile or so from the village lies **Castel Odo**, an Iron Age fort providing evidence that there have been five different occupations of the peninsula dating back to the 4th century BC.

UWCHMYNYDD
15 miles SW of Pwllheli off the B4413

Situated on the wild and beautiful tip of the Llyn Peninsula, it was from here that, in the Middle Ages, the first pilgrims set out to Bardsey Island. On the summit of Mynydd Mawr the National Trust has converted an old coastguard hut into a small information point. The National Trust is responsible for much of the land towards the tip of the Llyn Peninsula, including the ecologically outstanding coastal heath of **Braich-y-Pwll**, where the ruins of St Mary's Church, once used by the pilgrims, can still be seen. This heath is the spring and summer home of a variety of plant life and birds, including fulmars, kittiwakes, cormorants, guillemots and the rare chough. A similar variety has its home on the tiny islands of Dinas Fawr and Dinas Bach. Five miles east of Aberdaron, on the south side of the Peninsula, Porth Ysgo and Penarfynndd cover 245 acres of beaches and cliffs, while two miles northwest of the village Mynydd Anelog is a 116-acre area of ancient commonland with the remains of prehistoric hut circles. Here, as in the

other NT stretches of coastland on the Peninsula, is found our friend the chough, a relative of the crow with a distinctive red bill. Apart from here, this rare bird is found only in Pembrokeshire and on a part of the western coast of Scotland. The curiously named **Porth Oer** (Whistling Sands), located off the B4417 by Methlem, are worth a visit as at certain stages of the tide the sands seem literally to whistle when walked upon. The noise is caused by the rubbing together of minute quartz granules.

BARDSEY ISLAND
17 miles SW of Pwllheli off the B4413

Settlement of the island is thought to have begun during the Dark Ages, although it was the death of St Dyfrig on Bardsey, that saw the beginning of pilgrimages. At one time it was considered that three pilgrimages to this holy island was equivalent to one to Rome. Little remains of the 12th century monastery, and the island is now an important bird and field observatory. Boat trips around the island can be made from Aberdaron.

The island's name is Norse in origin and the Welsh name, **Ynys Enlii**, means Island of Currents - an obvious reference to the treacherous waters that separate Bardsey from the mainland.

LLANBERIS

This former slate-producing community has many attractions to keep the visitor occupied although it is, perhaps, best known for the nearby mountain, **Snowdon**. Rising to some 3,560 feet, this is the highest peak in Wales and the most climbed mountain in Britain. On a clear day, the view from the summit is fantastic, with Ireland sometimes visible, but before setting out for the summit it is worth remembering that the weather

Llanberis

Llanberis Lake Railway (see panel below) takes a short trip during which there are several different views of the mountain. The railway lies in **Padarn Country Park**, which gives access to 800 acres of Snowdonia's countryside and also includes Llyn (Lake) Padarn. The Kingfisher Trial is designed specifically for wheelchairs. By the side of the lake is Cwm Derwen Woodland and Wildlife Centre, with a woodland discovery trail and a timewalk exhibition with an audio-visual display. Here, too, is the **Welsh Slate Museum** (see panel on page 98) which tells the story of the slate industry

changes dramatically up here and walkers and climbers should always be prepared. Many reach the summit the easy way, with the help of the **Snowdon Mountain Railway**, a rack and pinion system built in 1896 that has carried millions to the top of the mountain over the years. It is not surprising that this mountainous and inhospitable area is also steeped in legend and mystery. The eagles of Snowdon have long been regarded as oracles of peace and war, triumph and disaster, and Snowdon's peak is said to be a cairn erected over the grave of a giant who was killed by King Arthur.

For those wanting another train ride or are content with a more sedate journey, the

LLANBERIS LAKE RAILWAY

Llanberis, Gwynedd LL55 4TY
Tel: 01286 870549
website:
www.greatlittletrainsofwales.co.uk

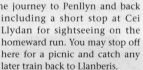

The Llanberis Lake Railway will be ahighlight of your visit to Snowdonia. From your seat in the comfortable enclosed coaches you can enjoy spectacular views of Snowdon and the surrounding high mountains. Starting at Gilfach Dclu station in the Padarn Park at Llanberis, the trains take approximately 40 minutes to make the journey to Penllyn and back

including a short stop at Cei Llydan for sightseeing on the homeward run. You may stop off here for a picnic and catch any later train back to Llanberis.

The railway is very popular with visitors to Wales wishing to ride one of the "Great Little Trains of Wales" without spending too much money or time doing so. Even cheaper fares are available for families, pre-booked coach parties and school groups. Guidebook available. Station cafeteria open Easter to late October offers a selection of refreshments in pleasant surroundings. A specially adapted coach is now available for wheelchair users. Toilets with disabled access are situated within the park. Please call to check times of trains.

colony by David Cox and other eminent Victorian countryside painters; their work inspired others, and the coming of the railway in 1868 brought the tourists to what soon became a busy holiday centre. The Old Church, near the railway station, has been in use since the 14th century and remained the town's major place of worship until the influx of visitors required a larger and more prestigious building. A major attraction is the **Motor Museum**, whose unique collection of vintage and post-vintage cars includes a fabulous Bugatti Type 57. The Museum is open daily from 10.30 to 6 from Easter to October.

As the village is close to the point where the Conwy, Lledr and Llugwy rivers meet, it seems natural that these waterways should play an important role in the development, building and beauty of Betws-y-Coed. Thomas Telford's **Waterloo Bridge**, a marvellous iron construction, built in 1815, gracefully spans the River Conwy, while the **Pont-y-Pair**, dating from around 1470, crosses the River Llugwy; further downstream, an iron suspension footbridge spans the river by the church. However, the main attractions that draw people to this area are the waterfalls: the spectacular multi-level **Swallow Falls** on the River Lugwy, **Conwy Falls**, **Machno Falls** and **Fairy Glen Ravine**. Next to the railway station

Swallow Falls

is the **Conwy Valley Railway Museum** and shop, a popular place to visit in the summer. The village's most famous, and certainly most curious, attraction is **Ty Hyll**, the Ugly House, which stands close by the River Llugwy. Apparently this building, which looks like it was literally thrown together, is an example of hurried assembly in order to obtain

freehold on common land. The house was often used as an overnight stop by Irish drovers taking cattle to English markets. The scenery around Betws-y-Coed is truly magnificent, and within minutes of leaving the town centre there are numerous well-marked walks lasting anything from an hour to all day and suiting all energy levels.

CAPEL GARMON
15½ miles E of Llanberis off the A5

Surrounded by the spectacular scenery of the Snowdonia mountain range, this tiny village has an additional attraction for the superstitious visitor as there are two legends associated with the village inn. The first involves the daughter of a long ago innkeeper, who fell in love with a local farmhand. One night the young man rode up on his white horse and the girl climbed down from her bedroom window and rode off with him, never to be seen again. The second legend concerns a friendly fair-haired lady who watches over all the events here but no one knows for sure whether the two are connected.

Close by the village is the **Capel Garmon Burial Chamber** which dates from around 1500 BC; the remains of a long barrow with three burial chambers, one with its capstone still in position, can be seen.

NANT PERIS
2 miles SE of Llanberis on the A4086

Once known as Old Llanberis, the village lies at the opposite end of Llyn Peris from its larger namesake - Llanberis - and at the entrance to the Pass of Llanberis. The **Well of Peris**, which lies just north of the village centre, was, until relatively recently much visited for its healing

Continued on page 104

TY-GWYN HOTEL & RESTAURANT

Betws-y-Coed, Conwy LL24 0SG
Tel: 01690 710383/710787
e-mail: mratcl1050@aol.com website: www.tygwynhotel.co.uk

On the outskirts of the village, **Ty-Gwyn** is a centuries-old coaching inn with flowers and greenery at the front and woods rising imposingly behind. The inn, run by partners Tim and Martin Ratcliffe and Nichola Bradbury, has 14 beautifully appointed bedrooms, most with bathrooms en suite, and guests start the day with a hearty breakfast that sets them up for a day in the glorious countryside or by the sea. The inn has a beamed lounge bar and cosy tv lounge, and fresh local produce is a feature of the bar meals, à la carte menu and vegetarian dishes, all complemented by an extensive choice of wines.

DOLWEUNYDD GUEST HOUSE

Pentre Du, Betws-y-Coed, Snowdonia National Park,
North Wales LL24 0BY e-mail: jenny.dolweunydd@virgin.net
Tel: 01690 710693 website: www.snowdonia-dolweunydd.co.uk

"Hospitality is our first language." Jenny and Rob Shepherd have proven this as Regional and National runners up of the Welcome Host of the Year Awards. Recently refurbished, **Dolweunydd** has five en suite letting bedrooms, one of which is a peaceful, secluded cottage in the garden with a beamed double bedroom, shower room and lobby entrance. All rooms have tv and hospitality tray, and guests can unwind in a cosy lounge. Rob is a talented chef and provides an excellent breakfast and optional evening meal using fresh local produce. Guests enjoy a 25% discount at Betws-y-Coed Golf Club. Well-behaved children are welcome. Sorry no pets. Strictly non-smoking .

WALK 3

Lledr Valley

Start	Dolwyddelan
Distance	6½ miles (10.5km)
Approximate time	3 hours
Parking	Dolwyddelan, car park and picnic area by station
Refreshments	Pubs and cafés at Dolwyddelan
Ordnance Survey maps	Landranger 115 (Snowdon), Outdoor Leisure 17 (Snowdonia – Snowdon & Conwy Valley areas)

This is a walk that provides a succession of outstanding views over the surrounding mountains, especially of Moel Siabod and Snowdon, plus attractive woodland and riverside walking, for only a modest effort. The first half is along a broad and undulating track, much of it through woodland, and the return is along tree-lined paths and lanes and across lush meadows bordering the lovely River Lledr.

The village of Dolwyddelan is situated below the spectacular rugged slopes of Moel Siabod in the Lledr valley. It has a small, largely unrestored 16th-century church, and about ¾ mile (1.2km) to the east is Dolwyddelan Castle, reputed birthplace of Llewellyn the Great. The castle is in sight for much of this route and was one of the principal residences of the princes of Gwynedd. During the English conquest it was occupied by Llewellyn ap Gruffydd, last native prince of Wales, before being captured by Edward I in 1282. At the end of the Middle Ages it fell into disuse and ruin; the main surviving parts are the fine 12th-century keep, which was partially rebuilt in the 19th century, and the 13th-century west tower.

Start by turning left out of the car park and picnic area, turn left again to cross the railway bridge and at a T-junction bear left along a lane. Walk up hill and where the lane ends by the last house, turn left on to a track, **A** passing in front of houses.

Keep along this clear, broad, winding and gently undulating track for the next 2½ miles (4km), negotiating several gates and stiles. At the start there are some abandoned slate-quarries and for much of the way the track passes through attractive woodland. The more open stretches provide some superb views to the left across the Lledr valley, with Snowdon and Moel Siabod prominent on the skyline, plus the impressively sited Dolwyddelan Castle. Because of the lack of waymarks, it is necessary to look out carefully for where a slaty path crosses the track diagonally. Turn sharp left **B** on to it, almost doubling back, and the path heads down through trees and bears right to pass under a railway bridge to a gate. Go through, walk along an enclosed track which descends towards a farm, bear right in front of the farmhouse and after going through two gates, the path turns left Ⓒ alongside the foaming, rushing waters of the River Lledr.

Keep beside the tree-shaded riverbank to a ladder-stile, climb it, continue up hill through dense woodland and later bear right and gently descend along a walled path to a gate. Go through, head down to go through another one and continue once more beside the Lledr. The riverside path – boggy in places – leads to a T-junction where you turn right through a metal gate, cross a drive and continue along an enclosed up hill path to emerge on to a tarmac drive. Continue up hill along it, passing to the left of an hotel, to join a narrow lane Ⓓ and keep along the lane, passing Pont-y-pant

station, to where it ends at a farm. Keep ahead through a metal gate and walk along an undulating track, later keeping beside the railway line on the right. Go through a metal gate, turn right through another to pass under a railway bridge and turn left along a path across lovely riverside meadows. Now come more splendid views of the river, Moel Siabod and Mount Snowdon.

Pass to the right of farm buildings, go through a gate and keep ahead along a track, passing by an attractive old clapper-bridge over the Lledr on the right. The tarmac track continues across meadows, keeps to the left of another farm – there are some gates to negotiate here – and leads directly back to the starting point. ●

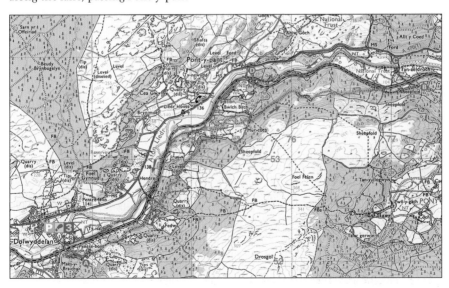

powers, as well as for wishing. A successful request was said to be signalled by the appearance of a sacred fish.

DOLWYDDELAN

11 miles SE of Llanberis off the A470

Here can be seen the stark remains of **Dolwyddelan Castle**, which is unusual among Welsh castles in that it was constructed by a native Welsh prince rather than by either the English or the Normans. Built between 1210 and 1240 by Llywelyn the Great to control a strategic pass through the mountainous region of his kingdom, the fortress fell to Edward I in 1283. In 1488, the place was acquired by Maredudd ap Levan, who built the village church that now houses his kneeling brass effigy. After Maredudd's death the castle fell into ruin and the modern roof and battlements seen today were added in the 19th century when the core of the castle underwent restoration. However, the beauty of the castle is very much its lonely setting and from here there are stunning mountain views. The Castle is now looked after by CADW - Welsh Historic Monuments.

PENMACHNO

14½ miles SE of Llanberis on the B4406

This delightful village of picturesque stone cottages, set in a wooded valley, lies on the River Machno, from which it takes its name. Not only is Penmachno surrounded by glorious countryside but it is also situated within an area that is a stronghold of Welsh culture and here can be found the traditional **Penmachno Woollen Mill**. Visitors to the mill can not only see the working power looms as they weave the cloth but can also browse through the shop among the finished articles and other Welsh craftwork on display.

To the northwest of the village centre and in the secluded Wybrnant valley lies **Ty Mawr Wybrnant**, the birthplace of Bishop William Morgan (1545-1604) who was the first person to translate the Bible into Welsh. Now restored to how it probably appeared in the 16th and 17th centuries, the house (now in the ownership of the National Trust) includes a display of Welsh Bibles, including Morgan's of 1588. A pleasant one mile walk starts at the house and takes in woodland and the surrounding fields.

To the northeast of the village and approached by a walk alongside the River Machno, lies **Ty'n y Coed Uchaf**, a small farm that gives visitors an insight into the traditional way of life of the Welsh-speaking community in this area.

PENTREFOELAS

19½ miles SE of Llanberis on the A5

Once an upland estate village, Pentrefoelas is now becoming a focal

THE RIVERSIDE CHOCOLATE HOUSE

The Little Chocolate House in the Hills
Pentrefoelas, Nr Betws-y-Coed, Conwy LL24 0LE
Tel: 01690 770366
website: www.riversidechocolates.co.uk

The **Riverside Chocolate House**, in this quiet village, is based on the Chocolate Houses of Continental Europe where high quality chocolates and patisserie are made and sold on the premises. Master chocolatier Roy Nesling creates luxury handmade chocolates using the very best cocoa beans for the shells and real spirits and real pure fruit compounds for the fillings. A viewing area allows visitors to watch Roy at work. He is also a Master Patissier, and in the tea room the most delicious desserts - Swiss tortes, cheesecakes and pastries - can be enjoyed.

point to the continuation and revival of crafts and skills which were used to maintain the estate; among the attractions is a working **Watermill**.

FFESTINIOG

13½ miles SE of Llanberis on the A470

Situated above the **Vale of Ffestiniog**, there is a delightful walk, beginning at the village church, to **Cynfal Falls**, just below the village. Above the falls stands a rock, known locally as Pulpud Huw Llwyd, that recalls a local mystic who preached from here. Three miles to the northeast, **Gamallt** is a remote 300-acre moorland that supports a variety of plant life as well as water beetles,

sandpipers, ring ousels, wheatears and meadow pipits. Archaeological remains include a large Iron Age settlement, and the important Roman road known as **Sarn Helen** crosses the property, which is in the care of the National Trust.

MAENTWROG

13½ miles SE of Llanberis on the A496

Lying in the Vale of Ffestiniog, this peaceful and attractive village is home to **Plas Tan-y-Bwlch** where the 19th century terraced gardens not only provide glorious views of the surrounding area but where there are picturesque walks through woodland. Here, too, among the magnificent trees

CROCHENDY TWROG POTTERY

Maentwrog, Nr Porthmadog, Gwynedd LL41 3YU
Tel: 01766 590302

Trefor Owen produces unique wood-fired stoneware in a handsome complex of 18th century, Grade II listed farm buildings in the lovely Vale of Ffestiniog. He runs the pottery

with his wife Gill, and their pots, vases and other decorative and domestic ware are thrown by hand on the wheel. The glazes are made on site from raw materials, including ashes from pine, apple and rhododendron. The showroom displays an impressive collection of **Crochendy Twrog** pottery and a selection of pottery made by other Welsh craftspeople. The Pottery is open from 10 to 6 seven days a week.

and rhododendrons, is an oak wood that provides a small reminder of the vast oak forests that once covered much of Wales.

BLAENAU FFESTINIOG
12 miles SE of Llanberis on the A470

This was once the slate capital of the world and the industry still dominates the landscape and economy of this town and the surrounding area. Stretching across from the feet of Manod towards the Moelwyn Mountains, the legacy of the slate industry is visible everywhere - from the orderly piles of quarried slate waste to the buildings in the town.

Ffestiniog Railway

Today, the industry lives on in two slate mines: **Llechwedd Slate Caverns** and **Gloddfa Ganol Slate Mine** The slate caverns, the winners of many top tourism awards, take visitors underground to explore the world of a Victorian slate miner and the man-made caverns of cathedral proportions, while, on surface, there is a Victorian village to wander through. The Gloddfa Ganol mine, where digging began in 1818, was once the world's largest, and today slate is still being turned into commercial products. At the foot of Manod Bach, beside the waterfall at Bethania, **Pant-yr-ynn Mill** is the earliest surviving slate mill of the Diffwys Casson Quarry. Built in 1846, it later saw service as a school before being converted into a woollen mill in 1881. It worked until 1964, when it was closed down and the machinery scrapped. The original part of the building has been preserved and the waterwheel restored; it is now home to an exhibition dealing with Blaenau - the town, the communities, the landscape and the changes to it made by the 20

quarries in the vicinity. The exhibition, which includes drawings and paintings by resident artist and industrial archaeologist Falcon D Hildred, is open from 2 to 5 on the second weekend of the month between May and October. For visits at other times, call 01766 830540.

As well as having a mainline train service, Blaenau Ffestiniog is the end, or the starting point, of the narrow gauge **Ffestiniog Railway**, which runs through the vale to Porthmadog (see panel on page 92). Built to carry slate down to the sea for shipping off around the world, the railway has since been renovated by enthusiasts and volunteers. There is a comprehensive service giving passengers the chance to admire the scenery of the vale on their journey to the coast. There are many stopping off points so walkers can take advantage, en route, of **Tan-y-Blwch County Park** and other beauty spots.

To the northwest of the town, at First Hydro's power station, is the **Ffestiniog Visitor Centre**, the ideal place to discover the wonders of hydro-electricity. Opened in 1963 by Her Majesty the Queen, the station consists of reservoirs and underwater passages constructed inside the mountains and the displays and exhibitions at the centre explain not only how the electrical power is generated but also the development of electricity over the years.

BEDDGELERT

7½ miles S of Llanberis on the A498

This village's setting, surrounded by mountains and, in particular, the 2,566 feet of **Moel Hebog**, is reminiscent of the Swiss Alps. In the 6th century a Celtic monastery was founded here that went on to become one of the foremost religious houses in Wales. Later, in the 12th or 13th century, the monastery was succeeded by a small Augustinian priory given both land and support by Llywelyn the Great and Owain Gwynedd.

However, Beddgelert was much more than just a religious centre in medieval times. This was thanks to the River

Glaslyn being navigable as far as Pont Aberglaslyn, the stone bridge at the narrowest point of the gorge. Shipping remained an important mainstay of life here until the Porthmadog embankment was constructed in the early 19th century. The **Pass of Aberglaslyn**, through which the racing waters of the salmon river flow, lies to the south of the village; it is a delightful pass with steeply wooded slopes and an abundance of rhododendrons.

The village's name translates to "Gelert's Grave" and it refers to Llywelyn the Great's faithful dog Gelert, which he left to guard his little son. When he returned, he found the dog covered in blood and the child nowhere to be seen. He concluded that Gelert had killed his son, so in his fury he killed the dog. Only then did he realise that his son was alive, saved by Gelert from a wolf, whose

Continued on page 110

BRYN EGLWYS HOTEL

Beddgelert, Gwynedd LL55 4NB
Tel: 01766 890210 Fax: 01766 890485
website: www.bryneglwyshotel.co.uk

Kevin and Lyn Lambert put out the welcome mat at **Bryn Eglwys Country House Hotel**, which enjoys a stunning setting within the Snowdonia National Park. Their Georgian former country farmhouse has been extensively refurbished while retaining much of its original charm, and the well-equipped en suite bedrooms provide character, comfort and superb views. There's a cosy, friendly feel throughout, and guests will find easy relaxation in the lounge and bar. In the elegant restaurant a daily changing menu puts local and Welsh produce to fine use in such dishes as fillet of Colwyn Bay plaice with herb butter, rack of lamb with garlic and rosemary, and extra mature rump steak with pepper sauce.

The hotel, which lies off the A498 south of Beddgelert, has ample parking facilities and a large, attractive garden. The scenery all around is truly breathtaking, and there are many popular walking routes providing anything from a gentle stroll to a serious climb. The lovely River Glaslyn flows almost past the door and the impressive mass of Moel Hebog looms beyond. Gelert's Grave is just one of many historic attractions nearby.

WALK 4

Llyn y Gader and Beddgelert Forest

Start	Rhyd-Ddu, National Park car park
Distance	5 miles (8km)
Approximate time	2½ hours
Parking	Rhyd-Ddu
Refreshments	Pub at Rhyd-Ddu, ¼ mile (400m) north of starting point
Ordnance Survey maps	Landranger 115 (Snowdon), Outdoor Leisure 17 (Snowdonia – Snowdon & Conwy Valley areas)

This walk is through terrain that lies just to the west of Snowdon, and the last part of it uses a section of the Rhyd-Ddu Path, which is one of the most popular routes to the summit of Wales' highest mountain. For much of the way the austere Llyn y Gader is in sight, and there are dramatic views of Mynydd Mawr, the Nantlle ridge and Moel Hebog to the west, and Yr Aran, the most southerly peak of the Snowdon range, to the east. The route also touches the northern fringes of the extensive Beddgelert Forest.

From the car park cross the road and go through a metal kissing-gate at a public footpath sign. As you walk along a slabbed path there is an imposing view ahead of the precipitous cliffs of Y Garn, part of the Nantlle ridge. On reaching the Afon Gwyrfai, follow the path to the left and then turn right to cross a footbridge over the river.

Climb a ladder-stile and turn right along a path which crosses a track to the left of a whitewashed farmhouse and continues across rough grass to join another track. Walk along the track, climb a ladder-stile on to a road and immediately turn left **A** through a metal gate, at a public bridleway sign, and continue along a path by a low wall and wire fence on the right. Head up to

climb a ladder-stile and continue to a large boulder with white arrows painted on it. On the next part of the route you enjoy fine views of the Nantlle ridge ahead, and to the left across Llyn y Gader to Yr Aran.

Continue past the boulder – the route here is marked by a series of white arrows on rocks – heading steadily uphill all the while, ford two streams and pass a spectacular waterfall to eventually reach a ladder-stile. Climb it, keep ahead to enter the conifers of Beddgelert Forest, pass through a wall-gap and descend to a crossroads **B**. Turn left and continue steadily downhill along a wide and curving track, initially along the left inside edge of the forest and later through the trees. At a T-junction, turn left and continue steadily downhill, passing beside a barrier and keeping ahead to a road **C**.

Turn left and after nearly ½ mile (800m), turn right **D** through a metal gate at a public footpath sign to Snowdon. Walk along a tarmac drive which bends left up to Ffridd Uchaf farm, go through a metal gate, turn right between farm buildings and bear left to a gate. Go through, head uphill, by a wall bordering a conifer wood on the left, go through a metal kissing-gate and continue uphill. To the right are grand views of Snowdon, and to the left Llyn y Gader, Y Garn and the Nantlle ridge come into view again.

Climb a ladder-stile, keep ahead across grassy moorland – although the

path is only faint there are regular marker-stones – and pass to the right of a group of rocks to reach a T-junction in front of a wall **E** . Turn left to join the Rhyd-Ddu Path and descend between rocks to a ladder-stile. Climb it and as you continue steadily downhill along a winding path, glorious views open up looking along the length of Llyn Cwellyn towards Caernarfon and the Menai Strait.

Climb two more ladder-stiles, keep ahead between old quarry workings, pass beside a metal barrier and continue to a metal kissing-gate. Go through and turn left along a track back to the start. ●

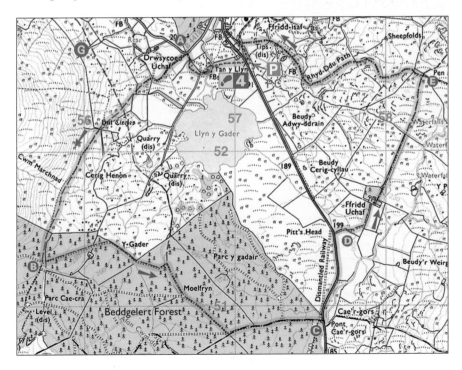

Beddgelert

has been reopened as a remarkable and impressive example of Welsh industrial heritage where visitors can see the maze of underground tunnels and chambers, the massive stalactites and stalagmites and the copper ore veins that also contain traces of gold and silver. Audio commentaries give details of each stage of the mining process, with lighting and sound effects, which all contribute to this fascinating glimpse of the past.

Just a short distance further along this road lies **Dinas Emrys**, a hill fort that is thought to be associated with the legendary 5th century battle between the two dragons - one red and one white - that was prophesied by the young Merlin. The lake nearby, **Llyn Dinas**, is also associated with Merlin the Magician and legend claims that the true throne of Britain is in the lake and will only be revealed when a young person stands on a certain stone.

body lay nearby. The reputed grave of Gelert is in a riverside meadow, just south of the village, though the stones found here were apparently erected by a local landlord during the 18th century, perhaps hoping to attract more business with the grave as a local place of interest. The land around the grave was bought in 1987 with grants from the Countryside Commission and the Portmeirion Foundation in memory of Sir Clough Williams-Ellis. There's another animal connection: Alfred Bestall, the original illustrator of Rupert Bear, lived in Beddgelert. This attractive village won the "Wales in Bloom" small village section in 2001.

To the northeast of the village, on the road to Capel Curig, lies the **Sygun Copper Mine**, which was abandoned in 1903. However, today, the former mine

HARLECH

Harlech means "Bold Rock" and there is no doubting the fact as the town clings to the land at the foot of its spectacularly sited Castle. Another of Edward I's Iron Ring of fortresses, which was begun in 1283, **Harlech Castle** is perched on a rocky outcrop for added strength and it is, today, a World Heritage Site which is in the hands of CADW. The Castle's situation, close to the sea, has not only proved a great defence but was also useful during its blockade by Madog and his men in 1294, when supplies transported in from Ireland enabled the 37 men inside to hold fast. If the use of power and strength to impress and intimidate an indigenous population was ever aided by architecture then Harlech is a prime example. Situated 200 feet above sea level, its concentric design, with lower outer walls, by architect James of St George, used the natural defences of its site to emphasise its impregnability. However, in 1404 Owain Glyndwr managed to capture the castle and held it for five years while using the town of Harlech as his capital.

The song, *Men of Harlech*, has immortalised the siege during the War of the Roses when the Castle was held for the Lancastrian side for seven years before it finally became the last stronghold to fall to

Harlech Castle

the Yorkists in 1468. The last time Harlech saw action was 200 years later, during the Civil War, when it again withstood attack and was the last castle in Wales to fall to Cromwell's forces. The panoramic views from the Castle's

battlements take in both Tremadog Bay and the mountainous scenery behind the town.

Though not as imposing as the Castle, **The Lasynys Fawr** is another building worth a visit while in Harlech. The

YR OGOF BISTRO

High Street, Harlech, Gwynedd LL46 2YE
Tel: 01766 780888

Regulars come from many miles around to enjoy the relaxed atmosphere and the excellent food at Julie and Andrew Jones's **Yr Ogof Bistro**. Behind the white-painted facade on Harlech's main street, the 56-cover restaurant is appointed in traditional style, the walls adorned with pictures, prints and old food advertisements from Julie's father's shop along the road. The owners are proud that everything on their evening

menu is cooked to order.

Many of the dishes have a local provenance, and one of the options is a three-course Welsh menu featuring such dishes as lamb with a redcurrant gravy or Welsh cheese and leek pie with a creamy mushroom sauce. These dishes are also available on an extensive à la carte selection that provides plenty of choice for all tastes, from a classic prawn cocktail to lemon sole in a celery and thyme sauce, garlic chicken, pepper steak and spaghetti bolognese. A splendid meal ends on a high note with mouthwatering puddings made by a local farmer's wife. Best to book ahead, especially at the weekend, as this is a deservedly popular place to spend an evening.

HAFOD WEN GUEST HOUSE

Harlech, Gwynedd LL46 2RA Tel: 01766 780356

Hafod Wen Guest House is situated on the A496 a mile south of Harlech on the sea side of the road - look for the large sign with a picture of the house. The location, in sloping gardens with magnificent views over Cardigan Bay and the Lleyn Peninsula, is just one of the attractions of Hafod Wen, where owners Reg and Jane Chapman offer excellent hospitality and top-class accommodation in seven beautifully furnished en suite bedrooms. Guests are pampered with extra-comfortable beds, soft towels and quality toiletries and fragrances.

Most of the rooms have French windows opening on to balconies that make the most of the stunning setting. Paintings from Jane's family hang in the hall and the lounge, where guests can browse through a pile of magazines round a coal fire in winter. In the summer, it's a real delight to sit outside on the sheltered veranda or stroll round the gardens. A generous breakfast sets guests up for a day in the open air, and in the evening a three or four course dinner provides a leisurely end to the day. There is a private path to the sea at Harlech, where a long sandy beach provides safe bathing. Harlech Castle is two minutes away, and it's only a short drive inland to the scenic glories and marvellous walking opportunities provided by Snowdonia National Park.

home of Ellis Swynne (1671-1734), one of Wales' most famous prose writers, the house is an excellent example of one of its period - it dates from 1600. Some of the scenes in the early James Bond film *From Russia With Love* were shot in Harlech. The famous Royal St David's golf course is just outside the town.

Just outside Harlech, to the north, lies **Morfa Harlech**, a nature reserve with woodland trails that occupies the flat land between the town and Llanfihangel-y-thaethau.

BONTDDU

9 miles SE of Harlech on the A496

Looking at this pleasant village it is hard to imagine that it was, over 100 years ago, a bustling centre of the Welsh gold mining industry. Apparently, there were 24 mines operating in the area around this village and it was one of these mines

that provided the gold for the Royal wedding rings.

BARMOUTH

9 miles S of Harlech on the A496

Occupying a picturesque location by the mouth of the River Mawddach, Barmouth was once a small port with an equally small shipbuilding industry. As the fashion for seeking out sea air grew in the 18th century, the character of Barmouth changed to accommodate visitors flocking here for the bracing sea air - those suffering from scurvy were even fed seaweed, which is rich in Vitamin C and grew in abundance in the estuary. However, the Barmouth seen today is, like many other seaside resorts, a product of the railway age and the Victorian architecture is still very much apparent. **Ty Gywn** is one of its older buildings, dating from the 15th century.

GWRACH YNYS COUNTRY GUEST HOUSE

Talsarnau, Nr Harlech, Gwynedd LL47 6TS
Tel: 01766 780742 Fax: 01766 781199
e-mail: cl@gwrachynys.co.uk website: www.gwrachynys.co.uk

Gwrach Ynys is a roomy, relaxing Edwardian country house where Gwynfor and Deborah Williams provide the warmest of welcomes. Seven tastefully decorated rooms (six en suite and a single with private facilities) offer everything needed for a comfortable stay, and guests have a choice of two lounges where they can relax and browse through the selection of books, magazines and files of local information. Mature trees fringe the pleasant lawns, and there are lovely views towards Snowdon and Harlech Castle. Dozens of footpaths offer a multitude of walks for all energy levels, and miles of golden sands are just minutes away.

The house, now the home to a Tudor exhibition, is said to have been built for Henry Tudor, Earl of Richmond, who went on to become Henry VII. It is thought to have been used as the meeting place where the plot to overthrow Richard III was hatched. The town is also home to the **Lifeboat Museum**.

The town's harbour, host to a regular regatta, is overlooked by **Dinas Oleu**, a small hill that was the first property given to the newly formed National Trust in 1895. It was a gift from the local wealthy philanthropist, Mrs Fanny Talbot, who

CHAPEL ANTIQUES CENTRE

High Street, Barmouth, Gwynedd LL42 1DS
Tel/Fax: 01341 281377 e-mail:jonestheantique@supanet.com

Danny Jones, a well-known Barmouth businessman and the Mayor in 2001-2002, has found an excellent new role for a handsome stone chapel built in 1881 on the town's main street. **Chapel Antiques Centre** is home to 20 antique dealers under one roof, carrying stock from glass and china to furniture, lighting, jewellery, pictures, books, maps and prints and a wide range of collectables and decorative items. Many of the original church fittings, including the organ, are still in place, while others, such as the pulpit, are part of the stock for sale. The Centre is closed Wednesdays off season.

BRYN MELYN HOTEL

Panorama Road, Barmouth, Gwynedd LL42 1DQ
Tel: 01341 280556
e-mail: bryn.melyn@virgin.net
website: www.brynmelynhotel.co.uk

Bryn Melyn Hotel, which stands in its own grounds, is an ideal base for a relaxing holiday. Hosts Peter Jukes and Mary Calland provide a real home from home feel, and the nine comfortable, en-

suite bedrooms have tv, telephone, hospitality tray and lots of little extras. In the restaurant the table d'hote menus offer plenty of choice, and special dietary requirements can be catered for with notice. The views from Bryn Melyn are stunning, and the whole area is a paradise for walkers. Panorama Walk, created as a tourist attraction in the 19th century, leads up to a rocky promontory.

LLWYNDU FARMHOUSE HOTEL

Llanaber, Nr Barmouth, Gwynedd LL42 1RR
Tel: 01341 280144   e-mail: intouch@llwyndu-farmhouse.co.uk
Fax: 01341 281236   website: www.llwyndu-farmhouse.co.uk

Inglenook fireplaces, mullion windows, exposed stone walls and sturdy old beams create a delightfully traditional look at Paula and Peter Thompson's 16th century **Llwyndu Farmhouse**. The setting is picturesque, tranquil and relaxed, with a genuine home-from-home ambience. Accommodation comprises seven rooms, all en suite, three of them in the main house, the others in a beautifully converted barn. All have tv, and two have four-posters. Peter is an excellent cook, and his breakfasts and candlelit dinners are occasions to look forward to with relish. Children and pets are welcome.

THE OLD FARMHOUSE

Tyddyn Du, Dyffryn Ardudwy, Gwynedd LL44 2DW
Tel: 01341 242711
e-mail: metcalfe.oldfarmhouse@virgin.net
website: www.ukworld.net/oldfarmhouse

The comforts of a well-run hotel and the friendliness and informality of a farmhouse. Those are the twin attractions of the **Old Farmhouse**, where John and Margaret Metcalfe are the most genial and welcoming of hosts, and where guests who arrive as strangers are sure to leave as friends. And those friends return year after year to enjoy the relaxed atmosphere, the comfortable accommodation, the lovely gardens overlooking Cardigan Bay and the magnificent local scenery.

The five en suite bedrooms all have teletext tv, radio alarm clock, tea/coffee trays and hairdryers; garden rooms are particularly secluded and cosy. Rooms are let on a bed and breakfast basis, with the option of an evening meal by prior arrangement. In the grounds is a heated swimming pool for summer use; a hot spa pool is available all year round. The Old Farmhouse has a super lounge with an open fire and lots of books to browse. John knows just about everything there is to know about the area, and his "specialist subjects" are classic cars and the local railways. The farmhouse is signposted from the A496 midway between Harlech and Barmouth.

YSTUMGWERN HALL FARM

Dyffryn Ardudwy, Gwynedd LL44 2DD
Tel: 01341 247249 Fax: 01341 247171
e-mail: ynys@ystumgwern.co.uk website: www.ystumgwern.co.uk

John and Jane Williams provide a warm Welsh welcome to **Ystumgwern**. A taste of luxury with a cosy, relaxed atmosphere. Lying between beach and mountains on the west coast of the Snowdonia National Park, this 16th century farmhouse and barn conversions, are furnished and equipped to the highest standards. Featuring oak beams, inglenook fireplace and central heating they sleep from two to eight guests in one to four bedrooms, many en-suite. There are landscaped areas for leisure activities and the farm is an ideal base for making the most of the glorious Welsh scenery. W.T.B 5 stars. Some disabled access.

was a friend of two of the Trust's founding members. Panorama Walk is a scenic walk created as a tourist attraction at the turn of the 19th century. There are several viewpoints along its route, the best being the one from the promontory at the end of the path. Built over 125 years ago and half a mile in length, the railway viaduct that spans the river mouth has a walkway on the bridge from where there are magnificent views of the town, coast and estuary.

LLANABER
8 miles S of Harlech on the A496

Found close to the clifftops, the village church here is said to have been used by smugglers, who hid their booty inside the tombs in the churchyard. Dating from the 10th century, this place of worship, which was once the parish church of Barmouth, has an interesting doorway that is one of the best examples of early English architecture.

DYFFRYN ARDUDWY
5 miles S of Harlech on the A496

Neolithic remains, as well as the remnants of Iron and Bronze Age settlements, abound in this area and in this village can be found two burial chambers. Perhaps the most interesting is **Arthur's Quoit**, the capstone of which

is said to have been thrown from the summit of Moelfre by King Arthur.

LLANBEDR
3 miles S of Harlech on the A496

This village is an excellent starting point for walks along the lovely valleys of the Rivers Artro and Nant-col and into the Rhinog Mountains. At 2,360 feet **Rhinog Fawr** may not be the highest local peak but, from its summit, there are superb views over the Coed y Brenin Forest to the Cambrian Mountains.

Those not so keen on walking may be interested in **Maes Artro Village** which was once the living quarters for pilots of fighter squadrons during World War II and, today, is a family attraction that includes a museum, aquarium and craft shops.

SHELL ISLAND
3½ miles S of Harlech off the A496

More correctly described as a peninsula that is cut off at high tide, Shell Island (see panel on page 116) is a treasure trove of seashells and wildlife and the shoreline, a mixture of pebble beaches with rock pools and golden sands, is ideal for children to explore. Seals are often seen close by and there is plenty of birdlife; surprising considering the fairly regular aircraft activity from the nearby Llanbedr airfield.

TAN Y RHIW

Llanbedr, Nr Harlech, Gwynedd
Tel/Fax: 01952 730212 e-mail: intogift@msn.com

Paul and Carol Richardson have refurbished this fine old stone cottage to provide delightful self-catering accommodation retaining its period character with up-to-date amenities. The cottage lies in the heart of Snowdonia, within easy access to the most beautiful scenery in Wales. Tan y Rhiw is set in private gardens surrounded by beautiful woodland, within walking distance of the village shops and eating places. The cottage has a large dining room and sitting room with beamed ceilings, timber floors and real fires. The generous double bedrooms cater for eight people.There is a bathroom and shower room, a full fitted breakfast kitchen and utility. Guests are provided with a welcome pack of groceries, wine and fuel for the fire.

LLANFAIR SLATE CAVERNS

Llanfair, Nr Harlech, Gwynedd LL46 2SQ
Tel: 01766 780247
e-mail: owen@llanfairslate.fsnet.co.uk
website: www.lokalink.co.uk/harlech/slatecaverns

The Owen family restored and re-opened **Llanfair Slate Caverns**, which had been the source of local prosperity between 1853 and 1906. A tour takes visitors down the main tunnel into the imposing man-made caverns where miners worked in arduous conditions by candlelight. Many industrial towns in Britain and Ireland still have original roofs of Llanfair slate. The site has a café and a souvenir shop, and a children's farm park with rabbits, lambs, goats and nature walks. The Caverns are open from Easter to October.

SHELL ISLAND

Llanbedr Mer, Gwynedd LL45 2PJ
Tel: 01341 241453 Fax: 01341 241501

Shell Island is located two and a half miles west of Llanbedr on the A496, three miles south of Harlech and seven miles north of Barmouth. The name refers to a small privately-owned peninsula which extends to 462 acres and provides an interesting day out and a fabulous camping site. The peninsula can be reached by a one mile tidal causeway - signs at the mainland end give clear instructions on when it is safe to cross.

At the centre of the peninsula is the holiday complex, open daily, which offers a snack bar for teas, coffees and light meals; a licensed bar for on or off sales; a restaurant for evening meals and Sunday lunch. Many visitors come here to enjoy the natural scenery and abundance of wildlife. The panoramic scenery is second to none - on a fine day you can enjoy views of Harlech Castle, the Lleyn Peninsula, the Snowdon range, the foothills of Cadair Idris and the coastline extending to Pembrokeshire.

Wild birds are found in great numbers on Shell Island and the estuary is a haven for all kinds of wildlife. Migrating birds can often be seen not far from the shore, a family of swans regularly visit with their young during the summer, and winter brings a variety of wintering birds. Wild Flowers are also found in great numbers with a number of rare species being found here. As the land has been left to its own devices for over 25 years large areas become smothered with wild flowers and aromatic roses growing side by side with tangles of wild strawberries and speedwell. Hedges burst with colour and the estuary turns a shade of pink in June as sea thrift blooms.

Most people come to Shell Island for the shells which can be found in abundance after the winter storms and high tides. More than 200 different varieties can be identified, some of them rare and difficult to find anywhere else in Britain. Some are so small that a magnifying glass is a necessary piece of equipment!

LLANFAIR

**1½ mile S of Harlech
on the A496**

Between 1853 and 1906, Llanfair was a prosperous slate mining village and the old, deep quarries, the **Chwarel Hên Llanfair Slate Caverns**, in use until 1906, are now open to the public (see panel above), who can don miner's helmets and set out on a self-guided tour.

BALA

This agreeable town is a good stopping off point when exploring Snowdonia National Park. Roman and Norman remains have been found here, but the town was really founded in around 1310 by Roger de Mortimer, who was looking to tame the rebellious Penllyn district. The town was by Tudor times a small, and by all accounts not very successful, market town, but it later became an important centre for the knitted stocking industry that flourished in the 18th century before the inventions and factory systems of the Industrial Revolution put paid to this established cottage industry. Today, though tourism is certainly an important part of the town's economy, it has remained a central meeting point and a market place for the surrounding farming communities.

Bala Lake

However, it is perhaps as a religious centre that Bala is better remembered. The Reverend Thomas Charles, one of the founders of the Methodist movement in Wales in the 18th century, first visited Bala in 1778 and moved here in 1783 after marrying a local girl. Working for the Methodist denomination, Charles saw the great need for Welsh Bibles and other religious books, and he joined forces with a printer from Chester to produce a series of books and pamphlets. The story of Mary Jones, who walked some 25 miles from Llanfihangel-y-Pennant to buy a bible from Charles, was the inspiration for the foundation of the Bible Society (see also under Llanfihangel-y-Pennant on page 126). Notable sons of

BALA LAKE COUNTRY HOTEL & RESTAURANT

Tel: 01678 521585
e-mail: robertalan.dehoxar@virgin.net
website: www.balalakehotel.com

Built 200 years ago as a hunting lodge, the **Bala Lake Hotel** enjoys a beautiful lakeside location on the B4403 just outside Bala. The hotel has 29 acres of woodland and pasture and a terrace with fine views of the Lake and mountains; it also has an outdoor swimming pool. Completely restored and refurbished by new owners Robert de Hoxar and his five partners, the hotel has 19 en suite bedrooms and a suite with access and facilities for disabled guests. All rooms have a shower, tv, telephone, tea/coffee making facilities and hairdryer, and superior rooms have both bath and shower and enjoy the best of the views. The hotel has an à la carte restaurant, and packed lunches are available if requested the night before; afternoon teas are served in season.

The large lounge also affords spectacular views, and other day rooms include a bar-lounge, a small games room and a chapel/quiet room. All public rooms are smoke-free zones, but some bedrooms are

reserved for smokers. The six partners of the Bala Lake Hotel are from different Christian traditions and have a welcome for visitors of all denominations, or none. Three of the partners are medically qualified, and all have some understanding of physical, mental and emotional illness. There are regular times of prayer in the chapel, which is open at all times for private prayer. The dining room and conservatory may be used for conferences and can accommodate up to 100 on a day basis, with buffet lunch included. Smaller groups (up to 40) are offered on-site accommodation and restaurant facilities, and additional accommodation is available locally.

GLASSBLOBBERY

Glanrafon Hall, Glanrafon, Nr Corwen, Denbighshire LL21 0HA
Tel: 01490 460440 Fax: 01490 460247
e-mail: wendy@glassblobbery.co.uk website: www.glassblobbery.co.uk

The old community hall in Glanrafon is the site of **Glassblobbery**, where David and Wendy Pryce-Jones create wonderful ornamental pieces in glass. Each piece is made freehand from varying thicknesses of glass rod over a flame that reaches 2,000°C, which is then fired and taken to the staining room, where Wendy applies mixtures of metal oxides to the surface to produce a range of hues. Also in the studio is a range of unusual craft objects in wood, ceramic and porcelain, many of them locally made, as well as original watercolours, limited edition etchings, sculptures and other objects of art.

BRYN TEGID COUNTRY HOUSE

Llanycil, Nr Bala, Gwynedd LL23 7YG
Tel/Fax: 01678 521645
e-mail: info@bryntegid.co.uk website: www.bryntegid.co.uk

Bryn Tegid is a greystone Victorian country house set in nine acres of lawns and woodland overlooking Bala Lake. The three guest bedrooms are en suite, with tv and tea/coffee-making facilities; two of which enjoy views of the Lake. Owner Rosina Jones produces lovely flower arrangements that are a feature throughout. A splendid breakfast is served in the bright, spacious dining room, where an evening meal is also available by arrangement. This is great walking, cycling and bird-watching country, and all the attractions of Bala Lake, and the National Whitewater Centre, are almost on the doorstep. Self-catering accommodation is also available.

CYSGOD Y GARN

Frongoch, Bala, Gwynedd LL23 7NT
Tel: 01678 521457
e-mail: carys@snowdoniafrongoch.co.uk
website: www.snowdoniafrongoch.co.uk

Cysgod y Garn is a small country farmhouse, which stands in its own grounds surrounded by beautiful farmland and spectacular rural Welsh views. Three miles from Bala, half a mile from White Water Rafting Centre. The farmhouse provides excellent

bed and breakfast accommodation in three comfortable, attractively furnished double/twin rooms. All have en-suite, whirlpool bath and sitting areas.

- 4 Star WTB.
- Evening meals by arrangement.
- A Welsh welcome awaits you.

Bala include Thomas Edward Ellis, a Liberal Member of Parliament who worked hard for the Welsh, and Owen M Edwards, who was a leading light in the Welsh educational system. There are statues to both these worthies in Bala. The son of Owen Edwards, Sir Ifan ab Owen Edwards, established the Welsh Youth Movement, which has a camp at Bala Lake. To the southwest of the town, **Llyn Tegid (Bala Lake)** is the largest natural lake in Wales and feeder of the River Dee. Four miles long, nearly three quarters of a mile wide and up to 150 feet deep, the Lake is a popular centre for all manner of watersports; it is also the home of Tegi, the Welsh version of Scotland's Nessie. Formed during the Ice Age, the Lake is an important site ecologically and has been designated a Site of Special Scientific Interest and a Ramsar site (Wetlands of International Importance).

Many uncommon wetland plants flourish on its banks, and the birdlife includes coots, mallards, pochards, wigeons and great crested grebes. The fish life is interesting, too, and Bala is the only lake in Wales which is home to the gwyniad, a white-scaled member of the herring family that feeds on plankton in the depths of the Lake. Along the eastern bank of the lake runs the narrow gauge **Bala Lake Railway**, which provides the perfect opportunity to catch a glimpse of the Tegi.

FRONGOCH
2 miles N of Bala on the A4212

Just to the west of the village lies the reservoir **Llyn Celyn** on whose banks is a memorial stone to a group of local Quakers who, centuries ago, emigrated to America to escape persecution. The modern chapel close by, **Chapel Celyn**,

---

THE NATIONAL WHITEWATER CENTRE

Canolfan Tryweryn, Frongoch, Nr Bala, Gwynedd LL23 7NU
Tel: 01678 521083 Fax: 01678 521158
e-mail: ct.bookings@virgin.net website: www.ukrafting.co.uk

Set in the heart of the glorious Snowdonia National Park, the **National Whitewater Centre** is a purpose-built facility on the banks of the River Tryweryn. The river has been used for kayaking and canoeing since the mid-seventies and has hosted two world championships and numerous international competitions. In 1986 the centre developed the first whitewater rafting operation in the UK, going on to become the largest and most respected rafting organisation in Britain.

The river is dam controlled, ensuring a fast flow of water all year round. "Raft Experience" is a taster session providing a spectacular introduction to the thrills of the sport, and after a briefing by

one of the qualified raft guides, it's time to run the whitewater course. 'Raft Extravaganza' is two hours of non-stop action, involving usually four runs in groups of 4 to 7 people in rugged, inflatable 14ft rafts that are virtually unsinkable. At the end of the runs participants return wet and exhilarated to the Centre for a hot shower, a change of clothing and something to eat and drink in the café overlooking the course. The Centre is internationally recognised as a centre of excellence for paddlesport coaching and white water safety and rescue training. The courses, all non-residential, are run by highly qualified coaches with many years' experience of delivering high-quality specialist coaching.

was built as a reminder of the rural hamlet which was drowned when the reservoir was created in the 1960s. Overlooking Llyn Celyn is **Arenig Fawr**, which has, on its 2,800 foot summit, a memorial to the crew of a Flying Fortress that crashed here in 1943.

LLANUWCHLLYN

4 miles S of Bala on the A494

This hamlet, at the southern end of Bala Lake, is the terminus of the Bala Lake Railway, which follows the lake for four miles with various stops where passengers can alight and enjoy a picnic or a walk.

Cadair Idris

Spreading up from the eastern banks of the lake is the **Penllyn Forest**, which can be reached and passed through via **Cwm Hirnant** on an unclassified road that weaves through the forest to

moorland and eventually reaches **Llyn Efyrnwy (Lake Vyrnwy)**.

DOLGELLAU

Meaning "meadow of the hazels", Dolgellau is the chief market town for this southern area of Snowdonia.

BALA LAKE RAILWAY

The Station, Llanuwchllyn, Nr Bala, Gwynedd LL23 7DD
Tel: 01678 540666 Fax: 01678 540535
e-mail: balalake@freenetname.co.uk
website: www.bala-lake-railway.co.uk

Run by the company and a team of voluntary helpers, the narrow-gauge **Bala Lake Railway** operates a four-times-a-day service between Easter and the end of September. Three steam and one diesel locomotive haul the trains from Llanuwchllyn to Bala, enjoying wonderful views along the lake shore on their 25-minute journey. The trains run on the track bed of what was once part of the standard gauge Great Western Railway line from Ruabon to Barmouth, a line that was closed under the Beeching proposals in the early 1960s.

The main station is at Llanuwchllyn ("the village above the lake"), where there is a buffet and souvenir shop. Here, visitors can see the engine being prepared for its journey to Bala and on most days can have a look in the loco shed. All trains stop at Llangower, the mid-point along the Lake, and at the other stops, Bryn Hynod and Pentrepiod, passengers can board by signalling to the driver and alight by telling the guard in advance. The trains all finish their day's work at Llanuwchllyn. Volunteers provide the train crews and fill other posts connected with the running and maintenance of the Bala Lake Railway, one of the Great Little Trains of Wales.

Pleasantly situated beside the River Wnion, with Cadair Idris rising in background, the town is very Welsh in custom, language and location. Owain Glyndwr held a Welsh parliament here in 1404, later signing an alliance with France's Charles VI. Now, the town's narrow streets can barely evoke those distant times and few early buildings remain. However, the seven-arched bridge over the river dates from the early 17th century and, before much of Dolgellau was built in an attempt to lure Victorian holidaymakers to the delights of Cadair Idris, there was a small rural Quaker community here. The **Quaker Heritage Centre** tells the story of this community and also of the persecution that led them to emigrate to Pennsylvania. North of the town, the seven mile **Precipice Walk** offers superb views. The local gold mines provided the

PIA

Eldon Square, Dolgellau, Gwynedd LL40 1RD
Tel/Fax: 01341 421384
e-mail: pia@dolgellau.org.uk
website: www.pialifestyle.co.uk

At the top of the town square opposite the Tourist Information Centre, **Pia** is a delightful shop which no visitor to Dolgellau should miss. On the ground floor of a fine old stone building on a corner, Glenys Kojs has filled her shop with a wide variety of attractive gifts, some made locally, others from all over the world. Greetings and art cards are hand-made, mostly to local Welsh designs, and there are small pieces of English furniture on display.

Among the other notable items are table and standard lamps in contemporary style from Italy; the Broste collection of Danish candles and glassware; Sia glass decorations; and hand-crafted gifts from Africa. Dolgellau is a lovely old market town that is very Welsh in custom, language and location, and Pia, with its connections from near and far, adds an international touch that manages to fit perfectly into the surroundings. Opening hours of Pia (it's the Welsh for the chiff-chaff bird) are 10 to 5 or 5.30 every day except Wednesday and Sunday.

THE ROYAL SHIP HOTEL

Queens Square, Dolgellau, Gwynedd LL40 1AR
Tel: 01341 422209 Fax: 01341 421027

Since arriving at the beginning of 2002, Bernhard and Angela Lanz have considerably enhanced the standing of the **Royal Ship Hotel**. An early 19th century coaching inn right in the middle of town, the hotel has been extensively modernised and extended, and behind its attractive ivy-clad façade there are two bars, a residents' lounge, a pleasant dining room and 23 bedrooms, 18 of which are en suite, the remainder with private allocated bathrooms. Robinsons Brewery provides an excellent range of beers and lagers, and as well as morning coffee and afternoon tea, the menu offered is available throughout the day.

gold for the wedding rings of both Queen Elizabeth II (then Princess Elizabeth) and Diana, Princess of Wales.

Rising to some 2,927 feet to the southwest of Dolgellau, **Cadair Idris** dominates the local scenery and on a clear day a climb to the summit is rewarded with views that take in the Isle of Man and the Irish coast as well as, closer to home, the Mawddach estuary. The mountain's name means "Chair of Idris" and traditionally it was named after a great poet and warrior. Those climbing to the top should also be aware of the local folklore that says anyone sleeping on the summit will either wake up a poet or a madman, or blind, or - in another version - not at all!

DOLGUN UCHAF

Nr Dolgellau, Gwynedd LL40 2AB
Tel: 01341 422269 Fax: 01341 422285
e-mail: dolgunuchaf@guesthousessnowdonia.com
website: www.guesthousessnowdonia.com

Dolgun Uchaf is a characterful 500-year-old building that started life as a Hall House and was later a Quaker meeting house. Owner Eleanor Meredith offers bed and breakfast accommodation (and an optional evening meal) in three delightful en suite bedrooms, all with central heating, tv and beverage facilities. Other options are self-catering accommodation in an adjacent house sleeping up to eight guests, and a camping and touring site on a small, level field with showers and electric hook-ups. The views are superb, and walks include the famous torrent walk that passes close by.

FRONOLEU FARM HOTEL

Tabor, Dolgellau, Gwynedd LL40 2PS
Tel: 01341 422361
e-mail: fronoleu@dfronoleu0fsnet.com
website: www.fronoleu.fg.co.uk

High above Dolgellau, with views of Cader Idris and the Mawddach estuary, **Fronoleu Farm Hotel** offers a winning combination of traditional warmth and character and modern comfort. Owners Dewi and Maggie Jones, here for 16 years, started with a modest bed and breakfast establishment and created a lovely

hotel acclaimed for its fine food and wine. Lighter meals are served in the Stable Bar, while in the restaurant the full evening menu is highlighted by the superb locally supplied lamb, beef and game. Most evenings, dinner is accompanied by the gentle strains of a harp.

Guest accommodation comprises 10 tastefully appointed bedrooms, most with en suite facilities,

some with four-poster beds. All have tv, tea tray and hairdryer; children are very welcome, and cots and high chairs can be provided. Day rooms include a cosy bar and lounge, both with log fires. The area around the hotel is wonderful walking country, and guests planning a day in the fresh air can start on the right foot with a sumptuous breakfast and set out with a packed lunch supplied by Dewi and Maggie. And if they return wet or muddy, there are washing, drying and ironing facilities at the hotel. Free fishing is available for residents on Dolgellau Angling Association waters, and pony trekking can be arranged.

AROUND DOLGELLAU

LLANELLTYD
2 miles NW of Dolgellau on the A470

This is the point at which the Rivers Wen and Wnion, boosted by other waters further upland, meet to form the Mawddach estuary. Close by, just across the River Wen, lies the serene ruins of **Cymer Abbey**, which was founded by Cistercian monks in 1198. This white-robed order was established in the late 11th century in Burgundy and they arrived in Britain in 1128 to seek out remote places where they could lead their austere lives. Cymer was one of two Cistercian abbeys created in the Snowdonia region during the Middle Ages - the other is Conwy Abbey - and Cymer held substantial lands in this area. Despite this, the abbey was poor and it also suffered badly during the fighting between England and Wales. In fact, by the time of the Dissolution in 1536 the abbey's income was just £51. Visitors to this CADW site can see the remaining parts of the church, refectory and chapter house set in particularly picturesque surroundings.

LLANFACHRAETH
3 miles N of Dolgellau off the A470

Close to the village is **Nannau Hall**, the ancient seat of the Vaughan family who owned much of the land in this area. It is said that an earlier house on the site belonged to Howel Sele, a cousin of Owain Glyndwr, who, during a dispute with Glyndwr over Sele's Lancastrian sympathies, shot at but missed his cousin while out hunting. Glyndwr was so enraged that he killed Sele and hid his body in a hollow oak. This hiding place was later to receive a mention in Sir Walter Scott's *Marmion* as "the spirit's blasted tree".

GANLLWYD
5 miles N of Dolgellau on the A470

This hamlet gives its name to the attractive valley in which it is found and which is, in turn, surrounded by the **Coed y Brenin Forest Park**, an area of some 9,000 acres around the valleys of the Rivers Mawddach, Eden, Gain and Wen. Originally part of the Nannau Estate, founded by Cadougan, Prince of Powys, in 1100, the forest was acquired by the Forestry Commission in 1922, when extensive planting of conifers took place. Ganllwyd was once a centre for gold mining and, during the 1880s, the nearby mine at Gwynfynydd was prosperous enough to attract some 250 miners. The mine had produced around 40,000 ounces of gold by the time it closed in 1917; it re-opened from 1981

DOLGELLAU HOLIDAY COTTAGE

The Gardens, Llanelltyd, Nr Dolgellau, Gwynedd LL40 2SU
Tel: 01341 422358

Standing in landscaped grounds with superb views towards Cader Idris, **Dolgellau Holiday Cottage** has three bedrooms (one with en suite shower room), a bath/shower room, an excellent fitted kitchen/diner, a lovely lounge with tv, video and feature inglenook, and a splendid conservatory. On the same site and in the same ownership as this excellent self-catering cottage is a nursery which has been in May Roberts' family for four generations. The area offers glorious scenery and great walking and cycling opportunities, and it's a five minute stroll from the cottage to the beautiful Mawddach estuary with salmon and trout fishing.

to 1989. The mine is on the route of one of the four waymarked trails, which also takes in waterfalls, forest nature trails and an old copper works. Orienteering is a good way to explore the park, which also offers some of the best mountain biking in the UK. Bikes can be hired at the Visitor Centre, which has a café, shop and exhibitions. There are also riverside picnic sites and a children's adventure play area. Broadleaved woodlands once covered the land and some of these woodlands still survive at the National Trust owned **Dolmelynllyn** estate. On the slopes of **Y Garn**, a path through this expanse of heath and oak woodland leads to **Rhaeadr Ddu** (the **Black Waterfall**), one of the most spectacular waterfalls in Wales. Also in the heart of the forest can be found a series of hundreds of steps, known as the **Roman Steps**, which climb up through the rocks and heather of the wild Rhinog Mountains. Certainly not Roman, they are thought to have been part of a late medieval trade route between the coastal region around Harlech and England.

TRAWSFYNYDD
10 miles N of Dolgellau off the A470

To the west of the village lies **Llyn Trawsfynydd**, a man-made lake developed in the 1930s as part of a hydro-electric scheme. There are walks around the lake, while on its northern shores stands **Trawsfynydd Nuclear Power Station**, which opened in 1965 and was the country's first inland nuclear station.

Down a minor road close to the power station are the remains of a small Roman amphitheatre that also served as a fort. Later used by the Normans as a motte, **Tomen-y-Mur** is associated with the legendary princes of Ardudwy. The story goes that the prince's men, after a raid into Clwyd, were returning with their bounty and Clwydian women when they were caught by the pursuing men and slain. The women, smitten by their captors, chose to drown themselves in a lake close to Ffestiniog rather than return to Clwyd.

In the village centre is a statue in honour of Hedd Wynn, a poet and shepherd who was awarded the bardic chair at the 1917 Eisteddfod while he fought and died in the Flanders fields during World War I.

DINAS MAWDDWY
8½ miles E of Dolgellau on the A470

During the Middle Ages, this now quiet village was a centre of local power but the only surviving building from those days is a packhorse bridge, **Pont Minllyn**. A gateway to the upper Dyfi valley, it was once alive with quarries and mines but all that today's visitors can see of past industry is the traditional

MEIRION MILL

Dinas Mawddwy, Powys SY20 9LS
Tel: 01650 531311 Fax: 01650 531447

Meirion Mill, known as the "Mill in the Mountains", lies just off the A470 between Machynlleth and Dolgellau. The Mill shop has a wide range of beautifully designed craftware and clothing, including a tremendous selection of woollen items, Portmeirion Pottery and Welsh Royal Crystal. Refreshments are available in the coffee shop, serving light meals and a tempting selection of cakes. The cheese scones are especially noted. Meirion Mill is open every day throughout the year. There's plenty of parking and a playground for the children.

weaving of cloth at **Meirion Mill**, where there is also a visitor centre, craft shop and café.

MALLWYD

9 miles SE of Dolgellau on the A470

This small village's inn, **The Brigand**, recalls the days during the 16th century when this area was menaced by a gang known as the "Red Robbers of Mawddwy". Eighty gang members were executed in 1554 and the survivors exacted some revenge by murdering their prosecutor, Baron Lewis Owen, at the nearby town of **Llidiart-y-Barwn**.

CORRIS

6 miles S of Dolgellau on the A487

This small village, surrounded by the tree covered slopes of the Cambrian Mountains, was home to the first narrow gauge railway in Wales. Constructed in 1859 as a horse drawn railway, steam locomotives were introduced in 1878 before the passenger service began in 1883. After finally closing in 1948, the Corris Railway Society opened a **Railway Museum** dedicated to the line in 1970 that explains the railway's history and also the special relationship with the slate quarries through displays, exhibits and photographs.

Industry of a different kind can be found at the **Corris Craft Centre**, which is home to a variety of working craftsmen and women. An excellent place to find a unique gift, the craft centre is also home to the fascinating **King Arthur's Labyrinth** - a maze of underground tunnels where visitors are taken by boat to see the spectacular caverns and relive tales of the legendary King Arthur.

The legend of King Arthur is first told in **The Mabinogion**, a collection of stories which evolved over 1,000 years.

KING ARTHUR'S LABYRINTH

Corris Craft Centre, Machynlleth, Powys SY20 9RF
Tel: 01654 761584   Fax: 01654 761575
e-mail: king.arthurs.labyrinth@corris.wales.co.uk website: www.kingarthurslabyrinth.com

King Arthur's Labyrinth is an exciting visitor attraction in mid-Wales which has captured the public imagination. An underground boat ride takes visitors into the spectacular caverns deep under the mountain at Corris near Machynlleth. As visitors walk through the caverns, Welsh tales of King Arthur are told with tableaux and stunning sound and light effects. The journey ends with a trip along the beautiful subterranean river into the grounds of Corris Craft Centre. The craft centre is home to six craft workshops, woodcraft, toymaking, pottery, jewellery, leather work and candle studio.

New for 2002 is the Bards' Quest- an outdoor floral Maze with tableaux illustrating the stories. It challenges you to go in search of the lost legends hidden in the Maze of Time. When you find them you will be enthralled by the mystical stories, echoing across the ages, and so help to save them from extinction.

GLANDWYRYD CERAMICS

Glandwyryd, Upper Corris, Nr Machynlleth, Powys SY20 9BE
Tel/Fax: 01654 761297 e-mail: ceramics@glandwyryd.fsnet.co.uk

Figurative ceramics designed and hand-made by Don and Jacky Bennett are on display in their studio-showroom and retail shop in Upper Corris. Every item is crafted by hand, and because clay is a variable media, figures may vary slightly in colour and design, making each piece unique. The limbs are hand-rolled, the clothes cut and layered just as they would be worn. The range includes glazed earthenware candle snuffers, bathers in hip baths, busy children, boaters, mounted horses and splendid nativity sets. The Bennetts gladly undertake commissions.Open most days between 10am-5pm but please phone if making a special journey.

Passed from generation to generation from the 4th century onwards, they were not written down in a surviving manuscript form until the 13th century. The *White Book of Rhydderch* and the *Red Book of Hergest* between them contain 11 stories, five of which centre round the exploits of King Arthur and his contemporaries. In these tales we meet Gwenhwyfar (Guinevere), Cei (Sir Kay), Bedwyr (Sir Bedivere), Myrddin (Merlin) and Gwalchmei (Sir Gawain). In the *History of the Britons*, written by the Welsh cleric Nennius around 830, we first read of Arthur's battles, some at least of which took place in Wales, from about 515 onwards. The last great battle, against his nephew Mawdred and his Saxon allies, marked the end of a phase of Celtic resistance to the Saxons; this battle has been dated to 537 and is located by some historians on the Llyn Peninsula. In Welsh tradition Merlin and the great bard Taliesin took the dying King Arthur to the magical Isle of Avalon, which recent research has identified as Bardsey Island, where St Cadfan established a monastery and where 1,000 Welsh saints are buried. The caverns of King Arthur's Labyrinth are the workings of the Braich Goch Slate Mine, which was operational between

1836 and 1970. At its peak, the mine employed 250 men and produced 7,000 tons of roofing slate annually.

TAL-Y-LLYN

5 miles S of Dolgellau on the B4405

This tiny hamlet lies at the southwestern end of the **Tal-y-llyn Lake**, which is overshadowed by the crags of Cadair Idris to the north. A great favourite with trout fishermen, the village has a simple early 17th century church with an unusual chancel ceiling of square panels decorated with carved roses.

LLANFIHANGEL-Y-PENNANT

7 miles SW of Dolgellau off the B4405

Just to the northeast of this small hamlet lie the ruins of **Mary Jones's Cottage**. After saving for six years for a Welsh Bible in the early 1800s, Mary Jones, the

Nant Gwynant, Snowdonia

daughter of a weaver, walked to Bala to purchase a copy from Thomas Charles. As Charles had no copies of the Bible available, he gave her his own copy and the episode inspired the founding of the Bible Society. Mary lived to a ripe old age (88 years) and was buried at Bryncrug, while her Bible is preserved in the Society's headquarters in London.

Close by lie the runs of **Castell y Bere**, a hill top fortress begun by Llywelyn the Great in 1223. Taken by the Earl of Pembrokeshire, on behalf of Edward I, in 1283, the castle stayed in English hands for two years before being retaken by the Welsh and destroyed.

ARTHOG
6 miles SW of Dolgellau on the A493

Overlooking the Mawddach estuary, this elongated village is a starting point for walks into Cadair Idris. Beginning with a sheltered woodland path, the trail climbs up to the two **Cregennen Lakes** from where there are glorious mountain views. The lakes are fed by streams running off the mountains and they have created a valuable wetland habitat that is now in the hands of the National Trust. Down by the river mouth, there is an **RSPB Nature Reserve** protecting the wealth of birdlife and wildlife to be found here.

FAIRBOURNE
8 miles SW of Dolgellau off the A493

This growing holiday resort lies on the opposite side of the Mawddach estuary from Barmouth and, from the ferry that carries passengers across the river mouth, runs the **Fairbourne Railway**. Originally a horse-drawn tramway, now steam-hauled, this 15" gauge railway runs from Fairbourne to the mouth of the

FAIRBOURNE & BARMOUTH STEAM RAILWAY

Beach Road, Fairbourne, Gwynedd LL38 2PZ
Tel: 01341 250362 Fax: 01341 250240
e-mail: enquiries@fairbourne-railway.co.uk
website: www.fairbourne-railway.co.uk

Originally laid in 1895 by Arthur McDougall of flour fame, the **Fairbourne & Barmouth Steam Railway** runs for a distance of 2½ miles between Fairbourne and Penrhyn Point. There is an intermediate stop at a place with 65 letters that means "the Mawddach station with its dragon's teeth on the northerly Penrhyn drive on the golden beach of Cardigan Bay". The service runs from Easter to mid-September, with some days later in the year, and the train connects at Pernrhyn Point with the ferry across the

Mawddach estuary to Barmouth.

The locomotives on this tiny railway are half-size replicas, among them *Sherpa*, a Darjeeling and Himalaya Class B engine built in 1978. The engine shed, café, ticket office and souvenir shop are all at Fairbourne, where free attractions are the museum, with 100 years of history in words and photographs and popular nameplate rubbings, and the Rowen Indoor Nature Centre with birds, mammals, fish, reptiles, amphibians, insects and a bubbling trout stream.

Mawddach estuary. Its midway halt was given an invented name that outdoes the 59 letters of LlanfairPG by eight. Translated from the Welsh, it means "Mawddach Station with its dragon's teeth on North Penrhyn Drive by the golden sands of Cardigan Bay".

TYWYN
14 miles SW of Dolgellau on the A493

This coastal town and seaside resort on Cardigan Bay has long sandy beaches, dunes and a promenade, as well as being the start (or the end) of the famous **Talyllyn Railway** (see panel on page 129).

The area inland from Tywyn is wonderful walking country, and marked walks include the new National Trail that runs between Machynlleth, Welshpool and Knighton. One of the stations on the line is Dolgoch, from which a walk takes in three sets of magnificent waterfalls. Four walks of varying lengths and difficulty start at Nant Gwernol station and provide an opportunity to enjoy the lovely woodlands and to look at the remains of Bryn Eglwys quarry and the tramway that served it.

ABERDOVEY
16 miles SW of Dolgellau on the A493

Also commonly known by its Welsh name, **Aberdyfi**, this now quiet resort, at the mouth of the River Dovey (or Dyfi), was once one of the most important

TYN-YR-EITHIN

Bryncrug, Tywyn, Gwynedd LL36 9LF
Tel/Fax: 01654 711823
e-mail: tynyreithin@ukonline.co.uk

Tyn-yr-Eithin is a handsome 200-year-old stone farmhouse surrounded by farmland. Owners Keith and Maureen offer top-quality bed and breakfast accommodation in two lovely en suite bedrooms in the main house and two more in an adjacent converted barn. Home-made preserves are a real treat at breakfast time, and evening meals are available by arrangement. A self-catering cottage is also available. Keith and Maureen have another outstanding talent, with jointly 65 years experience of working with wood, and in their studio is a display of wooden items of the highest craftsmanship, including bowls, table lamps and small tables and stools.

RIVERSIDE HOUSE

Abergynolwyn, Nr Tywyn, Gwynedd LL36 9YR
Tel: 01654 782235
e-mail: ronbott@talyllyn-freeserve.co.uk
website: www.snowdonia.wales.co.uk

Three large, comfortably furnished rooms - one of them with en suite facilities - provide homely bed and breakfast accommodation in a wonderful riverside setting below Cader Idris. **Riverside House**, built for the local quarrymaster, is the home of Ron Bott and Gillian Skinner, who regale guests with an excellent breakfast and, by arrangement, a memorable three-course evening meal. There are plenty of books and local information in the tv lounge, and Ron organises tours of the area, along the coast and up the valley of the River Dysynni.

Aberdovey

one particular occasion having 180 ships unloading or waiting for a berth. The town has been attracting holiday-makers since Edwardian times, when the railways made such seaside trips possible for many more people. It is a gentle, civilised spot, with all the best attributes of a seaside resort and none of the kiss-me-quick tat of many larger places. Aberdovey has given its name to a Victorian ballad called "The Bells of Aberdovey", recounting the legend that the sea drowned a great kingdom here and how on quiet summer evenings the bells can be heard ringing out from beneath the waves.

ports along the Welsh coast. Shipbuilding flourished here alongside the busy port, whose records show on

Talyllyn Railway

Wharf Station, Tywyn, Gwynedd LL36 9EY
Tel: 01654 710472 Fax: 01654 711755
e-mail: enquiries@talyllyn.co.uk
website: www.talyllyn

Volunteers come from all over the British Isles for the delight and privilege of working on the best known and best loved of all the Great Little Trains of Wales. **The Talyllyn Railway** was opened in 1865 to carry slate from the quarry at Bryn Eglwys to Tywyn for transfer to the newly built mainline coast railway. It also carried passengers, but by 1950, when it was running with the minimum of staff and the worn-out original Victorian equipment, it faced closure. In that year a group of individuals led by Tom Rolt formed a society to save and operate the railway, which became the world's first preserved railway and enjoyed investment and great success which has lasted to this day. The Talyllyn has six steam locomotives, all maintained at the Pendre sheds and workshop.

The oldest, *Talyllyn*, dates from 1864, the newest, *Tom Rolt*, from 1991. Three diesels are used for engineering duties and emergency replacements. The railway runs daily from Easter to the end of

October, with a few days also in other months except January. On some summer Sundays the special Talyllyn Vintage Train uses the original coaches pulled by an original locomotive; there are various other special events during the year, including certain evenings with entertainment included. The main terminal station at Tywyn, recently renovated and extended, has a shop and museum, and cafés at Tywyn and Abergynolwyn provide refreshments when the trains are running. The beautiful valley offers a series of walks which start and finish at stations on the line.

Once part of the old county of Montgomeryshire, this northern region of Powys is an area of varied landscape and small towns and villages. Situated between the high, rugged landscape of Snowdonia and the farmland of Shropshire, this is a gentle and pleasant region through which many rivers and streams flow. As well as being home to the highest waterfall outside Scotland, Pistyll Rhaeadr, one of the Seven Wonders of Wales, there is Lake Vyrnwy. Built in the 1880s to supply the expanding city of Liverpool with water, this large reservoir is not only famous for its splendid feats of Victorian engineering but also as a location for the film *The Dambusters*.

The major settlement here is Welshpool, a town situated on the banks of the River Severn which is also close to the English border. Originally known as Pool, the prefix was added to ensure that the dispute regarding its nationality was finalised once and for all. From the town leisurely canal boat trips can be taken along the Montgomery Canal but there is also a narrow gauge steam railway running westwards to Llanfair Caereinion. Near the town can be found the splendid Powis Castle, which is famous not only for the many treasures it houses but also for its magnificent gardens.

Machynlleth

Montgomery, a tiny anglicised town which gave its name to the county of Montgomeryshire, not only has a splendidly situated ruined borderland castle but it is also close to some of the best preserved sections of Offa's Dyke. Nearby Newtown, which despite its name was founded in the 10th century, is another interesting and historic market town that is also the home of the famous High Street newsagents WH Smith. The associated museum tells of the company's growth from its humble beginnings in 1792 and those who are interested in history, particularly social history, will find the Robert Owen Memorial Museum well worth a visit.

To the west and beyond the quaint town of Llanidloes lies Machynlleth, the home of Owain Glyndwr's parliament in the 15th century. A visit to the Welsh hero's centre, which is found in the part 15th century parliament house, tells the story of Glyndwr and his struggle against the English.

This is great walking country that takes in some of the finest scenery in Wales. The many marked established trails and walks include a large part of Offa's Dyke Path and Glyndwr's Way, a 123-mile walk that follows a circular route across dramatic landscapes from Welshpool to Knighton by way of Machynlleth.

LOCATOR MAP

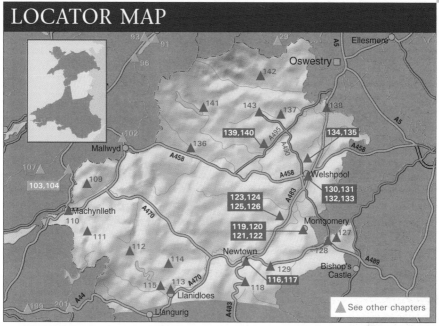

© MAPS IN MINUTES ™ 2002   © Crown Copyright, Ordnance Survey 2002

ADVERTISERS AND PLACES OF INTEREST

MACHYNLLETH

This small town is a popular but not overcrowded holiday centre in the shadow of the Cambrian Mountains. It was here that Owain Glyndwr held one of his parliaments in around 1404 and, on the site today, stands **Parliament House**, a part 15th century building. Revered as the last native prince of Wales, Parliament House is home to an exhibition of this legendary hero and the **Owain Glyndwr Centre** tells the story of his life, the rebellion he led against the English and details of the parliament from where he controlled most of Wales. The building also has a brass rubbing centre. Glyndwr's aims were independence for Wales, a church independent of Canterbury and the establishing of a Welsh university. After being refused redress when Lord Grey of Ruthin seized some of his land, he laid waste the English settlements in northeast Wales and spent the next few years in skirmishes; he established other parliaments in Dolgellau and Harlech, and sought alliances with the Scots, the Irish and the French. He resisted many assaults by Henry IV's armies, but eventually Henry V seized Aberystwyth and Harlech and Glyndwr soon disappeared from the scene, dying, it is thought, at the home of his daughter Anne Scudamore. It was while presiding over the parliament that Owain was nearly killed by his brother-in-law Dafyd Gam. The plot failed, and Dafyd was captured. He was granted a pardon by Owain and later fought at the Battle of Agincourt.

Opposite the house is the entrance to **Plas Machynlleth**, an elegant mansion built in 1653 that was given to the town by Lord Londonderry and which is surrounded by attractive gardens open to

Dovey Valley Shooting Ground

Brynmelin Farm, Llanwrin, Nr Machynlleth, Powys SY20 8QJ Tel: 01650 511252
e-mail: enquiries@doveyvalley.co.uk
website: www.doveyvalley.co.uk

Hugh Jones set up the **Dovey Valley Shooting Ground** over 20 years ago and it soon became one of the best simulated game shooting centres in the UK. Both beginners and occasional shots are welcome here, and one-to-one tuition at all times means that children can learn in safety. Brynmelin is a hill farm set high above the picturesque Dovey Valley, off the B4404 six miles northeast of Machynlleth, and as well as offering tuition the centre also provides perfect pre-season practice for more experienced shots. The 35 shooting areas give a superb range of natural coverts among the hills and valleys, and a shooting day can be tailored to individual or group requirements, with guns, cartridges and any other essential equipment provided.

Changing rooms, toilets and refreshments are all available at the centre, from where transport takes shooters to the first drive and then on to the other drives. Besides the excellent clay pigeon shooting, Dovey Valley Shooting Ground offers the thrill of quadbike trekking, in which parties of up to 10 ride for an hour or all day with full training given on riding skills and techniques plus the use of all-weather clothing and safety helmets. These guided rides provide not only immense exhilaration but also the opportunity to observe birdlife and wildlife in their natural habitats.

the public. This beautifully restored mansion is also home to **Celtica** (see panel), a museum and multimedia centre where the history and the legends of the Celts is uncovered. Along with the imaginative exhibits and displays, the museum, which was put together by the same team responsible for the Jorvik Centre in York, uses the latest information technology and is also host to a number of colourful and traditional Celtic festivals and events.

At the centre of the town is an ornate **Clock Tower** dating from 1872 which was built by public subscription to mark the coming of age of Lord Castlereagh, heir to the Marquess of Londonderry. Machynlleth's Tabernacle Chapel has been turned into a thriving arts and performance venue. The Cwysi Christmas Food Fair will be held in Machynlleth on November 27, 2002.

CELTICA

Y Plas, Machynlleth, Powys SY20 8ER
Tel: 01654 702702 Fax: 01654 703604
e-mail: celtica@celtica.wales.com
website: www.celtica.com

The Ancient Britons have never gone away says **Celtica** - a unique centre on the outskirts of Owain Glyndwr's parliament town of Machynlleth - which explores the history, culture and beliefs of the Celts through two special exhibitions. Located in a specially refurbished stately home, Celtica offers the chance to find out more about the fighting spirit that rattled the Romans, stung the Saxons and numbed the Normans, a journey through more than 2,000 years of Celtic history, legend and culture. For the under eights, there is also a

Celtic-themed soft play area Tir Na nOg. Open seven days a week, Celtica has excellent parking facilities for both cars and coaches, an outdoor adventure playground, gardens, gift shop and tea-room.

AROUND MACHYNLLETH

CARNO
10 miles E of Machynlleth on the A470

The dress and interior designer Laura Ashley, who was born in Wales, and her husband moved to Machynlleth in 1963 and later settled at **Carno**, which became the site of the headquarters of the Laura Ashley empire. It was in the churchyard of St John the Baptist, close to the

factory, that she was buried after her death due to a fall in 1985. In the hills of Trannon Moor near the village is the National Wind Power's Carno Wind Farm, a site containing dozens of turbines that generate enough electricity to meet the needs of about 25,000 homes. The Carno Wind Farm project was completed in 1996 and comprises 56 wind turbines each of 600 kilowatts maximum output. The plateau on which the farm is located is visited by over 30 bird species including red kite, hen harrier, buzzard, red grouse, curlew and golden plover. The site access road is located off the A470 at the northern end of Carno village. Visitors can walk along the marked public footpaths that cross the site; there is an information board at

TALBONTDRAIN GUEST HOUSE

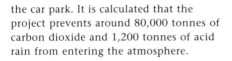

Uwchygarreg, Machynlleth, Powys SY20 8RR
Tel: 01654 702192
e-mail: hilary@talbontdrain.co.uk website: talbontdrain.co.uk

A 500-year-old stone farmhouse in beautiful, tranquil countryside provides
the perfect setting for a break. Owner Hilary Matthews and her staff are on
hand to make guests feel instantly at home. There are four guest bedrooms - a double with en suite
bathroom, an optional double/twin and two singles. A hearty breakfast with free-range eggs and home-
made preserves starts the day, and in the evening home-cooked suppers are served in generous portions,
with seconds usually available. In between, packed lunches sustain days spent in the wonderful
countryside that surrounds the house. No tv, no smoking.

the car park. It is calculated that the project prevents around 80,000 tonnes of carbon dioxide and 1,200 tonnes of acid rain from entering the atmosphere.

LLAN

8½ miles E of Machynlleth on the B4518

Found on the banks of the River Twymyn, this hamlet was the birthplace of Abraham Rees, who published an edition of *Ephraim Chambers Cyclopedia* between 1778-88 after having added over 4,500 new pieces of information. Llan was also the home, for many years, of the social reformer, Reverend Samuel Roberts (1880-1885), who worked hard for the principles of social equality and was a leader of non-conformist opinion. He was also an advocate of free trade, Catholic emancipation and temperance, and in 1827 he advanced a plan for an inland penny postal service. Between 1857 and 1867 he was in America with his brother Richard Roberts preaching racial equality.

DYLIFE

8½ miles SE of Machynlleth off the B4518

Apart from an inn and a few houses, there is little left of this once prosperous lead mining community. A footpath from the settlement passes close to a grassy mound which was once a Roman fort, built here, it is believed, to guard the nearby lead mines. The path

continues past more redundant lead mines that were last worked during the late 17th century before it meanders through a woodland, following the banks of River Clywedog, and on towards Staylittle. The final part of the route lies close to Bronze Age tumuli which suggest that mining occurred in the area even before the Roman occupation. Close to the village is **Glaslyn Nature Reserve**, a 540-acre tract of heather moorland that is the breeding site for the wheatear, golden plover, ring ousel and red grouse.

STAYLITTLE

11 miles SE of Machynlleth off the B4518

A one-time lead mining village, Staylittle is said to have derived its name from the village's two blacksmiths who shoed horses so rapidly that their forge became known as Stay-a-Little. Situated in a remote area high in the Cambrian Mountains, Staylittle is on the edge of the **Hafren Forest**, which has several waymarked trails through the forest, along the banks of the upper River Severn and up to **Plynlimon**, which rises to 2,500 feet.

LLANIDLOES

16½ miles SE of Machynlleth on the A470

This peaceful, small market town, which sits at the exact centre of Wales, is certainly one of the area's most attractive, and its adaptability, from a

THE STAR INN

Dylife, Nr Staylittle, Llanbrynmar, Powys SY19 7BW
Tel: 01650 521345

The venerable **Star Inn** - parts go back to 1640 - is situated in quiet countryside just off the B4518 nine miles northwest of Llanidloes on the road to Machynlleth. Susan Ward-Banks creates a relaxed, easy-going atmosphere in the day rooms, which feature beams, panelling, bench window seats, settees and armchairs. Pub classics such as garlic mushrooms, scampi, chilli, cottage pie and steaks are served in very generous portions, and children have their own selection of dishes. Daily specials include meat, vegetarian and fish dishes, and the last might feature rainbow trout, red snapper, moonfish, butterfish and shark, all simply cooked and delicious.

A super place to drop in for a drink and a meal, the Star is also a hub of the local community, with pool and darts teams playing in the local leagues. It's also a good place to stay for tourists exploring this lovely area; the en suite bedrooms, all with tea tray, are cosy and comfortable, and offer excellent value for money. At 1,300 feet above sea level, this is one of the highest points in what was once an important centre of the lead-mining industry. Dylife itself, once a thriving mining village, is now at the heart of miles of unspoilt countryside. Walking, fishing and sailing are popular pastimes hereabouts, and for sightseers the Pennant Valley waterfalls are a great attraction.

rural village to a weaving town and now to a centre for craftspeople, has ensured that it is likely to remain so for many years to come. John Wesley preached here three times in the mid 1700s and the stone from which he addressed his audience stands outside the town's old **Market Hall**, which dates from 1609 and stands on wooden stilts. It was used by Quakers, Methodists and Baptists before those religious groups had their own premises and has also been a courthouse, a library and a working men's institute. The upper floors of the building now house the **Llanidloes Museum**, where there are displays and information on the textile and mining industries that thrived in the area during the 18th and 19th centuries. There is also a natural history exhibition and the new red kite centre. In 1839, the town was a focal point of the bitter Chartist Riots after the Reform Bill of 1832 had failed to meet

demands that included universal suffrage and social equality. Cheap labour, cheap wool and efficient new machinery had led to a boom in the wool and flannel trade in Llanidloes, as in Newtown, Machynlleth and Welshpool. Workmen flooded in, and in 1858 the population was more then 4,000. But the boom did not last, the factories closed, and unemployment inevitably ensued. Chartist propaganda reached the town and the Llanidloes unions adopted the Charter. The crowds started to gather and to arm, the police moved in, the Chartist leaders were arrested then released by the crowd, the magistrates fled. The Chartists then ruled for a few days: mills were re-opened and the prices of goods fixed. Then the Montgomeryshire Yeomanry came on the scene, 32 arrests were made and the Chartist ringleaders put on trial at Welshpool. Three were transported, the

Continued on page 139

WALK 5

Llanidloes

Start	Llanidloes
Distance	5 miles (8km)
Approximate time	3 hours
Parking	Llanidloes
Refreshments	Cafés and pubs in Llanidloes
Ordnance Survey maps	Landranger 136 (Newtown & Llanidloes), Explorer 214 (Llanidloes & Newtown)

Two major recreational footpaths cross in Llanidloes; this walk follows sections of both. The Severn Way winds a massive 220 miles (354km) from the river's source high above Llanidloes to the famous bridges across its estuary near Bristol, whilst Glyndwr's Way National Trail plots an adventurous course through the rugged mid-Wales landscape once home to this Welsh leader. The walk initially follows the River Severn upstream, a short but steepish section rises up lanes over a low ridge giving superb views over the Severn and its neighbour, the Afon Clywedog. The return leg down the Clywedog valley is largely through beautiful oakwoods typical of mid-Wales and home to pied flycatchers. Keep an eye out, too, for red kite, with their distinctive forked tail, quartering the skies above.

The entrance to the riverside car park and bus station at Llanidloes is opposite the Mount Inn. Facing this pub, turn left into the centre of Llanidloes, where the half-timbered Market Hall has survived since around 1600 Ⓐ. Now a museum, it has seen stirring times. The town was a major centre for weaving in the early 19th century, but the wages were low and the harvests were poor. With the French Revolution still in the minds of many, not least the authorities, matters came to a head in Llanidloes between 30th April and 4th May 1839.

Chartists were active here, either encouring or responding to the discontented workers. This movement took its name from the People's Charter of 1838. This demanded votes for all men, equal electoral districts, vote by secret ballot, annually elected parliaments, the payment of MPs and the abolition of

property qualifications for membership. Many advocated peaceful reform, based on "moral force", but some extremists were prepared for violence. A chief focus of hatred was the newly built workhouse at Caersws – now a hospital. The Poor Law Act of 1834 had replaced poor-relief with workhouses. Wages were low and working conditions bad. Rents were high, and the workers were crowded into insanitary living accommodation. Not surprisingly, interest in Chartism was strong.

A public meeting was held early in 1839 at which a Chartist leader, Hetherington, from London, spoke about the Charter. He later promoted the stock-piling of fire-arms at a private meeting with the leading Llanidloes Chartists. The younger ones were easily swayed and "borrowed" guns from local farmers. One home-made dagger was found when the authorities investigated.

T.E. Marsh, a local landowner and former mayor, determined to stamp out the perceived threat to his interests. He en-listed his tenants as "special" constables, while three constables arrived from London. The next morning, 30th April, saw a confrontation between the weavers and the 'specials' when news came that three Chartist leaders had been arrested. The weavers, some with guns, managed to release them, whilst badly beating up one of the London policemen.

Moderate Chartists managed to quieten the mob, but Marsh rode to the Lord Lieutenant to ask for troops to quell the rioters. They marched at break-neck speed from Brecon and arrived on the morning of 4th May. They were relieved to find their services were not required. Marsh seems to have influenced the magistrates, however. The town was sealed off on 6th May and 32 arrests were made. Despite the doubtful evidence, 30 were convicted, with sentences ranging between two months' hard labour and 15 years' transportation to Australia.

Turn left along Short Bridge Street and left again along Penygreen Road beyond the bridge across the Severn. In ½ mile (800m) fork left (signed for Llangurig), cross Felindre Bridge **B** and take the second lane on the right, waymarked as the Severn Way. Stay with this peaceful lane above the Severn for nearly 1 mile (1.6km) to a stile on your right, about 200 yds (183m) past a gated forestry road on your left. Walk to the foot of the field, go through the gate and cross the foot-bridge over the Severn. Once over, trace the track up to the right to reach a lane and turn left along this **C**.

Look for the lane on the right in about 600 yds (550m), opposite an old chapel in Glan-y-Nant and signed for Deildre. Climb this steepening back lane, taking two sharp left bends along the way. In under

½ mile (800m) take the narrow, gated lane sharp back-right **D**, rising gently to the ridge crest and heading directly in line towards the imposing, distant hill of Bryn y Fan, high above Clywedog Reservoir.

The lane soon bends sharp right and passes through a gate into oakwoods. Remain with it until a point 50 yds (46m) before these woods give out. Here **E** turn left along the wide track, pass through the gate and follow this pleasant green lane all the way down to a solid footbridge over the River Clywedog. Cross this, turn right for a few paces then turn left along the obvious path, rising through the trees and, keeping the house and barns off to your right, climbing to reach a minor road. Turn right along this, pass above the caravan park and turn right at the junction to return to Llanidloes along the route of Glyndwr's Way.

Cross the bridge and turn right to return to the Market Hall and the starting point of the walk. ●

THE UNICORN HOTEL

Long Bridge Street, Llanidloes, Powys SY18 6EE
Tel: 01686 413167 Fax: 01686 413516

Visitors to he small, peaceful town of Llanidloes in the very centre of Wales will find plenty of interesting sights to see and things to do, and if it's hospitality they're looking for **The Unicorn Hotel** provides it in generous measure. Derek and Christine Humphreys are a very professional, personable couple, and their 300-year-old town-centre hostelry can be relied on for something good to eat, something good to quench a thirst and a comfortable bed for an overnight stay. The refurbished bar and lounge are invitingly traditional, with beams and wooden panelling, and the five elegantly furnished bedrooms, a mix of doubles and twins, have en suite facilities, tv, tea tray and quality toiletries.

On the food front, the choice is wide and varied, from toasties, jacket potatoes, basket meals and salads to chicken satay, peppers filled with cream cheese, lasagne, grilled salmon or tuna, honey roast duckling and sirloin steak. Rack of ribs is another popular order, and there are always main courses for vegetarians. Visitors can leave their cars on the road at the front or in a large lawn park close by. After visiting the sights of the town, including the Museum and the lovely old Market Hall standing on wooden stilts, tourists can easily take in the local sights such as Clywedog Dam and the Elan Valley.

MANLEDD

Y Fan, Llanidloes, Powys SY18 6NP
Tel: 01686 412461
e-mail: manledd@talk21.com

The warmest of welcomes from Ann and John Johnson awaits visitors to **Manledd**, their lovely home set in two secluded acres at the end of a track. Two comfortable non-smoking bedrooms are let on a bed and breakfast basis, with evening meals available with advance notice. The rooms - a double and a single - have courtesy beverage trays but no tv; avid watchers will find a set in the lounge. An alternative to the B&B is self-catering accommodation for two or four in an adjoining cottage. A stream runs through the garden, and there are stunning views of the surrounding woods and hills. The setting is outstandingly peaceful and serene, and Manledd is ideally located for walking, bird-watching, painting, photography, star-gazing or just revelling in the wonderful views and the pure, fresh air.

The day at Manledd starts with a wholesome breakfast that includes home-baked bread and home-made preserves, and the owners can supply a packed lunch for guests planning a day exploring the area. There's certainly no shortage of things to do and places to see, including the splendid old market hall on stilts in Llanidloes, Llyn Clywedog reservoir, Hafren Forest and many traces of the lead mines that once brought prosperity to the area. To find Manledd from Llanidloes, take the B4518 Staylittle road for about a mile; second right to Y Fan; left at the Post Office and along the track past the old lead mine - less than three miles in total.

rest served terms of hard labour. The Chartists originated in London in 1837, when a People's Charter was drawn up by the London Working Men's Association. Their six main demands were: equal electoral areas; universal suffrage; payment for MPs; no property qualifications for voters; vote by ballot; and annual parliaments. Support for the Charter spread quickly through Britain, with the Welsh miners especially vociferous. A petition with 1¼ million signatures was rejected by Parliament in 1839, and riots ensued in Lancashire, Yorkshire and Wales. In 1842 another petition, this one with 3½ million signatures, was rejected in 1842. The Chartist movement went into something of a decline, and the repeal of the Corn Laws in 1846 helped to better the lot of the working classes.

To the northwest of the town lies **Llyn Clywedog**, a reservoir that developed in the mid 1960s to regulate the flows of the Rivers Severn and Clywedog. Roads follow around both sides of the lake, with the B4518 curving round the slopes of the 1,580 foot **Fan Hill** where the chimneys of the now disused **Van Lead Mine** are still visible. It was once one of the most prosperous mines in this area of Wales, and it is recorded that in 1876 6,850 tons of lead were produced. The deserted houses and chapels of the village that grew up around the mine add a sombre, evocative note.

NEWTOWN

The name was only really appropriate a very long time ago, as Newtown's origins date from around AD 973; but the town only came to prominence after being granted a market charter by Edward I in 1279. This was a centre for textiles and weaving and, by the 19th century,

BARN VIEW COTTAGES

The Old Farmhouse, Drainbyrion, Llanidloes, Powys SY18 6PN
Tel: 01686 413527
e-mail: wendy-robert-barn-view@supanet.com

The Knight family came from London in 1992 and converted a row of old timber-clad stone barns into stylish self-catering accommodation. **Barn View Cottages** offer characterful living with beams, oak feature walls, traditional furnishings and neat, uncluttered decor. There are fitted carpets throughout, the kitchen is fully equipped for an independent stay and there are heated towel rails in the shower rooms. The Lower cottage sleeps five, the Middle four and the Top a cosy two.

Adjoining the cottages is a laundry room with washing machine, iron and board, clothes drier and vacuum cleaner. There's ample parking space, and behind the row is a garden with seats. The idyllic hillside location commands magnificent views through the Severn Valley, and scenic attractions within easy reach include Hafren Forest, the Elan Valley and Lake Vyrnwy. Walkers, birdwatchers, golfers, pony trekkers and clay-pigeon shooters can all indulge their pastimes in the vicinity, and permits for fishing on the Wye, Severn and Clywedog rivers can be obtained locally. To find the cottages, go west from Llanidloes through Glan-y-Nant, then take the second right.

Newtown was the home of the Welsh flannel industry that led it to be referred to as the "Leeds of Wales". Some of the brick buildings were built with a third or even fourth storey with large windows to let in light for the looms. One such building now houses the town's **Textile Museum**, which tells the story of this once important industry and also gives a very good impression of the working conditions of the people which Newtown's most famous son, Robert Owen, devoted much of his life to changing. Born in Newtown in 1771, Owen grew from a humble background to become a social reformer and the founder of the co-operative movement who lobbied vigorously for an improvement in the working conditions specifically within

Newtown

the textile industry. He is particularly associated with the New Lanark mills in Scotland, which he ran and partly owned. The workforce at New Lanark numbered 2,000, including 500 children, and Owen provided good housing, cheap goods and the first infants' school in

course options.

The real speciality of Jays is decorated cakes and confectionery; the owners are superb confectioners, and some of their handiwork is on mouthwatering display in the chilled cabinet. This skill has enabled them to build up an outside catering business for special occasions, and they have ingenious equipment that lets them reproduce photographs or pictures directly on to icing on the cake - edible of course. So their cakes are doubly delicious - fit for a king to eat and pretty as a picture! Jays is open from 9 to 4.30 Monday to Saturday, and should definitely be a stopping place on any visit to Newtown.

JAYS RESTAURANT

Ladywell Centre, Newtown, Powys SY16 1AF
Tel: 01686 625395

John and Ann Evans and Ann's twin sister Carol Russell-Jones make a friendly, energetic and professional team at **Jays Restaurant**, set in a modern brick building in the heart of a pedestrianised shopping precinct. The interior is bright, neat and inviting, with polished pine chairs set at polished pine tables, and the restaurant is open for teas, coffees, snacks and lunches; the choice changes daily, with salads, quiches and casseroles among the main

Britain. His remarkable life is told at the intimate **Robert Owen Memorial Museum** and he was buried by the river in the churchyard of St Mary's. The grave has magnificent Art Nouveau iron railings, and his monument depicts the man with his workers.

Another interesting visit to consider while in Newtown is to the **WH Smith Museum**, where the shop has been restored to its original 1927 layout and devotes much of its space to the history of the booksellers from 1792 onwards. The people of Newtown must certainly be an enterprising lot as it was here that the first ever mail order company was begun in 1859 by a man called Pryce-Jones. The business started in a small way with Welsh flannel but expanded rapidly, and Pryce-Jones even obtained the Royal seal of approval by having Queen Victoria on his list.

Two miles east of Newtown is **Pwll Penarth Nature Reserve**, a feeding and nesting site for many species of wildfowl. The reserve has a nature walk and two hides, one accessible to wheelchairs.

AROUND NEWTOWN

TREGYNON
4½ miles N of Newtown off the B4389

Just to the south of the village lies **Gregynon Hall Gardens**, which are now part of the University of Wales, and where visitors can wander through the extensive woodlands on waymarked paths. Renowned for its spring bulbs, the sunken lawns before the house are associated with an unfinished design by William Emes. There is also a remarkable golden yew hedge. The hall is the setting for an annual music festival.

SHARPE DESIGNS

Dolafan Road, Newtown, Powys SY16 2AP
Tel: 01686 623433
e-mail: info@sharpe-designs.com
website: www.sharpe-designs.com

In the centre of Newtown (Drenewydd in Welsh), **Sharpe Designs** provide a range of contemporary Celtic designs, hand-made in their own studio and workshop. Julia Sharpe, a talented artist and stylist of distinction, is inspired in her work by the patterns used on harness fittings, shield bosses and torques that were the principal forms of metalwork and decorative art practised by the British Celts, and also by pieces found at the site of the Sutton Hoo ship burial.

Sharpe Design's years of experience include producing new original designs for the British Museum, and the current range includes the award-winning Celtic Dragon, a large box decorated with bosses and roundels with the Celtic Dragon lid. All the pieces in the Curious Celtic Collection - many of them pots - are unique designs available only by direct order. The other main collection is the Cymru, reflecting and celebrating Wales: all the items feature a stylised outline of Wales, including Brass Cymru sand-cast in solid brass, art prints, greetings cards, postcards, mouse mats and T-shirts.

THE DOLFOR INN

Dolfor, Nr Newtown, Powys SY16 4AA
Tel: 01686 626531

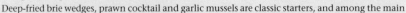

David and Olwyn Clapton moved with their teenage sons from Wiltshire to take over the **Dolfor Inn**, a 16th coaching house on the A483 three miles south of Newtown. A well-established and well-loved locals' pub with pool, dominoes and a friendly, sociable ambience, the inn has also gained a wider-flung reputation for its food. In the bars and restaurant, where brick walls and ancient beams (some originally ship's timbers) create a nice old-fashioned look, there are is space for 60 visitors to enjoy anything from a quick snack to a full à la carte meal.

Deep-fried brie wedges, prawn cocktail and garlic mussels are classic starters, and among the main

courses are several chicken dishes (chasseur, barbecue, curries both mild and Madras), Severn salmon with a creamy watercress sauce, lightly battered cod fillet, steaks, gammon, mixed grill and always a choice for vegetarians - perhaps brie, potato, courgette and almond bake or macaroni cheese and spinach. Sunday lunch is a really special occasion, when no fewer than five roasts served with Yorkshire pudding, plus a veggie roast, are on the menu. Soup comes first, and the meal ends with desserts and coffee; diners can opt for one, two or three courses, and children have their own dishes. The inn has plenty of parking.

LLANFAIR CAEREINION

9 miles N of Newtown on the B4385

This is the other end of the **Welshpool and Llanfair Railway**. Passengers at Llanfair can enjoy reliving the days of steam but also relax in the Edwardian style tea rooms at the station. The narrow-gauge railway was originally opened to carry sheep, cattle and goods as well as passengers. It now travels, without the animals and the goods, along the delightful Banwy Valley, its carriages pulled by scaled-down versions of steam locomotives from Finland, Austria, Sierra Leone, Antigua and Manchester. There are nine members of the narrow-gauge **Great Little Trains of Wales** (GLTOW):

Bala Lake Railway
Brecon Mountain Railway
　(Merthyr Tydfil)
Ffestiniog Railway
　(Porthmadog)

Llanberis Lake Railway
Rheilfford Eryri
　(Caernarfon)
Talyllin Railway
　(Tywyn)
Vale of Rheidol Railway
　(Aberystwyth)
Welsh Highland Railway
　(Porthmadog)
Welshpool and Llanfair Railway

MONTGOMERY

7 miles NE of Newtown on the B4385

An attractive market town with a pleasant Georgian character, there are also some surviving Tudor and Jacobean buildings that are worthy of note. Above the town the ruins of **Montgomery Castle** stand in affirmation of this borderland region's turbulent history. Situated in part of the Marshes, which are so called because this area was continually fought over and became regarded as something of a wasteland, the castle played a part in this territorial struggle. The castle was first built in around 1100 by the Norman, Roger de Montgomery. Stormed over the years by rebels, the castle was rebuilt in 1223 as a garrison as Henry III attempted to quell the Welsh, a consequence being that the town received a charter from the king in 1227. During the Civil War, the castle surrendered to Parliamentary forces but was demolished in 1649 in punishment for the then Lord Herbert's Royalist sympathies. The remains of the Castle are open at all times and entrance is free; access is up steep paths from the town or by a level footpath from the car park, and the visit is worth it for the views alone. Offa's Dyke passes close by and is another reminder of the military

THE BRICKLAYERS ARMS

Chirbury Road, Montgomery, Powys SY15 6QQ
Tel: 01686 668177
e-mail: sara.pezzack@bt.com website: thebricklayers.uk.com

Leading restaurant guides have recognised the outstanding talent of owner-chef Robert Jennings, who with partner Sara Pezzack has made the **Bricklayers Arms** one of the top eating places in Wales. Robert has devised an outstanding menu using the very best of local produce including meats, fruit and vegetables, free-range eggs and cream, cheese and honey. Typical dishes are millefeuille of seafood garnished with Ynyslas mussels in a noilly prat cream reduction, and loin of Shropshire lamb stuffed with mulled apricots, served with dauphinoise potatoes and a redcurrant jus. To accompany this superb food are fine wines and well-kept real ales.

R H BUNNER & SON LTD

Arthur Street, Montgomery, Powys SY15 6RA
Tel: 01686 668308 Fax: 01686 668564
e-mail: info@rhbunner.co.uk website: www.rhbunner.co.uk

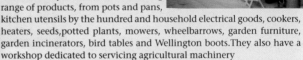

Just about everything of practical use for house and garden can be

found at **R H Bunner & Son Ltd**. Sisters Ann and Mary Udall stock an amazing range of products, from pots and pans, kitchen utensils by the hundred and household electrical goods, cookers, heaters, seeds,potted plants, mowers, wheelbarrows, garden furniture, garden incinerators, bird tables and Wellington boots.They also have a workshop dedicated to servicing agricultural machinery

DIANA FORRESTER

Kerry Street, Montgomery, Powys SY15 6PG
Tel/Fax: 01686 668005
e-mail: dianaforrester@ukonline.co.uk website: dianaforrester.com

Diana Forrester's eponymous shop in Kerry Street is filled with an amazing range of items, some practical, others ornamental, all unusual and highly desirable. The stock of distinctly different gifts and decorative accessories for the home and garden has been assembled from around the world, and many items are exclusive to Diana Forrester. There are ornaments in silver or glass, vintage-style greetings cards, terracotta pots, colourful tagines, garden lanterns..... the selection is truly impressive and the shop is open every day of the week for browsing and buying.

significance that this area once held. In Arthur Street, the **Old Bell Museum** has 11 rooms of local history including features on civic and social life, Norman and medieval castles, the workhouse and the Cambrian Railway.

The 13th century **St Nicholas' Church** has some interesting features, including wooden carved angels, carved miserere seats and the magnificent canopied tomb of Richard Herbert, Lord of Montgomery

Castle. In the churchyard is the famous Robber's Grave: John Davis, hanged in public in 1821 for murder, proclaimed his innocence and swore that the grass would not grow above his grave for at least 100 years!

To the west of the town the Iron Age hill fort **Fridd Faldwyn** tops a 750 foot hill that also provides stunning views to Cadair Idris and, eastwards, into England.

LITTLE BROMPTON FARM

Montgomery, Powys SY15 6HY
Tel/Fax: 01686 668371 e-mail: gaynor.brompton@virgin.net
website: www.littlebromptonfarm.co.uk

Gaynor Bright has been looking after guests for over 25 years at **Little Brompton Farm**, situated on the B4385 two miles east of Montgomery. In the delightful 17th century farmhouse, on a stock rearing farm, are three traditionally furnished ensuite bedrooms. Be cosetted with old fashioned comfort, ideal for the discerning guest looking for something rather special. Quality prevails with great value for money. There is abundant character, and a cosy guest lounge. This is magnificent walking country, with Offa's Dyke on the doorstep and wildlife all around, and Little Brompton Farm, four star WTB rated, is the perfect B&B base for lovers of nature and the countryside.

THE LION HOTEL

Berriew, Nr Welshpool, Powys SY21 8PQ
Tel: 01686 640452 Fax: 01686 640604

Owners Sue Barton and Tim Woodward have brought new standards of excellence to the **Lion Hotel**, whose black-and-white timbered facade has been a welcoming sight in the village since the 17th century. The black and white theme is continued inside, and the "Mind Your Head" sign on the low beams in the restaurant means what it says! The two bars are particularly cosy

and comfortable, and a full range of ales and beers is on sale at this free house. Lunchtime fare includes freshly made sandwiches and baguettes, traditional bar meals, fresh fish and home-made speciality dishes. The excellent à la carte menu provides plenty of choice and is based as far as possible on fresh local produce. One of the dining areas is designated non-smoking.

The hotel is also a splendid place to enjoy a break in picturesque, peaceful surroundings and is a good base for a walking or touring holiday. The seven bedrooms, including a family room, are all en suite, comfortable and particularly well appointed, with tv, telephone, radio-alarm and tea/coffee-makers. Berriew is as pretty a village as any in the county, with timbered buildings, their gardens bright with flowers, clustered around the church. Local attractions in the village are the Andrew Logan Museum of Sculpture and Silver Scenes (giftware manufacturer), and only a short drive away is Powis Castle.

BERRIEW

7½ miles NE of Newtown on the B4390

Over the years, this picturesque village of half-timbered houses, beside the River Rhiw, has won the "best kept village" award.

Like a number of other places in Wales, Berriew is associated with St Beuno who, it is recalled, apparently heard English voices while communing by the river and warned the villagers of the imposing threat. A large glacial boulder here has been named after him.

Berriew's 1870s church contains fine marble effigies of Arthur Price, Sheriff of Montgomeryshire in 1578, and his two wives. The memorial cross of 1933 in the churchyard is by Sir Ninian Comper, whose work can be seen in churches all over Britain.

The Gardens at **Glansevern Hall**, entered from the A483 by the bridge over the River Rhiew, were first laid out in 1801 and now cover 18 acres. Noted in particular for the unusual tree species, they also have lovely lawns, herbaceous beds, a walled garden, rose gardens, a lovely water garden and a rock garden complete with grotto. In the Old Stables are a tea room, a garden shop and a gallery with regular exhibitions of paintings, sculpture and interior design. A wide variety of herbaceous plants, all grown at Glansevern, can be bought. Surrounding a very handsome Greek Revival house, the gardens are themselves set in parkland on the banks of the River Severn. Built for Arthur Davies Owen Glansevern was the seat of the Owen family from 1800 until after the Second World War.

TREFNANT HALL FARM

Berriew, Nr Welshpool, Powys SY21 8AS
Tel: 01686 640262 e-mail: jane.trefnant@virgin.net
website: http://freespace.virgin.net/jane.trefnant/

Two miles from Berriew, **Trefnant Hall** is a delightful greystone farmhouse dating from 1742 set in a large garden. In the main house, which features a fine Georgian inlaid oak staircase, there are three spacious guest bedrooms, all with en suite facilities, central

heating, tv and tea/coffee trays, and a traditionally furnished lounge with views across the garden to the lovely surrounding countryside. Breakfast is served in a separate dining room. Adjoining the farmhouse is a self-catering unit converted from the old dairy, with a bedroom (double and single beds), bathroom and fully-fitted kitchen-lounge. No smoking throughout.

DYFFRYN VILLA

Dyffryn, Berriew, Nr Welshpool, Powys SY21 8AE
Tel: 01686 640244 Fax: 01686 640809

Dairy farmers Christine and Tudor Cookson have restored a charming 16th century cottage next to their farmhouse to provide top-class self-catering accommodation. The redbrick cottage, known as Alice's House after an earlier tenant, has two lovely bedrooms with exposed beams and furnishings in traditional style. The bathroom features a splendid old cast-iron bathtub. The fine kitchen has a Rayburn stove and all the up-to-date appliances needed for a comfortable, home-from-home stay. A small garden at the back of the cottage overlooks the River Severn. **Dyffryn Villa** (no smoking, no pets) is situated close to the pretty village of Berriew.

ANDREW LOGAN MUSEUM OF SCULPTURE

Berriew, Nr Welshpool, Powys SY21 8PJ
Tel: 01686 640689 Fax: 01686 640764
e-mail: info@andrewlogan.com
website:www.andrewlogan.com

Visit the amazing glittering fantasy wonderland of Andrew Logan, founder of The Alternative Miss World, a surreal art event for all round family entertainment. All the fantastic crown jewels - created by Andrew, from all 11 events, along with Host and Hostess costumes worn by Andrew and designed by Zandra Rhodes, Bill Gibb and

Ossie Clark, amongst other well-known designers, are on display.

The only museum in Europe dedicated to a living artist, it is overflowing with the most astonishing sculptures created in mirrored glass. Experience Andrew's humorous imagination, where butterflies are larger than birds and a throne is a velvet lily. Dance with an Indian Goddess, and encounter the roar of tigers and sounds of the Raj bursting from the "Singing Tree". *The Times*, "Museum of the Month", June 2002. Ranked 17th in *The Independent's Guide* to the top 50 museums in the country.

Jewellery and sculpture by Andrew is available for purchase, as owned by many of the famous including Elton John, Rula Lenska, Koo Stark and Amanda Barrie.

Children's activity packs and Café.

Chris Craymer - Italian Vogue

MELLINGTON HALL HOTEL

Mellington, Church Stoke, Powys SY15 6HX
Tel: 01588 620456 Fax: 01588 620928
website: mellingtonhallhotel.co.uk

Managers Lance and Vanessa Thomas have re-established the
reputation of **Mellington Hall Hotel.** Built in 1876 in Gothic style,
the hotel has two fine dining rooms with handsome panelling in
one and a William & Morris ceiling in the function room. There are five ensuite bedrooms, refurbished
to a high standard. Excellent food is produced by chef Lance Thomas who uses local produce for his
menus, which include roasted Welsh Lamb shoulder with mint gravy and chargrilled steak with various
sauces. A welcoming atmosphere awaits in elegant surroundings with wonderful parkland.

CHURCH STOKE
10½ miles E of Newtown on the A489

This attractive village lies right on the
Welsh-English border; just to the west,
can be found some very visible and well
preserved sections of Offa's Dyke. At
Bacheldre, two miles along the A489,
Bacheldre Mill is a fully restored
watermill producing award-winning
organic stoneground flour. Visitors can
enjoy a guided tour and even mill their
own flour.

ABERMULE
4 miles NE of Newtown on the B4386

Across the Montgomery Canal and River
Severn from this village, which is also
known by its Welsh name **Abermiwl**, lie
the scant remains of **Dolforwyn Castle**,
which was built in 1273 by Llywelyn the
Last (he was the last native ruler of

Wales). This was the last castle to have
been built by a native Welsh prince on
his own soil, and Llywelyn also tried to
establish a small town around the castle
to rival that of nearby, and much
anglicised, Welshpool. However, the
castle was only a Welsh stronghold for
four years before it was taken by the
English and left to decay into the
haunting ruins of today.

KERRY
2½ miles SE of Newtown on the A489

Found on the banks of the River Mule, a
tributary of the River Severn, this village
lies in the heart of sheep rearing country
and has given its name to the Kerry Hills
breed of sheep characterised by
distinctive black spots on their faces and
legs. Small, hornless and usually white
apart from the markings, the Kerry Hills

DREWIN FARM

Church Stoke, Montgomery, Powys SY15 6TW
Tel/Fax: 01588 620325 e-mail: ceinwen@drewin.freeserve.co.uk

Ceinwen and Robert Richards and their family offer a warm welcome
to guests at their 17th century farmhouse. **Drewin Farm** has two
centrally heated letting bedrooms
with en suite shower rooms
(bathroom available), tv and tea/coffee-making facilities. There's a
separate lounge for residents, and traditional home cooking is served
in the dining room. With the friendly, relaxed ambience, the great
outdoors and the glorious views of the Welsh borderlands, it is not
surprising that guests return year after year to this lovely spot.
Winner of AA Best Welsh Breakfast 1999/2000.

CEFN-Y-MYNACH

Kerry, Powys SY16 4PL
Tel: 01686 670332

Sheila Large and her husband took early retirement from academic careers to move into **Cefn-y-Mynach**, a former monastic farmhouse set in mature gardens with stunning views across the Vale of Kerry. In a newly converted wing they offer top-quality, centrally heated self-catering accommodation in two first-floor bedrooms, a double and a twin. Furnishings are traditional, and in the homely sitting room there's a television set, a radio, books maps and games.

The tiled kitchen has an oven, microwave and fridge, and with a little notice laundry facilities can be made available. Guests have their own patio and garden, with tables and chairs to make the most of sunny weather and to spot the great variety of birdlife that visits - 48 species have been recorded. Walking (the Kerry Ridgeway is close by) and cycling are popular activities, and sporting facilities in the vicinity include golf, riding, fishing and quad trekking. To find Cefn-y-Mynach, take the A489 from Kerry; turn right on to the B4368, and after about a mile right again on to a "no through road"; the farmhouse is half a mile along this road. No pets, no children under 5, no smoking.

have very dense fleeces that are particularly suitable for dyeing in pastel shades for knitting yarns. This breed is one of several variants on the Welsh Mountain Sheep; others include Black Welsh Mountain, Badger-faced Welsh Mountain, Beulah Speckle Face, Lleyn and Llanwenog.

The village church in Kerry has a chained Welsh Bible of 1690. There was, in former times, a custom at the church that the sexton would "patrol" the congregation during services and would ring a bell if he found anyone asleep.

LLANDINAM
5½ miles SW of Newtown on the A470

This quiet village was the home of David Davies, an industrialist who was instrumental in founding the docks at Barry in South Wales. Davies' bronze statue, made by the same Sir Alfred

Gilbert who was responsible for Eros in Piccadilly, stands in the village.

CAERSWS
4 miles W of Newtown on the A470

The village is built on the site of a 1st century Roman fort that was strategically positioned here by the Rivers Severn and Carno and, to the north, the remains of an earthwork fort can still be seen. In more recent times, Caersws was the home, for some 20 years, of the poet John "Ceiriog" Hughes, who was then the manager of the local Van Railway. Born at Llan Dyffryn Ceiriog in 1833, he took employment on the railways in Manchester when he was 17. In 1865 he became stationmaster at Llanidloes and six years later took over at Caersws, managing the six-mile railway that ran to the Van lead mines. It is said that many people came to Caersws just for the delight of having a chat to the affable poet. Hughes lies buried in the graveyard at the nearby village of Llanwnog. Near Caersws, signposted off the A470 Machynlleth road, Llyn Mawr Reserve is a 20-acre lake with wetland habitat noted for wetland birds such as the great crested grebe, tufted duck, snipe and the curlew.

WELSHPOOL

This bustling market town, which was granted a charter in 1263 by the Prince of Powys, was, for a long time, known as "Pool" - the Welsh prefix was added in 1835 to settle the long running dispute concerning its nationality as it is so close to the border with England. As is typical with many places in the upper Severn Valley, Welshpool has numerous examples of half-timbered buildings among its other interesting architectural features.

Housed in a former warehouse beside the Montgomery Canal is the **Powysland Museum**, which was founded in 1874 by Morris Jones. Earlier, many of the artefacts that formed the museum's original collection had been put together by the Powysland Club - a group of Victorian gentlemen who were interested in the history of mid-Wales. The museum covers various aspects of the region: the development of life in Montgomeryshire from the earliest times to the 20th century; local agriculture and farming equipment; and the building of the first canals and railways in the area. There are also some remains from Strata Marcella, the Cistercian abbey founded around 1170 by Owain Cyfeiliog, Prince of Powys; the

abbey was all but destroyed during the Reformation.

Along with the museum, the old warehouse is also home to the **Montgomery Canal Centre** where the story of this waterway is told. Completed in 1821, the canal carried coal and food from Welshpool to the upper reaches of the River Severn. Though, as with other canals, its decline came with the arrival of the railways, the section of the canal around Welshpool is once again open, now for pleasure cruises.

The town is also home to two other interesting buildings, the **Cockpit** and **Grace Evans' Cottage**. The only surviving cockpit on its original site in Wales, this venue for the bloodthirsty sport was built in the 18th century and

---

MONTGOMERYSHIRE WILDLIFE TRUST (YMDDIRIEDOLAETH NATUR MALDWYN)

Collot House, 20 Severn Street, Welshpool
Tel: 01938 555654
e-mail: montwt@cix.co.uk
website: www.wildlifetrust.org.uk/montgomeryshire

Montgomeryshire is home to some very special wildlife, including the red kite, otter and dormouse. It is also a landscape clothed with important habitats such as woodland, unimproved grassland and moorland. The **Montgomeryshire Wildlife Trust** is dedicated to conserving and enhancing wildlife habitats and protecting threatened species for the enjoyment of this and future generations. Why not enjoy the wildlife at any one of 13 fantastic nature reserves? Better still, become a member! Contact the Trust for further details.

F E ANDERSON & SON

5 High Street, Welshpool, Powys SY21 7JF
Tel: 01938 553340 Fax: 01938 590545
e-mail: feanderson@yahoo.co.uk
website: www.antiquesweb.co.uk

In a distinguished Jacobean century town house on the main street of Welshpool, Ian Anderson is carrying on a family business that was established by his ancestors in the same premises in 1842. F E Anderson & Son are well-known dealers in fine antiques and works of arts, and their customers come from all over Wales and from across the border. Items of furniture from the 17th, 18th and 19th centuries make up most of the stock, which also includes mirrors, decorative items, silver and glass. Besides holding this large stock on the premises, they also exhibit at major antique fairs including Olympia and LAPADA (London and Provincial Antique Dealers Association) fairs.

The building itself is an interesting period piece, with some fine old oil paintings alongside a very grand and striking Elizabethan staircase. An underground passage leads from the house, part of the Powis estates, to the Castle. Welshpool has numerous handsome half-timbered buildings among many interesting architectural features. The Castle contains the Clive Museum, recording the life and deeds of Clive of India, and another museum tells the story of the Montgomery Canal. From the town, the narrow-gauge Welshpool and Llanfair Railway travels through the Powis estates and the Banwy Valley to Llanfair Caereinion.

ROWLES FINE ART

The Old Brewery, Brook Street,
Welshpool, Powys SY21 7LF
Tel: 01938 558811 Fax: 01938 558822
e-mail: enquiries@rowlesfineart.co.uk
website: www.rowlesfineart.co.uk

An old brewery on Welshpool's inner ring road has been converted into one of the premier art galleries in Wales. Rowles Fine Art, owned and run by brothers Glenn and Mark Rowles, specialises in fine 19th and 20th century British and European paintings, and the three spacious, well-lit rooms house an interesting and constantly changing collection of works covering, among other themes, a range of popular classic subjects that are always in demand. Welsh landscapes attract a large local clientele, and sporting studies of gun dogs, leaping salmon and pheasants, still-life flowers and Victorian animal and child studies are in great demand from collectors all over the country and beyond, who know the high reputation which the brothers have built up.

The gallery provides a showcase for a number of exceptional contemporary artists, among them Kay Boyce, Nigel Hemming, John Silver and Terence Lambert. With years of experience and excellent connections in the world of fine art, the gallery's owners and staff are well placed to answer questions about any pictures, and are ready to provide information about particular works or artists, or valuations on customer's paintings.

remained in use until the sport was banned in Britain in 1849. Grace Evans is certainly one of the town's best known citizens as she was instrumental in rescuing Lord Nithsdale (who was in disguise as a lady) from the Tower of London in 1716. As Lady Nithsdale's maid, Grace fled with the couple to France but she returned to Welshpool in 1735 and lived at the cottage, which is said to have been given to her by a grateful Lord Nithsdale, until her death three years later.

At the southern edge of town on Severn Farm Industrial Estate is Severn Farm Pond, one of 13 nature reserves managed by the Montgomeryshire Wildlife Trust. This one is a particularly good site for dragonflies, damselflies and amphibia.

Long Mountain stretches four miles along the Welsh side of the border east of Welshpool. It is crossed by Offa's Dyke and on its highest point is an ancient hill fort known as Beacon Ring. It was on Long Mountain that Henry Tudor camped in 1485 before crossing the border, defeating Richard III at Bosworth Field and ascending the throne of England as Henry VII. Henry Tudor had a **Red Dragon** as his standard and as King he incorporated the Welsh dragon into the Royal arms. There it stayed until James I displaced it with the Scottish unicorn. In 1901 the Red Dragon was officially recognised as the Royal badge of Wales and in 1959 the Queen commanded that the Red Dragon on its green and white field should be the official Welsh flag.

Just to the southwest of the town lies one of the best known places in the area - **Powis Castle** (see below). Inhabited for around 500 years, the various alterations which have taken place here over the years now cause the castle to look more like a mansion.

Powis Castle

Welshpool, Powys SY21 8RF
Tel: 01938 551920 info line: 01938 551920
e-mail: ppcmsn@smtp.ntrust.org.uk

A mile south of Welshpool off the A483 stands one of the best known landmarks in the area. **Powis Castle** was originally built by Welsh Princes and later became the ancestral home of the Herbert family and then of the Clive family. One of the owners was Edward, son of Clive of India, and the Clive Museum houses a beautiful collection of treasures from India from the famous man's time there. Visitors can also see one of the finest collections of paintings and furniture in Wales.

The Castle is perched on a rock above splendid terraces and gardens both formal and informal. Laid out in 1720 in a style influenced by both French and Italian design, the gardens and terraces retain some splendid original features, including lead urns and statues, an orangery and an aviary. The woodland, which was landscaped in the 18th century, overlooks the Severn Valley. The Castle is open to visitors from 1 to 5 late March to early November, the gardens from 11 to 6. There's a plant sales area, a shop and a licensed restaurant.

Derwen Garden Centre

Guilsfield, Nr Welshpool, Powys SY21 9PH
Tel: 01938 553015 Fax: 01938 556170
e-mail: kath@derwengardencentre.co.uk
website: www.derwengardencentre.co.uk

Derwen Garden Centre, located just off the
B4392 two miles north of Welshpool, has
everything for gardeners and lovers of gardens,
rightly describing itself as a "world of imagination,
innovation and inspiration". The range of trees,
shrubs, roses, herbaceous perennials, alpines and
seasonal bedding plants is superb, and in the
greenhouse is a lovely selection of conservatory
and house plants. For water gardens there are pool liners, pumps, water features, aquatic plants and
fish. In another section pottery from all around the world is on display, along with garden statuary
and stoneware and a selective range of durable and attractive garden furniture. In the gift shop and
showroom is a unique collection of decorative ware and giftware, including the Sia Inspiration range,

and all kinds of garden aids and sundries. This is
definitely a place to linger and to browse and to
buy, and visitors can pause to enjoy delicious home-
cooked lunches, snacks, cakes and pastries in the
licensed café. Friendly, well-informed staff are
always on hand with a warm greeting and helpful
advice at this outstanding garden centre, which is
open from 10 to 6 every day except Tuesday, when
it is open from 2 to 6.

Adjacent to the garden centre, Derwen House is
a substantial, gracious former estate dower house
which now offers guest accommodation in two well-
appointed and generously sized self-contained
apartments, one with four bedrooms, the other with
three. Both are equipped with everything needed for a comfortable self-catering holiday, and both
have gardens and ample car parking space. Guests at the house are granted a 10% discount on anything
bought at the Garden Centre.

Five minutes' drive from Derwen Garden Centre and Derwen House, on the same B4392 across the
A490, lies Dingle Nursery and Garden, which throughout the year offers the discerning gardener the
inspiration to experiment with new ideas. As traditional nursery people, Barbara and Ray Joseph grow
and develop their own plant species on site so that customers can be assured that the plants, shrubs
and trees they buy are consistently of the
highest quality. The unique feature here
is the four-acre garden, mostly the work
of Barbara, who has planned it to look
splendid all year round, paying particular
attention to the winter. May is the time
for rhododendrons and azaleas, while in
June the herbaceous plants take over to
give a wide range of colour and interest.
A dingle is another word for a stream,
which the owners dammed to create two
charming pools. Opening hours are 9 to
5; closed Tuesday and Christmas week.
Tel: 01938 555145 Fax: 01938 555778.

Powis Castle, Welshpool

The remains of a Norman motte and bailey are thought to be from the original castle which is believed to have been built on this site in the early 12th century and was then destroyed during a dispute between Llywelyn the Great and Gruffydd ap Gwenwynwyn, a local landowner. Edward I granted the family a barony on condition that they renounced their Welsh title, which they subsequently did, and so the Castle seen today was built.

2002 marks the 50th year of the Castle being in the hands of the National trust. But it was a series of tragedies to the Powis family that led to the Castle being

acquired by the Trust. George, the 4th Earl of Powis, lost his elder son Percy at the Battle of the Somme in 1916, his wife died after a car crash in 1929 and his only surviving son Mervyn was killed in a plane crash in 1942. So, before his own death in 1952, the Earl ensured that the Castle, its treasures and its gardens were looked after for the future by leaving Powis to the National Trust. The golden anniversary has been marked by a series of events, all gold-themed, including an Easter Golden Egg Trail (see also the Powis Castle panel on page 151). From the town, the narrow gauge **Welshpool and Llanfair Railway** takes passengers on a steam train journey through the Powis estates and the delightful Banwy valley to Llanfair Caereinion.

GUILSFIELD
2½ miles N of Welshpool on the B4392

The large 15th century village church here is well worth a second glance as, not only does it have an unusual upper chamber above the south porch, but there is also a splendid panelled roof and

THE OAK

Guilsfield, Nr Welshpool, Powys
Tel: 01938 553391

The Oak is a 17th century black and white farmhouse standing back from the road in the picturesque village of Guilsfield. Timber-framed, it sports many original features, and landlords David and Helen are maintaining its reputation for hospitality for all ages and for home cooking that has earned great praise and several awards. A good range of beers and other drinks is served in the stylish open-plan bar area, and the snack

and à la carte menus provide a variety of tasty dishes both classic and more innovative. The Oak has plenty of outside seating at both front and rear, an area where children can play in safety and ample car parking space.

some fine 19th century vaulting.

Off the B4392 just outside the village, **Gaer Fawr** (it means Great Camp) covers most of a hilltop and includes a scheduled ancient monument. Great walks through woodland and grassland; splendid views.

LLANGEDWYN
10½ miles N of Welshpool on the B4396

Just to the northeast of the village and close to the English border, lies one of Wales' most nationalistic shrines, **Sycharth Castle**. A grassy mound is all

BANWY VALLEY NURSERY
Foel, Nr Welshpool, Powys SY21 0PT
Tel/Fax: 01938 820281
e-mail: banwy.valley@virgin.net website: www.powysweb.co.uk

Brown and white signs lead south from Foel to **Banwy Valley Nursery**, where owners Syd and Carol Luck grow and sell a wide selection of trees, shrubs and hardy perennials. There's always an excellent variety of magnolias and azaleas, as well as up to 40 types of rhododendron. Visitors can browse at leisure around the nursery, see plants growing in the tranquil gardens and get good advice on plant and gardening matters from the friendly, knowledgeable owners and staff. The nursery is open from 10 to 5 Tuesday to Sunday, also Bank Holiday Mondays. No credit cards.

LLANGEDWYN MILL CRAFT WORKSHOPS
Llangedwyn, Oswestry, Powys SY10 9LD

Set in the beautiful Tanat Valley, **Llangedwyn Mill Craft Workshops** are home to four separate craft enterprises.

MIRAGE GLASS, established in 1978 by Johan and Wolfe van Brussel, specialises in architectural and decorative stained glass designed and made to commission using both traditional and innovative techniques and inspired by the Welsh landscape and legend. Their workshop is open all year round and they also sell mirrors, lamps and jewellery and in summer run classes in the techniques of creating stained glass (Tel: 01691 780618, website/e-mail: mirageglass.co.uk).

CREATIVE WOODWORKING is the brainchild of Peter Phelps and Helen Speak, who create a range of quality Treen and gifts turned and carved from beautiful native timbers. Bowls and plates, salad servers, spoons, salt and pepper grinders and rolling pins are all both attractive and practical, and there are also some lovely traditional games and toys on display; they welcome commissions and are also open all year round (Tel: 01691 780065, e-mail: peterhelen@tiscali.co.uk).

THE NIMBLE THIMBLE, run by Chris Parkinson, specialises in charts and kits for the cross stitcher and also operates as a framing workshop. The shop holds a large selection of materials and linens, and the stock includes some unusual American charts and kits. They are stockists for, among others, The Drawn Thread, Moira Blackburn Samplers, Bent Creek, Twisted Thread, Shepherds Bush and Lavender & Lace, plus all the necessary accessories (Tel/Fax: 01691 780088, e-mail: chris@nimblethimble.co.uk).

At STUDIO BEE, Graham Parker is a highly qualified repairer and restorer of antique clocks and barometers, and a design jeweller who undertakes commissions in precious metals. He has made badges and chains of office for councils and livery companies, and also produced the Crown for an Eisteddfod. There are clocks and barometers for sale in his workshop (Tel: 01691 780642 or 830744, e-mail: Parkersbee@btinternet.comuk).

MALTHOUSE ANTIQUES

Pool Road, Four Crosses, Llanymynech, Powys SY22 6PS
Tel: 01691 830015

The old stone building on the A483 just south of Llanymynech looks full of interest and character, and those venturing inside are not likely to be disappointed. **Malthouse Antiques** is owned and run by Neville Foulkes, an expert in architectural salvage and antique and period furniture, fireplaces, baths and basins. The stock here, much of it made locally, changed constantly, with Welsh dressers, reconditioned baths, sink units and beaten copper buckets typifying the range. This is a fascinating spot where every item has its exact place - even if that place is known only to Neville!

that remains of one of Owain Glyndwr's principal houses, which was immortalised in a poem by Iolo Goch, which speaks of its nine halls, many guest rooms and a church. The poem appears in a translation by Anthony Conran in the *Penguin Book of Welsh Verse*:

Here are gifts for everyone
No hunger, disgrace or dearth,
Or ever thirst at Sycharth!

Haply the best of Welshmen
Owns the land, of Pywer's kin;
It's a strong, lean warrior owns
This most lovable of mansions.

MIDDLETOWN

5½ miles NE of Welshpool on the A458

To the north of this border village lies **Breidden Hill**, which is thought to have been the venue for a fierce battle between the Welsh and the forces of

CORNER HOUSE GALLERY

Meifod, Nr Welshpool, Montgomeryshire SY22 6BZ
Tel: 01938 500600 e-mail: kathy@kathygittins.com
Fax: 01938 500700 website: www.kathygittins.com

In a picturesque village in the valley of the River Vyrnwy, **Corner House Gallery** is a showcase for the work of artist, publisher and mother of four Kathy Gittins. Her career as an artist began at the age of 15 when she won a national painting competition, and after raising a family she was able to return to her profession and turn her attention to a collection of 70 watercolours inspired by the rural surroundings of Montgomeryshire. She launched her first exhibition in 1997, the success of which encouraged her to supply not only original works but limited edition prints and greetings cards in both English and Welsh. Her work is now marketed to over 200 outlets nationally. In 1998 Kathy bought a 300-year-old stone cottage in her local village, and converted it into the Corner House Gallery.

On view alongside her watercolours, prints and cards are some lovely glass, pottery and other artefacts from talented British artists. After attending exhibitions in North America and Japan, export

orders followed, along with distribution and licensing agreements. Floral still lifes are one of her specialities, and the delicacy and detail of her work appeals strongly to the Japanese market, while its uniquely Welsh character imparts a distinctive quality that is gaining growing recognition in the USA. Corner House Gallery, which serves light refreshments, is open from 10 to 5.30 Monday to Saturday and from 2 to 5.30 on Sunday; groups, clubs and other organisations are very welcome to visit outside these times by arrangements. The Gallery holds regular exhibitions by invited artists throughout the year.

Edward I in 1292. On the summit stands an obelisk, **Rodney's Pillar**, which commemorates Admiral Rodney's victory over the French off Domenica in 1782. A little way further along the A458 is the remote hamlet of Melverley, whose church, perched above the River Vyrnwy, is one of the most delightful in the region, with a "magpie" exterior, timber-framed walls and a tiny tower.

MEIFOD
5½ miles NW of Welshpool on the A495

This picturesque village, in the wooded valley of the River Vyrnwy, is remembered in Welsh literature as being the location of the summer residence of the princes of Powys. The village **Church of St Tysilio and St Mary**, which was consecrated in 1155, is home to an interesting 9th century grave slab that bears old Celtic markings as well as a Latin cross and a Greek crucifix. According to legend, in AD 550, when St Gwyddfarch was asked where he would like to built his first church, he is said to have replied, in Welsh, "yma y mae i fod" (here it is to be). So the village got its name and, after his death, the saint is thought to have been buried a short distance from the village. In the 9th century, while the princes of Powys had their main residence close by, Meifod became a religious centre and it is

thought that the grave slab is a memorial to one of the princes.

LLANFIHANGEL-YNG-NGWYNFA
10½ miles NW of Welshpool on the B4382

In the small church of this tiny village not only are there some interesting artefacts but there is also a memorial to the Welsh writer, Ann Griffith, and some 15th century graves lie in the churchyard. Born at a farm near Dolanog, in 1776, where she lived most of her short life, Ann only ever travelled as far as Bala, where she went to hear Thomas Charles preach. However, despite dying at the early age of 29 years, Ann wrote over 70 Welsh hymns, all dictated to a friend.

LLANWDDYN
14 miles NW of Welshpool on the B4393

The village lies at the southern end of **Lake Vyrnwy** (Llyn Efyrnwy), a four mile stretch of water that was created, in the years following 1881, by the flooding of the entire Vyrnwy Valley, to provide the people of Liverpool with an adequate water supply. Close to the dam, which is 390 yards long, 144 feet high and a splendid testament to Victorian engineering, is a monument that marks the beginning of the **Hirnant Tunnel** - the first stage of a 75 mile aqueduct that carries the water to Liverpool. Another

---

THE KING'S HEAD

Meifod, Nr Welshpool, Powys SY22 6BY
Tel: 01938 500788

The King's Head presents a handsome ivy-clad facade in the pretty village of Meifod . Guests relax over a glass of real ale warmed by an open fire in the bar in the winter or outside in the summer. The restaurant menu features excellent use of national produce, including Welsh Mountain lamb, Welsh Black beef and Welsh cheeses. Owner Robert Thomas offers "Gallery Special" luncheons and suppers in conjunction with partner Kathy Gittins' Corner House Gallery (see page 155). The five en suite bedrooms provide all the modern comforts while keeping their delightful traditional character.

Lake Vyrnwy

massive reservoirs in north and mid-Wales, the original village of Llanwddyn, home to some 400 people, was flooded along with the valley. On the hill south of the dam stands the "new" village and the church, built by Liverpool Corporation in 1887. Photographs in the Lake Vyrnwy Hotel show the original village with its 37 houses, all now along with the church submerged under the Lake's 13,000 million gallons of water. The reservoir's visitor centre not only tells the story of the construction but is also home to an RSPB centre; there are four RSPB hides at various points around the lake and guided tours can be arranged around the estate for schools and groups. A road circumnavigates the Lake but

striking building is the Gothic tower designed by George Frederick Deacon, engineer to the Liverpool Water Board. On higher ground is an obelisk that is a monument to the 44 men who died during the construction of the reservoir. To construct this, the first of several

LAKE VYRNWY HOTEL

Lake Vyrnwy, Llanwyddyn, Montgomery, Powys SY10 0LY
Tel: 01691 870692 Fax: 01691 870259
e-mail: res@lakevyrnwy.com
website: www.lakevyrnwy.com

Lake Vyrnwy Hotel is a magnificent stone mansion set high on a wooded hillside looking across the man-made lake set amid the 24,000 acres of the Vyrnwy Estate. The 35 bedrooms are individually furnished and decorated, with lake or countryside views; many have some fine antiques and several boast special features such as jacuzzis, four-posters or balconies. A holiday in this unique spot can be totally relaxing, with guests taking their ease in the sumptuous day rooms or enjoying gentle walks to take in the magical scenery, or all action: the hotel owns some of the country's best fishing together with sporting rights covering sailing, rowing, clay pigeon shooting, archery, cycling, tennis, quad trekking and climbing.

Another attraction is the award-winning candlelit restaurant, where the best fresh produce is used for the superb dinner menu, where typical choices run from salmon and herb boudin with dressed leaves and tomato dressing through rib of Welsh Black beef with lyonnaise potatoes, swede purée, creamed leeks and port wine jus to a classic pear Belle Hélène. Everything from the breakfast marmalade to the petits fours in the evening is made in the hotel's kitchens. Well-behaved dogs are welcome in the bedrooms but not in the day rooms; kennelling and stabling are available.

walking around the lake or on any of the nature trails, is an ideal way to observe the abundant wild and bird life that live around the shores. Another trail visits large wooden sculptures carved from local materials by local and visiting artists. Bethania Adventure, based at the Boat House, organises activities on and around the lake, including sailing, windsurfing, kayaking, canoeing, climbing and abseiling; the lake is also a favourite spot for anglers. With its lovely scenery and coniferous forests, the lake has doubled in films for Switzerland or Transylvania; it was also used for location shots in *The Dambusters*.

LLANGYNOG
16 miles NW of Welshpool on the B4391

Situated at the confluence of the River Tanat and Eirth and overlooked by the Berwyn range, the village's name recalls Cynog, the son of the 5th century Welsh prince, Brychan. Further up the wooded valley of the upper River Tanat, in the hamlet of **Pennant Melangell**, lies **St Melangell's Church**, where there can be seen two images that are said to be of a Welsh prince and the 7th century St Melangell. The story goes that a hunted hare took refuge in the saint's cloak and thus she became the patron saint of hares. They were once treated as sacred in this lonely area. A short distance

further upstream is a small waterfall that marks the start of the valley.

LLANRHAEADR-YM-MOCHNANT
13 miles NW of Welshpool on the B4580

Despite its relative isolation this village attracts many visitors who pass through on their way to **Pistyll Rhaeadr**, which lies up a narrow road to the northwest of the village. This is one of the Seven

Pistyll Rhaeadr

TAN-Y-FFRIDD

Caer Fach, Llanrhaeadr-ym-Mochnant,
Nr Oswestry, Powys SY10 0DT
Tel: 01691 701418 Fax: 01691 791437
e-mail: caerfach@aol.com
website: www.tanat-holidays.co.uk

Tan-y-Ffridd provides the perfect setting for a secluded self-catering holiday in glorious surroundings. Margaret Hart has two properties for letting, one a fine stone-built farm cottage sleeping six, the other a bungalow. The cottage, dating back some 200 years, has been sympathetically restored while retaining original features. It has a king-sized double, a double and a twin, plus a child's cot and a put-u-up bed. Both properties are fully equipped with the essentials for an independent break, and the owner maintains both in immaculate condition.

CAIN VALLEY HOTEL

High Street, Llanfyllin, Powys SY22 5AQ
Tel: 01691 648366   Fax: 01691 648307
e-mail: info@cainvalleyhotel.co.uk
website: www.cainvalleyhotel.co.uk

Cain Valley Hotel is a 17th century coaching inn
owned by keen sailor and climber Les Merrit. Behind
the smart black-and-white frontage eyecatching
features include heavy beams and a fine Jacobean
staircase. The 13 centrally heated, comfortably
furnished bedrooms all have en suite facilities, tv and courtesy tray. In the bar, an excellent range of
real ales and snacks is served, and Birches Restaurant offers a splendid à la carte menu and a well-
chosen wine list. There are some lovely walks in the area and plenty of exploring to be done in the
town and in the surrounding countryside.

Wonders of Wales and, with a drop of
240 feet, is the highest waterfall in
Britain south of the Scottish Highlands.
The English translation of the name is
Spout Waterfall, an obvious name as the
water drops vertically for 100 feet before
running into a cauldron, on through a
natural tunnel in the rock and then
again reappearing.

It was while vicar at Llanrhaeadr-ym-
Mochnant, in the late 16th century, that
Bishop William Morgan made his famous
translation of the Bible into Welsh. He
was granted permission to carry out this
work by Queen Elizabeth I, her father
Henry VIII having banned any official
use of the Welsh language. The villagers
here maintain a tradition that was once
common in the area - the Plygeiniau, a
form of Christmas carol service, where
groups of men wander from church to
church giving unaccompanied
performances of Welsh carols.

LLANFYLLIN

9 miles NW of Welshpool on the A490

This charming and peaceful hillside
town lies in the valley of the River Cain.
It was granted its charter as a borough in
1293 by Llewelyn ap Gruffydd ap
Gwenwynwyn, Lord of Mechain;
Welshpool is the only other Welsh
borough to have been granted its charter

from a native Welsh ruler. To celebrate
the 700th anniversary in 1993 of the
granting of the charter a large tapestry of
the town's historic buildings was created;
it can be seen in the parish church of St
Myllin, a delightful redbrick building
dating from 1706. Overlooking the town
is the beauty spot of **St Myllin's Well.**
Water from the well has, from the 6th
century onwards, been thought to cure
all manner of ailments and certainly the
view from the well, over the town and to
the Berwyn Mountains beyond, is
uplifting. St Myllin, a 7th century Celt, is
traditionally alluded to as the first cleric
to baptise by total immersion in his holy
well. Opposite the church is the brick
Council House, which has 13 wall
paintings in an upstairs room. These
were all done by a Napoleonic prisoner
of war, several of whom were billeted in
the town between 1812 and 1814. Ann
Griffiths, the famous Welsh hymn writer,
was baptised in Pendref Congregational
Chapel, one of the oldest Non-
Conformist places of worship in Wales,
established in 1640; the present building
dates from 1829.

Two miles southeast of Llanfyllin, off
the A490, **Bryngwyn** is a handsome
18th century house by Robert Mylne,
surrounded by 18th century and early
19th century parkland.

5 SOUTH POWYS WITH BRECON BEACONS NATIONAL PARK

This southern region of the large county of Powys is steeped in history and there is evidence aplenty of turbulent times past. From the Celtic standing stones and burial chambers, to the ruined castles at Builth Wells, Painscastle, Clyro and near Talgarth, the landscape is littered with the buildings and memorials left by many past inhabitants.

Llyn Y Fan Fach, Brecon Beacons

Continued on page 162

ADVERTISERS AND PLACES OF INTEREST

LOCATOR MAP

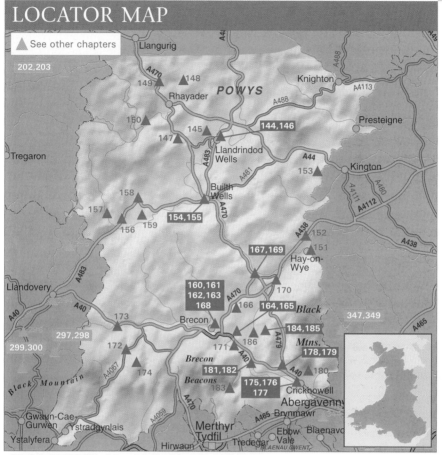

▲ See other chapters

202,203

© MAPS IN MINUTES ™ 2002   © Crown Copyright, Ordnance Survey 2002

In the heart of the county (the northern part of this region) can be found the four spa towns of Llandrindod Wells, Builth Wells, Llangammarch Wells and Llanwrtyd Wells. Still popular tourist centres today, though no longer primarily spas, these places all grew and developed as a result of the arrival of the railways and the Victorians' interest in health. Although the architecture of these towns suggests that they date mainly from the 19th and early 20th centuries, there are the remains of a Roman fort close to Llandrindod Wells, and Builth Wells saw much fighting in medieval times. As well as the spa towns, the region also has the border settlements of Knighton and Presteigne, the second-hand book capital of the world Hay-on-Wye and the ancient cathedral city of Brecon, but it is perhaps for its varied countryside that south Powys is better known. Close to Rhayader, in the Cambrian Mountains, are the spectacular reservoirs and dams that make up the Elan Valley. Built at the end of the 19th century to supply water to the West Midlands, not only are these a great feat of Victorian engineering but the surrounding countryside is home to one of Britain's rarest and most beautiful birds - the Red Kite.

Brecon Beacons

Further south lies the Brecon Beacons National Park, which takes its name from the distinctively shaped sandstone mountains of the Brecon Beacons; but there are two other ranges within the park's 519 square miles. To the east of the Brecon Beacons lie the interlocking peaks of the Black Mountains which stretch to the English border while to the west is Black Mountain, which, though its name is singular, refers to an unpopulated range of barren, smooth humped peaks.

LLANDRINDOD WELLS

The most elegant of the spa towns of mid-Wales, Llandrindod Wells, though not primarily a spa today, is still a popular place that has retained its Victorian and Edwardian character and architecture. This was only a small hamlet until 1749, when a hotel was built here and, for a time, until the hotel closed in 1787, the town had a reputation as a haunt for gamblers and rakes. Despite its chiefly 19th and early 20th century architecture, Llandrindod Wells has ancient roots and to the northwest of the town lies **Castell Collen**, a Roman fort that was occupied from the 1st century through to the early 4th century and whose earthworks are clearly detectable today. The first castle was of turf and timber, put up by Frontinus in about AD 75, and later versions were made of stone.

It was the Romans who first understood the possible healing powers of Wales' mineral rich waters - saline, sulphur, magnesian, chalybeate - but it was with the coming of the railway in 1867, along with the Victorians' enthusiasm for "taking the waters", that Llandrindod Wells really developed in to a spa town. People would flock to the town in their thousands (at its peak some 80,000 visitors a year) to take the waters in an attempt to obtain relief from complaints and ailments ranging from gout, rheumatism and anaemia to diabetes, dyspepsia and liver trouble. A complete system of baths and heat and massage treatments were also available. The most famous of the individual spas in Llandrindod during its heyday, **Rock Park** is a typically well laid out Victorian park where visitors coming to the town would take a walk between their treatments. With particularly fine tree

ROCK PARK HERITAGE RESTAURANT

Rock Park, Llandrindod Wells, Powys LD1 6AE
Tel: 01597 829267 Fax: 01597 824350

Rock Park is the site of the most popular of the spas that put the town on the map in Victorian times. Today it provides a tranquil, scenic setting for the Rock Park Heritage Restaurant, which has recently been re-opened by Richard and Caroline Mann. The owners are already realising their ambition to put this hidden treasure back in business as *the* place to go to enjoy a snack or meal in a relaxed, family-oriented atmosphere. The cheerful, stylish restaurant is open from 10 to 5 Monday to Saturday for coffee, cakes, snacks or a light lunch and from 12 to 5 for a leisurely traditional Sunday lunch.

With families in mind, an early supper is served from 5.30 to 7 Tuesday to Saturday, and from 7 to 9 the full à la carte menu is served. Local produce features prominently in Richard's repertoire, and his fish dishes enjoy particular acclaim. The food is complemented by a well-priced wine list that includes three by the glass. The restaurant and toilet are easily accessible to wheelchair users, and there are baby changing facilities. With its picturesque setting and happy atmosphere, the restaurant is an ideal venue for private parties - up to 70 can be accommodated.

Radnor Farm & Country Holidays Ltd

Highbury Farm, Llanyre, Llandrindod Wells, Powys LD1 6EA
Tel/Fax: 01597 822716
e-mail: highbury.farm@btinternet.com
website: www.farmbreaks.org.uk

Radnor Farm & Country Holidays Ltd is made up of a group of individuals who have worked together for some years to provide quality holiday accommodation in the serene, beautiful heart of mid-Wales. All of the properties are farmhouses, offering either bed and breakfast accommodation, or self-catering with some providing both options. Each has its own individual character and appeal, but what they all have in common is a warm welcome, a comfortable, relaxing atmosphere and a tranquil setting in lovely rural surroundings.

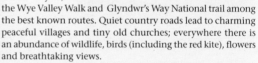

Many of the establishments are working farms, with a variety of farm animals which children can sometimes help to feed. At some of the farms evening meals and packed lunches are available by prior arrangement. Miles of footpaths, bridleways and cycle paths criss-cross the region, providing exercise that can be as gentle or energetic as required, with Offa's Dyke,

the Wye Valley Walk and Glyndwr's Way National trail among the best known routes. Quiet country roads lead to charming peaceful villages and tiny old churches; everywhere there is an abundance of wildlife, birds (including the red kite), flowers and breathtaking views.

Outdoor sporting activities include golf, mountain biking, riding, pony trekking, fishing and, for the more adventurous, the lure of canoeing or paragliding might prove irresistible. The area is steeped in history and includes castles and caves, old mine workings, Roman encampments, churches and monuments. The towns in this part of the world are also full of interest: Knighton, on the path of Offa's Dyke in the Teme Valley, with Powys Observatory; Presteigne, with its annual music festival; Llandrindod Wells, a Victorian spa town that is home to the National Cycle Museum; Rhayader, with the Kite Feeding Centre, gateway to the spectacular Elan Valley, whose five dammed lakes, called the Lakeland of Wales, are surrounded by magnificent scenery. Moving on to Hay-on-Wye, the secondhand book capital of the world. Come and discover the unspoilt beauty of mid-Wales.

planting and shrubberies, the park is still a pleasant place today, and here and elsewhere in town, visitors can still take the waters or experience some of the more modern therapies.

As well as the evidence of the town's heyday that is all around, visitors can find out more about the spa's history at the **Llandrindod Wells Museum** where not only is there a collection of Victorian artefacts but also relics excavated from Castell Collen. A splendid attraction in the Automobile Palace is the **National Cycle Collection**, an exhibition that covers more than 100 years of cycling history, through an amazing collection of over 200 bicycles and tricycles that date back as far as 1818, spanning every development from the hobby horse and bone-shaker to the high-tech machines of today. Also here are old photographs and posters, historic replicas, the Dunlop tyre story and displays on cycling stars.

Just outside Llandrindod Wells, off the A44 Rhayader road, there is free access to **Abercamlo Bog**, 12 acres of wet pasture that are home to water-loving plants, breeding birds such as the whinchat and reed bunting, and a variety of butterflies. Not far away, at Ithon gorge, is **Bailey Einion**, woodland home to lady fern, golden saxifrage,

pied flycatchers, woodpeckers and cardinal beetles.

Wales is famous for its amazing little narrow-gauge railways, but it also has some full-size trains, too. One of the most popular tourist lines is the **Heart of Wales Line** that runs from Shrewsbury

LLANDRINDOD WELLS VICTORIAN FESTIVAL

Victorian Festival Office, Town Hall, Memorial Gardens, Llandrindod Wells, Powys LDI 5DL
Tel: 01597 823441 Fax: 01597 825905

Each year Llandrindod Wells hosts a Victorian festival *Coming of Age*. 2002 will see it celebrating its 21st year. Held in the last full week of August before the Bank Holiday, this popular festival is going from strength to strength and has now become one of the premier Victorian festivals in Britain today.

As Llandrindod was a thriving spa resort in the Victorian era it is natural to base the festival on the Victorian theme. The town's unspoilt architecture provides a perfect backdrop to the celebrations and, on Temple Gardens, there is an ideal venue for the many different types of street entertainment provided free for the visitors and townsfolk throughout the day.

The aim of the festival is to provide a family fun festival and to cater for all ages and tastes, whilst keeping to a Victorian theme. Attracting some 40,000 visitors to a town that has a population of only 5,000 is no mean feat, but the apparent ease with which it is done is largely due to the transformation achieved in the town's reversion to the Victorian era. The effect of horses and carriages, Victorian window displays and the townspeople and some visitors sporting a whole range of appropriate costumes creates an atmosphere, the effect of which is nothing short of miraculous.

At the end of the nine days, the proceedings are closed in the grandest of manners with the moving torchlight procession and fireworks display over the lake - a spectacle not to be missed.

ARGOED MILL GALLERY

Argoed Mill, Doldowlod, Nr Llandrindod Wells, Powys LD1 6HH
Tel: 01597 860470
e-mail: info@argoed-mill.co.uk website: www.argoed-mill.co.uk

Argoed Mill Gallery is owned by artist Deborah Leeton and her husband Tim, who have together created a truly beautiful centre for the promotion of local art and craft. The works for sale, each one unique and of the highest quality, have all been produced within a 40-mile radius of the Gallery. From handmade soaps to paintings and sculptures, ceramics and jewellery, there is something to suit all purses. Exhibitions by resident artists, including Deborah herself, are held throughout the year, along with demonstrations and workshops in many crafts, among them painting, woodturning and basket making.

to Swansea, "one line that visits two viaducts, three castles, four spa towns, five counties, six tunnels and seven bridges". Dolau, six miles to the northeast of Llandrindod Wells, is the best starting point on the line to walk to the top of Radnor Forest, the highest point in the old county of Radnorshire. Llanbister Road and Llangunllo are nearby request halts ideally placed for discovering the remoter scenic delights of the area.

ABBEY-CWM-HIR
6 miles N of Llandrindod Wells off the A483

Cwmhir Abbey, founded by the Cistercians in 1143, is reputed to have been attacked by Owain Glyndwr in 1402 who thought that the monks were English sympathisers, while earlier it had been all but destroyed by Henry III in 1231. It is a place of peace and tranquillity in the lonely Clywedog Valley that is well worth visiting; there is a memorial stone among the abbey ruins to Llywelyn the Last that marks, many believe, the grave of his headless body.

RHAYADER
6½ miles NW of Llandrindod Wells on the A44

Often referred to as the Gateway to the Lakeland of Wales, Rhayader lies at the entrance to the magnificent Elan Valley and the impressive collection of dams and reservoirs it contains. This town,

whose name means "Waterfall of the Wye", dates back to the 5th century, though the waterfall all but disappeared with the construction of a bridge over the river in 1780.

The town's castle, built here by Rhys ap Gryffydd in the 12th century, was destroyed centuries ago, while more recently Rhayader was the scene of some of the Rebecca Riots protesting against toll gates. The men, who dressed up as women and so earned themselves the nickname "Rebecca's Daughters", destroyed turnpikes in protest at the high toll charges. Many tall stories have grown up around these riots and some of them concern Rebecca herself, who is said to have appeared as an old blind woman at the toll gate and said, "My children, something is in my way." The first gate to be destroyed was at Yr Efail Wen, where "Rebecca" proved to be a huge man called Thomas Rees. Many toll gates were demolished by the protesters until, in 1844, the remainder were removed legally.

Welsh Royal Crystal, a manufacturer of hand-crafted lead crystal tableware and gift items, is located in the town and the factory takes visitors on a guided tour to watch the craftsmen at work. Rhayader is at one end of the beautiful Wye Valley Walk, which follows the river valley, criss-crossing the border, through Builth Wells and Hay-on-Wye to

GILFACH NATURE RESERVE

Gilfach Farm, St Harmon, Rhayader, Powys LD6 5LF
Radnorshire Wildlife Trust,
Tel: 01597 870301
e-mail: radnorshirewt@cix.co.uk

This important Site of Special Scientific Interest enjoys a beautiful setting at the mouth of the Marteg Valley in the Cambrian Mountains, just off the A470, seven miles from Llangurig and three from Rhayader. In the care of the Radnorshire Wildlife Trust, the farm is a complex pattern of rocky outcrops, ancient oak woodlands, hill-land, hedgerow enclosed meadows, green lanes and boundary walls.

This varied landscape supports a tremendous abundance of plants and animals within a comparatively small area, and four waymarked trails offer visitors the opportunity to enjoy not only the richness of the wildlife but also the outstanding views. Part of the Visitor Centre complex at the heart of the Reserve is the ancient Gilfach Longhouse, a traditional Welsh building of local rubble stone that is an attraction in its own right. Facing this house, across the farmyard, is another fine old building, The Barn, comprising hay barn, byre and stables and built of stone. There is parking at the farm and wheelchair access to the centre, toilet facilities and some of the trails.

OAK WOOD LODGES

Llwynbaedd, Rhayader, Powys LD6 5NT
Tel: 01597 811422
e-mail: info@oakwoodlodges.co.uk
website: www.oakwoodlodges.co.uk

Oak Wood Lodges, under the personal supervision of resident proprietors Sue and Tim Dobb, provide abundant comfort, peace and relaxation in one of the most beautiful parts of the country. The lodges are built of solid Norwegian logs, and with their sturdy construction and efficient central heating they are as well suited to a winter break as to a summer holiday. Each lodge has two bedrooms (a double and a twin) with two fold-up beds enabling up to six guests to sleep in each, a shower room, open-plan lounge, dining area and well-equipped kitchen, tv and French windows opening on to a south-facing veranda.

The elevated position of the lodges commands superb views, and there are plenty of opportunities in the locality for walking, mountain biking, fishing, golf and pony trekking. It is also an excellent area for birdwatching, with the renascent red kites often spotted. Oak Wood is a fine place to take a lazy break and is an ideal centre for touring, with the beautiful Elan Valley and the Cambrian mountains on the doorstep. The market town of Rhayader, just two miles away, has plenty of shops and pubs, a Tourist Information Centre and a leisure centre with a swimming pool.

Hereford, Monmouth and Chepstow. An extension is due to open in the autumn of 2002 beyond Rhayader to Llangurig and the slopes of Plynlimon, where it will join the Severn Way in Hafren Forest.

The area around Rhayader is still very rural and on the outskirts of the town lies **Gigrin Farm**, where visitors can see red kites at close quarters as they are feeding.

Craig Goch Reservoir, Elan Valley

ELAN VILLAGE
8 miles W of Llandrindod Wells off the B4518

The village is close to the beautiful reservoirs of the **Elan Valley** - a string of five dammed lakes that are together around nine miles long and were constructed between 1892 and 1903. Formed to supply millions of gallons of water to Birmingham and the West Midlands, the first of the dams was opened in 1904 by Edward VII and Queen Alexandra and the final dam, the Claerwen dam, was finished in 1952. Dubbed the "Lakeland of Wales", the five man-made lakes are surrounded by magnificent scenery and this is a popular area for walkers, cyclists and

birdwatchers. The **Elan Valley Visitor Centre** (see panel below), as well as incorporating a tourist information office, also has an exhibition telling the story of the building of the reservoirs and lots of information about the red kite.

Percy Bysshe Shelley visited his cousin Thomas Grove at Cwm Elan after being expelled from Oxford for writing a treatise supporting atheism. Soon after this visit he eloped with the schoolgirl Harriet Westbrook and married her in Scotland. They returned to Wales and for a brief spell in 1812 stayed at a house in the area called Nant Gwyllt. Like Thomas Grove's house, it is now submerged under the waters of **Caben Coch** reservoir, but when the water level is low the walls of the garden can still be seen. In 1814 Shelley left Harriet for Mary Godwin, and soon after Harriet drowned

THE ELAN VALLEY

Elan Valley Visitor Centre, Elan Valley, Rhayader, Powys LD6 5HP
Tel: 01597 810880
website: www.elanvalley.org.uk

The Elan Valley is 70 square miles of the Cambrian Mountains in mid-Wales - a special area for wildlife with reservoirs and dams, rivers, woodlands and moorland. There is a well signposted Visitor Centre open from the middle of March to the end of October every day from 10am to 5.30pm which has a wildlife exhibition, cafe, shop, toilets, a large car park suitable for coaches and cars and a picnic area beside the River Elan. The Valley has several leafleted walks and many guided walks and wildlife events are led by the team of Countryside Rangers.

herself in the Serpentine. Shelley married Mary, who was later to write *Frankenstein*. In 1822 Shelley himself drowned off the Italian coast.

ST HARMON
8 miles NW of Llandrindod Wells on the B4518

The diarist Francis Kilvert was vicar here in 1876-77, after his time at Clyro. Kilvert was born near Chippenham in 1840 and was educated at Wadham College, Oxford. He was curate to his father in Wiltshire before taking up a post at Clyro in 1865, where he started his famous diaries. Detailed, vivid and very personal accounts of life in the remote Welsh countryside in mid-Victorian times. Back to England, then a year here, then back to Bredwardine in Herefordshire, where he married. He died five weeks later of peritonitis; he was 39 years of age. To the southwest of the village lies **Gilfach**, a lovingly restored Welsh longhouse at the centre of an extensive nature reserve. Oak woodland, meadows and upland moorland support a rich diversity of wildlife, and at the longhouse there are exhibitions on the building's history and the surrounding wildlife.

KNIGHTON

Situated in the Teme Valley on the border of Powys and Shropshire, Knighton lies on the path of Offa's Dyke. The Welsh name for the town is Tref-y-Clawdd which means "town of the dyke" and Knighton is home to the **Offa's Dyke Centre** where there is information about the long distance footpath that runs from Prestatyn to Chepstow. Here, too, visitors can find out more about the historic background to the 8th century dyke and the bloodshed of the battle that continued in the borderlands for hundreds of years.

Knighton Church

Knighton and its near neighbour, the border town of Presteigne, saw many battles between the Anglo Saxons and the Celts. "It was customary for the English to cut off the ears of every Welshman who was found to the east of the Dyke (Offa's), and for the Welsh to hang every Englishman found to the west of it", wrote George Borrow in his 19th century book, *Wild Wales*.

Beginning in Knighton, **Glyndwr's Way** follows the route taken by Owain Glyndwr, one of Wales' favourite sons, as he fought the English for Welsh independence in the 1400s. This scenic and important route travels southwest to Abbey-cwm-hir, passing by the ancient abbey ruins, before heading northwards into the old county of Montgomeryshire and the market town of Llanidloes. The 128 miles of the path takes in some of the finest scenery in mid-Wales before reaching Machynlleth, from where it heads southeastwards and finally ends at the border town of Welshpool.

Beside the banks of the River Teme is **Pinners Hole**, a natural amphitheatre that is strengthened on one side by a superb section of Offa's Dyke where there is a stone that commemorates the opening of the footpath. Across the river lies **Kinsley Wood**, a sizeable area of native oak woodland. Sited on a hillside, trees of different species were planted to form the letters "ER" to commemorate the Coronation of Her Majesty Queen Elizabeth II.

PRESTEIGNE
5 miles S of Knighton on the B4362

Once the county town of Radnorshire, Presteigne remains a charming and unspoilt place on the southern bank of the River Lugg. A border town distinguished by its handsome black and white half-timbered buildings, Presteigne grew up around a Norman castle that has long since been destroyed; the site is now occupied by a pleasant park. Presteigne's history is as turbulent as that of most of the region: it was captured by the Mercians in the 8th century, besieged by Llywelyn in 1262 and pillaged by Owain Glyndwr in the early 15th century. By Tudor times the town had got its breath back and had become a peaceful market centre, but it was its position on a major mail coach route between London, Cheltenham and Gloucester and Aberystwyth that brought it prosperity and importance.

One of the town's most outstanding buildings is **The Radnorshire Arms**, which dates from 1616. Originally built as a house for Sir Christopher Hatton, one of Elizabeth I's courtiers, this superb timber framed building became the property of the Bradshaw family before becoming an inn in 1792. The best

known member of this family was John Bradshaw, who was Lord President of the Parliamentary Commission that brought Charles I to trial. He headed the list of signatories to the King's death warrant, refusing to let him speak in his defence. The town also claims the oldest inn in Radnorshire, the **Duke's Arms**, for which records show that an inn on the site was burnt to the ground by Owain Glyndwr in 1401. The rebuilt inn became a local headquarters for the Roundheads during the Civil War and, in later centuries, was an important coaching inn.

Although the **Judge's Lodging** only dates from 1829, it is another fascinating attraction in Presteigne. Designed by Edward Haycock and built on the site of the county gaol, this was the judicial centre for Radnorshire and the home of the Radnorshire Constabulary. Today, the house, with its adjoining court, has been furnished as it would have appeared in 1870, and visitors can explore the world of the judges, their servants and the felons.

OLD RADNOR
8½ miles S of Knighton off the A44

Situated on a hill, Old Radnor was once home to King Harold. The motte by the church was the site of his castle, while the church itself contains interesting examples of 14th century building design, as well as a huge font made from a glacial boulder. Motte and bailey castles were introduced into Britain by the Normans. They basically comprised a ditch or moat surrounding an earth mound with a palisade protecting the tower, or keep. By the tower was a flat area, the bailey, used for outside purposes such as stabling.

NEW RADNOR
8½ miles SW of Knighton off the A44

Once the county town of Radnorshire, the village is overlooked by the remains

of its 11th century motte and bailey **Castle**. Like many other strongholds in this border region, New Radnor Castle suffered at various hands: it was destroyed by King John, rebuilt by Henry III and destroyed again by Owain Glyndwr in 1401. New Radnor was the start point in 1187 of a tour of Wales by Archbishop Baldwin, who was accompanied by the scholar and churchman

Hay on Wye

Giraldus Cambrensis. They preached the Third Crusade, and after the tour Baldwin, the first archbishop to visit Wales, made a pilgrimage to the Holy Land, where he died. Baldwin was the Bishop of Worcester before becoming Archbishop of Canterbury, in which capacity he crowned Richard I.

HAY-ON-WYE

This ancient town, tucked between the Black Mountains and the River Wye in the northernmost corner of the Brecon Beacon National Park, grew up around its Norman castle. Found across the river from the main town centre today, the original motte and bailey was replaced by a stone castle although this was all but destroyed in the early 1400s by Owain Glyndwr. However, a Jacobean manor house has been grafted on to part of the remaining walls and, close by, there are traces of a Roman fort.

Historic though this town may be, it is as the second hand book capital of the world that Hay-on-Wye is best known. Among the town's many buildings can be found a plethora of book, antique, print and craft shops. The first second-hand

bookshop was opened here in 1961 by Richard Booth, owner of Hay Castle, and since then they have sprung up all over the town - the old cinema, many houses, shops and even the old castle are now bookshops, at least 35 in all and with a stock of over a million books. The annual **Festival of Art and Literature**, held every May, draws many to the town, from Germaine Greer and Stephen Fry to Paul McCartney and Bill Clinton.

The impressive **Hay-on-Wye Craft** Centre offers visitors a change from books as well as the opportunity to see craftspeople working at age-old skills such as glass blowing, wood turning and pottery.

GLASBURY

4 miles S of Hay on the B4350

This town was once the site of a Roman station and also of a Celtic monastery, from which the village takes its name - Clas-ar-Wy.

Bronydd Holiday Cottages

Bronydd, Hay-on-Wye, Herefordshire HR3 5RX
Tel/Fax: 01497 820766 website: www.hay-on-wye.co.uk

Bronydd Holiday Cottages, managed by resident owners Gillian and Albert Haver, offer high-quality self-catering accommodation in a superb setting above the hamlet of Bronydd. Recently converted, the five delightful cottages are all comfortably furnished and well equipped. They range from single-storey "Ivy" and "Honeysuckle", sleeping two, through "Chestnut" and "Pine", sleeping four, to "Elm" with four bedrooms on two floors. Each cottage has a fully fitted kitchen with microwave, deep-fryer, toaster and fridge-freezer. Cots are available, and laundry facilities. No pets.

Offa's Dyke Lodge

Gladestry, Nr Kington, Powys HR5 3NR
Tel: 01544 370341 Fax: 01544 370342
e-mail: odl@offtec.ltd.uk
website: www.offas-dyke-lodge.co.uk

Offa's Dyke Lodge lies in the beautiful and tranquil Welsh Marches on the edge of the tiny village of Gladestry. Since buying the property Steve and Una White have completely redecorated and refurnished the Lodge to provide guest accommodation with king-size beds, en suite or private bathrooms, central heating, tv's, bathrobes and tea-making facilities.

Una is a great cook, so guests start the day with a super breakfast. Packed lunches and evening meals can be provided with notice, otherwise there are some outstanding eating places in the vicinity including, the Michelin starred Stagg Inn at Titley, The Waterdine near Knighton and Penrhos Court just outside Kington. The Marches offer exciting entertainment for all the family, including castles, steam trains, and Red Kite feeding. Walking, in particular on Offa's Dyke Path, is a major attraction as are other outdoor pursuits such as cycling, riding and golf. The Lodge has a heated outdoor swimming pool and ample car parking but does not accept pets, smoking or credit cards.

CLYRO

2 miles NW of Hay on the A438

Although little remains of the Roman station that was here, the remains of a motte and bailey castle, built by the fiendish William de Braose, can still be seen. The diarist Francis Kilvert was curate in the village between 1865 and 1872 and, in his journal, he describes both life in the village and the surrounding area. There are Kilvert memorabilia in his former home, now a modern art gallery.

A little way north of Clyro, Cwm Byddog is a 15-acre ancient woodland with pollarded oaks, bluebells in spring, the remains of a motte and bailey castle and a variety of birds, including the blackcap and the garden warbler.

PAINSCASTLE

5 miles NW of Hay on the B4594

Sometimes known as **Castell Paen**, the early motte built in 1130 by Payn FitzJohn was later rebuilt in stone and, by the late 12th century, was in the hands of the notorious William de Braose. The cruelty of de Braose has earned him a place in Welsh folklore and, while he was given the nickname the "Ogre of Abergavenny", his wife Maud is thought to have lived long after his death as a witch. Their names have also been given to several breeds of cattle in Wales including the de Braose Maud and the de Braose David.

In 1198, de Braose's stronghold of Painscastle was attacked by Gwenwynwyn, Prince of Powys, but William and his English army slaughtered over 3,000 of Gwenwynwyn's men and the prince's dreams of a united Wales died along with them. However, de Braose met his match - for cruelty - in King John, who stripped him of his land; de Braose died a pauper.

After her husband's death, Maud suggested that John had also killed his nephew Prince Arthur and for this accusation both she and her youngest son were imprisoned in Corfe Castle with little food to keep them alive. So legend has it that when, some 11 days later, the dungeon door was opened, both prisoners were dead and, in an attempt to keep herself alive, Maud had half eaten the cheeks of her son.

Close to the castle remains is an altogether more pleasant place to visit, the **Tawny Owl Animal Park and Craft Centre**, which lies in the shelter of beautiful hills. Opened in 1998, the park is named after the wild owls that live in the broad leafed woodlands surrounding the farm and, as well as the owls (which are not caged), visitors can also see a whole range of farm animals at close quarters. Along with the animals and the farm trails, there are also traditional country crafts on display and for sale which have been made using methods passed down from generation to generation.

BUILTH WELLS

Another spa town of mid-Wales, Builth Wells lies on the River Wye, which is spanned at this point by a six-arched bridge. The discovery of the saline springs in 1830 helped Builth Wells develop from a small market town into a fashionable spa that became more popular with the arrival of the railways towards the end of the 19th century. As a result, many of the town's original narrow streets are littered with Victorian and Edwardian buildings.

However, the town's history dates back much further than just a couple of hundred years; it grew up around a Norman castle that changed hands many times during the struggles with the

English. The inhabitants of Builth Wells earned the nickname "traitors of Bu-allt" because of their refusal to shelter Llywelyn the Last from the English in 1282 and, as a result, some 20 years later, Llywelyn partly destroyed the Norman stronghold. At the **Castle Mound** only the earthworks remain of the town's 13th century castle that was built by Edward I on the site of the earlier motte and bailey structure. The earthworks can be reached by a footpath from the town centre.

Since the 1963 opening of the **Royal Welsh Show Ground** at nearby **Llanelwedd**, the annual Royal Welsh Show, held in July, has gained a reputation as being the premier agricultural show in the country. Builth Wells is regarded as the centre for farming and agriculture in Wales and the show provides an opportunity for the farming communities to come together

DOL-LLYN-WYDD

Builth Wells, Powys LD2 3RZ
Tel: 01982 553660

Dol-Llyn-Wydd is a charming 17th century farmhouse situated down a quiet farm lane off the B4520 a mile and a half from Builth Wells in glorious walking, touring and bird-watching country. Owner Biddy Williams provides very comfortable bed and breakfast accommodation in four centrally heated bedrooms - one en suite, the others sharing two bathrooms. There's off-road parking and a lock-up garage for bikes. Children over 16 are welcome at the farmhouse, which is a non-smoking establishment. Evening meals by arrangement.

THE PLOUGH HOTEL

26-28 Market Street, Builth Wells, Powys LD2 3EF
Tel: 01982 552553 Fax: 01982 551037

Set on a raised pavement in the centre of Builth Wells, the **Plough Hotel** is a 300-year-old building with a spacious car park at the back. It's owned and run by Andrew Davies who in his time here has refurbished the place to a very high standard and made many improvements to the amenities. Exposed stone walls are among the original features retained, and in the open-plan bar there are plenty of tables and chairs for relaxing with a social drink, a snack or a meal. The food is all freshly prepared, from a sandwich or a snack to a full evening menu.

Guests staying overnight, or longer, have the choice of bed and breakfast or self-catering accommodation. Some on the ground floor which are disabled friendly, others under the eaves. All apartments have a bedroom, fitted oak kitchen, bathroom or shower room and living room.Rooms

have tv, tea tray and toiletries. The Plough also serves as a lively and popular local, with pool, darts and domino teams playing in the local leagues. There's plenty to see in the spa town of Builth Wells, which lies on the River Wye, spanned by a fine six-arched bridge. Spa treatments are a thing of the past, but the town offers excellent fishing, walking, cycling, bird-watching, golfing and bowls. The town also has an indoor swimming pool and a cinema. Builth Wells is central to the Brecon Beacons National Park, Elan Valley Dams and Hay-on Wye bookshops.

at what is considered to be one of the finest and most prestigious events of its kind.

Although spa treatments are no longer available here, Builth Wells remains a popular touring centre and base. As well as the many shops and the weekly market on Mondays, visitors can also enjoy the wide variety of arts and cultural events held at the **Wayside Arts Centre** or take a pleasant riverside stroll through **Groe Park**.

Builth Wells

On the summit of the nearby mountain, **Cefn Carn Cafall**, is a cairn that is said to have been built by King Arthur. The stone on top of the cairn bears the imprint of a dog's paw that, according to local legend, was left by King Arthur's dog, Cafall, while they were out hunting. Arthur built the cairn, placing the stone on top, and then named the peak. The story continues that if the stone is removed it will always return to this spot.

ERWOOD

12 miles S of Llandrindod Wells on the A470

Pronounced "Errod", the village's name is actually a corruption of the Welsh "Y Rhyd" (the ford), a name that harks back to the days when the shallow crossing of the River Wye here was used by drovers. The station at Erwood, closed in 1962, has been turned into a centre for local art and craft.

CILMERY

7½ miles SW of Llandrindod Wells on the A483

It was at this village on the banks of the River Irfon, in 1282, that Llywelyn the Last, while escaping after the abortive battle of Builth, was killed by the English. According to legend, the place where Llywelyn fell and died was once

covered in broom which then ceased to grow on the site - in mourning for the loss of the last native Prince of Wales. Thirteen trees have been planted here to represent the 13 counties of Wales. The rough hewn stone **Memorial to Llywelyn the Last** describes him as "ein llyw olaf" (our last leader) while the English tablet beside the monument calls him 'our prince' Following his death, Llywelyn's head was taken to London and paraded victoriously through the city's streets.

LLANWRTYD WELLS

14½ miles SW of Llandrindod Wells on the A483

Surrounded by rugged mountains, rolling hills and the remote moorland of **Mynydd Epynt**, it was here, in 1792, that the sulphur and chalybeate spring waters were discovered by a scurvy sufferer. As visitors came here in the 19th century, to take the waters in relief of numerous complaints, the town developed. Today, despite being listed as the smallest town in Britain in the *Guinness Book of Records*, Llanwrtyd Wells is still a popular holiday centre, particularly with those who enjoy bird watching, fishing and walking. However, anyone visiting Llanwrtyd

CARLTON HOUSE HOTEL

Llanwrtyd Wells, Powys LD5 4RA
Tel: 01591 610248 Fax: 01591 610242
e-mail: info@carltonrestaurant.co.uk website: www.carltonrestaurant.co.uk

Alan and Mary Ann Gilchrist have earned accolades in hotel and restaurant guides for the **Carlton House Hotel**. The hotel has six well-furnished bedrooms, all with private bathrooms, tv and tea-makers. Downstairs there is a cosy sitting room and a comfortable and well-appointed south-facing dining room, with original 19th century wood panelling. Mary Ann uses only the best produce to create wonderful menus in the restaurant, complemented by an excellent wine list. The restaurant is closed on Sunday evening, when residents can dine in the owners' Bassets Brasserie a minute's walk away.

KILSBY COUNTRY HOUSE

Kilsby, Llanwrtyd Wells, Powys LD5 4TL
Tel: 01591 610281 Fax: 01591 610873
e-mail: kilsbybb@aol.com website: www.kilsbybb.co.uk

Kilsby Country House is an elegant 19th century house, standing in extensive grounds with magnificent views over the upper Irfon

valley. Bed and breakfast accommodation comprises a double/family room and a twin-bedded room with an optional third bed. The rooms are provided with tv, tea and coffee making facilities and hairdryers and guests have exclusive use of a bathroom with shower, separate shower room and WC. Kilsby is a great base for relaxing or walking, mountain biking, pony trekking, fishing or bird-watching, and packed lunches are available on request. Owners Sue and Chris Cooper also offer self-catering accommodation in a delightful two-bedroom cottage.

THE TROUT

Beulah, Nr Llanwrtyd Wells, Powys LD5 4UU
Tel/Fax: 01591 620235
e-mail: suejones123@hotmail.com

Sue Jones and Mike and Liza Crossland are family partners in **The Trout**, an attractive refurbished inn on a prominent corner site where the A483 Llandovery-Builth Wells road meets the B4358 road up to Newbridge and Rhadyer. Tourists, walkers and cyclists take a break from their exertions and join the locals in the bright, cheerful bar for a drink (one or two cask ales always available) and something to eat from the extensive menu, from snacks to a three course meal. Also available are the Oriental boards and Trout Treats.

The Trout is also a good base for a stay in this scenically stunning part of the world, and the five en-suite bedrooms comprise three doubles, a treble and a family room. Tables are set outside under sunshades, and children have an area where they can romp in safety. The owners support various charities throughout the year, including bingo every four weeks. Quizzes take place from time to time, and there's occasional live musical entertainment. Trekking and golf can be arranged at the inn.

Wells will be surprised that somewhere so small could have so many events and festivals throughout the year. The home of the "Man versus Horse" race in May, a Folk Weekend in spring and a late autumn Beer Festival. However the most unusual of all the events held here is undoubtedly the annual **World Bog Snorkelling Championship** that takes place each August.

In the 18th century, William Williams, the poet, hymn writer and one of the leaders of the Methodist revival lived in the town, while another claim to fame is that the Welsh rugby folk song, *Sosban Fach*, was written here in 1895.

On the outskirts of the town lies the **Cambrian Woollen Mill**, which recalls the rich history of Wales' rural past. The first mill was founded in the 1820s, but its modern form dates from 1918, when it was opened by the Royal British Legion for the benefit of servicemen disabled in the Great War. A tour of the mill allows visitors to see traditional cloths being woven while, in the factory shop, there is a wide choice of beautifully finished items to buy.

Found in the hills to the northwest of the town is **Llyn Brianne**, the latest of Wales' man-made lakes, which was opened in 1973.

The dam that holds the water is the highest of its type in the country - at 300 feet - and the grand scale of the lake has to be seen to be believed.

LLANGAMMARCH WELLS

12 miles SW of Llandrindod Wells off the A483

Situated where the Rivers Irfon and Cammarch meet, Llangammarch Wells was the smallest of the Welsh spas and was renowned for its barium chloride carrying waters that were thought to be useful in the treatment of heart and

THE LAKE COUNTRY HOUSE HOTEL

Llangammarch Wells, Powys LD4 4BS
Tel: 01591 620202 e-mail: info@lakecountryhouse.co.uk
Fax: 01591 620457 website: www.lakecountryhouse.co.uk

Fifty acres of immaculate parkland provide a delightfully peaceful and picturesque setting for one of the truly outstanding hotels in Wales. Fine antiques, beautiful paintings, sumptuous sofas and log fires set a traditional, civilised scene in the richly furnished lounges, and pleasant, well-trained staff do their jobs quietly and efficiently. Traditional Welsh tea is a treat to savour every day, served beside log fires in the drawing room or under the chestnut tree in the garden overlooking the River Irfon. In the elegant award-winning restaurant fresh produce and herbs from the garden are used to excellent effect in dishes that combine classic skills with flair and imagination; the fine food is complemented by an outstanding wine list compiled with real knowledge and enthusiasm.

Each of the hotel's superbly comfortable bedrooms has its own charm and character, with fine fabrics, period furniture, pictures and books; every room has a private bathroom, telephone and television. **The Lake Country House** grounds are a haven for wildlife, and guests can fish for trout in the lake. Fishing can also be arranged on the Wye, the Irfon and the Chewfru, and other amenities include a tennis court and billiards room. The area around the hotel is wonderful walking country, and for motorists there's easy access to some of the finest scenery in the whole country.

rheumatic complaints. The old
well and pumphouse are
contained in the grounds of the
Lake Hotel. As well as being the
birthplace in 1559 of John Perry,
who was hanged in London in
1593 for treason, this now sleepy
little town was also the home of
the Theophilus Evans. He was
vicar here, and also wrote a
classical historical interpretation
of the area entitled *View of the
Primitive Age*.

Abergwesyn Pass

ABERGWESYN

14 miles SW of Llandrindod Wells off the B4358

Situated in an isolated spot in the Irfon
Valley, Abergwesyn lies on an old
drovers' route that twists and climbs
through the **Abergwesyn Pass**. Known
as the "roof of Wales", this is a beautiful
pathway that, centuries ago, consisted of
nothing more than dirt tracks, along
which the drovers would shepherd cattle
and other livestock from one market
town to the next. There are actually a
number of drovers' routes which can be
followed - some in part by car. Many of
the roads are narrow and in the south
one such route begins at Llandovery and
travels across the Epynt mountain and
crosses the ford at Erwood.

THE BEACONS

16 Bridge Street, Brecon, Powys LD3 8AH
Tel/Fax: 01874 623339
e-mail: beacons@brecon.co.uk
website: www.beacons.brecon.co.uk

Taking its name from the mountain range that dominates Brecon
and the National Park, **The Beacons** is a handsome Georgian town
house that started life as a riverside farm. Melanie and Stephen Dale
are maintaining a long tradition of hospitality, by concentrating
on personal service and the comfort of guests. The hotel has 14
well-equipped bedrooms, each with its own style and appeal, and
guests can take their ease in an elegant lounge. A good choice of
breakfasts starts the day, and eating by candlelight in the restaurant
provides a relaxed, leisurely end to the evening.

The hotel combines modern comfort and amenity
with abundant period charm: the original spiral staircase,
moulded ceilings and even the meat cellar (now a cosy
bar) all add to the character of this really charming place,
from where it is only a five-minute walk across the River
Usk bridge to the centre of town with its markets,
museums, cathedral and heritage centre. And the Brecon
Beacons National Park offers inspiring scenery,
wonderful walks, all kinds of outdoor activities, and a
legacy that is rich in history.

BRECON

Famous for its ancient cathedral, Georgian architecture and annual Jazz Festival, Brecon lies on the banks of the River Usk, at the confluence of the Rivers Honddu and Tarrell in the heart of the National Park. The first evidence of a settlement in the area are the remains of the Roman fort **Y Gaer** which lie to the west of the town. First built in around AD 75, the fort was rebuilt twice before it was finally abandoned in about 290. A garrison for the 2nd Legion and the Vettonian Spanish cavalry, parts of the fort were excavated by Sir Mortimer Wheeler in 1924 and sections of the outer wall - in places 10 feet high - and traces of gates can be seen.

A walk along the promenade beside the River Usk leads to the remains of medieval **Brecon Castle** which can be found partly in the Bishop's Garden and partly at the Castle Hotel. The town grew up around this castle, which was built in the late 11th century by Bernard of Newmarch. Besieged first by Llywelyn the Last and again during Owain Glyndwr's rebellion in the early 15th century, by the time of the Civil War Brecon considered its growing cloth trade of paramount importance and remained neutral with the townsfolk going so far as to begin dismantling the castle.

Close by stands **Brecon Cathedral**, an impressive and magnificent building that originated from an 11th century cell of the Benedictine monastery at Battle in Sussex. The Priory Church of St John the Evangelist was elevated to a cathedral in 1923 and inside there are many interesting examples of religious artefacts and of the chapels dedicated to craftsmen which once filled the aisle - only that to the corvisors (shoemakers)

BRECON CATHEDRAL - HERITAGE CENTRE, SHOP & PILGRIMS RESTAURANT

Brecon Cathedral Close, Brecon, Powys LD3 9DP
Tel: 01874 625222 Fax: 01874 625894
e-mail: hazelbar@aol.com

For over 900 years the Church of St John the Evangelist has stood on the hill overlooking the Honddu river. It was elevated to cathedral status in 1923 as the Cathedral of the new Diocese of Swansea and Brecon. A 16th century tithe barn in the grounds has been restored and now houses the Cathedral's Heritage Centre that includes an exhibition on the history of the Cathedral from priory church to the present day. Also found here are a shop selling a wide range of gifts and souvenirs, and Pilgrims Restaurant (Tel: 01874 610610).

In addition to providing excellent food in peaceful, friendly surroundings, Pilgrims is a favourite place for celebration lunches or suppers, special occasion dinners and theme evenings. Full inside and outside catering services are offered, and Pilgrim Hampers, hand-prepared and beautifully presented, with traditional and classical recipes faithfully recreated, make superb gifts. The Cathedral is open daily from 8.30 to 6, the Heritage Centre and Shop 10.30-4.30 Monday to Saturday and 12-3 Sunday, the Restaurant 10-5 daily. Access and toilets for wheelchairs, parking next to the Cathedral.

THE GEORGE HOTEL

George Street, Brecon, Powys LD3 7LD
Tel: 01874 623421/2 Fax: 01874 611579
e-mail: reservations@george-hotel.com
website: www.george-hotel.com

The George Hotel enjoys a central location in the historic
town of Brecon, with easy access to the scenic glories of
the Brecon Beacons National Park. Independent owner Ian
Blair has retained all the best features and character of the
building's 17th century origins while providing the up-
to-date comfort and amenities expected by today's visitors;
one of the most striking of the traditional elements is the
handsome 300-year-old central staircase.

The 16 centrally heated en suite bedrooms include a number of suites and family rooms; many
rooms enjoy the luxury of a whirlpool bath, including the
romantic honeymoon suite with its four-poster bed. The
bar, open all day to residents and non-residents, serves a
good selection of real ales, wines from around the world
and bar snacks, and the full à la carte menu is available in
the bar, restaurant and conservatory. Across the courtyard,
Mr Dickens, the hotel's Victorian eating house, specialises
in dishes cooked on a traditional open stone kiln. The
George is a popular venue for special occasions, private
functions and conferences; the Regency Suite can
comfortably seat 120 and has its own bar facilities.

BOOKS, MAPS & PRINTS
AND MOUNT STREET GALLERY

7 The Struet, Brecon, Powys LD3 7LL
Tel/Fax: 01874 622714

Books, Maps & Prints is a Welsh interest bookshop
with a large stock of books, walking guides, South
Wales engravings and antiquarian maps of the area,
cards and photographs. The shop, housed in 15th
century premises, also provides a complete picture
framing service. The shop is owned and run by
Wimke and Andrew Wakley. Wimke has a

background in interior design for the hotel and leisure industry and Andrew has long family connections
with Brecon; they took over the Struet business in January 2001.

The shop is linked by a stone spiral staircase to
the Wakleys' other enterprise, Mount Street Gallery,
which was opened in May 2002 by Roger Williams,
MP. The bright, spacious gallery holds regularly
changing exhibitions showcasing high-quality
artwork by Welsh artists or artists with Welsh
connections.. The inaugural exhibition covered
painting, hand-spun textiles, pottery, woodturning,
photography and jewellery. Entry is free to the gallery,
which is open from 10 to 5 Monday to Saturday
except Wednesday afternoons.

remains. Housed in a 16th century tithe barn is the cathedral's imaginative **Heritage Centre.**

Found in another of the town's old buildings, the elegant former Old Shire Hall, is the **Brecknock Museum** where visitors can see the old assize court as well as take in the extensive collection of artefacts and other items from past centuries including the museum's large collection of Welsh love spoons. The

Abergavenny Canal, Brecon

town's second museum is equally fascinating and the **South Wales Borderers Museum** features memorabilia of the regiment's famous defence of Rorke's Drift. Over 300 years of military history are recorded here through various displays that include armoury, uniforms and medals - the regiment has taken part in every major campaign and war and has won 29 Victoria Crosses and over 100 Battle Honours. However, though its history is long and varied, it is the regiment's participation in the Zulu wars that is best remembered and which

PETERSTONE COURT

Llanhamlech, Brecon, Powys LD3 7YB
Tel: 01874 665387 Fax: 01874 665376

On a site that dates back at least as far as the 14th century, **Peterstone Court** was built in 1741 and retains 18th century style and proportions. Comfort and convenience are watchwords here, and the eight guest bedrooms, together with four split-level studios in converted stables, guarantee a quiet, relaxing stay. All the rooms have en suite facilities and a host of thoughtful extras, from dressing gowns and quality toiletries to videos, cassette players and a complimentary glass of sherry. The hotel's restaurant has built up a fine reputation for its award-winning cuisine, which makes imaginative use of local produce and is complemented by an extensive wine list.

A private salon is available for intimate dinner parties, and the hotel is a popular venue for wedding receptions, banquets and small conferences. Guests have unlimited access to the Health Club, whose amenities include a gym, sauna, spa bath and solarium. Llanhamlech is situated off the A40 between Abergavenny and Brecon, close to Llangorse Lake and all the delights of the Brecon Beacons National Park.

OLD FORD INN

Llanhamlach, Brecon, Powys LD3 7YB
Tel: 01874 665220 (accommodation) 01874 665391 (bar &
restaurant) e-mail: enquiries@theoldfordinn.co.uk
website: www.theoldfordinn.co.uk

In a spectacular setting on the A40 on a ridge looking across to
the Brecon Beacons, the **Old Ford Inn** combines a well-preserved
traditional charm with the up-to-date comfort that today's traveller needs. In the cosy oak-beamed
bars and non-smoking restaurant food is served lunchtime and evening, with real ale and a selection
of wines to accompany. Upstairs, the inn has eight comfortable bed and breakfast rooms with en suite
facilities, tv and beverage tray. Private parties and functions can be catered for by forward booking.

CAEBETRAN FARM BED & BREAKFAST

Felin Fach, Brecon, Powys LD3 0UL
Tel/Fax: 01874 754460 e-mail: hazelcaebetran@aol.com

Caebetran Farm, standing high on a hillside commanding breathtaking
views, is a traditional Welsh longhouse dating from the 17th century
which owners Gwyn and Hazel have modernised without losing any of
its period character. All the guest bedrooms are en suite, with tv, tea-
making facilities, hairdryer, iron and many little extras. There is a comfortable lounge, and in the
dining room guests can enjoy good home cooking featuring home-reared beef and lamb and local
produce. Visitors are free to look round the farm, and all round the property there are quiet country
lanes, ancient hedgerows and abundant wildlife. Caebetran is a non-smoking establishment.

LLANGOED HALL

Llyswen, Brecon, Powys LD3 0YP
Tel: 01874 754525 Fax: 01874 754545
e-mail: llangoed_hall_co_wales_uk@compuserve.com
website: www.llangoedhall.com

The site on which **Llangoed Hall** stands has been occupied by a
number of distinguished buildings down the centuries, possibly
including the home of the first Welsh Parliament in 560 AD.
The present building dates from the 17th century, but was
restored and largely redesigned by Sir Clough Williams-Ellis of Portmeirion fame, who transformed it
into a magnificent Edwardian country house. Splendidly situated in a valley of the River Wye, the
hotel owes much of its splendour and its status as the top hotel in Wales to the endeavours of its
owner, Sir Bernard Ashley, many of whose marvellous paintings grace the walls of the Great Hall and
other public rooms, which also boast open fires, Oriental rugs and handsome antique furniture.

A sweeping staircase leads up to the large, sumptuously appointed bedrooms, each one with its
own style and charm, and all generously supplied with thoughtful extras such as fresh fruit and
spring water. The bathrooms are equally opulent, with huge towels and luxurious toiletries. The food

at Llangoed Hall is as outstanding as the accommodation,
and chef Richie Herkes and his brigade produce dishes that
are both visually stunning and a delight to the palate; the
fine food is complemented by a wine list long in choice
and quality. A regal breakfast starts the day in style, and
guests can spend a happy hour or two in the maze or on
the tennis court or croquet lawn. Fishing is available a few
minutes' walk away.

was immortalised in the film *Zulu* starring Michael Caine. It recalls the heroic defence of Rorke's Drift in 1879, when 141 men from the regiment were attacked by 4,000 Zulus; nine VCs were awarded here in a single day.

As well as having the River Usk flowing through the town, Brecon is also home to the **Monmouthshire and Brecon Canal**, a beautiful Welsh waterway which once used to bring coal and limestone into the town. There are attractive walks along the canal towpath along with pleasure cruises on both motorised and horsedrawn barges while the canal basin in the town has been reconstructed and is now proving to be an attraction in its own right.

Anyone thirsty from all the sightseeing can either take advantage of the many pubs, inns, restaurant and cafés in the town or pay a visit to the **Welsh Whisky**

BRECKNOCK WILDLIFE TRUST

Lion House, Bethel Square, Brecon, Powys LD3 7AY
Tel: 01874 625708. Fax: 01874 610552
e-mail: brecknockwtgcix.co.uk
website: www.waleswildlife.co.uk

The Brecknock Wildlife Trust is part of the UK wide movement of county based Wildlife trusts. It is a registered charity operating in the county of old Breconshire, now the southern portion of Powys. To achieve its objectives of protecting wildlife and the habitats required for wildlife to thrive, the Trust owns and manages 18 nature reserves, provides advice to planners, landowners and farmers, operates species projects and promotes a greater understanding of wildlife and the environment through lifelong learning opportunities for adults and children. The Brecknock Wildlife Trust is a membership organisations and its members play a significant role in carrying out the work of the Trust. In a voluntary capacity, members work with local schools, undertake practical projects on nature reserves and in the local community, carry out surveys, adopt local roadside verges and campaign for wildlife.

Distillery and Visitor Centre An audio-visual presentation explains the history of whisky making through the ages and, after a tour of the distillery, visitors can sample a tot in the well-stocked gift shop. Well-known natives of Brecon include Dr Hugh Price, founder of Jesus College, Oxford, and the actress Sarah Siddons. Besides the Jazz Festival, the town holds a monthly farmers' market, and November 15th 2002 sees the start of the three-day Georgian Festival, which

THE GRIFFIN INN

Llyswen, Brecon, Powys LD3 0UR
Tel: 01874 754241 e-mail: info@griffin-inn.freeserve.co.uk
Fax: 01874 754592 website: www.griffin-inn.co.uk

Rena and Peter welcome visitors to the **Griffin Inn**, a splendid 16th century coaching inn located in the beautiful Wye Valley. Behind the ivy-clad facade the old-world charm survives intact, with old beams and fireplaces creating a cosy, inviting atmosphere. Local produce and fish delivered fresh from

Cornwall feature on the daily-changing menu, and there's always a good choice for vegetarians. For guests staying overnight there are comfortable, well-appointed en suite bedrooms, one with a four-poster. Rooms are let on a bed and breakfast or dinner, bed and breakfast basis.

THREE COCKS HOTEL AND RESTAURANT

Three Cocks, Nr Brecon, Powys LD3 0SL
Tel: 01497 846215 Fax: 01497 847339
website: www.threecockshotel.com

The Three Cocks Hotel and Restaurant is a rambling, old-fashioned hostelry of great charm and character. Dating back in part to the 15th century, it is owned and run by Michael and Marie-Jeanne Winstone, who have given the place a unique ambience. The hotel is richly furnished with antiques, oil paintings and Oriental rugs, and the seven immaculate en suite guest bedrooms have been tastefully modernised. Mouthwatering dishes using top-quality organic ingredients, accompanied by carefully chosen wines and beers , are served in the dining room overlooking the tranquil garden. Well-behaved children welcome .

includes a costume ball and a sedan chair race.

LLANFRYNACH

2 miles S of Brecon on the B4458

Housed in an 18th century warehouse, the **Canal Museum** tells the story of life on the canal. Horse-drawn boat trips start from here, and sometimes a blacksmith can be seen at work.

LIBANUS

4 miles SW of Brecon on the A470

To the northwest of this attractive hamlet, on Mynydd Illtyd common, lies the **Brecon Beacons Mountain Centre**, where visitors can find out about the **Brecon Beacons National Park** from

displays and presentations; there are also some interesting remains to be seen in the area. **Twyn y Gaer**, a Bronze Age burial chamber, and **Bedd Illtyd**, a more modest ancient monument said to be the grave of St Illtyd, the founder of the monastery at Llantwit Major. Brecon Beacons are a small part of the National Park. The Beacons, including the sandstone peaks of **Pen y Fan** and **Corn Du**, were given to the National Trust in 1965 and have become one of the most popular parts of the UK with walkers. (At 886 metres, Pen y Fan is the highest point in southern Britain.) The area is also important for sub-alpine plants and is designated a Site of Special Scientific Interest. But the very popularity of the Beacons with walkers has caused great problems, exacerbated by military manoeuvres and the sheep that have grazed here since Tudor times. Erosion is the biggest problem, and the National Trust has put in place an ambitious programme of footpath and erosion repair. There are many ways in which members of the public can help the Trust, and information is available from the National Trust, Dan-y-

Pen y Fan

CAMBRIAN CRUISERS

Ty Newydd, Pencelli, Brecon,
Powys LD3 7LJ
Tel: 01874 665315
e-mail: cambrian@talk21.com
website: www.cambriancruisers.co.uk

Bob and Nicola Atkins operated a hotel boat on the Monmouthshire & Brecon Canal before taking over **Cambrian Cruisers** as a going concern in 1998. They are based three miles south of Brecon at the northern end of the canal, hiring out modern narrow boats designed and built specifically for use on the Mon and Brec. Comfortable, spacious and well-planned, the boats have every modern convenience. They are powered by quiet, water-cooled diesel engines which provide plenty of steaming hot water and also charge the batteries that power the electric equipment (fluorescent lights, fridge, razor point, tv, radio/cassette player, hairdryer). The boats, which sleep two or four, are available for hire from mid-March to late October. Weekly hire or short breaks available. Pets allowed on some boats. All the boats are annually inspected by the tourist board.

With the Black Mountains and the Brecon Beacons as a backdrop, the Mon and Brec is definitely a jewel among waterways. At Brynich, an aqueduct takes the canal high above the River Usk. The boats travel through a 360-metre tunnel at Ashford as well as under many traditional-style stone bridges and lift-bridges. There are only six locks in the 35 cruising miles, and the 24-mile lower pound is one of the longest lock-free sections of canal in Britain.

Gyrn, Blaenglyn, Libanus, Brecon, Powys LD3 8NF. Tel: 01874 625515.

YSTRADFELLTE
12 miles SW of Brecon off the A4059

This small village is a recognised hiking centre and the area of classic limestone countryside around it is one of the most impressive in the British Isles.

The narrow road heading north from the village climbs sharply and squeezes its way along a narrow valley between **Fan Llia** on the east side and **Fan Nedd** on the west. The **Maen Madog** is a nine-foot high standing stone with a Latin inscription proclaiming that Dervacus, son of Justus, lies here.

To the south of Ystradfellte is **Porth-yr-Ogof**, a delightful area with a collection of dramatic waterfalls as the River Mellte descends through woodland.

Porth-yr-Ogof

YSTRADGYNLAIS

18½ miles SW of Brecon on the B4599

Situated at the top end of the Tawe Valley, which stretches down to the city of Swansea, and close to the boundary of the Brecon Beacon National park is Ystradgynlais, a former mining community. A place rich in industrial heritage, iron was produced here as far back as the early 17th century and the legacy of this industrious past can still be seen, although the area surrounding Ystradgynlais is known as waterfall country and is popular with walkers, ramblers and cavers.

A local legend tells of three cauldrons, filled with gold, that are buried beneath **Y Garn Goch** - the red cairn - on the summit of Mynydd y Drum, to the east of the town. The story goes that one day a young girl will come to claim the treasure which until then is protected by demons. To prevent anyone trying to take the gold, the legend also tells of a wizard and his apprentice who attempted to overcome the demons with their magic. While the elements raged, a spirit on a wheel of fire swept the apprentice out of the protective circle he had made and gave him a lighted candle, saying that as long as the candle burned his life would last. As soon as the candle was spent the apprentice died and the wizard, terrified, fled from the mountain.

CRAIG-Y-NOS

15½ miles SW of Brecon on the A4067

The **Dan-yr-Ogof Showcaves**, the largest complex of caverns in northern Europe, lie to the north of this village. Discovered in 1912, the caverns have taken 315 million years to create and they include both the longest and the largest showcaves in Britain. Exploring these underground caverns is only one aspect of this interesting attraction as there is also an award winning **Dinosaur Park**, where life size replicas of the creatures that roamed the earth during Jurassic times can be seen, and the **Morgan Brothers' Shire Horse Centre**, where the massive horses, the wagons they pulled and other farm animals are on show. The replica **Iron Age Farm** gives a realistic idea of how the farmers lived so long ago.

To the east of the village lies **Craig-y-Nos Country Park**, where visitors can enjoy the unspoilt countryside and the landscaped country parkland of the upper Tawe Valley. The mansion in the country park, known as **Craig-y-Nos Castle**, was once the home of the 19th century opera singer Madame Adelina Patti. She bought the estate in 1878 as a home for her and her second husband, the tenor Ernesto Nicolini. She installed an aviary, a little theatre modelled on Drury Lane and a winter garden that was

subsequently moved to Swansea's Victoria Park. Patti was born in Madrid in 1843, the daughter of a Sicilian tenor, and achieved fame in New York at an early age. Her first husband was the Marquis de Caux, her second Ernesto Nicolini and her third the Swedish Baron Cedarström, whom she married in the Roman Catholic church at Brecon in 1898.

SENNYBRIDGE

7½ miles W of Brecon on the A40

Situated along the southern edge of the Mynydd Epynt and on the northern border of the Brecon Beacons National Park, this village is very much a product of the industrial age as it only began to develop after the railways arrived here in 1872 and Sennybridge became a centre for livestock trading. However, the remains of **Castell Ddu**, just to the west

of the village, provides evidence of life here from an earlier age. Dating from the 14th century and believed to stand on the site of an 11th century manor house, this was the home of Sir Reginald Aubrey, a friend of Bernard of Newmarch. two new waymarked walks have been opened on the Sennybridge army training area, beginning at **Disgwylfa Conservation Centre** on the B4519. The centre has an interactive learning centre and military and conservation displays. One of the walks is accessible for disabled visitors.

CRICKHOWELL

Situated in the beautiful valley of the River Usk and in the shadow of the Black Mountains that lie to the north, Crickhowell is a charming little town with a long history. The town takes its

LLWYNON SADDLERY

Trecastle, Nr Brecon, Powys LD3 8RG
Tel/Fax: 01874 638091
e-mail: enquiries@llwynonsaddlery.co.uk
website: www.llwynonsaddlery.co.uk

Graham Butt and his team run one of the best equipped saddleries and suppliers of riding accessories in the land. **Llwynon Saddlery**, voted the best tack shop in the UK two years running, carries a range of items to suit all needs and all budgets, and the services offered include saddle

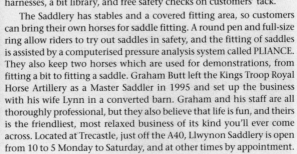

repairs, saddle fitting, rug washing and repairs, hand-stitches made-to-measure tack and harnesses, a bit library, and free safety checks on customers' tack.

The Saddlery has stables and a covered fitting area, so customers can bring their own horses for saddle fitting. A round pen and full-size ring allow riders to try out saddles in safety, and the fitting of saddles is assisted by a computerised pressure analysis system called PLIANCE. They also keep two horses which are used for demonstrations, from fitting a bit to fitting a saddle. Graham Butt left the Kings Troop Royal Horse Artillery as a Master Saddler in 1995 and set up the business with his wife Lynn in a converted barn. Graham and his staff are all thoroughly professional, but they also believe that life is fun, and theirs is the friendliest, most relaxed business of its kind you'll ever come across. Located at Trecastle, just off the A40, Llwynon Saddlery is open from 10 to 5 Monday to Saturday, and at other times by appointment.

MAESWALTER

Heol Senni, Nr Brecon, Powys LD3 8SU
Tel: 01874 636629
e-mail: maeswalter@talk21.com

Maeswalter is a 300-year-old farmhouse centrally located in the Brecon Beacons National Park in the quiet, picturesque valley of Heol Senni. The centrepiece of a no longer working farm, Maeswalter provides a warm welcome from owner Joy Mayo and comfortable bed and breakfast accommodation in three bedrooms (one en suite) with tv, tea/coffee making facilities and magnificent views across the Senni Valley. Beams and open fires create a lovely traditional atmosphere, and home cooking adds to the attractions of a stay here. Heol Senni is a small farming community of quiet, unspoilt beauty.

The nearest shops are four miles away in the market village of Sennybridge, and the numerous attractions and amenities of Brecon are an easy nine-mile drive to the east. Maeswalter is an excellent base for a short break or a more extended stay. Tourists, sportsmen and lovers of the great outdoors are in their element, and the house itself is surrounded by breathtaking scenery in an area that is a haven for wildlife, including the red kite.

THE CHEESE PRESS

18 High Street, Crickhowell, Powys NP8 1BE
Tel: 01873 811122 Coffee Shop: 01873 810167

The Cheese Press is a family business established in 1980 in the main street of Crickhowell, a charming little town in the beautiful valley of the River Usk. The current owner is Garth Roberts, and throughout the ground-floor and basement the shop is stocked with an amazing range of gifts for all ages and tastes. Greeting and art cards, books for children and grown-ups, soft toys, framed pictures, jugs and mugs and bowls, lamps, china ornaments, clocks, trinket boxes, hats and scarves, fabrics, nightwear, pottery by Nicholas Mosse and Emma Bridgewater..... the list

goes on, and the gifts are not the only attraction, as one end of the shop is set with rustic tables and chairs to cater for the many locals and tourists who combine browsing with a cup of tea or coffee or a glass of wine, perhaps accompanying a delicious home-made cake, a salad or a slice of quiche.

With its castle and its famous bridge, Crickhowell is a good place for pottering, but no serious potterer should leave before looking in at The Cheese Press, a splendid combination of Aladdin's Cave and favourite refreshment stop where every visit is guaranteed to produce fresh ideas for gifts and fresh cakes for tea.

name from the Iron Age fort, **Crug Hywell** (Howell's Fort) that lies on the flat-topped hill above the town that is aptly named Table Mountain. The remains of another stronghold, **Crickhowell Castle** - once one of the most important fortresses in this mountainous region of Wales - can be found in the town's large park. Built in the 11th century, only the motte and two shattered towers remain

Crickhowell

of the Norman fortress that was stormed by Owain Glyndwr and abandoned in the 15th century.

The picturesque and famous **Crickhowell Bridge**, which dates from the 16th century, spans the River Usk in the heart of the town. Still carrying traffic today, the bridge is unique in that it has 13 arches on one side and only 12 on the other! For the rest, this is a pleasant place, with some fine Georgian architecture which, due to its close

Continued on page 193

THE BEAR HOTEL

High Street, Crickhowell,
Powys NP8 1BW
Tel: 01873 810408 Fax: 01873 811696
e-mail: bearhotel.co.uk
website: www.bearhotel.co.uk

Built as a coaching inn over 500 years ago, the **Bear Hotel** maintains its tradition of hospitality under proprietors Judy Hindmarsh and her son Stephen. Famed far beyond the boundaries of Wales this most atmospheric and likeable of country inns offers an exceptional combination of welcoming ambience, great character, fine food and comfortable accommodation that has won it many top accolades, including Best Pub in Britain (twice). Though renowned far and wide, it's also a great favourite with the local community, and the bar, with its log fire, low beams and antiques, is a marvellous place to meet for a drink and a chat.

The bar menu and the à la carte restaurant menu both make excellent use of fresh seasonal local produce and home-grown herbs in dishes that combine the best ingredients - salmon from the Usk and Wye, local game, Welsh lamb - with well-practised skills and a generous measure of flair. Most of the bedrooms are set around a courtyard which in summer boasts a splendid show of colour from flower tubs and hanging baskets. The rooms, each with its own front door leading off the balcony, all have en suite bathrooms, tv telephone, hairdryer and tea/coffee making facilities. Some of the rooms feature beautiful antiques, and the top-of-the-range rooms boast four-poster beds and jacuzzis. A delightful suite with separate sitting room is located in a converted cottage at the end of the garden.

WALK 6

Mynydd Llangorse

Start	Cockit Hill. Small parking area on bend at highest point of minor road 1¾ miles (2.8km) east of Llangors village
Distance	5½ miles (8.9km)
Approximate time	3 hours
Parking	Parking area at Cockit Hill
Refreshments	none
Ordnance Survey maps	Landranger 161 (Abergavenny & The Black Mountains), Outdoor Leisure 13 (Brecon Beacons National Park – Eastern area)

This circuit of Mynydd Llangorse provides superb and ever-changing views for remarkably little effort. The only strenuous section is the steep climb between Ⓐ and Ⓑ out of the valley of Cwm Sorgwm on to the moorland plateau. The walk along the western slopes is particularly enjoyable; the path is tree-lined at times and there are spectacular views over Llangorse Lake to the line of the Brecon Beacons.

First head southwards down the lane and after a few yards bear right on to a track which keeps parallel to the lane but later bears gradually right away from it. Follow the track along the side of Cwm Sorgwm and below the eastern slopes of Mynydd Llangorse for about 1¼ miles (2km). About 100 yds (91m) before reaching a metal gate, bear right Ⓐ on to a grassy path which heads up the hillside, clips a fence corner and then continues more steeply uphill.

Follow the path first around a sharp right-hand bend, then around a left-hand bend, bear right to reach the top and continue along a grassy path through bracken and heather to a

prominent cairn Ⓑ. The only strenuous part of the walk is now over and from the cairn there are superb views over the Black Mountains and the Usk valley.

Continue past the cairn to join another path and bear right along it to head over the open, breezy moorland on top of Mynydd Llangorse. Stay on the main path all the while, keeping right at two successive forks, to reach a crossroads of paths and tracks just in front of a small group of stunted trees, a rarity on this windswept plateau.

Here turn left on to a broad, grassy track and follow it across the moorland, gradually curving left and heading gently downhill to a crossroads by a fence corner and another cairn **C**. Turn right to keep parallel to the fence on the left and where it ends continue ahead. Now there is the first of a series of superb and ever-changing views across Llangorse Lake and the Usk valley to the main peaks of the Brecon Beacons. The path curves to the right to contour along the western slopes of Mynydd Llangorse. Descend to go through a gate, continue, passing to the right of a cottage and on across a meadow, before descending again through conifer woodland. Bear right, go through a gate and continue down through the wood. Cross a track and keep ahead along an attractive tree-lined path, by the bottom edge of woodland and with a wire fence on the left.

Go through a gate to leave the wood and continue, keeping by a fence on the left for almost the remainder of the walk. The western slopes of Mynydd Llangorse are more wooded than those on the eastern side and this part of the walk makes a striking contrast with the early section.

Ford a stream and continue, taking the

right-hand, upper path at the fork just in front. Ahead the view is now dominated by the distinctive bulk of Mynydd Troed. Eventually the path veers slightly right away from the fence and then leads directly back to the starting point. ●

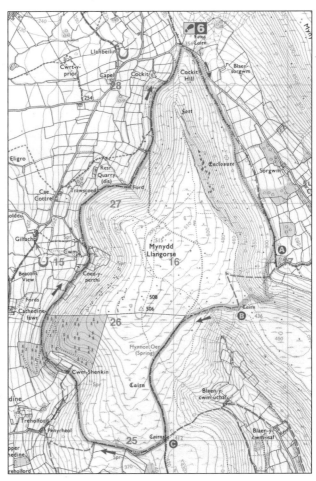

GLIFFAES COUNTRY HOUSE HOTEL

Crickhowell, Powys NP8 1RH
Tel: 01874 730371 Fax: 01874 730463
e-mail: calls@gliffaeshotel.com
website: www.gliffaeshotel.com

Fishing is one of the favourite pastimes at Gliffaes Country House Hotel, where Susie and James Suter are the third generation of the Brabner family to be at the helm. The house was built in the 1880s in Italianate style, with a dominant campanile at each end, and at the same time a superb Victorian garden was created that was redesigned in 1948 and is to this day one of the hotel's

many delights. Quality, comfort, relaxation, great food and wine, genuine friendliness and a host of activities are what Gliffaes is about, and the 22 bedrooms, all with private bathrooms, offer space, style, elegance and views of either the gardens or the river. Cots or camp beds can be put into the rooms for younger children, and a simple early evening supper can be laid on for children in the conservatory.

The sitting room and drawing room are superb places for taking it easy, and the 33 acres of stunning landscaped gardens and woodland are perfect for gentle strolls. For the sportier guests there's a tennis court, croquet lawn and golf putting green and practice net, while snooker players have the use of a full-size table. But above all Gliffaes is a fishing hotel, and

certainly one of the best in the land: the hotel overlooks the River Usk, and two and a half miles of beats provide superb salmon and brown trout fishing. The hotel offers packages of two days trout fishing and either a bar lunch or packed lunch on each day plus a fly box of 10 Usk flies. Dogs are welcome in the grounds but not inside the hotel. With so much to do, visitors need never leave the grounds, but there is also a host of attractions in the locality, including walking in the Brecon Beacons or the Black Mountains, playing golf at several excellent courses, boating, riding, cycling, and visiting the many castles and historic sites.

NANTYFFIN CIDER MILL INN

Brecon Road, Crickhowell, Powys NP8 1SG
Tel/Fax: 01873 810775
e-mail: cidermill@aol.com
website: www.cidermill.co.uk

Top-quality bistro food brings the crowds from near and far to **Nantyffin Cider Mill** at the junction of the A40 and A479. This multi-award winning historic drovers' inn, widely regarded as one of the very best food pubs in the UK, is run by chef-owner Sean Gerrard and Jessica and Glyn Bridgeman. Welsh produce is showcased in superb dishes like old spot pork and Caerphilly cheese stuffed mushrooms or roast Glanusk mallard with blackberry and cassis sauce and poached figs. A mile away is sister establishment The Manor Hotel.

THE MANOR HOTEL

Brecon Road, Crickhowell, Powys NP8 1SE
Tel: 01873 810212 Fax: 01873 811938

High on a hillside in the Black Mountains range, **The Manor** is a lovely country house hotel with 23 individually styled, en suite bedrooms with tv and telephone. The views are spectacular, the food excellent, and the hotel's other attractions include a leisure suite and swimming pool. Half a mile west of Crickhowell on the A40, The Manor is run by the same team as the nearby Nantyffin Cider Mill. These and nine other independent businesses form The Silurian Retreats, whose aim is to provide the best in food, accommodation or both in the Brecon Beacons.

proximity to the Black Mountains and the National Park, is popular with those looking for outdoor activities including walking. Close by is **Pwll-y-Wrach Nature Reserve** in a steep-sided valley. Owned by the Brecknock Wildlife Trust, this woodland reserve has a waterfall and also a great variety of flora, for which it has been designated a Site of Special Scientific Interest.

LLANGATTOCK

1 mile SW of Crickhowell off the A4077

The village church, which was founded sometime during the early 6th century, is dedicated to St Catwg, one of Wales' most honoured saints. Born in around AD 497, by the end of his life, in around 577 Catwg, had become a Bishop and had taken the name Sophias.

RED LION INN

Llanbedr, Crickhowell, Powys NP8 1SR
Tel/Fax: 01873 810754
e-mail: redlion@barbox.net

The Red Lion, in the heart of the Black Mountains, is one of the most delightful and welcoming little inns in the region. Dating back to the 16th century, with abundant period character provided by low beams and open fires, the inn is owned and run by Jackie and Owen Hart, whose regular local custom is boosted by a growing following of walkers, cyclists and tourists in cars. Thirsts are quenched by a wide selection of well-kept real ales (Hancocks HB, Brains Reverend James) and hungers satisfied by wholesome home-cooked meals using local produce as far as possible.

To the southwest of the village, towards the boundary of the Brecon Beacons National Park lies the **Craig-y-Cilau Nature Reserve**. With over 250 plant species and over 50 kinds of birds breeding within the reserve, this is one of the richest in the National Park.

LLANGYNIDR

4 miles W of Crickhowell on the B4558

Rising to the south of this riverside village on the open moorland of Mynydd Llangynidr, lies the **Chartists' Cave**, where members of the movement stored ammunition during their active years in the mid-19th century.

TRETOWER

2½ miles NW of Crickhowell on the A479

This quiet village in the Usk Valley is the home of two impressive medieval buildings - **Tretower Court and**

Tretower Castle (both in the hands of CADW). The elder of these historic sites is the castle where all that remains on the site of the original Norman motte is a stark keep that dates from the 13th century. The castle was built in this valley to discourage Welsh rebellion but, nonetheless, it was besieged by Llywelyn the Last and almost destroyed by Owain Glyndwr in 1403. Adjacent to the bleak castle remains lies the court, a magnificent 15th century fortified manor house that served as a very desirable domestic residence particularly during the less turbulent years following Glyndwr's rebellion. While the 15th century woodwork here and the wall walk, with its 17th century roof and windows, are outstanding, it is the court's **Gardens** that are particularly interesting. The original late 15th century layout of the gardens has been

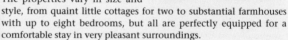

recreated in such a manner that the owner of the time, Sir Roger Vaughan, would have recognised them. Among the many delightful features there is a tunnel arbour planted with white roses - Sir Roger was a Yorkist - and vines, an enclosed arbour and a chequerboard garden. Tretower Court's Gardens are best seen in the early summer.

TALYBONT-ON-USK
7 miles NW of Crickhowell on the B4558

Just beyond this attractive village, the Monmouthshire and Brecon Canal passes through the 375 yard long Ashford Tunnel while, further south still, lies the **Talybont Reservoir**. In this narrow wooded valley on the southeastern slopes of the Brecons there

are several forest trails starting from the car park at the far end of the reservoir.

LLANGORSE
8 miles NW of Crickhowell on the B4560

To the south of the village lies the largest natural lake in South Wales - **Llangorse Lake** (Llyn Syfaddan). Around four miles in circumference and following its way round a low contour in the Brecon Beacons the waters of this lake were, in medieval times, thought to have miraculous properties. Today, the lake attracts numerous visitors looking to enjoy not only the setting but also the wide variety of sporting and leisure activities, such as fishing, horse riding and sailing, that can be found here. There is also a Rope Centre, with

THE USK INN

Station Road, Talybont-on-Usk, Brecon, Powys LD3 7JE
Tel: 01874 676251 Fax: 01874 676392
e-mail: stay@uskinn.co.uk website: www.uskinn.co.uk

Hands-on owners Michael and Barbara Taylor have a combined time in the business exceding 50 years! No wonder they have succeeded in transforming this formerly run down pub into a Village Inn that's aim is to exceed customers expectations, and does so time and again. Established in the 1840s around the time of the Brecon-Merthyr railway the inn has seen much change over the years even though it now enjoys its original name. Thanks to the efforts of the Taylor's and their enthusiastic staff it is now a popular destination for visitors to the National Park whether simply as tourists, enjoying the great outdoors or touring around in classic cars.

The rooms, all individual in size, decor and character, are named after birds found along the nearby river Usk, some have queen size beds, and there is a four-poster. The Usk is definately food led, having been awarded a rosette and named pick of the pubs by the AA. A seasonal menu is backed up by two blackboards which both make excellent use of the produce of the park.

Dishes include shank of lamb, and pork loin from Cae Crwn Farm at Battle, not forgetting Venison from Middlewood Farm in Bwlch and there's also lots of fish, which brings the inn yet another award.Lunch times are much more laid back with their own menu and in addition for just £10 there is a three course lunchtime table d'hote, which includes a glass of wine! The wine list is extensive and good beer is available - largely from within Wales. When it's cold there's a log fire in the cosy bar and children are welcome in an inn that provides high chairs, a kids menu and even a toy basket.

ABERCYNAFON LODGE

Abercynafon, Nr Talybont-on-Usk, Brecon, Powys LD3 7YT
Tel/Fax: 01874 676342
e-mail: gaynor.gatehouse@virgin.net
website: www.visitourbeacons.com

Jill Carr and her family welcome visitors to **Abercynafon Lodge**, which is idyllically situated in an acre of garden at the head of Talybont Reservoir. Guest accommodation, in a separate wing of the house, comprises three centrally heated bedrooms - a twin with en suite shower room, and a double and a single with private bathrooms. Guests also have their own lounge overlooking the garden, and there's a separate dining room where breakfasts and the optional evening meals are served. Special diets and packed lunches can be catered for by prior arrangement.

SHIWA LODGE & THE LAURELS

Llangorse, Powys LD3 7UG
Tel: 01874 658631 e-mail: marie-gray@shiwa-lodge.fsnet.co.uk
Fax: 01874 658144 website: www.shiwa-lodge.fsnet.co.uk

Proprietors Marie and John Gray offer two properties of immense character for bed and breakfast accommodation near Brecon. **Shiwa Lodge**, in the small village of Llangorse and overlooking the lake of the same name, is a former farmhouse now totally restored under the inspiration of a house in Northern Zambia called Shiwa N'Gandu (the Lake of Royal Crocodiles). Marie grew up in Zambia and has filled her guest house with African wall hangings and artefacts. The house has three letting bedrooms with tv and hostess trays offering disabled, family and twin or double accommodation with en suite shower rooms. Breakfast is served in the conservatory overlooking the garden, the lake and the Brecon Beacons. This room, the lounge and the garden are at the disposal of guests throughout the day, and the house is a perfect base for a touring holiday, or for walking, birdwatching, painting or boating on Llangorse Lake. The aim of the owners at Shiwa Lodge is to offer a glimpse of Africa, and also to help people in Zambia and Zimbabwe who are struggling to survive in

difficult financial conditions. Some of the objects in the house are donated to the Grays, who make payment by way of supporting Zambian charities. Smoking is not allowed here or at the owners' other bed and breakfast property, **The Laurels**, in Church Street, Bronllys, Powys LD3 0HS Tel: 01874 712188 Fax: 01874 712187. The Laurels is a large Victorian family house offering comfortable accommodation in en suite bedrooms with tea/coffee-makers. The house has a roomy guest lounge with tv, plenty of parking and a lock-up for cycles.

THE OLD VICARAGE COTTAGE

Llangorse, Brecon, Powys LD3 7UB
Tel: 01874 658639 Fax: 01874 658161
e-mail: maryanderson@oldvic45.fastnet.co.uk
website: www.tuckedup.com

Next to the Old Vicarage in Llangorse, the Cottage is set in quiet, attractive grounds in the centre of the village but away from the road. Mary Anderson's cottage is a lovely spot for a self-catering holiday, with all the amenities and the wonderful scenery of the Brecon Beacons within easy reach. Accommodation comprises a dining/sitting room with tv and a piano, a fully equipped kitchen and a cloakroom/WC and upstairs, reached by a wide staircase, two double bedrooms with a bathroom and WC. A cot or extra bed is available on request.

Llangorse Lake

cruel and greedy princess. Though her lover was poor, she agreed to marry him only if he brought her great riches. So the lover set out to complete his task and in so doing robbed and murdered a wealthy merchant, giving the riches to his princess. However, the merchant's ghost returned to warn the happy couple that their crime would be avenged, not on them but on the ninth generation of their family. One night, years later, a great flood burst from the hills, drowning the surrounding land and its inhabitants; it is still said today that a city can been seen under the water.

climbing, abseiling, potholing, log climbing and a high-level rope course.

Naturally, the lake is associated with a legend and local stories suggest that the land beneath the lake once belonged to a

DOLYCOED

Talyllyn, Brecon,
Powys LD3 7SY
Tel: 01874 658666

Dolycoed is a substantial Edwardian house set in lovely gardens four miles east of Brecon within the Brecon Beacons National Park. Mary Cole and her family moved here from the Home Counties in the mid-1980s and began providing bed and breakfast accommodation; the family have now gone, but Mary, the most charming of hosts, continues to offer guests a warm, personal welcome and a comfortable stay in bedrooms that are quietly furnished in a style that is in keeping with the origins of the house. A glazed front porch leads into the hall with its brightly tiled floor and ground floor rooms that retain all their original wood and plasterwork.

Dolycoed is a very pleasant, civilised place for a break in the country, and guests start the day with a good breakfast before setting out for a day exploring the local places of scenic and historic interest. It's an easy drive from Dolycoed to Brecon, famous for its ancient cathedral, fine Georgian buildings and annual jazz festival. Even closer is the lovely Llangorse Lake, the largest natural lake in South Wales. Four miles round, it attracts visitors with its scenic setting and its wide variety of sporting and leisure activities.

TALGARTH

10½ miles N of Crickhowell on the A479

Lying in the foothills of the Black Mountains, Talgarth is an attractive market town with narrow streets that boasts many historic associations as well as some fine architecture. The 15th century parish **Church of St Gwendoline** has strong links with Hywell Harris (1714-73), an influential figure in the establishment of Welsh Methodism. Harris was also instrumental in establishing a religious community, The Connexion, which was organised on both religious and industrial lines.

Although this is now a quiet and charming place, Talgarth once stood against the Norman drive into Wales. Some of the defensive structures can still be seen today - the tower of the church and another tower that is now incorporated into a house - though it has also served time as the jail.

On the outskirts of Talgarth lies **Bronllys Castle** a well-preserved centuries old keep built by the Norman baron Bernard of Newmarch. Originally a motte and bailey castle, it was later replaced with a stone edifice and now it is a lone tower standing on a steep mound that is in the hands of CADW - Welsh Historic Monuments.

6 CEREDIGION

Ceredigion's countryside features some of the most beautiful landscapes in Wales and this county also attracts many rare species of birds, wildlife and plants. In particular, it is home to the graceful red kite and keen birdwatchers are well served by nature reserves around the Teifi and Dyfi estuaries and at Llangranog, New Quay and Cors Caron.

Ceredigion means the land of Ceredig, son of the Celtic chieftain Cunedda. Dating from around AD 415, the region is steeped in history and tradition. It is renowned for its unique brand of Welshness and, within Wales, its inhabitants are affectionately known as "Cardis". The patron saint of Wales, St David, was born in Ceredigion and many famous Welsh princes are buried in the ruins of Strata Florida Abbey. The region is not as well endowed with castles as the counties further north, but Aberystwyth and Cardigan castles both saw fighting before they were left to ruins, and Cardigan is credited with being the venue for the first recorded Eisteddfod in 1176.

Teifi Valley, Cenarth

Perhaps, though, this county is best known for its coastline on the great sweep of Cardigan Bay. Many of the once fishing villages have now become genteel resorts but few seem to have attained the great degree of brashness that is associated with other seaside holiday destinations. In the north of the county and close to the mouth of the River Dyfi is the great expanse of sand at Borth while, further south, the coastline gives way to cliffs and coves - once the haunt of smugglers.

While much of Ceredigion can be classed as very Welsh and very rural, it is also an important area of learning. St David's College at Lampeter, a world renowned ecclesiastical establishment, is now, as University College, part of the University of Wales, while Aberystwyth is home not only to the first university in Wales but also to the National Library of Wales.

LOCATOR MAP

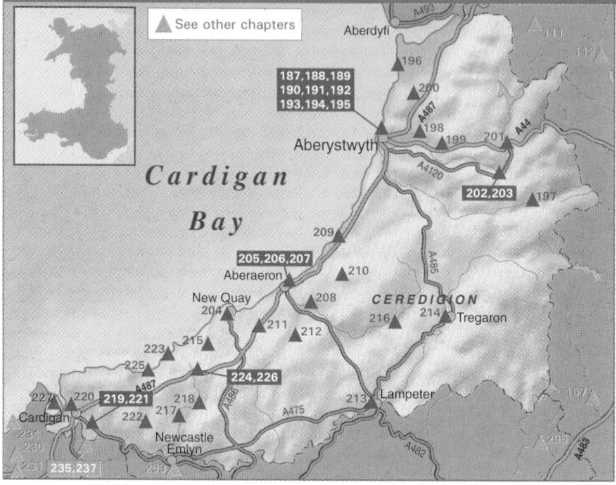

See other chapters

Aberdyfi

Cardigan

Bay

187,188,189
190,191,192
193,194,195

Aberystwyth

202,203

209

205,206,207
Aberaeron

New Quay
204

208   210   *CEREDIGION*
216   214   Tregaron
211   212

223
225
224,226
219,221   218   213   Lampeter
220   217
Cardigan   222

Newcastle
Emlyn

235,237

© MAPS IN MINUTES ™ 2002   © Crown Copyright, Ordnance Survey 2002

ADVERTISERS AND PLACES OF INTEREST

ABERYSTWYTH

The largest town in Cardigan Bay, the seat of local government and the home of the University College of Wales and the National Library of Wales, Aberystwyth is not only the unofficial capital of mid-Wales but also a cosmopolitan coastal resort. Although there is evidence that the town is older, Aberystwyth as we know it can certainly be traced back to the late 13th century when, in 1277, Edward I began building **Aberystwyth Castle** and also granted a charter that made the settlement around the new fortification a free borough with a ditch and wall, a guild of merchants, a market and two fairs. Constructed to subdue the Welsh, the castle withstood a siege in 1282 by the Welsh but in 1404 it fell to Owain Glyndwr during fighting that destroyed the surrounding town. Glyndwr made the castle his base for four years and it became an important seat of government until, in 1408, it was recaptured by Prince Henry (who later went on to become Henry V). In 1637, Thomas Bushell was given permission to set up a mint within the castle, and during the Civil War the silver coins minted here for Charles I were needed to pay the Royalist soldiers, as Cromwell had taken control of the mints in London. However, the castle finally fell to the Parliamentarians in 1646 and Cromwell destroyed the building some three years later. Today, the ruins, standing on the rocky headland, remain an impressive sight. Also on Castle Point can be found the town's **War Memorial**, a splendid monument that was commissioned the year after World War I ended; it is the work of the Italian sculptor Mario Rutelli.

In the years following the turmoil of the Civil War, and before the arrival of the railways, Aberystwyth remained essentially a fishing town, but with a

---

THE TREEHOUSE ORGANIC FOODSHOP & RESTAURANT

14 Baker Street, Aberystwyth, Ceredigion SY23 2BJ
Tel: 01970 615791 website: www.aber-treehouse.com

At the **Treehouse**, the aim of Jane Burnham and her partners is to produce and sell high-quality organic food grown in a way that causes the least impact on the environment and brings the most benefit to the local community.

The foodshop, open from 9 to 5 Monday to Saturday (to 7 on Friday) sells an amazing selection of fresh organic fruit and vegetables, organic meat from Graig Farm in Powys, and a great choice of dairy produce, wholefoods, bread, eggs and other organic produce. The shop can deliver boxes of the best seasonal produce to pick-up points in the Aberystwyth area.

Meals served in the restaurant above the shop are cooked with

seasonal organic fruit and vegetables, many grown in their market garden. Hot meals are served from 12 to 4 Monday to Saturday, and teas, coffees and cakes can be enjoyed all day, from 9.30 to 5.30. Burgers, quiches, pizza and filled baked potatoes are joined by daily specials that could be anything from broccoli bake to dressed crab to a warm tortilla wrap filled with roast chicken, rice, cottage cheese, chilli, garlic and grapes, served with a salad garnish. Teas, coffees, soft drinks and organic beers and wines provide the liquid accompaniment

VALE OF RHEIDOL RAILWAY

Park Avenue, Aberystwyth, Cerdigion SY23 1PG
Tel: 01970 625819 Fax: 01970 623769
website: www.rheidolrailway.co.uk

2002 is Centenary Year for the **Vale of Rheidol Railway**, which offers passengers an unforgettable journey through the spectacular Rheidol Valley by narrow-gauge steam train. Trains leave Aberystwyth from a station adjacent to the British Rail station, setting out on a journey of almost 12 miles to Devil's Bridge that is a delight from beginning to end. The train has to surmount a height difference of over 600 feet on its journey, affording superb views of the valley.

At Devil's Bridge there are toilets, a café and a picnic area. The famous Mynach Falls, Jacob's Ladder and the Devil's Punchbowl are tourist attractions within walking distance of this station. Trains run daily from Easter until the end of October with some exceptions in low season. The V of R opened in 1902 to serve the lead mines, the timber trade and the passenger traffic of the valley. The gauge is only 1' 11¾" but the three locomotives are more than eight feet wide and each weighs more than 25 tons. For most of its life the V of R was in the hands of the Great Western Railway, and the Swindon-built locomotives had (two of them still have) all the familiar GWR trappings of green livery, copper-capped chimneys and brass nameplates for the locomotives and a chocolate and cream livery for the carriages.

The locomotives are 7 *Owain Glyndwr*, 8 *Llewelyn* and 9 *Prince of Wales*. The line survived many changes of ownership and threats of closure; by 1968, all steam had disappeared from BR except this little line, which was then in the hands of the London Midland Region. It passed into private hands in 1989, since the owners have undertaken major renovation programmes that have seen the rebuilding of the rolling stock, the renewal of the track and the opening up of marvellous views not seen for decades. Truly, The Vale of Rheidol Railway is one of the Great Little Trains of Wales.

growing shipbuilding industry. Although much of this industry has now ceased, **Aberystwyth Harbour and Marina** is still a bustling place that can accommodate over 100 vessels, and at the town quay all manner of fish and seafood are landed.

The arrival of the railways in the 1860s saw the town expand rapidly as first the Victorians and then the Edwardians made their way here to enjoy the sea air and the beauty of the great sweep of Cardigan Bay. The town's 700 foot long **Pier** was constructed in 1864 and the Pavilion at the end was added in 1896 to provide a capacious venue for light entertainment. Just to the north, along the coast from the town centre, lies the longest electric **Cliff Railway** in Britain (see panel on page 205) - another product of the Victorian development which still carries passengers up the cliff

Aberystwyth War Memorial

THE OLD WELSH CELLAR

19 Pier Street, Aberystwyth, Ceredigion SY23 2LJ
Tel: 01970 627121
e-mail: tatchbowden@angelfire.com

2002 saw the opening of an excellent new delicatessen in the centre of Aberystwyth. **The Old Welsh Cellar** is owned and run by Andy Tatch, and his spacious shop is literally chock full of good things. Andy is an expert on cheese, and the 50 or so on display include 10 Welsh varieties. He also stocks a good range of sugar-free chocolates, vegetarian cheeses and patés, pasta, Welsh mead and fruit wines, as well as a wonderful range of chilli products, including sauces and condiments.

PLAS ANTARON HOTEL

Southgate, Aberystwyth, Ceredigion SY23 1SF
Tel: 01970 611550 Fax: 01970 627084
e-mail: plas.antaron@tinyworld.co.uk

Top-to-toe refurbishment by owners John and Gloria Gifford has added to the long-established appeal of **Plas Antaron Hotel**, whose overnight accommodation comprises 10 bedrooms with an Edwardian theme and smart new fabrics. All have en suite or private bathroom, tv and tea-making facilities; several are suitable for families, and a cot and high chair are available. Plas Antaron is not only a comfortable hotel but also a popular local meeting place serving a good range of beers, snacks and meals. A large function room is used for wedding receptions, parties, conferences and meetings.

THE MECCA TEA & COFFEE MERCHANTS

25 Chalybeate Street, Aberystwyth,
Ceredigion SY23 1HX
Tel: 01970 612888

Devotees of fine coffee can follow their noses to
The Mecca Tea & Coffee Merchants, located
behind a traditional, red-painted shop front in the
centre of Aberystwyth. Using their knowledge of

the tea and
coffee trade,
Iain Halliday

and Elaine Dean moved to Wales to open this marvellous little place,
where 68 different coffees and numerous flavoured varieties provide
what could be the largest choice in the country for lovers of the
magical bean.

The coffee is sold in various quantities, either as beans or ground
to customers' requirements. The range of teas is no less impressive,
and the shop also stocks a wide selection of coffee and tea makers
and accessories. The shop is open from 8 in the morning to 7 in the
evening Monday to Saturday. This is where you buy, while over the
road at 26 is where you get to taste the delicious brews.

In addition to the over-the-counter sales, products are also
available by mail order.

THE MECCA COFFEE HOUSE

26 Chalybeate Street, Aberystwyth, Ceredigion

This wonderful little coffee house, its walls adorned
with art deco mirrors and moody café photographs,
stands opposite The Mecca Tea & Coffee Merchants
and is run by that owner's partner Elaine Dean.
Customers come to **The Mecca Coffee House** to
enjoy a cup or two of some of the best tea or coffee
they'll ever taste. The teas run from the Mecca
Breakfast Blend to speciality teas such as Ceylon
Pekoe, jasmine or rooibos to tisanes, while the coffee
options include regular filter, the traditional French

favourite café au lait and several variations on
espresso - espresso con panna is "graced by a
crescent of whipped cream".

To accompany the refreshing cup are fresh-
baked croissants, Danish pastries and viennoiserie
and some wonderful, individually hand-made cakes
from a superb local chef-patissier. For the savoury
tooth there are sandwiches with tempting fillings
like brie with cranberry, hummus with an olive
tapenade, or chicken, apricot and walnut in a
creamy mayonnaise. This always busy place keeps
the same hours as the Merchants opposite - 8 till 7
Monday to Saturday.

face at a sedate four miles an hour. From the summit there are panoramic views over the bay and, inland, to the Cambrian Mountains. Opened nearly 100 years after the railway was laid, and also on the cliff summit, is the **Great Aberystwyth Camera Obscura**, housed in an octagonal tower. A faithful reconstruction of a popular Victorian amusement, the huge 14 inch lens - the biggest in the world - gives visitors an even better view from this excellent vantage point.

Aberystwyth by Night

While the town today certainly seems to cater to holidaymakers' every need, Aberystwyth is also a seat of learning. The **Old College** was originally built, to JP Seddon's design, in the 1870s and it was intended to be a hotel designed to accommodate the influx of Victorian visitors. However the venture failed and in 1872 the high Gothic building was

sold, becoming the first university in Wales and now home to the departments of Welsh, Education and Theatre, Film and Television. With such an intellectual heritage it is not surprising that the town is also the home of the **National Library of Wales**, one of only six copyright libraries in Great Britain and the keeper of the majority of materials that relate to the Welsh people

ABERYSTWYTH CLIFF RAILWAY

Cliff Railway House, Cliff Terrace, Aberystwyth, Ceredigion SY23 2DN
Tel/Fax: 01970 617642

Aberystwyth's Constitution Hill boasts two unique attractions. One is the world's biggest camera obscura, the other Britain's longest electric cliff railway.

Aberystwyth Cliff Railway, the only one in Wales, was opened in 1896 and rises 430 feet in its 778 feet of undulating track. It travels at a sedate four miles per hour, and passengers arriving at the summit enjoy superb views over the bay and, inland, to the Cambrian Mountains.

The camera obscura is on the summit, along with a gift shop and a café serving afternoon teas and home-cooked snacks. The railway is managed as a charitable trust by Margaret Walters, who was once a driver on it.

Trains run every few minutes from 10 to 5 mid-March to early November (10 to 6 in July and August).

MARINE HOTEL

The Promenade, Aberystwyth, Ceredigion SY23 2BX
Tel: 01970 612444 Fax: 01970 617435
e-mail: marinehotel@barbox.net
website: marinehotel@aberystwyth.com

A warm Welsh welcome awaits guests at the **Marine Hotel**, whose
attractive blue-and-white frontage has long been a feature on the
promenade at Aberystwyth. Nerys Evans and her staff pay every
attention to the comfort of their guests, many of whom have become old friends, and the 35 bedrooms,
all en suite, with tv and tea-makers, provide everything needed for a peaceful, comfortable stay; the
top-of-the-range suites include extras such as saunas or jacuzzis. A hearty breakfast starts the day,
which might be spent exploring the lovely coast and countryside, which are ideal for walking and for
picnics - the hotel can provide hampers for guests wanting to make the most of a day in the open air.
In the evening, dinner in the elegantly appointed dining room makes use of the finest local produce,
and the spectacular Cardigan Bay sunsets add an extra touch of magic.

The lounges, bars and restaurants all enjoy ocean views, and the hotel has a leisure suite with
sauna, steam room, sunbeds and keep-fit equipment. There are
conference facilities for up to 200 delegates, and the Atlantic
ballroom is a popular spot for wedding receptions and other special
occasions. Nerys Evans also owns a new luxury guest house set in
peaceful surroundings on a sheep farm four miles from Aberystwyth.
Llety Ceiro Country Guest House (Tel: 01970 821900) has 10 well-
equipped bedrooms, including one specially designed for disabled
visitors, and serves bar meals and evening meals.

ABERYSTWYTH ARTS CENTRE

University of Wales, Aberystwyth, Ceredigion SY23 3DE
Tel: 01970 622889 Fax: 01970 622883
e-mail: lla@aber.ac.uk website: www.aber.ac.uk/artscentre

Aberystwyth Arts Centre is a vital part of the life and work of the
University of Wales and is situated at the heart of the campus, well
signposted from the A487 going north from the town centre. After the
completion of a £4 million redevelopment programme, the 2000/2001
season was the start of a new era for the Centre, and its impressive facilities
have made it, as the *Western Mail* put it, "a
national flagship for the arts". The
programme, with participants from all over
the world, attracts 76,000 visitors to 373
live performances, and 37,000 attendees at
2,469 classes, workshops and other
educational events each year.

On the visual arts side, the year saw 25 exhibitions and 958
educational events; there were festivals of classical music, literature and
ceramics, and 360 screenings in the cinema. 2002 is just as busy and
promises to be even more successful, with a non-stop run of events that
range from a theatre production of *My Beautiful Laundrette* to a Japanese
modern dance group, a summer music festival, a David Bailey exhibition
and courses on activities as diverse as banner making and belly dancing.
The Centre has a stunning glass-fronted craft and design shop and a
number of cafés and bars.

and their culture. Founded in 1909 and eventually opened in 1937 by George VI, the library holds many early Welsh and Celtic manuscripts among which is the *Black Book of Carmarthen*, a 12th century manuscript that is the oldest in Welsh. An enhanced Visitor Centre and other new facilities opened in 2002. Housed in a beautifully restored Edwardian music hall, right in the centre of the town, is the **Ceredigion Museum**. Described as "probably the most beautiful museum interior in Britain", it tells the history of Cardiganshire through an interesting collection of materials: the history of seafaring, agriculture and silver and lead mining are all well chronicled. St Michael's Church is the home of the **Welsh Christian Centre**, with an exhibition and film about the history of the Christian faith in Wales. Those interested in all things equestrian will enjoy a visit to the **Welsh Pony and Cob Museum**, where the history of these animals, which have been so important to the Welsh economy, can be traced.

ANIMALARIUM

Borth, Ceredigion SY24 5NA
Tel: 01970 871224

Borth is home to one of the top visitor attractions in mid-Wales. At their **Animalarium**, Jean and Alan Maidens have a wonderful collection of exotic, unusual and interesting creatures brought in from rescue centres, the RSPCA, other zoos or pet shops. Also here are breeding pairs and colonies of endangered species whose natural habitat is under threat. The reptile house is a favourite with visitors, and there's always a crowd at feeding time for the piranhas and crocodiles. The Animalarium shelters a wide mix of animals and birds, including fruit bats, iguanas, lemurs, lynxes, meerkats, parakeets, pygmy goats, snakes and wallabies. Open all year round.

BORTH

5½ miles N of Aberystwyth on the B4353

The original settlement of this now popular seaside resort lies on the slopes of Rhiw Fawr and it is there that some of the older fishermen's and farmer's cottages can still be seen. The growth of the village began with the arrival of the railway linking it with Aberystwyth in the 1860s and its long, safe, sandy beach, along with the spectacular views out over Cardigan Bay and inland to the

Continued on page 211

ESGAIR WEN

Tyllwyd, Cwmystwyth, Nr Aberystwyth, Ceredigion SY23 4AG   Tel: 01974 282216
website: www.welshaccommodation.co.uk

The Welsh-speaking Raw family offer a true Welsh welcome "Croeso Cymreig!" at Esgair Wen, their delightful self-catering cottage overlooking the upper part of the Ystwyth Valley. This W.T.B. four star graded property is on a 1,300-hectare sheep farm, located on one of the AA's 2001 most scenic routes in Britain. It has been sympathetically modernised to retain the charm and character of its past, with a great sense of place. Seven guests can be accommodated in style and comfort. It is a perfect place for visiting the many local places of interest or relaxing in the peace and tranquillity of this quiet unspoilt countryside.

Borth and Sarn Gynfelyn

Start	Borth
Distance	6 miles (9.7km)
Approximate time	3 hours
Parking	Borth
Refreshments	Pubs and cafés at Borth
Ordnance Survey maps	Landranger 135 (Aberystwyth), Explorer 213 (Aberystwyth & Cwm Rheidol)

The walk follows the spectacular clifftop path, which is narrow and often near the edge, from the seaside resort of Borth to the intriguing shingle ridge of Sarn Gynfelyn, said to be an ancient causeway belonging to the submerged land of Cantre'r Gwaelod. The route then takes a grassy lane inland to join the B4572 to Borth. Although this is a back road it can be busy at times and due care should be taken.

Borth was changed from a tiny fishing hamlet to a resort – boasting a 4-mile (6.4km) beach with a fossil forest at its northern end – with the coming of the railway in 1863. You can still arrive here by train on the line between Aberystwyth and Shrewsbury. Borth also has a good bus service to and from Aberystwyth, and the 108-mile (174km) long-distance Dyfi Valley Way terminates here.

Begin from the car park and bus-stop beside the lifeboat station. Facing this, go left to walk with the sea on your right. Turn right along a "no through road" to keep above the sea and at the end of the road continue along the clifftop path. Reach the war memorial **A** .

Continue along the coastal path going south from Borth, keeping the sea on your right. Look out for Sarn Gynfelyn extending into the sea. Imagine, whilst walking above the sea, that you are overlooking a fertile plain. This would be the legendary Cantre'r Gwaelod "Lowland Hundred". Scientists agree that it did exist, perhaps around 3500 BC, when there may have been some earthquake or other natural disaster at a similar time to the submerging of land around the Scilly Isles that gave rise to the legend of Lyonesse. If so, the rich legends of its drowning are extremely old. These are usually reckoned to date from about AD 500.

Sarn Gynfelyn extended from Wallog to the principal settlement of Cantre'r

Gwaelod, Caer Wyddno, the city of Gwyddno Garanhir, who protected his territory with sea walls and appointed Seithenyn as a gate-master. One night Seithenyn was drunk and neglected his duties, with the result that the sea broke through and drowned the land. The drunkard's sons tried to atone for their negligent father by taking holy orders, so they can be traced to 6th-century churches. Gwyddno ended his days as an impoverished fisherman at Borth. One day his son, Elphin, fished a baby boy out of the River Dyfi and named him Taliesin – but that is another story.

Descend to the start of Sarn Gynfelyn at Wallog **B**. Cross a footbridge over the stream here and leave the coastal path by turning left inland along a track. Go through a gate, pass below a house on your right, continue through a second gate and keep with this track all the way to its junction with the B4572 road **C**.

Turn left to follow this road the 2½ miles (4km) back to Borth. If conditions

permit, you could extend this walk by continuing along the beach past the fossil forest to Ynyslas Nature Reserve, which is situated at the mouth of the River Dyfi.

PLAS DOLAU COUNTRY HOUSE

Y Gelli, Lovergrove, Aberystwyth, Ceredigion SY23 3HP
Tel: 01970 617834
e-mail: pat.twigg@virgin.net website: www.dolau-holidays.co.uk

A drive off the A44 west of the junction with the A4159 leads to the **Plas Dolau Holiday Centre**, where owner Patricia Twigg offers a variety of accommodation to, meet most requirements. First along the drive is Y Gelli, a modern guest house in Swedish farmhouse style, providing bed and breakfast accommodation with packed lunches and evening meals by arrangement. The family suite includes a jacuzzi bathroom and an interlinked room with full-size bunk beds and a cot. Other bedrooms are a single, a double and two twins upstairs and an en suite twin downstairs.

All rooms have tv and tea/coffee making equipment and there's a comfortable guest lounge with tv and video. Further along the drive is Plas Dolau, a former dower house that provides warm and comfortable accommodation for groups and

individuals. The west wing has three bedrooms, one en suite, a lounge-dining room with tv, video and piano and a kitchen with Aga, gas cooker, microwave, dishwasher and fridge. In the main house are five dormitory rooms with a mixture of beds and bunks, kitchen, dining room and spacious lounge.

The west wing and the main house can between them sleep up to 45, making a convenient base for a wide range of groups. Among those who have appreciated its capacity and freedom are school and youth groups, family reunions, walkers, fishermen - even a German church choir. There's plenty to explore around Plas Dolau, including mountains and moorland, forests and meadows, valleys and coastland, and Aberystwyth, just a couple of miles along the road, offers shops, pubs, restaurants and a wealth of leisure amenities, as well as plenty of historic sites and buildings. Plas Dolau is in the Vale of Rheidol, and the V of R railway, one of the Great Little Trains of Wales, is a popular local attraction.

The grounds include a small farm, mainly pasture grazed by cattle and sheep, with a couple of ponies and goats. There are wooded lanes for walks, and the old gardens are being restored to allow space for barbecues and other outdoor activities, and additional parking.

mountains, have ensured that it is still a much used holiday destination.

At a very low tide it is possible to see the remains of a submerged forest that, according to local legend, once formed part of the dynasty of Cantre'r Gwaelod (the Lower Dynasty) which extended out into the bay and was protected by a huge sea wall. One night the gatekeeper is said to have had too much to drink and had forgotten to close the gates against the rising tide that, with the help of a storm, drowned the forest and the dynasty.

To the east of the village lies **Borth Bog** (Cors Fochno), an important area of raised coastal peat mire (one of only two such areas in Europe) that supports an abundance of wildlife.

YNYSLAS
7½ miles N of Aberystwyth off the B4353

Situated at the northern end of Borth beach, Ynyslas - the name means Green Island - extends to the Dovey estuary, where there are broad expanses of sand, particularly at low tide, although the swimming is unsafe. The **Ynyslas Sand Dunes and Visitor Centre** explains the natural beauty of the Dyfi in wildlife displays and slide shows. There is also a conservation shop selling books, stationery and "green" pocket money gifts. From the centre there are glorious views over the river mouth to Aberdovey.

EGLWYS FACH
11 miles NE of Aberystwyth on the A487

Found in the sheltered waters of the Dovey estuary, the **Ynyshir RSPB Nature Reserve** is the home of a great many species of birds, in particular waders. It has an extensive network of walks, with bird watching hides, where visitors in winter can observe the reserve's unique flock of Whitefronted Geese from

CWMWYTHIG FARMHOUSE & COTTAGES

Cwmwythig, Capel Bangor, Nr Aberystwyth, Ceredigion SY23 3LL Tel/Fax: 01970 880640
e-mail: pwll@ukgateway.net website: www.pwll.ukgateway.net

In Cwmwythig Farmhouse & Cottages, farmer's wife Mrs Evans offer a choice of bed and breakfast and self-catering accommodation at Capel Bangor, four miles east of Aberystwyth off the A44 road to Llangurig. The four star farmhouse overlooking the Vale of Rheidol has a double ensuite and twin bedroom on the ground floor and private facilities and a single, double and twin upstairs. Each has a tv, beverage tray and numerous thoughtful extras, and guests have their own comfortable lounge and the use of a pleasant garden. Guests are regaled with a complimentary Welsh tea on arrival.

There's a golf club almost on the doorstep, and a riding school nearby. On the other side of the A44 are a number of self-catering cottages, some detached, others adjoined, sleeping from four to twelve guests. All are single-storeyed, tastefully furnished and equipped with all the modern conveniences; cots and high chairs are available on request. Guests can relax in the garden or on the patios, admiring the views or perhaps enjoying a barbecue. Guests at the farmhouse and the cottages can travel on the famous Vale of Rheidol narrow-gauge railway at a discount.

LLETY CEIRO COUNTRY GUEST HOUSE

Lon Ceiro, Llandre, Bow Street,
Nr Aberystwyth, Ceredigion SY24 5AB
Tel: 01970 821900 Fax: 01970 820966
website: www.marinehotelaberistwith.com

Llety Ceiro is a new luxury guest house set in the peaceful Eleri Valley four miles from Aberystwyth and just two from the popular seaside resort of Borth. The house is furnished and fitted to the highest standards, and the 10 en suite bedrooms are superbly equipped with everything from tv and

telephone to an iron, trouser press, hair dryer and a safe. One room is fully adapted for disabled guests, and top of the range is a romantic suite complete with jacuzzi.

Llety Ceiro has a bright, roomy conservatory lounge, a licensed bar serving home-cooked dishes and a stylish restaurant for evening meals. There are private car parking facilities, and bicycles can be supplied for touring the locality. It's also a good base for walkers, and the Aberystwyth Group of the Ramblers' Association has produced a leaflet with details of two pleasant walks from Bow Street.

Greenland and also the smaller flock of Barnacle Geese. It is the most important breeding site in Wales for lapwings and redshanks. The nature reserve's Visitor Centre has much information on the various species of birds found here.

FURNACE
10½ miles NE of Aberystwyth on the A487

This quaint old village was, in the 18th century, home to a iron ore smelting foundry and, today, **Dyfi Furnace** is an important early industrial site that has one of the country's best preserved charcoal burning blast furnaces. The bellows that pumped the air into the furnace were powered by a huge waterwheel driven by the River Einion and visitors here can see the wheel (now restored to working order) as well as tour this industrial heritage site and museum.

The road opposite Dyfi Furnace leads up the **Cwm Einion** - Artists' Valley - which is so called because it was once a favourite haunt of 19th century watercolourists. As well as seeing the remains of a silver lead mine, walkers climbing up the valley will find pleasant woodland trails and picturesque picnic spots.

TRE'R-DDOL
8 miles NE of Aberystwyth on the A487

The former medieval deerpark, **Lodge Park**, is now managed by Forest Enterprise, who have restored this semi natural woodland and have also preserved the northern boundary of the park that comprised a ditch and bank. The Wesleyan chapel in Tre'r-ddol was bought, in 1961, by a Mr RJ Thomas to house his folk object collection. He left this collection to the National Museum of Wales and it is now administered by

LLYWERNOG LEAD & SILVER MINE

Ponterwyd, Aberystwyth, Ceredigion SY43 3AB
Tel: 01970 890620 Fax: 01545 570823
website: www.silverminetours.co.uk

The mining of silver-rich lead ore was an important industry in the Plynlimon Mountains of mid-Wales in the 1860s. Most of the mines were later abandoned but **Llywernog Lead & Silver Mine** survived and was saved from dereliction by the late Dr Stephen Harvey and his son Peter, who now run this seven-acre heritage site. Visitors can follow the Miners Trail, take the underground tour to the Great Chasm and see the working water wheels, mining machinery and mineral displays. The site, which has a souvenir shop and tea room, is open from mid-March to the end of October; closed Mondays except Bank Holidays and July/August.

Aberystwyth's Ceredigion Museum.

TRE TALIESIN

7½ miles NE of Aberystwyth on the A487

This village was the home, in the 6th century, of one of the earliest recorded British poets, Taliesin. He is thought to have been buried here. The standing stone behind the village, **Bedd Taliesin** (Taliesin's Grave), actually dates from the Bronze Age (around 15000 BC) and while it marks a burial chamber it is unlikely to be that of the poet.

PENRHYNCOCH

4 miles NE of Aberystwyth off the A487

This is another village associated with one of Wales' great poets: Dafydd ap Gwilym was born just a short distance from Penrhyncoch. Although little remains of Gwilym's house except a small pile of stones, his medieval poetry lives on.

LLANBADARN FAWR

1 mile E of Aberystwyth on the A44

Although this village has now become a suburb of Aberystwyth, it was once a town in its own right and, in the 6th century, St Padarn established a small monastery here. For over 600 years, the monastery and the church were dominant despite the merging of the bishopric at Llanbadarn - the oldest in

Wales - with that of St David in the 8th century. The present **Church** dates from the 13th century and contains St Padarn's tomb as well as two Celtic crosses that are associated with St Samson, Padarn's brother.

LLYWERNOG

9 miles E of Aberystwyth on the A44

Just to the north of the village lies the **Llywernog Lead & Silver Mine** (see panel above), a museum that covers the

Llywernog Lead and Silver Mine

history of this major rural industry in mid Wales. This mine opened in 1740 and had its most prosperous period between 1850 and 1879. In the slump that followed most of the mines closed for good, but Llywernog refused to die and was briefly reopened in 1903 as a zinc prospect. It was saved in 1973 by the present owners.

PONTERWYD
10 miles E of Aberystwyth on the A44

An inn called the Borrow Arms remembers George Borrow, who came here to dry out after falling into a peat bog. Norfolk born, Borrow was a noted philologist and linguist who travelled widely overseas, acting for a time as an agent for the British and Foreign Bible Society. Later, he tramped around England and Wales, sometimes with his step-daughter, and in 1862 published his best-known work *Wild Wales*. Close by is the **Nant yr Arian Visitor Centre**, a Forest Enterprise centre with forest walks and trails, a mountain bike trail, orienteering course, tea room, local crafts, and picnic and play areas. Here, too, is the **Kite Country Centre** and feeding station. Designated the Bird of the Century in 1999, the **Red Kite** was a fairly common bird in the Middle Ages, seen even in London scavenging in the

streets. It was at that time considered useful and was even protected by the Crown, but with the passing of the Enclosures Act in the 16th century this impressive bird was among many species thought to be a threat to agriculture. Persecuted as vermin, they disappeared entirely from England and Scotland, but a few pairs remained in mid-Wales. With care and conservation efforts from individuals and organisations, the numbers gradually increased, so that now there are more than 300 breeding pairs in Wales. At 2 o'clock each afternoon throughout the year the kites swoop down to be fed, joined by other species looking for an easy meal, including crows, buzzards and ravens. Other red kite feeding stations in Wales are at Gigrin Farm near Rhayader, Powys, and Tregaron in Ceredigion, the latter feeding in winter only. More information on red kites is available from the Welsh Kite Trust, Tel: 01597 825981.

YSBYTY CYNFYN
10½ miles E of Aberystwyth on the A4120

Found in the circular wall of the village church, which dates from the 19th century, are the remains of a Bronze Age **Stone Circle**. Two of the stones have been moved from their original positions

HAFOD ARMS HOTEL

Devils Bridge, Aberystwyth, Ceredigion SY23 3JL
Tel: 01970 890232 Fax: 01970 890394
e-mail: enquiries@hafodarms.co.uk
website: www.hafodarms.co.uk

Built in 1787 as a shooting lodge, the **Hafod Arms** enjoys a spectacular setting at the head of the world-famous Mynach Falls. The views are shared by most of the 23 well-appointed bedrooms, which include the elegant Duke of Newcastle suite. The restaurant offers a good choice of traditional home cooking, and in the delightful Victorian Tea Room home-made cakes, bara brith and light snacks are served in the summer months. Janet Green's hotel is an ideal starting point for walks and drives through some of the most glorious scenery that Wales has to offer, but without even leaving the premises guests can enjoy the wonderful views.

DEVIL'S BRIDGE FALLS

Devil's bridge, Aberystwyth, Ceredigion
Tel: 01970 890233

Take a walk along the Nature Trail and
see the spectacular 300ft waterfalls and
the view of the three bridges which span
the breathtaking woodland gorge. The
first bridge is reputed to have been built
by the Devil but in reality it was built in
the 11th century by the monks; the middle
bridge was built in 1708, wider than the
lower bridge, to take horse drawn
vehicles; the top bridge was built in 1901
to cope with modern traffic.

    Cross the humped bridge spanning over the Mynach river at the
bottom of the waterfalls and begin to ascend the other side of the
gorge. Go into Robbers Cave, an old hide out place next to the waterfall.
Alternatively, chose the easier, short walk to view the three bridges
and the Devil's Punchbowl. Discover the legend, of how an old lady
and her dog outwitted the Devil.

Allow at least half hour for the long walk, (but you can stay longer). 10
mins for the short walk. Wear sensible shoes. Not suitable for elderly
or disabled due to steps. Open all year.

to form the gate posts but many of the
other ancient stones remain very much
as they have for centuries.

DEVIL'S BRIDGE

10 miles SE of Aberystwyth on the A4120

The terminus of the **Vale of Rheidol
Railway** (see page 202), the narrow
gauge railway that runs from
Aberystwyth through the Rheidol valley,
Devil's Bridge attracts many people who
come here to see the splendid waterfalls
that drop some 300 feet through this
breathtaking gorge (see panel above).
While the scenery is marvellous, there
are also three interesting bridges here -
dating from the 11th, 18th and 20th
centuries - which were built one on top
of the other. An iron bridge built in
1901 straddles the top of the falls and,
just below it, there is a stone bridge of
1708 while, further down stream again,
lies the original **Pont-y-gwr-Drwg**
(Bridge of the Devil). Thought to have
been built by the monks of Strata Florida

Abbey. Local legend
suggests that the bridge
was built by the Devil
and that he would
claim the first soul to
cross to the other side.
However, an old
woman, wanting to
retrieve her stray cow,
outwitted the Devil by
throwing a crust across
the bridge which her
dog chased after. The
Devil had to make do
with the soul of the dog
and the old lady safely
retrieved her cow.

    Along with the
footpaths and nature
trails that descend the
94 steps of Jacob's
Ladder to view the falls,
other paths lead to another vantage
point - **The Hafod Arch**. It was erected
by Thomas Johnes, the squire of Hafod,
in 1810 to honour the Golden Jubilee of
George III, the farmer king; Johnes also
transformed the area with forestation,
planting the surrounding countryside
with over four million trees as if in
anticipation of the Forestry Commission
who now own the land. The Arch, which
marks the highest point on the former
Hafod Estate of the old Aberystwyth-
Rhayader road, is one of many points of
interest on the **Pwllpeiran Trail**, a four-
mile trail that affords exciting views over
Hafod and the Upper Ystwyth Valley and
provides information on the agriculture,
forestry, wildlife and history to be seen
along its route. One section of the walk
joins the Cambrian Way Long Distance
Path through Myherin Forest; on its way
it passes through Gelmast farmyard,
which was Thomas Johnes' original
experimental farm. Elsewhere on the
Trail, below some new oak woodland, is

the Bwlch yr Oerfa scheduled monument, an agricultural settlement that is thought to be part of the former Cwmystwyth Grange of the Old Cistercian Abbey at Strata Florida.

NEW QUAY

Cei Beach, New Quay

This small yet busy resort, whose harbour now boasts more yachts than fishing boats, built its economy on both shipbuilding and coastal trading. However, although these traditional ways of life declined in the 19th century as the rail links developed, New Quay has retained much of its maritime charm. The first vessel to be built here was a 36 ton sloop; the subsequent shipping boom brought a great deal of employment to the area and this caused the population to rise to 2,000. Hand in hand with the shipbuilding and fishing industry, smuggling was also rife and, in 1795, New Quay was described as a place of "infamous notoriety" and the headland was reputedly riddled with a network of caves where contraband was stored.

New Quay's natural surroundings as a port and harbour of refuge led to its being considered, at one time, as a suitable place from which direct communication could be made with Wicklow and Dublin. Today's visitors will find charter boats operating out of the harbour offering a wide range of trips including deep sea and inshore fishing outings. The **Heritage Centre** has displays on the town's history, including local characters, shipbuilding, smuggling and fishing. It also details what is being done to protect the area's botttlenose dolphins, grey seals and porpoises.

The sands and boating facilities at New Quay have long been an attraction for holidaymakers and the town's **Yacht**

Club welcomes all visitors. The north beach leads to the rocky headland, **New Quay Head**, where an invigorating path follows the line of the sheer cliffs to **Bird Rock**, the home of many sea birds. Inland, lies the **Bird and Wildlife Hospital** which treats and returns to the wild any birds or mammals needing veterinarian treatment and particularly birds involved in oil spillages.

The coast to the south of New Quay is best described as rugged and there is a Heritage Coastal path that threads its way along the clifftops down through Cwmtudu to Llangranog and beyond. Whilst, to the northwest of the town are the long sandy beaches of **Treath Gwyn** (White Beach) and **Cei Bach** (Little Quay) that were once a hive of shipbuilding activity and are now peaceful and secluded places.

Along with Laugharne in Carmarthenshire, New Quay lays claim to being the original Llareggub in Dylan Thomas' *Under Milk Wood*. Thomas had an ambiguous relationship with New Quay: it is said that he was disliked in the town not least for his failure to pay his bills. It would seem he had his revenge, however, as Llareggub reveals its true meaning when spelt backwards!

disaster, rowed out to rescue the stricken sailors. Once safe, the family, unable to understand the language spoken by the shipwrecked strangers, sent for a monk who told them that they had saved King Ina. In thanksgiving, the king built a church from which the present church, **Ina's Church**, takes its name. **Cerrig Ina**, Ina's Stones, can be seen offshore and mark the spot where the original church stood.

Aberaeron
4½ miles NE of New Quay on the A487

Situated at the mouth of the River Aeron, this is a delightful small town with charming Georgian houses, particularly around **Alban Square**. These are the result of astute town planning initiated in the early 19th century by the Reverend Alban Gwynne, who was happy to spend his wife's inheritance on dredging the Aeron estuary and creating this new port. This was instrumental in turning the settlement from a small fishing hamlet into a bustling port that also became famous for its shipbuilding.

Although the industry here has all but gone, there can be found, on the quay, the **Aberaeron Sea Aquarium** where not only can all manner of sea life be viewed

AROUND NEW QUAY

Llanina
1 miles E of New Quay off the A486

This tiny village, with a long tradition of fishing, is also associated with the legend of King Ina of England. One day, in the early 8th century, a ship was wrecked on the rocks close to the village during a violent storm, and a local fisherman, his wife and daughter, having seen the

Aberaeron Harbour

Y PERL RESTAURANT

Aberaeron Craft Centre, Aberaeron,
Ceredigion SA46 0DX
Tel: 01545 571721

A stylish modern craft centre in traditional farm buildings provides an atmospheric setting for **Y Perl Restaurant**. With international chef Mark Whitford in the kitchen and his wife Margarette a lively, entertaining hostess, the restaurant is open long hours for anything from a snack to a full meal.

Y Perl is spread over two floors, one in bright Mediterranean style, the other sporting whitewashed walls and heavy black beams. In the daytime, morning coffee, pastries, lunches and afternoon teas are served in informal surroundings, while in the evening candlelight, table linen and crystal glassware set a much more romantic scene.

The evening à la carte menu offers diners plenty of choice, with starters such as deep-fried brie with a fruit coulis and main courses typified by poached salmon and tiger prawns in a lime and lemon butter, or pork loin steak in a cider and pear sauce. There are always main -course choices for vegetarians, and a selection of sweets rounds off splendid meal. The popular Sunday lunch always features a choice of roasts as the centrepiece.

COASTAL VOYAGES & THE SEA AQUARIUM

2 Quay Parade, Aberaeron, Ceredigion SA46 0BT
Tel: 01545 570142   Fax: 01454 570160
e-mail: coastalvoyages@btclick.com
website: www.coastalvoyages.co.uk

In its heyday the delightful small town of Aberaeron was a bustling fishing port and an important centre of

shipbuilding. These industries have all but gone, but the maritime influence is still strong and visitors can experience several aspects of this through **Coastal Voyages & the Sea Aquarium**. The Aquarium provides a fascinating insight into the marine life of Cardigan Bay's coastal waters. The tanks contain a wide variety of the fish and shellfish to be found in the Bay, and a very interesting film show runs throughout the day.

In the same premises by the harbour is the booking office of Coastal Voyages, a unique and exhilarating boating experience that explores the Bay's marine ecology and the heritage coast. The voyages offer the opportunity to see , in their natural habitat, a wide variety of wildlife, including dolphins, porpoises, seals, razorbills, guillemots, kittiwakes, gannets and gulls, shags and shearwaters. The *Atlantic Leopard* is a multi-purpose vessel which, in addition to carrying passengers, also operates as a commercial fishing boat and undertakes scientific research.

from the shore but the aquarium also offers visitors the chance to discover Cardigan Bay's marine ecology and heritage coast. It also contains small fish and lobster hatcheries.

Just inland from the town lies **Aberaeron Wildlife Park**, the home of llamas, red deer, parrots, owls and Jimmy, who is believed to be the world's only albino crow and who starred in the television series *Gormenghast*. As well as the animals at the park, there are natural trails, a miniature railway and plenty of other activities to keep all the family amused.

Although animals, birds and fish abound in this area, Aberaeron also has a **Craft Centre**, housed in traditional farm buildings, where visitors can not only see the beautiful products being hand-made but have the opportunity to buy a unique reminder of their time in the town.

ABERARTH

6 miles NE of New Quay on the A487

Although often bypassed because of the charm of its more illustrious neighbour, Aberaeron, Aberarth is a picturesque village overlooked by **St David's Church**. Founded in the 6th century, and originally hidden from the sea, the church was rebuilt in 1860 but its' still contains three early Christian inscribed stones from the 9th and 10th centuries.

THE HIVE ON THE QUAY

Cadwgan Place, Aberaeron, Ceredigion SA46 0BU
Tel: 01545 570445

Established in 1976, the Holgate family's **Hive on the Quay** is one of the best restaurants in Wales, with a reputation for quality that is second to none. It specialises in Welsh recipes, using honey, organic flour and free-range eggs in most of the baking. Everything is home-made, including bread, cakes and the wonderful ice cream. West Wales has been the heartland of organic agriculture for many years, and at Hive on the Quay local organic produce is used wherever possible. A menu of cakes, sandwiches and light snacks is available all day, and the lunch and dinner menus offer a splendid variety of superb dishes, with zingy fresh seafood (the restaurant has its own boat) a treat that is not to be missed.

The printed menu is always supplemented by a long list of daily specials that might include grilled Aberaeron mackerel with lemon chutney, honey chicken with basmati rice and a dipping sauce, and toad in the hole with mashed potato and onion marmalade. Many of the dishes can be served in children's portions, and the lucky little things also have their own menu of sandwiches, salads, pies and boiled egg and soldiers. The ice creams, all containing honey, come in a great variety of mouthwatering sundaes, including banana split, black cherry meringue and chocolate nut parfait. The restaurant is bright, airy and very welcoming, with lots of greenery, 70 spaces, counter and conservatory areas, and a take away kiosk that, like the restaurant, gets extremely busy in the summer. Just across the courtyard, the Fish on the Quay shop is equally popular. Café-Restaurant open Spring Bank Holiday to mid-September 10.30am -5.00pm; August 10.00am-9.00pm. Honey Ice Cream open Easter to November; afternoons only in low season.

LLANERCHAERON

Nr Aberaeron, Ceredigion SA48 8DG
Tel: 01545 570200 info line: 01558 825147
e-mail: glnest@smtp.ntrust.org.uk

The National Trust's latest opening in Wales is
Llanerchaeron, a small 18th century gentry estate
which has survived virtually intact. The house was
designed and built by John Nash in 1796 and was
bequeathed to the Trust by JP Ponsonby Lewes in
1989. Llanchaeron was a self-sufficient estate,
which is evident in the dairy, laundry, brewery
and salting room as well as the home farm

buildings from the stables to the threshing barn.

Llanerchaeron today is a working organic farm,
and the two walled gardens also produce organic
fruit and vegetables. Following extensive
restoration, the house and servants quarters, service
courtyard and Pamela Ward exhibition were opened
to visitors for the first time in June 2002. The house
is located 2½ miles east of Aberaeron off the A482.

PENYCASTELL FARM HOTEL

Llanrhystud, Aberystwyth, Ceredigion SY23 5BZ
Tel/Fax: 01974 272622
e-mail: info@penycastell.co.uk website: www.penycastell.co.uk

Penycastell Farm Hotel is a delightful rural retreat set in glorious
countryside. Owner Jean Blackwell-Vickers offers a choice of
comfortable en suite accommodation: seven rooms are in the
old farmhouse and three in the new barn conversion, all centrally heated, with up-to-date amenities
and lots of thoughtful little extras. One room has an 18th century American four-poster bed and
American wallpaper of the period. Penycastell, a non-smoking establishment, has a large, restful lounge
and a dining room where excellent breakfasts and evening meals are served. No children or pets.

MONACHTY MANSION

Pennant, Nr Aberaron, Ceredigion SY23 5JP
Tel: 01545 570215 Fax: 01545 571707
e-mail: monachty@btopenworld.com

Four spacious, well-appointed guest bedrooms offer top-class
accommodation in a handsome Regency country mansion set in
magnificent grounds. There are fires in each bedroom, one room has
a four-poster bed and all have private bathrooms. The Georgian flagstone entrance hall with magnificent
staircase sets the dignified tone of the interior, and guests have an elegant drawing room for relaxation.
Breakfasts are served in the breakfast room and four-course candlelit dinners are enjoyed, on request,
in the convivial company of owners Nigel and Wendy Symons-Jones. Fishing, riding and shooting are
available on the estate, together with wonderful woodland walks.

LLANRHYSTUD

11½ miles NE of New Quay on the A487

To the south of the village, which lies near the confluence of the Rivers Wyre and Carrog, are the two former hill forts of **Castell Bach** and **Castell Mawr** which are separated by a vale known as "the dell of slaughter" - a reference to an ancient battle. More remains can be found to the east - those of the castle **Caer Penrhos**. Built in around 1150 by Cadwaladr ap Gryffydd, the castle was razed to the ground some 50 years later to avoid it falling into a rival's hands.

PENNANT

8 miles E of New Quay on the B4577

In the 19th century, this village was the home of a recluse named Mari Berllan Piter (Mary of Peter's Orchard). Supposedly granted magical powers, her exploits were legendary: when a miller refused to grind her corn she made his mill wheel turn the wrong way, a young girl who stole an apple from Mari's orchard was forced to walk home backwards and sometimes, it is said, that Mari turned herself into a hare. The ruins of Mari's cottage, known locaqlly as The Witch's Cottage, can still be seen surrounded by her now overgrown orchard.

LLANARTH

2½ miles SE of New Quay on the A487

A local story tells that one night the Devil tried to steal the bell from Llanarth Church. However, he made such a noise that he woke the vicar who, armed with a bell, a book and a candle, climbed up into the belfry to investigate. By solemnly repeating the name of Christ, the vicar managed to drive the Devil to the top of the tower and forced him to jump off and, in the graveyard, there is a

CROCHENDY LLANARTH POTTERY

Llanarth, Ceredigion SA47 0PU
Tel/Fax: 01545 580584

Visitors can try their hand on the wheel at **Crochendy Llanarth Pottery**, which is signposted on the A487 coast road a mile north of Llanarth and three miles south of Aberaeron. David and Anne Farr recently took over at the Pottery, which was established over 20 years ago. In the pottery behind the showroom would-be potters can have a go at throwing a pot; they can take their handiwork home or have it fired and sent on later.

Decorating a ready made pot is another way of getting involved in this fascinating craft, and children can try hand-building a pot or modelling with clay. In the showroom is an exciting range of pots that are both practical and beautiful, in many varieties, glazes and styles, from eggcups to bread crocks. decorative items include bowls and vases, and as everything is made by hand each piece is unique. Parking and admission are free, there's easy access for visitors in wheelchairs, and the Pottery is open from 10 to 3 and from 4 to 6 every day except Tuesday. In an annexe to the house bed and breakfast accommodation is available in three en suite rooms with tv and beverage tray.

COED-Y-GOG

Rhosgoch Ganol, Mydroilyn, Nr Lampeter,
Ceredigion SA48 7RN Tel: 01545 580328

Mary Kitson and her husband run a dairy and beef farm and also let out a self-catering bungalow which stands at the entrance to the drive that leads to the farmhouse. It provides excellent accommodation, with the accent on comfort, in three bedrooms (a double , a twin and a single). The well-furnished lounge/diner has an open fire (in addition to the central heating), TV and radio. The kitchen with oven, microwave, freezer and washing machine supplies everything needed for a self-contained, independent stay.

Coed-y-Gog stands in a sheltered garden with a barbecue, garden table and chairs and ample parking for two cars and a boat trailer. Pets are welcome (only one dog at a time, please!). Sandy beaches and sheltered coves are a 10-minute drive away, and red kites are often seen from the farm. Sea and fresh-water fishing can be arranged, and attractions as varied as the ancient abbey of Strata Florida and the new National Botanic Garden with its Millenium Dome, near Carmarthen are within easy reach. New Quay and Lampeter are both well provided with shops, pubs and restaurants.

strangely scarred stone that is said to bear the marks made by the Devil when he landed.

CROSS INN

2 miles S of New Quay on the A486

To the south of the village lies **New Quay Honey Farm** - the largest honey farm in Wales - which is housed in an old chapel. Visitors here have the chance to see for themselves the amazing life of a honey bee as the top floor of the chapel has been turned into an exhibition illustrating the mysteries of bees and honey. Here, too, is a colony of leaf-cutting ants. On the ground floor of the chapel is a charming tea room where there is definitely "honey still for tea", and also mead, the oldest alcoholic drink that contains honey. Mead, honey and bee-keeping equipment are among the items on sale in the farm shop.

LAMPETER

Lampeter has long been the centre for this part of the Teifi Valley and an important meeting place for drovers but today it is best known as being the home of University College. Founded in 1822 by Bishop Thomas Burgess of St David's, **St David's College**, as it was first known, is a world renowned ecclesiastical and predominantly Welsh speaking college that is the oldest institution in Wales. The main university buildings include CB Cockerell's original stuccoed quadrangle of buildings dating from 1827 which were designed to mimic an Oxbridge College and, underneath these buildings, lies the town's old castle motte. Since 1971, the college has been integrated with the University of Wales - hence its new name **University College** - although the campus still retains its own unique atmosphere.

While the students add a certain bohemian flavour to Lampeter during term time, this is essentially a genteel and very Welsh town with a pleasant mixture of Georgian and Victorian buildings. Back in the 17th century, on what is now Maesyfelin Street, stood the home of the Lloyds of Maesyfelin. When the only daughter of the family, Elen, became engaged to Samuel Pritchard, the son of a poet priest called Rhys Pritchard from Llandovery, her four brothers, fearing the loss of their inheritance, tied her lover underneath a horse and galloped him from Lampeter to Llandovery. Samuel died of his injuries and the brothers threw his body in nearby River Teifi. On hearing what had happened Elen was driven mad with sorrow and died soon afterwards. Samuel's father, Rhys, put a curse on the family and, just a short while later, their family house caught fire and burnt to the ground; the eldest brother, out of remorse or perhaps due to the curse, killed his brothers and then himself.

AROUND LAMPETER

PONTRHYDFENDIGAID
15 miles NE of Lampeter on the B4343

Just a short distance from the village, and close to the ford of the Blessed Virgin, lies **Strata Florida Abbey**, a Cistercian house founded in 1164. This austere order was renowned for seeking out remote and isolated sites for its religious establishments and Strata Florida - the vale of Flowers - is one such site. Even though the abbey is in ruins today, it is still an evocative place for visitors. Just two years after its foundation the abbey's lands were overrun by Rhys ap Gryffyd but, in 1184, he refounded the abbey; most of the

PENLANMEDD

Llanfair Road, Lampeter, Ceredigion SA48 8JZ
Tel/Fax: 01570 493438
e-mail: penlanmedd@coombes-e.freeserve.co.uk

Peace, comfort and glorious scenery are among the attractions of **Penlanmedd**, a secluded 18th century farmhouse set in working farmland above

the River Teifi three miles north of Lampeter. Elaine

Coombes offers double, twin or family accommodation in three cosy en suite bedrooms appointed in an elegant style that gives a traditional look to modern fittings and furnishings. Two of the rooms can interconnect to make a perfect arrangement for families.

The gardens and grounds of the house are delightful for strolling, and the views across the quiet valley towards distant hills are stunning. This part of Ceredigion is a paradise for walkers and nature lovers, and fishing and riding are other activities that can be enjoyed locally. Nearby Cors Caron National Park is home to rare flora and fauna, and birdwatchers might see red kites, buzzards and sparrowhawks among the numerous species recorded. The university town of Lampeter is very close by, and it's only a 30-minute drive to Cardigan Bay with its fine beaches, coastal paths, dolphins and seals.

buildings now seen in ruins date from this time. During the 12th and 13th centuries, Strata Florida became not only one of the most important religious centres in Wales but also a place that was to influence Welsh culture as it was patronised by both princes and poets. Some of the last native princes and princesses of Wales were buried here, as was Dafydd ap Gwilym, probably the most famous of all Welsh medieval poets, who was born near Aberystwyth. In 1238, the Welsh princes swore their allegiance to Llywelyn the Great's son, Dafydd, at the abbey. This was also the time when the abbey flourished in terms of wealth, mainly through wool from the sheep that grazed on its vast lands.

After the Dissolution in the 16th century, the abbey and its lands passed through various hands and the ruins today, which are now in the ownership of CADW, consist mainly of the cloister and the chapter house by the church that now serves as Pontrhydfendigaid's parish church. Inside, remains have been integrated into the church, and in the north transept stands a memorial to the poet Dafydd ap Gwilym. The yew tree that stands amidst the abbey's remains is thought to mark his grave.

One legend associated with the abbey suggests that the Holy Grail, which was given to the monks at Glastonbury by Joseph of Aramathea, later ended up at Strata Florida. When the abbey, which formed part of the Nanteos estate, was left to fall into ruins, the cup, which had pieces bitten out of its sides by pilgrims convinced of its healing powers, was stored at Nanteos mansion.

TREGARON
9 miles NE of Lampeter on the A485

This small market town - a meeting place for 19th century drovers - still serves the remote farming communities in the Teifi valley. The surrounding land is sheep country and Tregaron, a natural centre point for the area, also became famous for its woollen industry and, in particular, hand-knitted woollen socks. While many of the socks were transported to the mining communities of South Wales, David Davies, an engineer from Llandinam, found another use for the wool - he used it to form a stable bed on which to lay the railway across Cors Caron bog. In the town's main square stands a statue of Henry Richard (1812-1888), the Liberal MP and son of Tregaron, who was a vociferous supporter of disarmament and an advocate of arbitration in international disputes; he became known as the "Apostle of Peace".

Housed in the Old National School, which opened in 1873, the **Tregaron Kite Centre and Museum** is an interesting and informative place which is dedicated to the red kite. With the dual aims of providing people with a better understanding of these

Strata Florida Abbey

beautiful birds of prey and with ensuring their survival in this part of mid Wales, visitors to the centre can also see the kites being fed daily here during the winter months. Also at the museum are artefacts from Ceredigion Museum that relate specifically to Tregaron and the surrounding area.

Although Tregaron is chiefly associated with sheep and wool, it is also the location of the **Welsh Gold Centre**.

To the north of the town lies **Cors Caron**, an ancient bog that is home to rare flora and fauna. The land was originally covered by a glacier, and at the end of the last Ice Age this glacier melted to create a natural lake which filled with sediment and vegetation. The peat surface grew, creating three distinctive domes above the original lake bed level. The **Old Railway Walk**, along the trackbed of the old Manchester-Milford Haven railway, provides visitors with the chance to observe some of the over 170 species of bird recorded here, including red kites, buzzards and sparrowhawks.

RHIANNON THE CELTIC DESIGN CENTRE

Main Square, Tregaron, Ceredigion SY25 6JL
Tel: 01974 298415 Fax: 01974 298690 website: www.rhiannon.co.uk

In the heart of a small Welsh speaking town surrounded by spectacular scenery, the **Rhiannon Celtic Design Centre** is an outstanding showcase of all that is best in Celtic jewellery, arts and crafts. The centre was established in 1971 by Rhiannon Evans, a jewellery designer with an international reputation for her original and unique interpretations of the Welsh and Celtic artistic traditions.

This very special attraction has recently been extended to include even more facilities. You can watch Rhiannon's jewellery being handcrafted by her own skilled goldsmiths in the **Exhibition Workshops**, where they create special jewellery in silver and gold, and also using rare and precious Welsh Gold, mined a few miles away in north Wales. As well as original Celtic knotwork and traditional Welsh images, many of Rhiannon's distinctive jewellery designs draw their inspiration from the landscape and wildlife of this most beautiful part of Britain. Other designs are

based on old Celtic legends, or derived from pieces of jewellery made thousands of years ago by the Celts themselves. All of the j ewellery is displayed in the **Welsh Gold Centre**, and there is also a comprehensive mail order catalogue if you can't visit.

The **Museum of Celtic Jewellery** traces the development of Celtic artistic styles and techniques, and includes many archaeological finds and exquisite pieces ofjewellery. It provides a special insight into the way Celtic jewellery was made and used many of the skills involved have hardly changed in 2000 years.

The **Celtic Gallery and Shop** features guest artists and themed exhibitions, as well as the very best Welsh and Celtic crafts. This is certainly not your average Welsh Craft Shop. Slate carvings, lampworked glass, sculptural ceramics, steel dragons, as well as many other examples of the very best in contemporary Celtic artwork and handmade crafts are displayed. Rhiannon and her family search the Celtic countries relentlessly to find the best craftspeople, and when they can't find just the right product, they even commission their own exclusive pieces for the shop.

Finally, the **Traditional Welsh Tearoom** provides a welcome chance to relax and enjoy the legendary Welsh welcome, as well as traditional Welsh food like cawl, bara brith, or a glorious afternoon tea. There is also the best coffee in the area, healthy, light snacks and deliciously fresh juices to drink.

The Rhiannon Celtic Design centre is open from Monday to Saturday throughout the year, except between Christmas and the New Year, and on St David's Day. Open Sundays July, August and Bank Holidays.

NEUADD FARM COTTAGES

Neuadd Farm, Llwyndafydd, Llandysul,
Ceredigion SA44 6BT
Tel & Fax: 01545 560324
e-mail: mheadley@btconnect.com
website: www.neuadd-farm-cottages.co.uk

Over the past 20 years Malcolm and Karina Headley
have converted a series of buildings, some of them near-
derelict, into the most delightful self-catering cottages,
all built, furnished and fitted to the very highest
standards. **Neuadd Farm Cottages** sleep from two to
six guests, and each is equipped to full residential
standards, including fitted carpets, original paintings
by Darby and Dulcie Headley, flowers, garden furniture,
tv and video players, with a library of films available,
and books, puzzles and games. Initial stocks of cleaning
materials are supplied, and a welcome tray with home-
made cookies, tea
and coffee and
milk in the fridge
greets arrivals.

The owners can provide a mouthwatering choice of meals from
the farm freezer. Each cottage has an electric cooker, microwave,
fridge freezer and coffee maker, and most have a dishwasher,
barbecue and wood-burning stove. They all have irons and ironing
boards, and there's a shared laundry room with washing machines
and tumble dryer. Among the cottages - there's a choice of 10 -
are the Hayloft, whose en suite bedroom has an Italianate balcony
to catch the sun and the views, and the two-bedroom Farmhouse
Cottage in a self-contained wing of the old farmhouse, with its
own walled and cobbled courtyard.

One of the best features of Neaudd is the 35 acres of stunning
gardens and grounds, almost permanent winners of the annual
Wales   in

Bloom awards and home to a wide variety of flora
and fauna (that's apart from the lambs, ducks,
geese, rabbits, ponies and other family pets). The
gardens have lots of little corners to sit in seclusion,
secret footpaths, ponds full of fish, and masses of
gorgeous flowers. The all-weather tennis court is a
superb amenity, so, too, the swimming pool. The
children's play area includes a tractor and Wendy
House among its attractions. Red kites, buzzards,
peregrines and choughs can be seen in the skies
above the cottages, and seals and dolphins are often
seen in the nearby coves (Cwm Tydu Cove is less
than two miles away). The gardens, the beaches,
the wildlife, the walks, the caring owners always
on hand.....it all adds up to the perfect escape from
the daily routine, a haven to which many guests
return year after year.

CEREDIGION

THE THREE HORSESHOE INN

Llangeitho, Nr Tregaron, Ceredigion SY25 6TW
Tel: 01974 821244 website: www.cardigan-bay.co.uk

Mike and Jane Williams welcome visitors to their fine old white-painted inn, which stands at a road junction in the centre of the village. The interior is cosy and traditional, and for warmer weather there are plenty of seats out in the garden. Regularly changing guest ales supplement the permanent choice in the bar, where pool, and darts are played. A new kitchen provides excellent food for the 24-seat dining room, one of the highlights being top-quality meat from a local butcher. For visitors touring this beautiful, peaceful part of the world the **Three Horseshoe Inn** provides an excellent base with a two-bedroom self-catering apartment on the first floor.

The walk starts from the car park near Maesllyn Farm on the B4343, 2 miles north of Tregaron.

LLANDDEWI BREFI
7 miles NE of Lampeter on the B4343

This traditional country village was host, in AD 519, to a synod which was attended by St David. The meeting was called to debate the Pelagian heresy, a doctrine advocating freedom of thought rather than the biblical version of original sin that determined the morality of the time. **St David's Church**, in the village, stands on a mound said to have risen up as St David preached during the synod. The church itself dates from the 13th century and, inside, contains some old inscribed stones: one is known as St David's Staff and another has an inscription in the obscure Ogham language thought to commemorate a heretic of the type that St David was denouncing.

Close by are the sites of several hill forts including **Llanfair Clydogau**, where the Romans mined for silver, and which sit beside the Sarn Helen - a military road. The road once connected a gold mine in the south, at Dolaucothi, with a fort at Bremia in the north.

CAPEL DEWI
8½ miles SW of Lampeter on the B4459

Close to the village lies **Rock Mills**

Woollen Mill, which was established in 1890 by John Morgan and whose descendants still weave here. The machinery is powered by a waterwheel which also drives a small alternator to provide lighting. The mill once provided power to the neighbouring church. From pure new wool, the mill produces all manner of woollen goods, including bedspreads, blankets and rugs, and it is one of the last traditional mills where the entire process, from fleece to fabric, may be viewed.

LLANDYSUL
11 miles SW of Lampeter on the A486

Set in the deep and picturesque valley of the River Teifi, this traditional little Welsh town was another centre of the woollen industry and it was also the birthplace, in the early 19th century, of Christmas Evans, a Baptist minister who was famed for his fiery, emotional sermons. The son of a cobbler, he was orphaned early in life; he became a Baptist minister instead of a Presbyterian minister because the Presbyterians required qualifications which he did not have. Today, this tranquil little town is renowned for its outstanding scenic views, fishing and white water canoeing as well as for the delights of its Victorian town centre.

A few miles up the the A486, **Ffostrasol** is the setting for the annual Cnapan Folk

CURLEW WEAVERS

Troedyraur, Rhydlewis, Ceredigion SA44 5RL
Tel/Fax: 01239 851357 e-mail: CWeavers@FSBdial.co.uk
website: www.curlewweavers.co.uk

Set in attractive countryside midway between Llangrannog and Newcastle Emlyn, **Curlew Weavers** is a family firm specialising in the production of a very wide range of woollen fabrics. Roger Poulson has recently invested in machinery to expand the business, which serves the retail, wholesale and

export trades. The fabrics include tweeds, flannels, dress materials and curtain and upholstery fabrics. Items can be made to individual requirements, and the whole process, from the yarn to the finished article, takes place here at the mill. When commissioned, the new machinery will process from the fleece form.

The garments (Curlew Tweedsters) range from casual tops, skirts and dresses to

capes and coats, and the mill also produces travel rugs, throws, bedspreads, blankets, shawls, scarves, tablecloths and ties, as well as made to measure curtains. Besides the mill's products, the shop stocks a selection of high-quality Welsh products including pottery, ceramics and jewellery. The shop and the mill (free tours, with disabled access) are open Monday to Friday all year; closed Bank Holidays.

BRONIWAN

Rhydlewis, Llandysul, Ceredigion SA44 5PF
Tel/Fax: 01239 851261
e-mail: broniwan@compuserve.com

A lane off the B4334 at Rhydlewis leads to a private drive, at the end of which is **Broniwan**, a small farm centred round a greystone house with ivy growing round the porch, overlooking a garden terrace. Built for the local doctor in 1867, it is now the home of Allen and Carole Jacobs, who offer guest accommodation in two

pretty bedrooms with en suite or private facilities; a single room is also available. Books, paintings, flowers and country antiques furnish the cosy sitting room, and in the dining room guests can watch finches, nuthatches and even the occasional woodpecker at the feeder outside the window.

Home-produced eggs, beef, fruit and vegetables feature in the excellent meals, and the soups, cakes and marmalade are all home-made. Guests can walk anywhere around the farm. There are two friendly dogs willing to act as guides to the stream or up to the high fields. The Welsh Botanic Gardens, Aberglasney Garden and the Welsh Wildlife Centre are all within easy reach, while fishing, pony trekking and the sandy beaches of Cardiganshire's coast are an easy 10 minute drive away. Allen runs reading groups locally, Carole writes. Their weekend breaks for reading and book reviews are becoming a speciality. Members of the Soil Association. Wales Tourist Board Farmhouse Award, Three Stars.

Festival, the largest Celtic folk music event on the British mainland.

CARDIGAN

Once the busiest port in Wales, Cardigan is an ancient borough which received its first charter in 1199 and it was, in the 12th century, a power base of Lord Rhys, one of the last Welsh princes to rule an independent principality. The few remains of **Cardigan Castle**, which stand beside the river, conceal a turbulent history: built in the late 11th or early 12th century by Gryffydd ap Rhys, the fortifications were strengthened around 1170 before it passed into the hands of the Earl of Pembroke in 1240. Thought to be the site of the first Eisteddfod in 1176, the castle fell to Parliament in 1645 during the Civil War.

The River Teifi, which provides Cardigan with its Welsh name Aberteifi, continues to be fished for trout and some still use the traditional coracle. Dating from pre-Christian times, coracles were once common on many of Britain's rivers and they have changed little over the centuries. The silting up of the Teifi estuary, along with the arrival of the railway, were the main causes of Cardigan's decline as a major port which had, at one time, over 300 ships registered here.

However, while the river is no longer at the centre of the town's economy it is still a place of charm enhanced by the six-arched **Teifi Bridge** - an ancient structure which was rebuilt in 1726.

Housed in an 18th century warehouse on Teifi Wharf, the **Cardigan Heritage Centre** tells the story of this former

ROSEHILL FARM

Llangoedmor, Cardigan,
Ceredigion SA43 2LJ
Tel/Fax: 01239 612019
website: www.rosehillfarm.co.uk

Rosehill is a 15th century stone farmhouse on the banks of the River Teifi providing bed and breakfast facilities in three well-equipped bedrooms. Owner Judy Moss, who has lived here for almost 30 years, is an excellent hostess and a superb cook, so the optional evening meal is something to be considered very seriously. In addition to the B&B, she also offers self-catering accommodation in two cottages, a 16th century coach house and a recently converted barn available for letting from March to October.

The cottages sleep four or six, the coach house five and the barn eight. All the properties have open log fires, modern fitted kitchens (farmhouse style with a Rayburn in the coach house), well-appointed bedrooms and bathrooms, tv and video, patio with furniture, own or shared barbecues and the use of Judy's washing machine and tumble dryer. The farm grounds comprise 91 acres of woodland and

pasture that are ideal for those who enjoy walking and are also home to a wide variety of animal and bird life. And it's a great place for fishing: the river is tidal and varies from deep pools to the gorge and rapids, opening out to provide superb places for the fly fisherman. Golf and riding are also available nearby, and the historic town of Cardigan is only two miles away.

THE CUSTOM HOUSE SHOP & GALLERY

44-45 St Mary Street, Cardigan,
Ceredigion SA43 1HA
Tel: 01239 615541 Fax: 01239 615310
e-mail: info@customhousecardigan.com
website: www.customhousecardigan.com

Close to the River Teifi and the remains of the old castle wall, Cardigan's original 18th century Custom House is now home to a vast range of work by makers and designers based in Wales, alongside an exclusive range of creative home accessories. The owner of the gallery is Karina Servini, a young, go-ahead industrial designer who has assembled an eclectic gathering of the very best in contemporary design and art, including oil paintings by local artists, carved wooden ornaments and exquisite work in copper and brass.

There are also antiqued leather suites, a vast range of home accessories, chinaware, lamps, artists cards and prints. The smaller items are displayed cheek by jowl in one area, while the larger pieces are on show in the original customs space with lofty ceiling and exposed beams. On display in the main window is one of Karina's strikingly original pieces, the Servi-Cue. This is a permanent structural barbecue with a combined cooking, serving and entertaining area. The materials used include cast iron, cast aluminium and hand-finished cast concrete, and this remarkable piece is the highlight of a collection that cannot fail to interest and sometimes intrigue.

The Custom House is open from 10 to 5 Monday to Saturday. Apart from the shop and gallery, it offers a mail order and comprehensive design service. Details and examples can be seen and purchased on the Custom House website. When the Custom House was built in the 18th century, Cardigan was a major port, with over 300 vessels registered locally. The River Teifi silted up long ago and the maritime trade dried up, but there are still reminders of the prosperous days, notably in the fine old warehouse buildings and the six-arched bridge over the river.

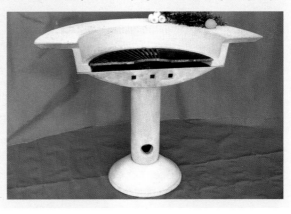

county town, from prehistoric times through to the present day. From its origins in the medieval age to its heyday in the 18th and 19th centuries, the port, in particular, is explored through the eyes of those who lived here. In addition to the permanent exhibitions, there is a programme of temporary exhibitions covering a range of topics. Those looking for performing arts and other cultural events will also not be disappointed as the **Theatr Mwldan**, in the town, is one of Wales' leading theatrical venues.

Beside the river, just outside the town, lies the **Welsh Wildlife Centre**, a nature reserve that provides a variety of habitats, including reed beds, woodland and meadow. As well as an extensive network of footpaths and being home to a surprisingly wide variety of flora and fauna, the reserve also has an excellent visitor centre.

AROUND CARDIGAN

GWBERT-ON-SEA
2½ miles N of Cardigan on the B4548

This small resort on the eastern banks of the River Teifi estuary is an excellent place for cliff walking and for looking out over the estuary and observing its wildlife. To the north of the village, and lying some 200 yards offshore, is **Cardigan Island**, a nature reserve to which there is no unauthorised access and which is inhabited by a flock of wild Soay sheep. Back on the mainland, **Cardigan Island Coastal Farm Park** is an ideal place from which to look out over the island from the headland and also to observe the rare choughs that nest on the cliffs. In the caves below, a colony of seals breed and some lucky visitors may also spot Cardigan Bay's bottle-nosed dolphins. The farm is home, too, to

SHEPHERD'S COTTAGE

Treforgan Farm, Llangoedmor, Cardigan,
Ceredigion SA43 2LB
Tel: 01239 614973
e-mail: colin.lewis@amserve.net

Resident owners Colin and Joan Lewis look forward to greeting guests at **Shepherd's Cottage**, where the friendly, informal atmosphere, the fresh air and the magnificent, unspoilt scenery add up to the perfect choice for a break from the stresses of city life. Shepherd's Cottage is a self-contained stone cottage converted by the owners from traditional farm buildings and with a charm and character in keeping with its surroundings. It has three bedrooms, a double and a twin on the ground floor and a single in the beamed gallery, a fully fitted modern kitchen and a very comfortable lounge with a log fire.

Luxurious furnishings and fabrics add to the feeling of well-being, and fresh flowers and Welsh tea

on arrival are typical thoughtful touches provided by Colin and Joan. The cottage, which earns the Wales Tourist Board's highest grading of five stars, stands in its own private garden overlooking the rolling farmland and a conservation pond around which ducks,chickens and lambs enjoy a happy, healthy life. Shepherd's Cottage stands off the B4570 a mile east of Cardigan, a pleasant and popular little town beside the River Teifi. Among the many local attractions are Poppit Sands, with half a mile of lovely sand and dunes, and the National Trust cove at Mwnt with its clifftop church.

friendly farm animals, including goats, sheep, pigs, ponies and ducks, as well as a llama, a wallaby and rare breed cows.

MWNT

3½ miles N of Cardigan off the A487

This beauty spot was on the Pilgrims' Route to Bardsey Island - the burial ground of over 20,000 Celtic saints - in the north. The tiny **Church of the Holy Cross** dates from around 1400 and stands on the site of a much earlier Celtic church, originally built in a hollow to hide it from view and to protect it from possible raiders coming by sea. Much of the coastline here, including the cliffs, the rocky headland and the safe family beach, is owned by the National Trust. This area is a geological SSSI (Site of Special Scientific Interest) and is part of the Ceredigion Heritage Coast; it is especially rich in maritime flora. The bay was the site of a battle in 1155, when

Fleming invaders were repelled by the local forces.

FELINWYNT

3½ miles NE of Cardigan off the A487

The village is home to the **Felinwynt Rainforest and Butterfly Centre** where, in a large tropical house, visitors are transported to the jungle to see the beautiful free-flying butterflies that live amidst the exotic plants. There is also a rainforest exhibition, which explains the delicate ecology of this interesting habitat, a tea room and a gift shop.

ABERPORTH

6 miles NE of Cardigan on the B4333

The original village of Aberporth consisted of small, single storeyed cottages with thick mud walls and thatched roofs that reflected the simple and hard lives of those living in this fishing and farming community. At one

PENWERN FACH HOLIDAY COTTAGES

Pont Hirwaun, Cardigan, Ceredigion SA43 2RL
Tel: 01239 710694 Fax: 01239 710854
e-mail: enquiries@penwernfach.co.uk
website: www.penwernfach.co.uk

Penwern Fach is the perfect place for a holiday, whether it's a quiet, relaxing break enjoying the beautiful countryside or taking part in more active pursuits such as walking, riding, canoeing, fishing and golf. Once a principal farm in the region, Penwern Fach is no longer a working farm, but the original stone stables and barns have been skilfully converted into four superb self-catering cottages. The cottages, which are named after local rivers, retain original features such as stone walls and exposed beams while providing all the up-to-date amenities needed for a comfortable, carefree holiday. Each cottage has a fully equipped kitchen, well-furnished sitting/dining areas, fitted carpets and tv, and a private patio with table, chairs and outside lighting.

Gwaun Cottage has one bedroom, Cych and Teifi each have two, and Towy, converted from the old stables and hayloft, can sleep up to eight guests in four bedrooms. The grounds and gardens in front of the cottages provide a large area for children to play in complete safety, and other amenities include a games room with pool and soccer tables, a golf-driving range and a stone barbecue with a picnic table. Penwern Fach is located off the A484 just south of Pont Hirwaun.

Aberporth

the coast is the National Trust's beach at **Penbryn**, an SSSI, part of the Ceredigion Heritage Coast, and a good spot for insect, bird and dolphin spotting. The approach to this popular, sandy beach is by way of Hoffnant Valley from the Trust's car park at Llanborth Farm, where a shop, café and WCs are open in season. The valley is known locally as Cwm Lladron, Robbers Valley, probably because of old-time smuggling connections.

time Aberporth became famous for its herring industry as great shoals of the fish came to feed and spawn in the shallow waters of this sheltered part of the Cardigan Bay coast. Today, and particularly in the summer months, the village is a small yet thriving resort that is popular with yachtsmen. A little way up

LLANGRANOG
9½ miles NE of Cardigan on the B4334

Lying in a narrow valley and rather reminiscent of a Cornish fishing village, Llangranog is not only one of the most attractive villages along the Ceredigion

THE SHIP INN & PENTRE ARMS

Llangranog, Ceredigion SA44 6SL
The Ship Tel: 01239 654423
The Pentre Arms Tel: 01239 654345

Kevin, Dee and Mike are partners in running two very popular pubs by the water's edge in Llangranog. Built in typical "Welsh coastal" style in local slate and stone, the **Ship Inn and the Pentre Arms** are separated by a mere 100 yards, and both offer a warm Welsh welcome and bags of old-world atmosphere. All three partners are talented, experienced chefs, and the food is a big attraction at both inns. The Ship, whose side wall is adorned with a large painting of a galleon under full sail on

a breezy sea, has two bars and a function room with seating for 70.

The Pentre Arms has another string to its bow in the shape of 10 letting bedrooms for bed and breakfast. The rooms are a mix of singles, doubles and twins, some en suite, some with tv, all with beverage trays. An adjacent cottage offers self-catering accommodation. The Pentre Arms is the closest inn to the sea in Ceredigion. Llangranog is a popular, picturesque resort, and the neighbouring cliffs and headlands provide stunning views and exhilarating walks.

WERVIL GRANGE FARM

Pentregat, Nr Llangranog, Ceredigion SA44 6HW
Tel/Fax: 01239 654252

A Welsh Georgian farm-house of substance provides a very high standard of accommodation in lovely countryside 10 minutes from Llangranog Beach.

Wervil Grange Farm is owned by Ionwen Lewis, a well-known lady farmer and Welsh Director for Farm Stay UK who built a high class restaurant business nearby before changing direction to offer top-quality bed and breakfast holidays.

The welcome here is always warm, and the comfortable farmhouse is beautifully furnished and decorated. No detail has been overlooked in the elegant, spacious bedrooms, whose facilities range from slipper baths and bathrobes to hairdryers, televisions and hospitality trays.

One room has a fine four-poster bed, and all have armchairs and gentle bedside lighting. Superb breakfasts make a memorable start to the day at Wervil Grange, which is very much a working farm, with a flock of breeding ewes and a herd of Welsh Black cattle.

The house stands in formal landscaped gardens that include lakes where guests can fish free of charge. The farm is signposted off the A487 Aberystwyth to Cardigan coast road a short way south of Plwmp and Pentregat.

The village of Llangranog is one of the most attractive along the Ceredigion coast, and the cliffs and headlands to the north offer exhilarating walks and dramatic scenery.

To the east of Llangranog, and very close to Wervil Grange, is one of the area's gems, the Walled Garden at Pigeonsford, set in grounds that inc-lude shrubberies, woodland and river-side walks.

coast but also one of the most popular resorts in the area. The headland and cliffs to the north of the village (now property of the National Trust) offer excellent walks and dramatic scenery. The sheltered coves around Llangranog helped to sustain a thriving shipbuilding industry but they also proved perfect landing and hiding places for contraband and the area was rife with smuggling activity.

Llangrannog

SELF-CATERING APARTMENTS AT PENTRAETH

Tresaith, Cardigan, Ceredigion SA43 2JL
Tel/Fax: 01239 811711

Pentraeth is an attractive 19th century building a few steps from Tresaith beach, with three spacious, self-contained apartments let on a self-catering basis by Oliver and Di Hadley. "Dolphin" has two double bedrooms, bathroom, fully fitted kitchen/dining room and a sitting room with a large southerly terrace overlooking the sea. "Mermaid" has a bed-sitting room, bathroom and small kitchen area, and "Crow's Nest" has a double bedroom, bathroom, kitchen/living room and a sheltered south facing terrace. All have tv, radio and sea views. Smoking is not permitted in the apartments.

THE NEW INN

Pentregat, Llandysul, Ceredigion SA44 5PT
Tel: 01239 654285

Ian and Tracey Gunn and their young children took off from the bustle of life near Heathrow and landed in this lovely part of Wales to take over the reins at the New Inn. They welcome singles, couples, groups and families of all ages to their old white-painted coaching inn, where low beams contribute to the traditional look and where classic pub games are played.

Food is a big attraction here, from sandwiches to full meals, and they also serve teas and coffees as well as a good free house selection of beers. The Sunday roast always brings in the crowds, and the regular menu served in the non-smoking restaurant is supplemented by daily specials such as pork and lemon schnitzel, teriyaki chicken and peppered ribeye steak. An over-60s club operates every Thursday lunchtime.

To the east of the village lies the **Walled Garden at Pigeonsford**, a Georgian walled garden which has been rep-lanted with botanical collections of herbaceous plants and shrubs as well as vegetables and fruits. Maintained as a working garden, the walled garden is set in large and less formal grounds that include shrubberies, woodland and riverside walks.

HENLLAN
11½ miles SE of Cardigan on the B4334

This village is home to the **Teifi Valley Railway**, another of Wales' famous little trains. This narrow gauge railway, which originally served the slate quarries, was created from a section of the Great Western Railway (also known as God's Wonderful Railway) that served the rural areas of West Wales. Today's passengers can enjoy a 40 minute steam train journey through this delightful valley

while, at the Henllan terminus, there are plenty of attractions to keep the whole family amused: woodland walks, crazy golf, the station tearooms and a gift and souvenir shop.

ST DOGMAELS
1 mile W of Cardigan on the B4546

Situated on the western banks of the mouth of the River Teifi, it was here that the Lord of the Manor, Robert Martyn, founded **St Dogmael's Abbey** in the 12th century for the monks of the Benedictine order brought over from Tiron in France. An earlier Welsh abbey on the site was sacked by the Vikings. Adjacent to the abbey ruins is a church which features an inscribed Sagranus stone whose markings and Latin inscriptions provided the key to deciphering the ancient Goidelic language. Close to the abbey is **The Mill** (Y Felin), a water-powered flour mill.

TRENEWYDD FARM HOLIDAY COTTAGES

St Dogmaels, Cardigan SA43 3BJ
Tel: 01239 612370 Fax: 01239 621040
e-mail: cherylhyde@trenewyddfarm.fsnet.co.uk
website: www.trenewyddfarm.fsnet.co.uk

Trenewydd Farm Holiday Cottages provide the very best in self-catering accommodation, and the numbers of guests who return year after year testify that this truly is a home from home. The farm has also gained professional recognition, earning the "Hospitality Award for the Best Self-Catering Accommodation in Wales" from the Wales Tourist Board. Five beautifully appointed cottages are available, with sleeping room for any number from two right up to nine - and for three-family group holidays, two of the cottages can be linked as one. All the cottages are fully heated for winter warmth, with night storage heating and individual heaters in each of the bedrooms and bathrooms.

Each cottage is fully equipped with everything needed for a self-contained holiday, and there are a variety of fresh farmhouse meals of excellent quality available. Accessories include a full complement of patio ware for use by the heated swimming pool in the landscaped gardens adjoining the farmhouse.

Also on the premises is a large children's play area with swings and a see-saw. Trenewydd has eight acres of peaceful rolling farmland with wooded valleys and a superb stretch of coastline nearby. The farmhouse pets include a donkey, a pony and lambs in springtime. Just three miles away is the glorious Poppit Sands, and there are several other safe, sandy beaches in the region, including the National Trust's Penbryn and Mwnt - the latter is a favourite spot for dolphin-spotting.

Pembrokeshire, which is known as Sir Benfro in Welsh, is home to Britain's only coastal national park - the Pembrokeshire Coast National Park. Visitors flock to this leading European holiday destination to see the spectacular grandeur and tranquil beauty of the countryside and take in some of the 186 mile coastal clifftop path.

Carreg Sampson, nr Abercastle

The coastal region offers wonderful walking and glorious views and is a paradise for bird-watchers. Incorporating one of the most fantastic stretches of natural beauty in Europe, the Pembrokeshire Coast National Park begins (or ends) on the south facing shoreline near Tenby. Running right around the ruggedly beautiful south western tip of Wales, around St Brides Bay and up along the north facing coast almost to Cardigan, the Park also includes quiet fishing villages, the huge cliffs at Castlemartin, sweeping golden beaches and small, often busy harbours. Although not strictly on the coast, the labyrinthine Cleddau river system also lies within the Park's boundaries and here there are delightful little villages such as Cresswell and Carew as well as the superb sheltered harbour of Milford Haven.

Pembroke Castle

Offshore there are various islands, including Grassholm, Ramsey, Skokholm and Skomer, which have changed little since they were named by Viking invaders. Many are now bird and wildlife sanctuaries of international importance. Grassholm is home to thousands of gannets, Skokholm has Manx shearwaters, Skomer has shearwaters and puffins. Ramsey harbours such species as choughs and the red-legged crow, and is also the resting place of many Welsh saints. One island, Caldey, has for over 1,500 years been the home of a religious community which continues today to live a quiet and austere life. Between their devotions, the monks of Caldey scrape a living from the land and are famous for their range of perfumes and toiletries inspired by the island's wild flowers. Pembrokeshire is the home of the corgi, which was brought to the notice of the Kennel Club by Captain Jack Howell. He presented Princess Elizabeth with her first corgi, and the rest, as they say, is history.

LOCATOR MAP

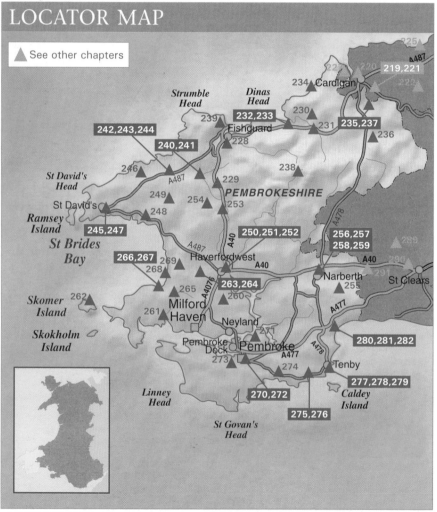

ADVERTISERS AND PLACES OF INTEREST

WEST WALES ARTS CENTRE

16 West Street, Fishguard, Pembrokeshire SA65 9AE
Tel/Fax: 01348 873867
e-mail: westwalesartsconnect.com
website: http://home.btconnect.com/WEST-WALES-ARTS/

Close to the centre of Fishguard, **West Wales Arts Centre** comprises three floors of elegant display areas behind a Georgian frontage housing a large and impressive collection of contemporary paintings, sculptures, ceramics, glassware and artistic cards. The director of the Centre is Myles Pepper, a family man of high profile in the world of art. Under his enthusiastic leadership the Centre holds regular exhibitions and promotes concerts and other cultural events in West Wales and Southern Ireland in conjunction with Celtic Connections. Among the main artists who regularly show at the Centre are David Tress and James MacKeown. London-born David Tress has lived in Pembrokeshire since 1976 and in 1999 he was one of 48 British artists and designers commissioned to design a stamp for the Millennium special stamp issue.

His works are on show here and in the National Museums and Galleries and the National Library of Wales, in the County Hall Collection of Dyfed County Council and at Clare Hall, Cambridge.

James MacKeown is the grandson of the late Tom Carr, one of Belfast's most distinguished painters, and his works take their inspiration from the landscapes and seascapes and people of County Down, of Pembrokeshire, where he lived in the 1980s, and of Normandy, where he has been based since 1988. He is renowned for his interiors and for his figures, especially of children.

His work has been featured in many one-man and group exhibitions in the UK, France and Hong Kong, and his paintings are in private collections in France, Ireland, Britain, Canada, the USA, Saudi Arabia, Japan, Switzerland and China.

Other artists and craftspeople who have recently exhibited at the West Wales Arts Centre include Catrin Webster, Sara Philpott, Ian Robertson, Andie Clay, Michael Payne, Mark Mawer, Monica Groves, Veronica Gibson, Brendan Stuart Burns, Josh Partridge, John Ward and Mark Raggett, and the summer 2002 exhibition features recent work by David Tress, James Campbell and Emma Maiden. Gallery events also include concerts, poetry readings and talks. The Centre is open Monday to Saturday 9.30am to 5.30pm

FISHGUARD

Situated at the mouth of the River Gwaun, from which the town takes its Welsh name Abergwaun, the geography of Fishguard can be somewhat confusing to visitors. The picturesque old harbour, a pretty little quayside lined with fishermen's cottages, is Lower Fishguard, which was the location for the fictional seaside town of Llareggub used in the filming in the 1970s of Dylan Thomas' play, *Under Milk Wood*, starring Richard Burton. The new harbour, built at the beginning of the 20th century, lies across the bay at Goodwick and it is from here that the ferries depart for Ireland. On the high ground between the two harbours lies the main town of Upper Fishguard, a bustling place packed with

Fishguard Harbour

shops, restaurants and pubs.

It was here, in February 1797, that the last invasion of Britain took place when a poorly equipped band of Frenchman landed at Carregwastad Point. Under the command of an American officer, Colonel William Tate (who hoped to start a peasants' rebellion), the 1,400

HEATHFIELD

Letterston, Pembrokeshire SA62 5EG
Tel: 01348 840263
e-mail: angelica.rees@virgin.net
website: www.p-net.co.uk/heathfield

Set high on a hill just outside the village of Letterston, **Heathfield** is a Grade II listed Georgian country house situated in 16 acres of beautiful pasture and woodland. It is run as a private guest house by Angelica and Clive Rees, she a former language teacher, he a retired Rugby Union international. The accommodation is very spacious and comfortable, and all the rooms have en suite or private bathrooms and splendid views over rolling countryside. Breakfast is English or Continental, and evening meals, with a choice of wines, are available by prior arrangement. Self-catering accommodation is also provided in a spacious, well-appointed and self-contained wing of the house, suitable for six adults and two children.

In the grounds is an attractive, traditional Welsh cottage sleeping two adults and two children. The atmosphere at Heathfield is relaxed and informal, the owners friendly and hospitable, and the grounds are ideal for walking and watching wildlife. There are fishing rights along a stretch of the Western Cleddau and shooting rights over 120 acres. Heathfield is situated at the end of a drive off the B4331. The nearby A40 provides quick and easy access to Fishguard and Haverfordwest. St David's is only 12 miles away, and it's just four miles to beautiful unspoilt beaches and the Pembrokeshire Coast Path. There are excellent golf courses in the vicinity, and horse riding is one of many outdoor activities that can be arranged locally.

strong French expeditionary force, who were mainly ex-convicts, stole drinks and looted the local farms. Unchecked by the local militia, the unruly invaders set up headquarters at a nearby farm and, according to local tradition, several local women, dressed in red cloaks, advanced on the French soldiers. The women were led by Jemima Nicholas, who carried a pitchfork, and the drunken invaders fled in terror mistaking the ladies for the

British army. The French retreated to the beach below Goodwick, where they formally surrendered to Lord Cawdor just two days after landing. Jemima Nicholas, who is said to have captured 12 Frenchmen singlehanded, became famous as the "General of the Red Army". She died in 1832 and is buried in St Mary's Church.

Housed in St Mary's Church's hall is **The Last Invasion Embroidered**

PENCRUGIAU ORGANIC FARM SHOP

Felindre Farchog, Pembrokeshire SA41 3XH
Tel/Fax: 01239 881265
e-mail: sales@organicfarmshop.uk.com
website: www.organicfarmshop.uk.com

Pencrugiau Organic Farm Shop has been growing organic produce for more than 21 years - long before the supermarkets jumped on the bandwagon! Mike Ray and his father opted for the country life when they started the business, which is located on the B4582, with delightful countryside all around and the coast very nearby. Their food is grown with sun, rain and natural goodness built up over years of organic growing - and not a chemical in sight.

Their seven acres produce an amazing range of over 200 crops: 10 types of lettuce; 5 varieties of tomato; 3 sorts of cucumber; white, red and savoy cabbage; curly, black and red kale; eating and cooking apples; garlic; leeks; bananas; dates; figs; citrus fruits; walnuts - that's just a short sample! Winter-storable roots such as potatoes and carrots can be purchased in bulk at discounted prices. The shop is open five days a week (closed Wednesday and Sunday) from April to October, three days a week (Thursday to Saturday) November to March.

HENLLYS FARM PARK

Felindre Farchog, Newport Crymych, Pembrokeshire SA41 3UX
Tel: 01239 820578 e-mail: dramaq3@btinternet.com

Henllys Farm is a place of unique appeal, where visitors can enjoy excellent food, planned walks and the company of friendly farm animals. One walk highlights the wonderful views and vistas, while another concentrates on woodland and wildlife. Each walk takes about an hour, after which a visit to the restaurant at the farmhouse is highly recommended. Owner Jenny Murray Threipland is renowned for her delicious light lunches and cream teas, and the Sunday roast is so popular that booking is essential. The farm is open from 10.30 to 5 from May to September; closed Monday (except Bank Holidays) and Tuesday.

Tapestry, which was created to mark the Bicentenary of this bizarre event. Designed by Elizabeth Cramp RWS and worked by more than 70 embroiderers, the 100-foot long tapestry is in the style of the famous Bayeux Tapestry and depicts scenes from the invasion. The tapestry has its home here, but sometimes goes on tour. To track it down, phone 01348 874997.

AROUND FISHGUARD

Dinas

3½ miles NE of Fishguard on the A487

The village is situated at the base of **Dinas Island** which is, in fact, a promontory that culminates in **Dinas Head**. Now no longer a true island, the land was given this name because at the end of the Ice Age it was indeed separated from the mainland. In the care of the National Trust, the headland is an important nesting site for sea birds, and grey and Atlantic seals can often be seen swimming offshore.

Newport

6½ miles E of Fishguard on the A487

As its name would suggest, Newport was once an important port; it had a brisk wool trade until the time of the great plague, when trade was diverted to Fishguard. Newport was also the capital of the Marcher Lordship of Cemaes - the only one not to have been abolished by Henry VIII - and the **Lords' Castle**, which was built in the 13th century, has now been incorporated into a mansion house (not open to the public).

Today, this is a pretty little seaside town with a fine beach that still retains the charm of its fishing port. An excellent place from which to explore the Preseli Hills to the south, just to the

Cnapan

East Street, Newport, Pembrokeshire SA42 0SY
Tel: 01239 820575 e-mail: cnapan@online-holidays.net
website: www.online-holidays.net/cnapan

Cnapan, "a country house for guests", is a fine period building in the attractive village of Newport. Family owned and run by John and Eluned Lloyd and Michael and Judith Cooper, it has a welcoming and relaxing feel, which, combined with old-fashioned standards of courtesy and service, accounts for the very high level of repeat business it enjoys. The spacious hallway, with its handsome oak Welsh dresser, sets the traditional tone of the house, and the guest lounge has a wood-burning stove. Around the house are bookcases full of maps, local information, books and magazines, and the bar is a cosy spot to meet for a drink. In the summer the sunny, sheltered garden is a perfect place for afternoon tea.

The five en suite bedrooms all have their own individual charm. Some face towards the sea, others towards the hills; one is a family room. Cnapan has a well-earned reputation for the quality of the cooking, and Eluned and Judith work together in the kitchen to come up with new ideas for their mouthwatering menus. Breakfast brings a really excellent choice and lunchtime sees wholesome

favourites like vegetable soup, home-baked ham and fisherman's pie. In the evening the ladies really come into their own with superb dishes such as herby roulade with creamy wild mushrooms, grilled breast of Gressingham duck with a bitter orange and lemon sauce, and damson sorbet with a blackcurrant coulis. An alternative to the main accommodation is a self-catering cottage annexe for six, totally self-contained with its own private garden; guests here have everything they need to be self-sufficient, but many are drawn to the delights of the restaurant!

CARREG COETAN

Waunwhiod, Newport, Pembrokeshire SA42 0QG
Tel: 01239 820822 website: www.scarey.clara.net
e-mail: susan.carey@btinternet.com

Susan Carey and her husband welcome all ages, singles,
couples and families to their self-contained modern
cottage just outside Newport on the road to Pen-y-
Bont and the coast. **Carreg Coetan** has two generously
sized bedrooms, one with a double bed, the other with
twin beds; a cot can be provided if required. The rooms
share a bathroom and adjoining WC, and the day
rooms comprise a well-appointed kitchen and a comfortably furnished lounge/diner with tv. The
window in the lounge overlooks the patio, a large lawned area and the countryside beyond; there's a
car port and ample parking for three cars in the private driveway.

The creeper-clad cottage is situated just yards from the Pembrokeshire Coastal Path and a few
minutes from Newport, a small village with pubs, restaurants and shops stocking everything needed

for a self-catering stay and a beach holiday. Newport nestles
between the Preseli Mountains and a long, sandy beach;
the beach is called Traeth Mawr (Big Beach) and has masses
of golden sand with rock pools and caves to explore. The
Coastal Path provides just one of many lovely walks near
Carreg Coetan, and there are excellent opportunities nearby
for birdwatching, riding and golf. Places of historic interest
include, almost on the doorstep, Carreg Coetan Arthur, a
burial chamber which according to legend holds the
remains of King Arthur; also close by is the 6th century
church at Nevern with its famous Celtic Cross.

BLUEBERRY ANGORAS

Spinning, Weaving, Hand Knitting Studio
Ffynnon Watty, Moylegrove, Nr Cardigan,
Pembrokeshire SA43 3BU Tel: 01239 881668

Close to the spectacular North Pembrokeshire coastline,
a warm welcome will be found at **Blueberry Angoras**,
the home of Graham and Sylvia Sexton and their flock
of Angora goats. The Moylegrove studio is open seven
days a week throughout the year for sales, demonstrations and tuition.

Their finest kid mohair is spun into soft, airy knitting
yarns which are hand dyed by Sylvia in over 50 shades.
Luxurious hand-knitted garments line the shelves and
can be custom made especially for you.

Cushions, scarves and knee rugs are hand-woven in
the studio. Mohair from the older goats is woven into
rugs and throws. Also stocked are mohair socks, cobweb
scarves, collectors bears and a range of spinning and
weaving equipment.

From the centre of Moylegrove village, take the
narrow turning by the chapel to Ceibwr. The studio is
signposted on the left.

north of the town is **Carreg Coetan Arthur**, a burial chamber reputed to hold the remains of King Arthur.

NEVERN

8 miles E of Newport on the B4582

The village of Nevern's most interesting features can be found at the **Church of St Brynach**, which is dedicated to the 5th century Irish saint whose cell was on nearby **Carn Ingli** - the Hill of Angels. Inside the church are two carved stones: the Maglocunus Stone, dating from the 5th century, commemorates Maglocunus, the son of Clutor and it bears both Latin and Ogham inscriptions; and the Cross Stone, which bears a Viking cross and dates from the 10th century. Outside in the churchyard stands one of the finest Celtic crosses in Wales - **St Brynach's Cross**. Dating from the 10th or 11th century, the cross stands some 13 feet tall and, according to tradition, the first cuckoo to be heard each year in Pembrokeshire sings from the top of the cross on St Brynach's Day (7th April).

To the northwest of the village are the remains of **Nevern Castle**, which was originally a local chieftain's fortress until, in around 1100, the Marcher Lord of Cemaes, Robert Martyn, built a motte and bailey castle on the site. The castle came into the hands of Rhys ap Gryffydd at the end of the 12th century and he added the stone castle, parts of which can still be seen today among the overgrown ruins.

EGLWYSWRW

11½ miles E of Fishguard on the A487

To the west of the village lies **Castell Henllys**, an Iron Age fort that is still being excavated by archaeologists. While the dig is continuing throughout the summer months, visitors to this late prehistoric site can also see the thatched roundhouses and outbuildings created to give as true as possible an insight into the lives of Iron Age man. Events throughout the season help to portray the wide spectrum of Celtic culture, from story-telling and craft demonstrations to the celebration of ancient festivals.

CILGERRAN

15 miles NE of Fishguard off the A478

The remains of **Cilgerran Castle**, one the most picturesque in Wales, can be seen sitting on a rocky promontory overlooking the River Teifi. A tranquil site today, this land was once hotly disputed territory and the castle's defences reflect this - there are almost sheer drops on two sides of the building, while the 13th century twin round towers and curtain walls protect the flank away from the cliff. The building of the castle is thought to have begun around 1093 but it was strengthened by Gerald de Windsor, to whom it was granted by Henry I. Thereafter it changed hands many times, being partially sacked by Rhys ap Gryffydd in 1164, retaken by the Earl of Pembroke in 1204 and finally falling to Llywelyn the Great in 1233.

The castle is forever associated with the legend of Princess Nest, the Welsh Helen of Troy, who, in 1109, was abducted by the besotted Owain, son of the Prince of Powys. Nest's husband, Gerald of Pembroke, escaped by slithering down a chute through the castle walls. One of the first major tourist attractions in Wales - in the 18th and 19th centuries it was fashionable to take a river excursion to the ruins from Cardigan - today, these romantic ruins still provide inspiration to artists, as they have done for centuries, and both JMW Turner and Richard Wilson are known to have visited here. Brown tourist signs

SNAIL TRAIL HANDWEAVERS

Martin and Nina L Weatherhead, Penwenallt Farm, Cilgerran,
Nr Cardigan, Pembrokeshire SA43 2TP
Tel/Fax: 01239 841228
e-mail: martin@snail-trail.co.uk website: www.snail-trail.co.uk

Snail Trail Handweavers offer accredited residential weaving, spinning and
dyeing courses in a delightful and secluded setting south of Cardigan,
surrounded by open farmland and overlooking the wooded Teifi Valley. Tutor
Martin Weatherhead is a full-time designer-craftsman who specialises in Ikat.
He exhibits widely and gives lectures and workshops throughout the UK.

Courses are held weekly from April to October subject to demand. Have fun creating colour with
dyes ancient and modern, relax to the rhythm of spinning fleece into yarn and enjoy taking home
your own handwoven tapestry, scarf, bag, cushion, floor rug or length of fabric. Try all three crafts or
choose to concentrate on just one. With an average of three or four students and never more than six,
classes are small and personal, so whether you are a complete beginner or have more experience, you
can work at your own pace and be surprised by your achievements in only one week.

Nina will look after you in the family's comfortable listed
Georgian farmhouse next to the studio. Her delicious wholefood
cooking includes fresh locally grown vegetables and free range
eggs when available. There is also an interesting and varied menu
for vegetarians or those on special diets.

Bed and breakfast is offered throughout the year.

The studio is open to visitors most weekdays from 10am to
5pm where Martin's work is available for sale.

WENDY BRANDON HANDMADE PRESERVES

Felin Wen, Boncath, Pembrokeshire SA37 0JR
Tel: 01239 841568
e-mail: w.brandon@btinternet.com
website: www.wendybrandon.co.uk

A converted barn in a 18th century corn mill is the centre
of operations of **Wendy Brandon Handmade Preserves**.
Wendy and her son Ian employ a skilled team in
producing a range of some 150 different preserves - jams,
jellies, marmalades, chutneys, pickles, fruit mustards,
fruit vinegars and flavoured oils. Everything is made in
small batches from fresh fruit and vegetables, and visitors
can watch them being made and have a taste before
moving on to the shop to make their purchases. They
sell their outstanding products to shops, hotels and
restaurants in the UK and overseas. They also offer a
mail order and gift service.

The jars have one of three different coloured labels:
red for traditional preserves sweetened with cane sugar;
green, sweetened with apple juice, so no added sugar -
and no salt; and orange, sweetened with a mixture of cane sugar and apple juice - these are mainly
marmalades. They are all superb, and among the more unusual items are ugli fruit marmalade, lemon
mustard and an old-fashioned green bean chutney. The shop and kitchen are open all year, Monday
to Friday and Saturday morning; also by appointment at other times and Bank Holidays. Wendy
Brandon Handmade Preserves lies in lovely countryside a mile from Boncath on the road to Bwlchygroes.

THE WELSH WILDLIFE CENTRE

Cilgerran, Cardigan SA43 2TB
Tel: 01239 621212 Fax: 01239 613211
e-mail: wildlife@wtww.co.uk
website: www.wtww.co.uk

The Welsh Wildlife Centre is set in 265 acres of the best wildlife habitats in Wales, from the Cilgerran Gorge to Cardigan town. The Teifi Valley has long been one of the most important landscape features in West Wales and was also a major player in agriculture, the slate mining industry and shipbuilding in the river's lower reaches. From the 18th century onwards the valley's dramatic gorges, castles and ruins attracted lovers of history and nature, and when the Cardi Bach railway was opened from Whitland to Cardigan the important water meadows were created. The railway has gone, the industry largely gone, too, so the valley has returned to its former tranquillity, a haven for wildlife in a great variety of habitats. More than 130 species of bird have been recorded, and more than 20 mammals, including otter, red deer, voles, badgers and many different bats, and the plant and insect life is equally varied. The Visitor Centre is open from April to October, and the Nuthatch Restaurant offers light meals and panoramic views of the river and reserve. In the Otter Holt gift shop visitors can buy a variety of mementoes of their visit to this magnificent wildlife centre.

The Welsh Wildlife Centre and Teifi Marshes Reserve is one of many nature reserves managed by the Wildlife Trust of South and West Wales based at Tondu near Bridgend. Tel: 01656 724100

lead from the point where the A478, A484 and A487 meet to the **Welsh Wildlife Centre** (see panel above), an excellent place for spotting birds, wild flowers, butterflies and otters. Wild footpaths pass through woodland, reed beds, meadows, marsh and riverside, providing the chance to see a vast variety of wildlife in different habitats.

LLANFAIR-NANT-GWYN

12½ miles E of Fishguard on the B4332

Bro-Meigan Gardens, to the east of the village, is a delightful place to spend a few hours meandering through the carefully designed gardens. With panoramic views over the Preseli Hills, the backdrop to the gardens, visitors to Bro-Meigan will see an incredible range of plants from all over the world, all grown from seed. While enjoying the superb horticultural displays, visitors can

also rest at the gardens' traditional tea rooms housed in a 300-year-old barn, enjoying home-made cakes and scones served on bone china.

CROSSWELL

10 miles E of Fishguard on the B4329

This village, on the northern slopes of the Preseli Hills, is home to **Pentre Ifan Burial Chamber**, one of the grandest megalithic remains in Wales. An ancient chamber with a huge 16-foot capstone, the monument is made of the same Preseli bluestones that somehow found their way - though no one has yet come up with a fully convincing explanation - to Stonehenge on Salisbury Plain. The site is managed by CADW.

PONTFAEN

4½ miles SE of Fishguard off the B4313

The village lies on the western edge of

Continued on page 250

WALK 8

Cilgerran and the Teifi gorge

Start	Cilgerran Coracle Centre. Follow signs to "River" from the main street in Cilgerran
Distance	5½ miles (8.9km)
Approximate time	3 hours
Parking	Coracle Centre car park at Cilgerran
Refreshments	Pubs and café at Cilgerran
Ordnance Survey maps	Landranger 145 (Cardigan), Outdoor Leisure 35 (North Pembrokeshire)

From the banks of the River Teifi the walk begins by heading up into Cilgerran, passing the castle and church, and it continues across fields and through woodland, with attractive views over quiet countryside. It is a twisting route and some muddy sections can be expected but it is well waymarked throughout; simply keep an eye out for the regular yellow arrows. The highlight comes at the end: a glorious stroll through the Teifi gorge with the romantic scene of the towers of Cilgerran Castle rising above the wooded cliffs.

Cilgerran occupies the ridge above the western side of the Teifi gorge, making it an ideal defensive site. The castle, which dates mainly from the early 13th century, and the church, which apart from its fine 14th century tower is mostly a 19th century rebuilding, are both in picturesque settings. The Teifi is one of the few rivers in Britain where fishing from traditional coracles can still be seen. It is difficult to believe that this tranquil backwater was once a busy commercial waterway, carrying salmon and later slates downstream to Cardigan. The modern Coracle Centre, where the walk begins, traces the varied history of Cilgerran and its river through the ages.

Facing the river, turn left along a track through the gorge and after a few yards turn left at a footpath sign, following directions to "Castle and village", along an uphill path, which is stepped in places. This goes through the remains of former slate quarries, now almost hidden by trees and scrub. In the 19th century Cilgerran became an important slate-quarrying centre with about 300 men employed in the industry.

Keep following the signs to "Castle and village", heading up to pass beneath the castle walls, turning left at the top of steps and

turning right along a track in front of a house. By the castle entrance, turn left along a tarmac track towards the village; the main part of the village is to the left but the route turns right here along a lane Ⓐ. The lane soon curves to the left and continues towards the church, heading downhill to pass to the right of it. In front of a bridge over a small stream, turn left onto an uphill wooded path to a road. Turn left and after about 100 yds (91m) turn right Ⓑ, at a public footpath sign, along a winding, hedge-lined track from which there are pleasant views across fields to hills dotted with woodland.

About 100 yds (91m) before reaching a farm, turn right over a stile and then left to head downhill across a field, passing below and to the right of the farm buildings. Continue through a hedge gap, keep ahead and turn left through a metal gate, immediately turning right Ⓒ along an enclosed path. Climb a stile, ford a small stream and turn left alongside it. Keep ahead, passing through two hedge gaps, and then walk gently uphill to climb another stile. Continue, passing through another hedge gap, bear slightly right and walk across the middle of a field to a stile. Climb that, bear right

WALK 8

along the right-hand edge of a field, by a line of trees on the right, climb another stile and turn left to continue along an enclosed track.

A few yards after this track bends to the right, turn left over a stile, head uphill across a field corner to climb the wire fence and turn left along a winding, uphill track. The track later levels out to reach a junction of several tracks; here turn left to continue along a pleasant, tree-lined track. After about 100 yds (91m), turn right over a stile and walk along the left-hand edge of a field, by a hedge on the left. Climb a stone stile and continue along the edge of the next field, turning left over another stone stile in the field corner. Now keep along the right-hand edge of a field, by a line of trees on the right, enjoying the fine views ahead of the Teifi valley. After 50 yds (46m), turn right over a stile, walk diagonally across a rough meadow to climb another stile and bear right to a third stile in the corner of the next meadow.

Climb the stile, turn left along an enclosed path that heads downhill into a wooded valley and turn left over a stile at the bottom. Turn right to cross a plank over a stream and head up to climb a stile. Continue along the left-hand edge of a field, by a wire fence on the left, climb a stile and turn right along the right-hand edge of a field, veering slightly left to climb another stile in the field corner. Turn left through a metal gate and walk along a hedge-lined track to a road  .

Turn left towards a chapel and almost immediately turn right along a tarmac track signposted to Rhosygilwen. Just after the track curves left, turn right at a public footpath sign and continue along a hedge-lined track, following it gently downhill. At a crossing of tracks climb the stile ahead, continue downhill, turn left at a T-junction and almost immediately turn sharp right onto a woodland path.

For the next 1¾ miles (2.8km) follow the path through attractive mixed woodland, taking care to look out for the indispensable yellow waymarks. In particular watch for a sharp right-hand turn downhill, shortly followed by an equally sharp

bend to the left. Another deviation from an otherwise fairly straight route is when you turn left in front of a metal gate and head uphill to turn right over a stile, continuing along the right-hand edge of a sloping meadow and where the wire fence on the right ends, turning right downhill to a track. Turn left along this track and, where it bends right, turn left over a stile, bear right uphill to join a woodland path and turn right along it. Continue through a particularly attractive stretch of lovely broad-leaved woodland, climbing a series of stiles and crossing several small streams, and finally walk along an enclosed path that heads up to go through a gate and continues to a narrow lane E.

Turn left along the lane for ½ mile (800m) to a T-junction on the edge of Cilgerran. Turn right along the road and at a public footpath sign turn left F onto a path at the side of the Masons' Arms. The path soon bends right and heads downhill into the Teifi gorge. Turn left to continue down to the river and follow it back to the start - a superb finale through the thickly wooded gorge.

the **Preseli Hills**, whose highest point, **Foel Cwmcerwyn** (1,759 feet) lies to the southeast; the views stretch as far as Snowdonia to the north and the Gower Peninsula to the south. These hills have seen many inhabitants come and go and they are littered with prehistoric sites. There are Iron Age hill forts, Bronze Age burial cairns and standing stones scattered along the "Golden Road", the ancient bridleway across the range.

In the foothills of the Preselis is the **Gwaun Valley**, a truly hidden place that runs from the hills to Fishguard. Some of the locals in this area still celebrate New Year on 12 January, in keeping with the custom that predates the introduction of the Gregorian calendar in 1752.

Located in the heart of the Gwaun Valley, **Gerddi Gardens** is the place to see an abundant display of miniature plants, dwarf conifers and alpines that are all set in attractive landscaped surroundings through which runs a fast flowing stream.

ROSEBUSH

8½ miles SE of Fishguard off the B4313

Lying in the shadow of Foel Cwmcerwyn, Rosebush is full of memories of the old slate quarries and now that the stone extraction has ceased the village and surrounding area has returned to being a peaceful rural community surrounded by lovely natural scenery. The local quarrymaster in the 1870s was one Edward Cropper; it is said that he had a special siding for his own railway carriage so that his wife did not have to mingle with the riff-raff! Rosebush slate was renowned and was used in many grand buildings, including the Palace of Westminster. Rosebush is thought to have been the first Welsh village with piped water.

THE POST OFFICE RESTAURANT

Rosebush, Nr Maenclochog, Pembrokeshire SA66 7QU
Tel: 01437 532205 Fax: 01437 532635
e-mail: oldpo_rosebush@hotmail.com

Set in the heart of the Preseli Mountains, the **Post Office Restaurant** is run by Ruth and Neal Jones, who are continuing a long tradition of hospitality at this well-established spot. The house was built in the 1870s of faced Rosebush slate for the owner of the local quarry, Edward Cropper. It later became a shop, then a post office, and many original features survive, along with memorabilia of the railway that served the quarry and evocative photographs of Rosebush 100 years ago.

The bistro-style restaurant, with half-panelled walls and a 1950s-style bar counter, is a cosy, unpretentious setting for enjoying a very varied choice of dishes to suit all tastes and appetites. Apart from the main evening menu, the offerings include vegetarian and vegan dishes, daily specials, light lunches, all-day snacks, afternoons teas and scrumptious home-made cakes and desserts. Next to the restaurant is a snug bar where visitors can enjoy a glass of wine or a pint of real ale (the ale choice includes a weekly changing special, so there's always something different). Booking is advisable, families are very welcome and the Post Office also offers bed and breakfast accommodation.

The other part of the building is a general store selling, among other things, local crafts and local ice cream. Outside is a patio area where visitors can sit with their dogs - water provided!

LLANGOLMAN

11½ miles SE of Fishguard off the A4313

Slate has been quarried in this area for centuries and, housed in a renovated 18th century corn mill, **The Slate Workshop** is a place where the art of handcrafting quality Welsh slate items continues. A wide range of articles is made here, including high quality plaques, sundials, clocks and objets d'art, and many illustrate the great skill required to work and carve the slate. To the south of the village lies another interesting building, **Penrhos Cottage**, which is one of the few lasting examples of an overnight house. If a man, with the help of his friends, could build a dwelling between sunset and sunrise, he was entitled to all the land that lay within, literally, a stone's throw from the door. This particular overnight house dates from the 19th century and still contains the original furnishings.

GOODWICK

1 mile W of Fishguard off the A487

This once small fishing village is now effectively the base for Fishguard harbour, which was built here between 1894 and 1906 by the Fishguard and Rosslare Railways and Harbours Company to provide a sea link between southwest Wales and Ireland. Still offering a much-used ferry service today, Goodwick is older than it first appears;

the settlement was known to ancient inhabitants as Gwlad hud a Lledrith - the Land of Mystery and Enchantment. The surrounding countryside certainly lives up to this name, although the tales told by James Wade, one of Pembrokeshire's best known storytellers, are rather far fetched, but nonetheless delightful. On one occasion Wade, who died in 1887, recounted that, while he was fishing on Goodwick beach, a great carrion crow swooped out of the sky and carried him, in its beak, across the sea to Ireland. On reaching land, the crow dropped Wade and he landed in a cannon where he spent the night. As he was waking the next morning, the cannon was fired and Wade was rocketed across St George's Channel and he landed beside his fishing rod in the exact spot from which he had been plucked!

Just a mile to the south of Goodwick lies **Manorowen Garden**, an interesting walled garden which has an historic gazebo. The garden was also involved in the French invasion of the 18th century, with a skirmish taking place between Colonel William Tate's invading army and the local militia.

STRUMBLE HEAD

4 miles W of Fishguard off the A487

This huge headland, with its lighthouse warning ships off the cliffs on the approach to Fishguard harbour, offers

MIRANDA'S PRESERVES

Ty'r Henner, Goodwick, Pembrokeshire SA64 0JB
Tel: 01348 872011 e-mail: miranda@preserves.freeserve.co.uk

Along the winding road from Goodwick to Strumble Head Lighthouse is a roadside stand filled with delicious homemade jams, marmalades, jellies, curds, boozy fruits, fruit cheeses and chutneys. **Miranda's Preserves** are made using traditional methods by Miranda James. As far as possible, locally sourced ingredients are used including home-grown fruit and vegetables. Miranda sells direct from Ty'r Henner, which is open every day from March to November, but what started as a small enterprise to earn pocket money has developed into a much larger, but still personal business, and her superlative produce is now available in many shops and by mail order.

THE WOOL GALLERY

Llain Farm, Mathry, Haverfordwest,
Pembrokeshire SA62 5JA
Tel: 01348 837634

The Wool Gallery is part of Llain
Farm, a 230-acre organic farm south
of Mathry - brown tourist signs show
the way from the B4330 and B4331.
Gareth and Linda Waters have been
farming here for 12 years, and four
years ago they opened the Wool
Gallery as an adjunct to the farming
side of the business. Their aim at the
farm is to keep and rear their animals

in the most natural way possible and
they specialise in some of the oldest
breeds in Wales.

The Welsh Black Cattle and Jacob
Sheep all graze freely with their young,
and the Oxford Sandy and Black Pigs
are also free-range, with pig arks for
shelter. The care with which the animals
are looked after is shown by the awards
which the owners have won at country
shows. In the farm shop a wide range
of meat from animals raised on the farm
is sold: Jacob and Welsh lamb and pork
on and off the bone, beef on and off
the bone and minced, sweet-cured
gammon, home-cured bacon, free-range chicken and turkey, sausages and burgers.

The choice is exceptional, with no fewer than 16 types of sausage and a dozen burgers. In the Wool
Gallery, woollen goods from
the sheep and from the farm's
Angora rabbits are on sale,
from woolly hats and scarves
to throws, baby fleeces and
lovely warm jerkins and wraps.
Linda herself does a lot of
spinning and weaving at the
Gallery. Visitors will also find
a selection of pottery and
carved wood furnishings and
ornaments produced by
talented local craftspeople. Tea,
coffee and light refreshments
are served at the Gallery and
Farm Shop, which are open
from 10.30 to 5 every day
except Monday; parking is
plentiful, and there are toilets
with access for wheelchairs.

Voyages Of Discovery

1 High Street, St David's, Pembrokeshire SA62 6SA
Tel: 01437 720285 Fax: 01437 721911 Freephone: 0800 854367

John Price, a marine biologist, is the principal of **Voyages of Discovery**, a business in St David's specialising in marine tours, cruises and fishing trips for individuals, families and groups. The most popular of the voyages is the tour to Ramsey Island on one of the powerful, sturdy inflatables, providing a combination of speed and exhilaration, wildlife observation and marvelling at the forces of nature. The island is home to a large colony of grey seals and to countless sea birds, and on most days porpoises can be seen during the trips. Ramsey is famous for its deep sea caves, and each tour includes navigating into them to wonder at nature's architecture. For a more relaxed outing to Ramsey Island, a traditional vessel, the *Treffgarne*, stops at points of interest and offers the chance to observe the bird and sea life. Fishing trips can also be arranged on the *Treffgarne*.

The Evening North Bishop Puffin Watch is a two-hour voyage to see North Bishop Island and to observe the puffins, seals and porpoises. The most powerful of the inflatables, the *Viking Pioneer*, undertakes voyages to the hitherto rarely visited islands of Grassholm and the Smalls, and apart from the superb birdwatching the vessel carries underwater hydrophones and will dedicate time to whale and dolphin watching. In conjunction with Voyages of Discovery, excellent self-catering accommodation in the heart of St David's can be booked by contacting Liz Taylor on 01437 720667. Three cottages sleeping from two to five all have fully-equipped kitchens, comfortable living rooms and off-street parking.

the Archbishop-designate of Canterbury, Dr Rowan Williams, into the Gorsedd of Bards, a historic order of Druids. The ceremony was held in a circle of standing stones fashioned, like the stones at Stonehenge, from Pembrokeshire rock. The ceremony involved the singing of Welsh Christian hymns and the Welsh National Anthem, the reading of a citation by the Arch-Druid and the wielding of a giant ceremonial sword - a burdensome task entrusted to Druid Ray Gravell, a former Welsh rugby international. Dr Williams is the third Archbishop of Wales to be a member of the Gorsedd. Speaking Welsh is a prerequisite for consideration for nomination, with one exception - the Queen.

Just outside the city, in a stunningly beautiful spot overlooking the sea, are **St Non's Well** and the ruins of **St Non's Chapel**. The bay too, is named after St David's mother - St Non - and legend has it that David was born here during a great storm in around AD 520. The waters

Whitesands Bay, St David's

of St Non's Well are said to have special powers for healing eye diseases and it was much visited during the Middle Ages by pilgrims to St David's. David's father was the chieftain Sant, his grandfather Ceredig, king of the region around Cardigan. Little is known about David, save that he received a formal education, gained great authority in the church and moved the seat of ecclesiastical government from Caerleon to Mynyw, now St David's. St David is a central figure in one of the many legends concerning how the leek came to be adopted as the national emblem of Wales. The legend states that just before a battle against the Saxons he advised the Britons to wear a leek in their caps to distinguish them from the enemy. St David's Day, March 1st, is the traditional national day of the Welsh, when Welsh people all over the world wear the national emblem, the leek, or the other national emblem, the daffodil. The Welsh words for leek and daffodil are the same, which could explain why both are national emblems.

Another coastal beauty spot, which is also steeped in legend, is **St Justinian's**, a rock-bound harbour that is home to the St David's Lifeboat Station. Justinian was a 6th century hermit who retreated across to **Ramsey Island**, a short distance offshore, to devote himself to

God. A strict disciplinarian, he must have been too severe with his followers as they eventually rebelled and cut off his head! Justinian is then said to have walked across the waters of Ramsey Sound, back to the mainland, with his head in his arms. Ramsey is a Norse name, a legacy of the Dark Ages when this part of the coast was terrorised by Viking invaders. Today, the island is an RSPB reserve that is home to an abundance of wildlife. There are boat trips around the island during which not only can the numerous sea birds be observed, but visitors may have a close encounter with colonies of seals.

SOLVA
16 miles SW of Fishguard on the A487

Situated at the end of a long inlet and well protected from the sometimes stormy waters of St Bride's Bay, Solva harbour is one of the most sheltered in Wales. Green hills roll down to the quayside and this picturesque view was the last sight of Wales for many 19th century emigrants who sailed from Solva to America for 10 shillings - the price of a one way ticket. Now no longer such a busy port, Solva is a charming old seafaring village that boasts a good range of craft shops. **Solva Woollen Mill**, in the beautiful valley of the River Solfach, has been in continuous production since

OCULUS
19 Main Street, Solva, Pembrokeshire SA62 6UU
Tel: 01437 729082

In the spring of 2000 two local girls, Joy Dixon and Karen Saunders, took over traditional shop premises on the main street of Solva and **Oculus** was born. Both skilled craftswomen, they invited fellow craftspeople to display their work, and the shop has since become a much visited showcase for the arts and crafts talents of the region. The walls, shelves and tables are filled with a wide variety of desirable handmade objects, each one a perfect gift for someone, from paintings and prints to framed photographs and items in glass, slate and stone, ceramics, metal and wood, fabrics and embroidery.

LLANDDINOG OLD FARMHOUSE AND COTTAGES

Llandeloy, Solva, Haverfordwest, Pembrokeshire SA62 6NA
Tel: 01348 831224 Fax: 01348 831191

Owner Stephanie Castle was a very successful rider and riding instructor before acquiring **Llanddinog Old Farmhouse and Cottages**, which she now lets as top-class self-catering holiday accommodation. The 13th century traditional stone farmhouse, set in 3½ acres on the edge of lovely rolling countryside, has four bedrooms, bathroom, shower room, two reception rooms, dining room and fully fitted kitchen. All the up-to-date essentials for a comfortable stay are provided, while retaining much of the period charm and character. A large patio area to the rear has garden furniture and barbecue facilities. In the grounds of the farmhouse are three self-catering cottages, similarly well-equipped for self-catering guests.

The Granary, converted from a 19th century granary building, is a detached cottage for up to six people and a baby in three bedrooms, and The Tackroom, part of the same range of farm buildings, has a similar specification. Both these, like the farmhouse, have tv, plenty of literature on activities and places to see in the area, and gravelled forecourts with ample parking space. The third cottage is The Stable, part of a series of outbuildings attached to the main house. A "minstrels' gallery' provides a unique family bedroom under the eaves. The Stable also has a sun-trap courtyard. Cycles can be hired and horse-riding arranged; there are golf courses nearby, and the whole area is a paradise for walkers and nature-lovers. The sandy beaches of Whitesands and Newgale, secluded coves, the harbour at Solva and the Pembrokeshire Coast Path are all a short drive away.

it opened in 1907; it now specialises in carpets and rugs, and visitors can usually see weaving in progress.

HAVERFORDWEST

This old county town, with its pleasant rural surrounding, lies on the banks of the labyrinthine Cleddau river system and is more or less in the centre of Pembrokeshire. Lining the steep streets of this hilly town there can be found some fine Georgian buildings that date back to the days when Haverfordwest was a prosperous port trading largely with Bristol and Ireland.

However, the town predates this trading boom by several centuries and its unusual name is a legacy of Viking raids.

Solva Harbour

Set on a hill overlooking the River Cleddau is the striking landmark of **Haverfordwest Castle**, which was built around 1120 by Gilbert de Clare. The town grew up around the fortress and throughout the 12th and 13th centuries it saw various inhabitants including

PEMBROKESHIRE ART AND FRAMING

Wyon House, 9 Market Street, Haverfordwest,
Pembrokeshire SA61 1NF
Tel: 01437 779524 e-mail: mail@pembsart.com
website: www.pembsart.com

At **Pembrokeshire Art and Framing** owner Gareth Roberts offers a comprehensive, high-quality framing service for the home or office. In spacious town-centre premises he stocks a range of over 600 frame mouldings and a wide selection of coloured and decorative mounts. Besides framing artwork to conservation and museum standards, he is skilled in the mounting and framing of all forms of needlework and fabric art, and 3D objects such as medals, trophies, sports shirts etc. He also offers advice on hanging and displaying pictures. Gareth is happy to supply framing materials and helpful advice to DIY framers. Works by local and internationally respected artists are displayed in the light and spacious gallery, ranging from original paintings and sculpture, to original prints, including etchings, lithographs and screenprints. There is also a range of limited edition prints, fine art posters and prints and a selection of greetings cards. Pembrokeshire Art and Framing is a member of The Fine Art Trade Guild and Gareth has achieved the guild's "Commended Framer" award.

THE SHEEP SHOP

7-11 Riverside Arcade, Haverfordwest,
Pembrokeshire SA61 2AL
Tel: 01437 760318
e-mail: HughJohnWilson@aol.com

Linda and Hugh-John Wilson, owners of Nant-y-Coy Mill in Treffgarne Gorge (see separate panel on page 262), have another string to their bow, this one in a modern shopping arcade by the River Cleddau. **The Sheep Shop** comprises three linked premises which between them stock an impressive range of woollens, jewellery, love spoons, paintings and craftware, soft toys, pottery, ceramics and greetings cards. The clothing range includes fleeces, waterproofs, sweatshirts and hand-knitted Arans made in Pembrokeshire; also made in Wales are ties, scarves, caps and splendid picnic rugs.

Visitors entering the shop might wonder why it isn't called the Bear Shop, as they are greeted by a display of bears of all kinds, notably the very valuable and highly collectable Steiff range, for which the shop is the local agent. Above the shop is a gallery featuring paintings by talented local artists specialising in local scenes; among them are Simon Swinfield, Graham Brace and Marianne Brand. Apart from being the home of woollen goods and princely bears, Haverfordwest has plenty of historic and architectural interest including fine Georgian houses, the remains of an Augustinian priory church and a museum and art gallery housed in the castle.

Gryffydd ap Rhys, Henry II and Edward I. Haverfordwest also saw fluctuating fortunes during the Civil War as the town changed hands several times before it was finally taken by Parliament's General Laugharne in 1645. He ransacked the Castle, and today, the tumbledown remains, whose inner wards were converted into a gaol in 1820, are home to the town's **Museum and Art Gallery**.

The remains of a **Priory Church**, founded by Augustinian Canons in the early 13th century, can be found by the Western Cleddau river. Excavations of the priory land have revealed that there were gardens here in the cloister and also between the priory buildings and the river. The riverside gardens, which were laid out in the mid-15th century, provide a rare example of the sort of garden that is often seen in medieval manuscripts and the narrow raised beds have been replanted with plant species appropriate to the period.

Close by is a strange, ghostly border that cannot be seen: known locally as the **Landsker** (or land scar) it divides the English speaking "little England beyond Wales" of south Pembrokeshire from the Welsh speaking north. This abrupt division of the county can be traced back to early medieval times when Norman invasions into these parts paved the way for Anglo Saxon and Flemish immigrants. A line of castles was built from Amroth right across to Roch and, although the Landsker is an invisible border, its significance has been profound in the past. It was unthinkable that a marriage should take place between a man and a woman from different sides of the line even though they may have lived along a short distance apart. The Landsker

NANT-Y-COY MILL

Treffgarne Gorge, Haverfordwest,
Pembrokeshire SA62 5LR
Tel: 01437 741671
e-mail: hughjohnwilson@aol.com

Nant-y-Coy Mill is an old corn mill that is part of a farm that was worked until 1971. It is now one of Pembrokeshire's main attractions, with a variety of things to see and do and a dramatic setting in Treffgarne Gorge. The old mill building contains a unique mixture of quality crafts and exhibitions of local history. In the old machinery and grinding rooms a shop has been created selling a wide range of knitwear, woollen rugs, pottery, toys, Celtic jewellery, pictures, prints, cards and lovespoons. These spoons were a traditional courting gift from a man to a woman, and many were ornately carved with symbols indicating a message of love. Visitors buying spoons at the Mill can have them engraved with their own messages.

In the Milking Parlour tea-room a range of cakes and snacks include Welsh specialities such as the hearty Welsh Cawl (a filling leek, meat and root vegetable soup) and home-made Bara Brith. The area surrounding the Mill is one of the most beautiful inland parts of the county, and the Mill's owners have devised a nature walk that leads up the secluded Nant-y-Coy Valley, across fields and up to the top of the Great Treffgarne Rocks. Easy to find on the A40 seven miles north of Haverfordwest, the Mill is open Monday to Saturday from Easter to October, also on Sunday in high season. The owners also have the Sheep Shop in Haverfordwest (see separate feature on page 260).

COLIN MORSE GALLERY

Priskilly Fawr Farm, Hayscastle, Haverfordwest,
Pembrokeshire
Tel: 01348 840650

Starting his professional life as a farmer, Colin Morse trained for four years before becoming a full-time illustrator and painter. He works from his farm studio, a bright, purpose-designed barn conversion next to the house where he and his wife Bobby live. On show in the **Colin Morse Gallery** is a

selection of his original works and limited edition prints depicting the countryside, coast and people of Pembrokeshire. The Gallery is open every day in

the summer months and can be approached from the A40/B4331 at Letterston or from the A487 by way of Castle Morris (from St David's) or Llangloffan Cheese Farm (from Fishguard). the scenery around the Gallery and farm is superb, and a new walk has been devised through the woods and fields.

borderlands feature delightful countryside and fascinating villages and hamlets with a rich heritage and many stories to tell.

AROUND HAVERFORDWEST

SCOLTON
4½ miles NE of Haverfordwest on the B4329

The Victorian **Scolton Manor House**, which dates from around 1840, along with its grounds is, today, a museum and **Country Park** that makes an interesting and enjoyable visit. The house, stable block and exhibition hall, as **Pembrokeshire's County Museum**, features a number of displays that illustrate the history of this southwestern region of Wales. While the past is concentrated on here, at the award winning **Visitor Centre** there is an exhibition which looks to the future and, in particular, green issues and the

wildlife of the surrounding park. Outside, the country park not only has nature trails, picnic areas and a play area but a greener lifestyle can also be experienced in the landscaped grounds.

LLYS-Y-FRAN
7½ miles NE of Haverfordwest off the B4329

The impressive dam built to form **Llys-y-fran Reservoir** in the 1960s has been constructed in sympathy with the surrounding countryside and, when it was officially opened in 1972 by Princess Margaret, the reservoir was able to meet the growing needs of the county's population and of the oil refineries at Milford Haven. Surrounded by the glorious **Country Park**, which lies in the shadow of the Preseli Hills to the north, there is a seven-mile perimeter path around the reservoir that provides an opportunity to possibly see some of the local inhabitants, including foxes, badgers, mink, squirrels and otters. The

THE WAGTAILS AND SWALLOWS NEST

Great Redford, Princes Gate, Narberth,
Pembrokeshire SA67 8TD
Tel: 01834 860035
e-mail: eleanor.macphee@virgin.net
website: www.pembrokeshirecountrycottages.co.uk

Set in attractive open countryside near the village of Princes Gate, **The Wagtails and Swallows Nest** are attractively restored former barns that provide a perfect self-catering getaway retreat. In the summer they are ideal for family holidays, with lovely sandy beaches just minutes away, but at anytime of the year they promise peace and relaxation in rural surroundings. The Wagtails has two bedrooms sleeping four guests plus a cot, a cosy lounge-dining room, well-equipped kitchen and bathroom with bath and shower; a small lawned area has patio furniture and a barbecue.

Swallows Nest has a twin room plus a cot, open-plan sitting/dining room with kitchen area, bathroom with walk-in shower, and a patio with furniture and a barbecue. Both are equipped with a full-size cooker, microwave oven, fridge, toaster, electric kettle, tv, video and micro hi-fi. Central heating is supplemented by log-burning fires, and The Wagtails has a washing machine. The owner of the cottages, Eleanor Macphee, can arrange salmon and trout fishing on the Eastern Cleddau. The beach at Amroth, just four miles away, is the starting point of the Pembrokeshire Coast Path, which runs around the coast for 180 miles, ending at Cemaes Head near Cardigan.

THE GOLDEN SHEAF GALLERY

25 High Street, Narberth, Pembrokeshire SA67 7AR
Tel: 01834 860407 Fax: 01834 869064
website: www.paul.sourcedirect.co.uk

Paul and Suzanne Morgan-Somers are the go-ahead young owners of the award winning **Golden Sheaf Gallery**. Approved by the Crafts Council for quality, the gallery is set in the attractive surroundings of a listed Georgian building. Here, you will find two floors of innovative, contemporary art, gifts and desirable goods, all specially and personally slected by Paul and Suzanne.

There are paintings by local artists, limited edition prints, handmade fine jewellery, ceramics and sculpture, toiletries by Neals Yard, L'Occitane, Green People and Savonnerie together with beautiful textiles, leather bags, alternative health and lifestyle books, a fantastic

selction of childrens toys and an exciting range of design led gifts for adults and children...... the list is almost endless and the stock continually evolves, so that no matter how many times this splendid place is visited, there will always be something new, original or amusing to buy.

The little town of Narberth, sited on an ancient hill, has a long and interesting history. It is mentioned in the Mabinogion and the ruins of the castle still remain. Today, Narberth is a thriving town notable for its fine shops and entertainments. Enjoy your visit!

ICHTHUS ANTIQUES

2 Market Square, Narberth, Pembrokeshire SA67 7AU
Tel: 01834 860416
e-mail: dichthus@aol.com

Antiques and collectables in great profusion and amazing variety fill every inch of space at **Ichthus Antiques**, located in a period house on a corner site in Narberth. Cheryl Evans, who lives "above the shop" and runs it with her daughter Lilian, has a keen collector's eye for spotting anything of interest or out of the ordinary, and to call her shop Aladdin's Cave is to do it scant justice! Among the merry jumble of items on display are pictures and prints; jewellery and trinkets; little wooden or plaster figurines; old Dinky toys; earthenware storage jars; mounted stag's horns; cups and mugs and jugs; folding chairs; photographic frames; plant holders; a Ming vase in a cabinet full of china, porcelain and crystal; a selection of bowler hats with an old hat stretcher, clocks of all sizes; small items of furniture and a beautiful selection of her speciality which is Welsh blankets and linens.

Part of the stock is a very unusual collection of period teaching aids including little figurines in national dress - a quaint reminder of one method of generating in schoolchildren an interest in and knowledge of foreign lands and peoples. The shop is full to bursting point with all these fascinating items, and customers can spend many a happy hour browsing for the perfect gift to take home. And they can be sure that the next time they are in this lovely part of the world there will be dozens or different little treasures to see. Opening hours are 10.30 to 5.30 Monday to Saturday.

fishing on the reservoir is some of the best in Wales and, regularly stocked with rainbow trout and with a steady population of brown trout, anglers can fish on the lake or from the banks.

CANASTON BRIDGE

7 miles E of Haverfordwest on the A40

To the south of the village can be found two very different attractions. **Blackpool Mill**, beside the Eastern Cleddau river, dates from the early 19th century and it is one of the finest examples of a water powered mill in Britain. Further south and hidden among trees lies **Oakwood**, Wales' premier theme park that is home to Europe's longest watercoaster, biggest wooden rollercoaster and largest skycoaster. As well as the outdoor rides there is an all-weather complex with a multitude of games, puzzles and rides and also Playtown, which is aimed at younger children.

NARBERTH

9½ miles E of Haverfordwest on the A478

This small old town, sited on a steep hill, is said to have been the legendary court of Pwyll, Prince of Dyfed. It is, however, a historical fact that Narberth grew up around its early Dark Ages' castle and that the town was burnt down by Norsemen in 994. **Wilson Castle**, in the southern part of the town, is one successor to the original fortification here; built in the 11th century, it was destroyed by the Welsh in 1115. Today, only a few fragments still stand of the castle rebuilt in 1264 by Sir Andrew Perrot and dismantled following the Civil War.

NARBERTH POTTERY

2 Market Street, Narberth, Pembrokeshire SA67 7AX
Tel: 01834 860732

Simon Rich and his daughter Bryony, are both acclaimed potters and Catherine, his wife, specialises in hand painted ceramics. They all produce a range of eye-catching pots, plates and dishes that have won acclaim far and wide. Simon's crystalline glazeware is of outstanding interest. He produces beautiful zinc crystals on pieces that come in all shapes and sizes. Their showroom is behind a traditional shop front. In it you will find Bryony's dazzling fumed copper raku, subtle terrasigilata, glorious lapis lazuli ware and Catherine's unique gold, silver and enamelled lustre ware. It is an ideal place to choose a very special gift or personal treat.

The Rich family's skills have gained recognition throughout the UK, and their quality and unique style are known far and wide. **Narberth Pottery** occupies premises close to the centre of Narberth, just off the main square. Narberth, sited on a hill, is rich in history and well worth a leisurely visit, but even without the literary and historical associations it's well worth taking time to admire the Rich family's work; the Pottery is open from 10.30 to 5.30 Monday to Saturday, with a short closure at lunchtime.

THE MALTHOUSE ANTIQUES CENTRE

Back Lane, Narberth, Pembrokeshire SA67 7AR
Tel: 01834 860303

The **Malthouse Antiques Centre** is located in one of the oldest buildings in Narberth, dating back some 300 years. Situated in the centre of this old market town which was once the main street, The Malthouse has become the most fascinating and popular antique centres locally and a "must see" on any tour of Pembrokeshire. Welsh country furniture, which is the particular expertise of the owner Paul Griffiths,is just one small part of the ever changing stock, which also includes general and garden furniture, stripped pine, mirrors, lamps and lighting, clocks, pots and vases and jugs, paintings, fireplaces and surrounds, Persian rugs, antiques of all kinds and collectables that range from cigarette cards to cannons.

All visitors are invited to browse at their leisure around this labyrinth of rooms, in an informal, relaxed and friendly atmosphere and whatever your interests something is bound to capture your eye. Antiques are bought and sold, and the centre undertakes house clearances. Connected to the centre is a trade warehouse offering a large selection of untouched, restorable furniture to which antique dealers and the public are welcome. Opening times are 10.00-5.30 Monday to Saturday. Narberth, originally Arberth, Court of the Prince of Dyfed has a wealth of fascinating stories to tell. It is a thriving colourful town where a friendly smile is high on the agenda.

RIITTA SINKKONEN-DAVIES HANDWEAVING

Mathom House, Moorland Road, Freystrop, Haverfordwest,
Pembrokeshire SA62 4LE
Tel: 01437 890712
e-mail: riitta@rasdavies.co.uk
website: www.rasdavies.co.uk

In the village of Freystrop, just south of Haverfordwest, **Riitta Sinkkonen-Davies** runs a small, interesting workshop specialising in linen weaving. Originally from Finland, Riitta married a Welshman and raised a family in Pembrokeshire while building up her workshop. A variety of work can be seen on display and in progress on different looms. During the summer Riitta also grows flax in her garden and processes it into linen to be used in her weaving. A wide selection of products can be purchased, from rugs, cushions and colourful table linen to pictures, wall hangings and handmade greetings cards incorporating woven samples.

Riitta accepts commissions for a variety of works. She has been involved in recreating many historic fabrics for several museums like Jorvik Viking Centre, Shakespeare's Birthplace and Sutton Hoo. Riitta

also gives talks and runs workshops on all aspects of her craft for both adults and children and can arrange courses at her workshop. Opening hours at the workshop are from 10 to 6 on Tuesdays, Wednesdays and Thursdays from April to October, otherwise by arrangement. From Merlins Bridge roundabout in Haverfordwest take the exit signposted Burton and Llangwm and follow for 2½ miles. At the crossroads in Freystrop turn right and immediately right again onto Moorland Road. Mathom House is the third on the left. Follow the arrows to the workshop at the back.

MARTLETWY

6 miles SE of Haverfordwest off the A4075

Cwm Deri Vineyard, to the south of
Martletwy and set in the Valley of the
Oaks, is the ideal place to see vines
growing from spring through to the
autumn harvest. At the vineyard shop
not only can visitors purchase estate
grown vintage wines but Cwm Deri also
produces fruit wines and liqueurs. Wine
tastings, of course, are always very
popular and, for younger members of
the family, the vineyard is home to
some rescued donkeys and there is also
a teddy bears' hideaway.

THE RHOS

3½ miles SE of Haverfordwest off the A40

East of the Cleddau toll bridge lies the
tidal estuary formed by the confluence of
the Western and Eastern Cleddau rivers,
into which also flow the Rivers Cresswell
and Carew. Winding a silvery ribbon
through the rural landscape, beside the
river banks are some of the Pembrokeshire
Coast National Park's most beautiful
treasures. Yet, this area is so often
overlooked by visitors that is has become
known as the Secret Waterway.

The Rhos, the only village in the
ancient parish of Slebach, overlooks the
Eastern Cleddau and here, close to the
river, lies **Picton Castle**, the historic
home of the Philipps family which is still
lived in by the direct descendants of Sir
John Wogan, who had the castle built in
the 13th century. The family, over the
centuries, has had its ups and downs:
they were awarded their Coat of Arms by
Richard the Lionheart following their
exploits during the Crusades; the
Philipps supported Parliament during
the Civil War; and, in the 18th century,
they took on prominent roles in the
economic, educational and social life of
Wales. Although the principal rooms

were remodelled in the mid-18th
century, some medieval features remain,
and, in the 1790s, the 1st Lord Milford
added the wing that now includes the
superb dining room and drawing room.

The castle is also home to an **Art
Gallery** with a permanent exhibition of
paintings by Graham Sutherland.
Outside, the gardens are equally
impressive and include a walled garden
with fish pond, rosebeds, culinary and
medicinal herbs and herbaceous borders.
In the extensive **Woodland Garden**
there is a fine collection of woodland
shrubs in among the ancient oaks,
beeches, redwoods and other
mature trees.

MILFORD HAVEN

6½ miles SW of Haverfordwest on the A40

As well as being the name of the town,
Milford Haven is also the name of the
huge natural harbour here. Described by
Nelson as "the finest port in
Christendom", the harbour offers some
of the best shelter in the world to large
ships as it is some 10 miles long by up to
two miles broad. Norsemen used the
harbour as did both Henry II and King
John who set sail from here to conquer
Ireland, but it was Sir William Hamilton
(husband of Lord Nelson's Lady Emma)
who, having inherited two nearby
manors, saw the potential of the Haven
as a major harbour. Hamilton was away
in Naples as an Envoy Extraordinary so
he appointed his nephew RF Greville to
establish the town around the harbour.
Greville contracted a Frenchman, J-L
Barrallier, to lay out the town and
dockyard in a square pattern that can
still be seen today. Although the docks,
completed in 1888, failed to attract the
hoped for larger ships, the Neyland
trawler fleet moved here and by the
beginning of the 20th century, Milford
Haven had become one of the country's

SKERRYBACK FARMHOUSE

Sandy Haven, St Ishmaels, Haverfordwest, Pembrokeshire SA62 3DN
Tel: 01646 636598 Fax: 01646 636595 e-mail: skerryback@pfh.co.uk

In an 18th century farmhouse Margaret Williams offers the perfect setting for a break from city life. The bed and breakfast accommodation at **Skerryback Farmhouse** comprises two double bedrooms with en suite facilities, and the guest lounge has tv, a log fire for chilly evenings and plenty of information on what to do in the area. Skerryback is a good base for exploring the nearby sandy beaches and secluded coves, for watching the birdlife of the estuary and the islands, and for visiting historic sites such as the ancient church at St Ishmaels. Margaret sees that guests start the day with a splendid breakfast, and evening meals are available by arrangement. No smoking at Skerryback.

leading fishing ports. During both World Wars, the Haven was busy with Atlantic convoys but after 1945 there was a decline and trawling also began to disappear. However, since the 1960s Milford Haven has developed as a major oil port and is still used by the leading oil companies.

Aptly housed in a former whale oil warehouse that dates from 1797, the **Milford Haven Museum** has a range of displays that follow the fortunes of the town and dockyard including hands-on exhibits tracing the town's history from a whaling port to a premier oil terminal. The **Discovery Centre** offers the opportunity to experience puzzles and illusions created by electronic and computer wizardry. The tomb of Sir William Hamilton can be seen in the graveyard of **St Katharine's Church**, while inside the church are a bible and prayer book presented by Lord Nelson.

SANDY HAVEN
8 miles SW of Haverfordwest off the B4327

The sheltered creek in this lovely village has been described as truly idyllic and, particularly at low tide in the spring and autumn, many birds can be seen feeding here. The picturesque banks of the creek are heavily clad with trees and a path from the village provides walkers with an excellent view of the entrance to Milford Haven harbour.

ST ISHMAEL'S
9 miles SW of Haverfordwest off the B4327

This small village on the Marloes and Dale Peninsula is named after a colleague of the 6th century St Teilo. Close by is evidence of early inhabitants of the area as, on the village outskirts, lies a motte that is Norman if not earlier while, just half a mile away, is the **Long Stone**, the tallest standing stone in the Pembrokeshire Coast National Park. During the 14th century, Sir Rhys ap Thomas of Carew Castle is said to have promised Richard III that if Henry Tudor passed through Pembroke it would be by riding over his body. When Henry landed at Mill Bay, to salve his conscience, Sir Rhys lay under Mullock Bridge (between St Ishmael's and Marloes) as Henry rode over the river and then Sir Rhys rode quickly to Carew Castle to welcome Henry.

DALE
11 miles SW of Haverfordwest off the B4327

A delightful little sailing and watersports centre, Dale lays claim to being one of the windiest places in Britain where gusts have been known to exceed 100 miles an hour. However, on the other side of the climatic coin, Dale is also one of the sunniest places in the country with an annual average of 1,800 hours a year - or five hours a day! To the south of the village, on the southern tip of the peninsula, is **St Ann's Head**, where a lighthouse and coastguard station keep a close watch over the dangerous rocky shores at the entrance to Milford Haven.

MARLOES

11 miles SW of Haverfordwest off the B4327

This inland village, on the road to **Wooltrack Point**, has a sandy bay to the southwest with **Gateholm Island** at its western extremity. Only a true island at high tide, the name comes from the Norse for Goat Island and there are traces here of a possible monastic settlement.

Right up until the end of the 19th century the ancient custom of hunting the wren, which was supposed to embody the evils of winter, was followed throughout Wales. In Pembrokeshire, the hunting took place on Twelfth Night

and the captured bird would be placed in a carved and beribboned "wren house" and paraded around the village by men singing of the hunt. A particularly fine example of a wren house, from Marloes, can be found in the Welsh Folk Museum, at St Fagans, near Cardiff.

Close by, at Martin's Haven, boats leave for Skomer and Skokholm Islands (see panel below).

NOLTON HAVEN

6½ miles W of Haverfordwest off the A487

The village sits at around the centre of St Brides Bay and the coastline here has steep, undulating cliffs and sandy beaches which have remained completely unspoilt despite being within easy reach of Haverfordwest and Milford Haven. As part of the Pembrokeshire Coast National Park, the coastline here is rich in outstanding natural beauty with a

Continued on page 273

SKOMER AND SKOKHOLM ISLANDS

The Wildlife Trust of South and West Wales
Tel: 01656 724100
e-mail: information@s&wwaleswt.cix.co.uk

Skomer Island National Nature Reserve and Skokholm and Grassholm provide some of Britain's best and most spectacular birdwatching. Boats leave from Martin's Haven, 12 miles west of Milford Haven, to Skomer and a world dedicated to wildlife. Skomer plays a vital role in the preservation of some of Britain's rarest wildlife, and its importance is recognised in its designation as a National Nature Reserve. Famous as the home of puffins and the Manx shearwater, Skomer's other visitors include guillemots, razorbills, fulmars, cormorants, shags, peregrine falcons, choughs and short-eared owls. Grey seals can be seen all year round, and in September visitors come from all over the world to see the pups being suckled.

The plant life on Skomer is also spectacular, with acres of bluebells, red campion, sea campion, thrift and heather, and the guided walks visit Britain's largest undisturbed Iron Age settlement, with hut circles, cemeteries and field systems dating back to 2000BC. Accommodation is available on Skomer (self-catering) and also on nearby Skokholm (full-board), another island wildlife paradise that is the site of Britain's first established bird observatory. The seas around the island are the natural habitat for grey seals, dolphins, porpoises and the occasional basking shark. In 1916, Trinity House built their first lighthouse on the Island, which is open to the public from the end of April to the end of August.

WALK 9

Broad Haven and Haroldston Wood

Start	Broad Haven
Distance	4 miles (6.4km)
Approximate time	2 hours
Parking	National park car park at Broad Haven
Refreshments	Pubs and café at Broad Haven
Ordnance Survey maps	Landranger 157 (St David's and Haverfordwest), Outdoor Leisure 36 (South Pembrokeshire)

The first half of the walk is mostly through lovely woodland and the second half is along the coast, descending into Broad Haven above the wide, sandy beach. This is an easy walk; the only steep climb is for those who opt for the higher of the two alternative paths through Haroldston Wood.

Start by taking the path that leads off to the left of the national park information centre, following "Woodland Walk" signs as the path winds around to a stile. Climb it, cross first a footbridge over a stream and then a track, and continue along the path opposite, signposted to Haroldston Wood, to immediately enter this beautiful area of woodland. At first the path keeps to the right of a stream but it soon crosses it via a footbridge and continues winding through this long, thin, secluded wood, confined within the sides of a narrow valley. There are plenty of boardwalks over the muddy sections.

At a footpath sign there is a choice between a high-level or low-level route **A**. To take the higher path, keep ahead up a flight of steps; the path is quite steep and narrow in places and winds along the top left-hand edge of the wood to a T-junction where you turn right to join the lower path coming in from the right a few yards ahead. To take the lower path, turn right along the route signposted to Haroldston West; this is an easier walk along a wider path to where it joins the higher path at a T-junction. At this junction **B** keep ahead if on the higher path or turn right if on the lower path and continue along an undulating path through the wood, eventually heading up to a footpath sign in front of St Madoc of Ferns' Church, the parish church for Haroldston West. Although on an ancient site, the present church was largely restored from ruins in 1883.

Ignore the direction of the footpath sign to the right and instead bear left and head up to climb a stile and keep ahead to a road **C**. Bear right along the road, passing to the left of the church and keeping ahead at a junction in the direction of Nolton. After ¼ mile (400m) turn left **D** along a lane sign-posted to Druidston Haven and about ¼ mile (400m) after a sharp right-hand bend turn left **E** at a coast path sign and walk along the right-hand edge of a field, by a wire fence on the right.

At the next coast path sign turn left **F** onto the coast path and follow it along the top of cliffs back to Broad Haven.

This is an open and relatively easy section of the path which passes above some impressive cliffs before descending above the wide, flat sands of Broad Haven to a road. Turn right along the road and after crossing a bridge over a narrow stream turn left **G** along a tarmac path to return to the car park. ●

ROGESTON COTTAGES

Portfield Gate, Haverfordwest, Pembrokeshire SA62 3LH
Tel/Fax: 01437 781373
e-mail: john@pembrokeshire-cottage-holidays.co.uk
website: www.pembrokeshire-cottage-holidays.co.uk

John and Paula Rees took up residence at Rogeston in 1974 and set about the considerable task of converting a ramshackle seven-acre smallholding into a tasteful and distinctive group of cottages offering top-quality self-catering accommodation. Such was their success in this venture that by the 1980s they had earned a commendation from the Royal Institute of Architects and a landscaping award from the Wales in Bloom Foundation. **Rogeston Cottages** and the Old Granary are located round a beautifully landscaped old cattle yard where banks of heather, rose bushes and old shrubs create a most attractive centrepiece, and all around the grounds, among the stone walls and grassland, the colour and scent of wild flowers are much in evidence. Most of the accommodation is within a long

row of buildings divided into five self-contained cottages, each with its own private patio and garden area.

Though all similar in layout, no two cottages are the same, so each has an individual charm. The Coach House is a two-storey building accommodating five guests plus a cot, while the others are all on a single floor: Little Rogeston Cottage accommodates two guests, Heather Cottage four, The Stables and Elderberry Cottage both four and a cot. The restored old granary is divided into two spacious apartments, each able to accommodate six guests plus a cot. Each of the restored 200-year-old cottages has a combined pine-fitted kitchen and sitting/dining room, bedrooms with floor-to-ceiling fitted pine wardrobes and shower room with pine-clad walls and ceramic tiled floors. The cottages are heated throughout and have wall-to-wall carpeting in the bedrooms and sitting rooms. In each cottage and the granary there is a television, books, cards and board games, maps of the area and local guide books. Guests have the use of a fully-equipped communal laundry in what used to be the old wash-house.

Children and babies are very welcome, and high chairs, cots, baby baths and other baby essentials are available free of charge on request. The farm atmosphere is an integral part of Rogeston's appeal, and the owners are always delighted to have children's help in feeding the ducks and hens, collecting eggs and feeding the pet Jersey cows. Guests needing a little gentle exercise have the use of a croquet lawn, a boules pitch and a grass badminton court. For something more energetic, windsurfing, riding, golf and many other outdoor activities are available close to the cottages. Rogeston is tucked away among country lanes five miles west of Haverfordwest and only two miles from the superb beach at Druidston.

Stack Rock, Little Haven

wide variety of natural amenities available to the holidaymaker including various short and longer distance footpaths from where an abundance of wildlife, sea birds and wild flowers can be seen. This area is a mecca for walkers, bird watchers, surfers, swimmers and sailors.

Roch

5½ miles W of Haverfordwest off the A487

Found on a rocky outcrop overlooking the village and the surrounding plain, are the remains of **Roch Castle**, which was originally built in the 13th century by the

East Hook Farm

Portfield Gate, Haverfordwest, Pembrokeshire SA62 3LN
Tel: 01437 762211 Fax: 01437 760310
e-mail: jen.patrick@easthookfarmhouse.co.uk
website: www.easthookfarmhouse.co.uk

In delightful countryside three miles west of Haverfordwest near to the coast, **East Hook** is a family run Georgian farmhouse formerly known as East Hook Estate. Howard and Jen Patrick, both from farming stock in Herefordshire, came here in 1997. Howard runs the 188 acre beef and sheep farm, Jen looks after the accommodation side.

In the immaculate three storey farmhouse, parts of which date back to 1600, the three guest bedrooms are models of good taste and attention to detail, with canopied headboards and superbly crafted antique and traditional furnishings.

All the rooms have en suite or private facilities.Large bedrooms with all the home comforts to suit your needs. A wide selection of breakfasts are available from the menu, served in the bright breakfast room. Meals are prepared from the local produce of Pembrokeshire. Dinner is also available. East Hook lies a mile off the B4341 road to Broad Haven among some of the most beautiful and unspoilt countryside in the world. The Pembrokeshire National Park and the Coastal Path are close by. Enjoy the wild flowers, birds and perfect country life. Awarded four stars by the Welsh Tourist Board.

ROSEMOOR COUNTRY COTTAGES

Rosemoor, Walwyn's Castle, Haverfordwest, Pembrokeshire SA62 3ED
Tel: 01437 781326 Fax: 01437 781080
e-mail: rosemoor@walwynscastle.com website: www.rosemoor.com

Guests at **Rosemoor Country Cottages** return year after year to enjoy a relaxed, carefree break in a lovely, unspoilt corner of Britain next to Rosemoor Nature Reserve, which is a delight for birdwatchers, botanists and lovers of the great outdoors. The main house sits on a hillside overlooking the reserve, and within the grounds are the cottages, all built of warm red sandstone and fully equipped for a go-as-you-please self-catering holiday. There are nine cottages in all, sleeping from two to eleven guests, and most of them are attractively grouped round an open courtyard. Completely renovated and adapted for 21st century living, they have comprehensively equipped kitchens, comfortable bedrooms with modern bathrooms, living room with tv, books and games, and a communal laundry. Children are very welcome, and cots, high chairs and other baby essentials are available free of charge on request. It's an excellent place to bring little ones, with large grounds and a playground well away from passing traffic, and an indoor games room for when the sun stops shining.

Owners John and Jacqueline Janssen are on the spot to see that the cottages are kept in superb order and to answer questions about the area or deal with any little problems that could arise. Each cottage is also supplied with a host of thoughtful extras and an information pack giving particulars of the wide range of activities available in the area. These include walking, fishing, sailing, water sports, golf and riding and some of the best and safest beaches in the whole of the United Kingdom.

LITTLE HAVEN POTTERY

Grove Place, Little Haven, Haverfordwest, Pembrokeshire SA62 3UG
Tel: 01437 781015
e-mail: litlehavenpottery@supanet.com

Since 1990 Philippa Lewis has been building up a very successful business at **Little Haven Pottery.** Trained at Art college in Cardiff, she produces a wide range of pots, bowls, mugs and jugs, many with a distinctive zigzag pattern, others in mottled blue and green or blue and white.. The craft studio can be visited at the back of the shop, where her pottery shares the well laid-out display space with a wide and interesting range of arts and craftwork, including carved wooden plants and creatures, water colour paintings by local artists, jewellery and soft toys.

Little Haven Pottery

Little   Haven Pottery and the shop - the Craftman Ship - occupy an old building painted a breezy bright blue that was built as a private residence and was converted to its present use many years ago. It stands almost on the seashore in St Bride's Bay in an area of outstanding natural beauty that attracts thousands of visitors from near and far. Philippa's Pottery and the shop have themselves become well-known visitor attractions, and many return regularly to browse at leisure and buy another sample of her handiwork.

THE CASTLE HOTEL

Little Haven, Haverfordwest, Pembrokeshire SA62 3UG
Tel: 01437 781445
e-mail: castlehotel@lineone.net

Mary Whitewright took early retirement from teaching to take over the reins at the **Castle Hotel**. Recently refurbished by the local brewery, the hotel is impressively well maintained, and its original role as a local pub has been considerably expanded to include a variety of eating options and comfortable overnight accommodation. Exposed stone, modern beams and bare varnished wooden flooring are used to good effect in the public rooms, which include two bars and a games room with a pool table and tv. The spacious bars, where a full range of beers, wines and spirits, tea and coffee are served, is open-plan, and separate from this is a cosy dining area with a traditional look enhanced by some well-chosen pictures on the stone walls, china jugs hanging from a shelf and a little spray of flowers on each neatly laid table.

The bar menu runs from Camembert-stuffed mushrooms and prawns in a filo tartlet to fish and chips, the Castle burger and Pembrokeshire fillet and ribeye steaks. Sandwiches and ploughman's platters (Pembrokeshire cheese of course!) make excellent lunchtime snacks, and the choice is supplemented by a long list of tempting blackboard specials: home-made smoked salmon pâté or scallops in a white wine sauce to start, then a dozen main courses that might include dressed Pembrokeshire crab and salad, chicken breast in a creamy mustard sauce, and Welsh lamb with a honey and rosemary sauce. The fine food is not the only reason to linger at the Castle, as the sea is a few steps away and the Pembrokeshire Coast National Park offers some of the most beautiful scenery in the whole country. Guest accommodation at the Castle comprises two new en suite rooms with tv and hospitality trays.

LION ROCK

Haroldston Hill, Broad Haven, Haverfordwest,
Pembrokeshire SA62 3JP
Tel: 01437 781645 e-mail: lion.rock@btinternet.com
Fax: 01437 781203 website: www.stayatlionrock.co.uk

Anthony and Jane Main offer a relaxed, home-from-home atmosphere at **Lion Rock**, which enjoys a breathtaking setting on the cliffs above St Bride's Bay. Their extended cottage has five guest bedrooms, all with en suite or private bath/shower room, tv and tea/coffee-making facilities. Kent and Terrace are single rooms, St Bride's and Pembroke are doubles, and Sun has twin beds and a conservatory. Guests start the day with a fine breakfast using local produce, setting them up perfectly for a day revelling in the glorious scenery of both land and sea. Walkers can set off in either direction along the 180-mile coastal path that runs nearby through Britain's only coastal National Park, enjoying the wonderful clean air and the outstanding natural beauty of an area rich in wildlife, sea birds and wild flowers.

There's easy access to the lovely beaches at Broad Haven, Marloes, Druidston, Newgale and Whitesands, and it's only a 25-minute drive to Martin's Haven, the embarkation point for trips to see

the bird sanctuary at Skomer Island. This 720-acre reserve is home to grey seals and to thousands of sea birds, including puffins, razorbills, guillemots, shags and fulmars. A few miles inland is the old county town of Haverfordwest, which has many attractions for the visitor. Lion Rock, then, is a perfect base experiencing everything that Pembrokeshire has to offer, but the relaxing ambience, the wonderful clifftop setting and the wild flowers that carpet the gardens right down to the cliff edge are excuse enough never to leave Lion Rock.

BUMPYLANE ORGANICS

Shortlands Farm, Druidston, Haverfordwest, Pembrokeshire SA62 3NE
Tel: 01437 781234 website: www.bumpylane.co.uk

Bumpylane Organics, perched on cliffs overlooking St Bride's Bay within the Pembrokeshire Coast National Park, is home to a variety of rare breeds of sheep, cattle and pigs. All the animals, bred for their traditional flavour, are born and reared on the farm, which is licensed by the Soil Association (G4793). Pam and David Williams sell their organic meat at farmer's markets in Haverfordwest and Fishguard, and freezer-ready packs by mail order. The Pembrokeshire Coast Path runs through the farm, which has a small caravan and camping site (electric hook-ups, shower and WC) with wonderful views and easy access to the beautiful, secluded beach at Druidston Haven.

feudal Lord of Roch, Adam de la Roche. A local story tells that de la Roche was told by a witch that he would be killed, one day, by a snake but, if he could pass a year in safety, then he need never fear vipers. Accordingly, de la Roche had the castle built in such a way as to be out of reach of any snake and so the fortress was constructed on this particularly well defended site. His year free from snakes began and de la Roche moved into the top floor of the castle and remained there, in constant fear, for a year. The very last night of his self-enforced imprisonment was bitterly cold and someone sent a basket of firewood to the castle to help Adam pass the night in comfort. The basket was taken to his room and, as de la Roche was putting the logs on the fire, an adder crawled out from among the logs and bit him. The next morning, Adam de la Roche was found dead in front of his hearth.

PEMBROKE

This historic town, with its long and unbroken line of well-preserved medieval town walls, is dominated by the mighty fortress of **Pembroke Castle** (see panel opposite). It was founded in the 11th century by the Montgomerys,

who established the first timber castle on a rocky crag above the River Cleddau.

Found opposite the castle is the charming **Museum of the Home** that houses a unique collection of household utensils and appliances and toys and games that span three centuries. Since 1924, when the town lost its naval dockyard, Pembroke has relied more and more on tourism to boost the local economy and this is a place that, whilst popular, is well worth visiting.

Just half a mile from the castle, and across Monkton Pill, stood **Monkton Priory** that was founded in 1098 by Arnulf de Montgomery for Benedictine monks and was given to St Albans in 1473. The priory church, with its long narrow barrel-vaulted nave and monastic chancel, was rearranged in the 14th century and, after lying in ruins for

Pembroke Castle

PEMBROKE CASTLE TRUST

Main Street, Pembroke, Pembrokeshire SA71 4LA
Tel: 01646 681510   Fax: 01646 622260
e-mail: pembroke.castle@talk21.com
website: www.pembrokecastle.co.uk

Open all year.

Looming magnificently above the main street of the town, **Pembroke Castle** is one of Britain's most impressive medieval monuments. It was founded in the 11th century by the Montgomerys, who established the first timber castle on a rocky crag above the River Cleddau.

The stone building which stands today is one of the foremost examples of Norman architecture in the country. It was commenced in the 12th century by Earl William Marshal, and his famous round Keep is nearly 80 feet tall with walls 19 feet thick. In 1454 the mighty fortress was held by Earl Jasper Tudor, and the castle is renowned as the birthplace of Jasper's nephew, Henry Tudor, who was to become Henry VII after defeating Richard III at the Battle of Bosworth - thus founding the Tudor dynasty.

During the Civil War the castle was held by both the Parliamentarians and the Royalists, and Cromwell travelled there to begin the siege that led to it finally falling under his control. Restoration work in the late 19th century and again in the 1930s has preserved many of the features of the castle that might otherwise have fallen into ruin. The walls, the towers, the turrets, the tunnels and the battlements resound with the history of the centuries, and are an irresistible attraction for lovers of history and for children.

Younger visitors are also fascinated by the brass rubbing gallery just outside the castle walls, where they can learn how to use gold or silver waxes to make pictures of knights of old. On Sundays during the summer months living history groups fill the Outer Ward and create a truly medieval atmosphere.

The castle is owned and managed by the Pembroke Castle Trust, a private trust that depends solely on income from visitors. The range of facilities inside the castle grounds includes lavatories, a snack bar (open in the summer) and a picnic area. Guided tours are available daily except Saturdays during the summer season and at other times by arrangement. Half a mile from the castle, on the opposite bank of the river, is Monkton Priory, which together with the castle is a visible representation of the twin symbols of medieval authority, the aristocracy and the Church.

POYERSTON FARM

Cosheton, Nr Pembroke,
Pembrokeshire SA72 4SJ
Tel/Fax: 01646 651347
e-mail: poyerstonfarm@btinternet.com
website: www.poyerston-farm.co.uk

Sheila and Philip Lewis are both farmers
and hosts at **Poyerston Farm**, their
delightful home and 400-acre farm. The
Victorian farmhouse, extended down the
years, is located down a tarmac drive off
the A477 close to the village of Carew
with its castle, millpond, restored tidal
mill and 11th century Celtic cross.

Many of South Pembrokeshire's main
attractions, both inland and coastal, are within easy reach, so the farm is an ideal base for a touring
holiday as well as being the perfect spot to relax and enjoy the peace, the fresh air and the lovely

views. The Lewis family accommodate their guests in
elegant, well-furnished en suite bedrooms, some on the
ground floor, all with central heating, tv, clock radio,
hairdryer, quality toiletries and a beverage tray with a cake
to welcome visitors on arrival. All rooms are non-smoking.
There's a good choice for breakfast, including
Pembrokeshire honey, home-made preserves and fresh
local produce that is traditionally home cooked on the
farmhouse Aga.

There is a delightful conservatory overlooking a slate
patio and the gardens, and a lounge with an open fire
and plenty of information about local places of interest.
Guests can enjoy gentle strolls round the farm paths and
the ponds, and watch the daily milking and all the seasonal activities of the working farm. For more

energetic interludes, the Pembrokeshire Coast Path is only four
miles away, and for serious sightseers the medieval town of
Pembroke is just one of the numerous local attractions. To
reach the farm: from Carmarthen take the A40 to St Clears
roundabout, then the A477 towards Pembroke Dock. Drive
through Milton; three-quarters of a mile further on, the farm
entrance is on the left opposite a Vauxhall garage.

THE OLD CROSS SAWS INN

109 Main Street, Pembroke, Pembrokeshire SA71 4DB
Tel: 01646 682475

World-travelled and worldly wise Victor Rees bought the
Old Cross Saws Inn in 2001 and runs it with his wife. Behind
a cheerful red facade, the 16th century inn has a single large
bar that runs the length of the building. Two real ales are
among the good choice of liquid refreshment, and in the
dining area the food ranges from light snacks to a full à la
carte menu. The inn is one of the most sociable and convivial
spots in town, with live music on Saturday nights and regular
jazz evenings and quiz nights. Pool is taken very seriously

here, with both
ladies and
gents teams
playing in the
local leagues.

The historic town of Pembroke, dominated by the
mighty fortress that is Pembroke Castle, deserves more
than a passing visit, and the Old Cross Saws is a very
agreeable place to base a stay. It has five letting bedrooms
for bed and breakfast, including a family room. All have
tv, tea/coffee tray and en suite or private bathroom. The
inn has a beer garden.

many years, was restored again in the
late 19th century.

AROUND PEMBROKE

UPTON

3 miles NE of Pembroke off the A477

Set in a secluded valley running down to
the River Carew, **Upton Castle Gardens**
has three raised formal terraces that drop
down from the medieval castle (not open

to the public). Along with the rose
gardens and herbaceous borders, there
are 40 acres of wooded grounds containing some 250 species of trees and shrubs.
There's also a medieval chapel from
which the walled garden can be seen.

CAREW

4 miles E of Pembroke on the A4075

Located on the shores of the tidal mill
pond, **Carew Castle** is one of the few
such buildings to display the

BOWETT FARM

Hundleton, Pembrokeshire SA71 5QS
Tel/Fax: 01646 683473 e-mail: bowett@pembrokeshire.com

Ann and Bill Morris make guests feel instantly at home at
Bowett Farm, a 250-acre working dairy and sheep farm a mile
west of Pembroke. The impressive creeper-covered farmhouse
offers excellent accommodation in two large bedrooms each

with private bathroom, radio, hospitality tray and hairdryer. A single room is also available for a party
of three travelling together. The house is furnished with some fine antiques, and guests have a sitting
room where they can relax with a book or watch tv. A substantial breakfast includes home-made
preserves. The house is set in a picturesque garden, and close by is an ancient wood that has a spectacular
show of bluebells and wild flowers in the spring.

ROSEDENE GUEST HOUSE

Hodgeston, Pembroke, Pembrokeshire SA71 5JU
Tel: 01646 672586 e-mail: eileen@rosedeneguesthouse.co.uk
Fax: 01646 672855 website: www.rosedeneguesthouse.co.uk

Escape - explore - relax in affordable luxury at Rosedene, a four star licensed guest house standing in cared-for grounds below the 13th century church and village green. Located midway between Tenby and historic Pembroke, Rosedene is an ideal touring base for the Pembrokeshire Coast National Park. Eileen and Frederick Fallon provide a friendly welcome for their guests whose enjoyment and comfort are their primary concern. There are seven en-suite bedrooms on the ground floor - six with private garden patios. All have tiled shower rooms and one luxury four poster room has both bath and shower. Each room is beautifully decorated and furnished, with little luxury touches giving additional pleasure. Colour TV (some with video), courtesy trays and information packs are provided whilst oil-fired central heating ensures a warm welcome whatever the season. One room is equipped for the less able, having ramped access to the patio and wheel-in shower room. All rooms are wheel-chair accessible and the car park is flat and immediately adjacent.

Meals are lovingly prepared using only the freshest of local and garden produce with multi choice menus suitable for gourmets, traditionalists or vegetarians. Candle lit dinners are served in the elegant dining room overlooking a small natural wood. A narrow lane alongside Rosedene winds to the Coastal Footpath and spectacular scenery, whilst numerous long sandy beaches are within a couple of miles.Eileen also offers self-catering accommodation in adjacent Rooks' Retreat, a converted stable. Built to residential standards with dishwasher and all other modern appliances, it sleeps six in three bedrooms - one en suite. Prices are fully inclusive of oil-fired central heating, making it an ideal choice for early or late season short breaks.

CASTLEMEAD HOTEL

Manorbier, Pembrokeshire SA70 7TA
Tel/Fax: 01834 871358
e-mail: castlemeadhotel@aol.com
website: www.castlemeadhotel.com

CASTLEMEAD HOTEL is superbly situated on the Pembrokeshire Coastal Path. A handsome period house with many original features, situated at the head of a small wooded valley, set in half an acre of mature lawns and grounds. The hotel overlooks the Bay and Norman Castle. Set in the heart of the village with a short stroll to the beach, Castlemead offers a tranquil peaceful atmosphere, the ideal spot to relax and unwind.

The restaurant with the glorious views and an enviable reputation is open nightly except for Sunday when a traditional lunch is served. As much local produce is used as possible in the varied and imaginative menues. There are eight pleasant bedrooms all with full facilities, three are at ground floor level in the converted Coach house ideal for the less mobile guest or those wishing to bring their dogs. Drinks on the lawn in the summer months, roaring log fires in the lounge and restaurant in the cooler months, a warm welcome awaits you at CASTLEMEAD.

development from Norman fortification (it was built between 1280 and 1310) to Elizabethan manor house. However, this site is much older, as archaeological excavations have found remains which go back some 2,000 years. Various remarkable individuals have connections with the castle, and the Great Tournament held here in 1507 was attended by 600 nobles; but the castle also gives an insight into the lives of servants, craftsmen, priests and common soldiers of the time.

During the summer months a wide variety of events is held in the castle grounds, including drama, school projects, holiday activities, battle re-enactments, country fairs and concerts.

Here too can be seen one of only three restored tidal mills in Britain. **Carew Tidal Mill** still retains its original

Carew Celtic Cross

machinery. The Story of Milling exhibition traces the history of milling through the ages and the mill's role in the local community. While touring this lovely four-storey building, visitors are given explanations of each stage of the milling process. As well as the castle and the mill, the Carew site also incorporates a causeway, a medieval bridge and an 11th century **Celtic Cross** that is one of the best examples of its kind in Wales.

ST FLORENCE
5½ miles E of Pembroke off the B4318

A small and quiet village located on the border of the National Park, St Florence is noted for its Norman church. To the northeast of the village lies **Manor House Wildlife and Leisure Park** where the original village manor house provides the perfect backdrop for the park's collection of birds, animals, fish and reptiles. Snake handling, bottle feeding and animal handling sessions all take place undercover in the Close Encounters Barn, while the wooded grounds and formal gardens are ideal places for both exploration and picnics. Ivy Tower Farm is the home of **St Florence Cheese**, where traditional cheese is made from both cows' and goats' milk. Also here are a farm shop, meadow walk and several mazes.

MANORBIER
5½ miles SE of Pembroke off the A4139

Manorbier is charmingly situated at the head of a valley that reaches down to the shore in a beautiful bay with a safe bathing beach. The village's name is thought to have been derived from Maenor Pyr (Manor of Pyr) and Pyr is believed to have been the first Celtic abbot of Caldey, living in the 5th century. Overlooking the bay of the same name, **Manorbier Castle** was

SLADE FARM

Manorbier, Nr Tenby, Pembrokeshire SA70 7SJ
Tel/Fax: 01834 871410

Greg and Marian Armstrong offer top-notch self-catering accommodation in two properties next to their home set in the seven secluded acres of **Slade Farm**. "Swallows" is a detached three-bedroom cottage converted from a part-stone outbuilding, furnished and equipped to a very high standard. Two bedrooms and a bathroom are upstairs, while on the ground floor are the third bedroom with en suite shower room, a comfortable lounge-diner, fully equipped kitchen and utility/cloakroom with washing machine, tumble dryer, WC and washbasin.

"Dovecote" is a one-bedroom self-contained annexe to the owners' house, all on one level, carpeted throughout, and also with everything needed for a relaxed, independent holiday. Both "Swallows" and "Dovecote" are centrally heated; well-behaved pets are welcome; smoking is not permitted inside the properties. The farm is 1½ miles from Manorbier with its lovely sheltered beach, castle and Norman church, and the Pembrokeshire Coast Path, which runs through the bay, provides magnificent walks and stunning views. The towns of Tenby and Pembroke are a short drive away. Swallows has a five star grading with the Welsh Tourist Board and Dovecote has a four star grading.

conceived by Odo de Barri in 1095 when he built a wooden hall within a defensive structure but it was his son, William, who began construction of the stone fortification in the early 12th century. Famous for being the birthplace, in 1146, of Giraldus Cambrensis, Gerald of Wales, a monk and chronicler who wrote the first account of life in medieval Wales, the castle was described by him as being "the pleasantest spot in Wales".

Today, life size wax figures placed at various points, including the impressive great hall, the turrets and the chapel, bring the history of this ancient building to life as atmospheric music captures the castle's spirit. The castle gardens were laid out by JR Cobb in the late 19th century and there is also a late Victorian cottage with appropriate herbaceous borders lining the castle walls.

LAMPHEY

1½ miles SE of Pembroke on the A4139

Just northwest of the village, in the 13th century, the medieval bishops of St David's built the magnificent **Lamphey Bishop's Palace** as a retreat from the affairs of Church and State. Though improved over a period of 200 years, the major building work was undertaken by the dynamic Bishop Henry de Gower between 1328 and 1347 and he was responsible for the splendid great hall. Although now in ruins, this is a peaceful and tranquil site where successive bishops were able to live the life of country gentlemen among the estate's orchards, vegetable gardens and rolling parkland.

ST GOVAN'S HEAD

5 miles S of Pembroke off the B4319

The cliff scenery is at its most spectacular at St Govan's Head where the tiny religious site of the 13th century **St Govan's Chapel** huddles among the rocks almost at sea level. Accessible by climbing down 52 stone steps, this minute chapel was built on the site of a holy well that once attracted pilgrims who believed the well's waters to have miraculous healing powers.

Inside is a vertical cleft in the rock which, according to legend, first opened so that St Govan could hide inside and escape his enemies. Closing behind him, the rock did not reopen until the danger had passed. Accordingly, a wish made while standing in the cleft and facing the rock will come true provided the person making the wish does not change his or her mind before turning round. Although many miracles have been credited to St Govan he remains a mysterious and little known man. Some believe him to have been a disciple of St David while others claim that he was a thief who, having miraculously found the hiding place, became a convert. St Govan is also thought by some to have been a woman named Cofen - the wife of a 5th century chief - who became a recluse.

BOSHERSTON
4½ miles SW of Pembroke off the B4319

To the east of the village and occupying part of the former Stackpole estate of the Earls of Cawdor are **Stackpole Gardens**, which were landscaped in the 18th century. Romantic in style and containing some interesting and well-engineered water features, including an eight arched bridge, these are intriguing gardens to explore and, although the original manor house has gone, the 19th century terraces, woodland

garden and summer house remain, along with a grotto, an ice house and three walled gardens.

PEMBROKE DOCK
1½ miles NW of Pembroke on the A477

Once an important naval dockyard, Pembroke Dock stands on the dividing line between the developed and the undeveloped shores of the Milford Haven. Downstream are the large petrochemical plants and oil terminals which take advantage of the Haven's deepwater channels while, upstream, are the enchanting waters of the Cleddau river system.

TENBY

Tenby's Welsh name, Dinbych y Pysgod, means "Little Fort of the Fishes" and certainly its most photographed scene is the pretty harbour with its pastel coloured Georgian houses. But the whole place is a real delight, prompting many eulogies such as this from the artist Augustus John: "You may travel the world over, but you will find nothing more beautiful: it is so restful, so colourful and so unspoilt." The artist was born in Tenby at Belgrave House, where a

Tenby Harbour

FOURCROFT HOTEL

North Road, Tenby, Pembrokeshire SA70 8AP
Tel: 01834 842886 Fax: 01834 842888
e-mail: hospitality@fourcroft-hotel.co.uk
website: www.fourcroft-hotel.co.uk

Chris Osborne is the third generation of his family to own and run **Fourcroft Hotel**, which enjoys a superb setting on the cliffs above Tenby's sheltered North Beach. Private paths lead from the hotel down to the beach through several levels of lovely landscaped gardens, and the town centre is only five minutes' walk away. Most of the 46 bedrooms overlook the bay, and all are appointed to ensure that guests have a very comfortable, pleasant stay: en suite bathroom, tv and radio, direct-dial telephone, central heating, hairdryer, tea and coffee bar.

The Hollywood Bar, with exotic decor and paintings of the great film stars on the walls, is a convivial place to meet for a drink and a chat, and the lounges and dining rooms enjoy views of the sea. Food options run from sandwiches and bar snacks to silver service dinners on à la carte and table d'hote menus that are both locally and internationally inspired. The Fourcroft has extensive leisure facilities for all the family, including heated open air swimming pool, an "aero-fitness" unit, spa pool, sauna, giant chess, children's playground and a games room with table tennis, table football, snooker, pool, carpet bowls and a classic pinball machine. The hotel is a popular venue for functions and conferences and also for weddings, for which it holds a civil marriage ceremony licence.

AUDREY BULL ANTIQUES

Upper Frog Street, Tenby,
Pembrokeshire SA70 7JD
Tel: 01834 843114

Audrey Bull founded her first antique shop in Cheltenham in 1946 with her mother Blanche Beck. 1957 saw the opening of this shop in Tenby, and in 1998 a branch opened in Carmarthen (see entry on page 293).

The two delightfully traditional shops are owned by Jane and Jonathan Bull, assisted by their daughter Quita, and their son Matthew manages the restoration workshop. They are

general antique dealers specialising in 19th and 20th century furniture, Welsh oak pieces, silver, porcelain and jewellery. The jewellery they buy and sell includes antiques, secondhand pieces, gem-set and modern designer creations.

The workshop prides itself on repairing and polishing in a way that preserves the original patination: they do not follow the fashion for making the furniture match the repair - they make the repair match the furniture. The shop is open from 9 to 5 Monday to Saturday, also on Sunday in summer.

THE EVERGREEN INN

The Green, Tenby, Pembrokeshire SA70 8EY
Tel: 01834 843364

A railway worker's cottage dating from the 19th century is now a bright, cheerful and very friendly public house. By the village green on the edge of the busy seaside town of Tenby, the **The Evergreen Inn** is run by Monique Brodie, who has maintained the period character of the place with such features as beamed ceilings and exposed stone walls. The traditional ambience is further assisted by time-honoured pub card games and dominoes. A good selection of ales, lagers, wines and spirits also encourages the relaxed, sociable atmosphere at the Evergreen.

collection of his works, and those of his sister Gwen, can be found. The town still retains its charming medieval character together with the crooked lanes that are enclosed within its surprisingly well-preserved 13th century town walls. On one particular stretch, **South Parade**, the walls are still at their full height and the two tiers of arrow slits are very much visible; the **Five Arches**, a fortified gateway on the walls, is perhaps the most famous feature. Unfortunately, the same is not true for **Tenby Castle**, the scant remains of which can be found on a small headland. However, the ruins are well worth a visit for the spectacular views out across Carmarthen Bay and along the Pembrokeshire coast. A statue to Prince Albert can also be found on the headland along with **Tenby Museum**, which began life in 1878. As well as having archaeological and historical material relating to the area, the museum has a fascinating maritime section and an impressive art gallery.

Close to the quay lies the **Tudor Merchant's House**, a relic of Tenby's prosperous sea-faring days and a fine example of a comfortable townhouse of the 15th century. Narrow and built with three storeys, the house, which is owned by the National Trust, has been furnished to recreate the atmosphere and environment in which a wealthy Tudor

family would have lived. With a Flemish chimney, early floral frescoes on some of the interior walls and a small herb garden outside, there is plenty at the house to evoke the times of around 600 years ago. The large and lavish **St Mary's Church** is another testament to the town's illustrious maritime past.

Perhaps of more interest to younger visitors to the town is the **Silent World Aquarium and Reptile Collection** housed in an attractive 19th century chapel. In these interesting, if somewhat unusual, surroundings there is a wide range of exotic fish, amphibians and invertebrates on display as well as fish and other creatures that live around the shores of Pembrokeshire. Upstairs are the reptiles and here visitors can see a fascinating collection of snakes and lizards from around the world. Gifts for all ages, some made by local craftsmen, are on sale in the shop, where grown-ups can enjoy coffee, tea and a snack while the youngsters play with toys, draw, do a brass rubbing or try one of the quizzes.

AROUND TENBY

SAUNDERSFOOT
2½ miles NE of Tenby on the B4316

This picture postcard perfect fishing village is centred around its harbour,

THE WOODLANDS HOTEL

St Brides Hill, Saundersfoot, Pembrokeshire SA69 9NP
Tel: 01834 813338 Fax: 01834 811480
e-mail: woodlands.hotel@virgin.net
website: www.woodlands-hotel.net

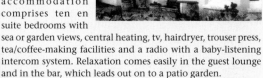

Owned and personally run by the Harwood family, the
Woodlands Hotel stands close to the sea in Saundersfoot, a
lively seaside village with sandy beaches, a picturesque
harbour and plenty of water sports activity. The family have

created a very
relaxed, friendly
ambience in their
substantial, white-
painted period home,
where the guest
accommodation
comprises ten en
suite bedrooms with
sea or garden views, central heating, tv, hairdryer, trouser press,
tea/coffee-making facilities and a radio with a baby-listening
intercom system. Relaxation comes easily in the guest lounge
and in the bar, which leads out on to a patio garden.

There's a good, varied choice for breakfast, snacks are
available in the bar, and an optional evening meal is served in
the restaurant, which is also open to non-residents. Locally
grown and sourced produce is used wherever possible on the
table d'hote dinner menus, which offer three choices per course
and feature mainly familiar classics such as roast chicken,
shepherd's pie, boiled ham and parsley sauce, sirloin steak garni
and the "new" classic chicken tikka masala.
Woodlands is situated within Pembrokeshire's
National Park, an area of outstanding natural beauty
with miles of glorious walks both inland and along
the coast - the 184-mile Pembrokeshire Coast Path
starts at Saundersfoot. The historic walled town of
Tenby, with its castle, church and Tudor merchant's
house, is close by; from here, boat trips can be arranged
to Caldey Island, where Cistercian monks have had a
settlement for hundreds of years.

which during the summer months is packed with colourful sailing craft. The harbour was constructed in the 1820s primarily for the export of anthracite, which was mined a short distance away and brought to the quay by tramway. Today, however, the industry has all but ceased and this resort, which has an attractive sandy beach, is probably one of the busiest watersports centres in South Wales. In the heart of the resort is a lovely surprise in the shape of **Stammers Gardens**, seven carefully developed acres with shrubberies, ponds, woodland and a bog garden.

AMROTH

4½ miles NE of Tenby off the A477

Lying at the south eastern most point of the Pembrokeshire Coast National Park, this quiet village has a lovely beach overlooking Carmarthen Bay. As well as the delightful surroundings the village is home to the enchanting **Colby Woodland Garden**, an eight acre area of woodland set round a Nash-style house in a secluded valley that is home to one of the finest collections of rhododendrons and azaleas in Wales. The carpets of bluebells follow the displays of daffodils in the spring and there is a mass of colour during the summer when the hydrangeas flower, before the garden is taken over by the rich colours of autumn. The garden is part of the National Trust's Colby Estate, which takes its name from John Colby, a 19th century industrialist.

STEPASIDE

4 miles N of Tenby off the A477

Between 1849 and 1877 this village, set in a wooded valley, had a thriving colliery and an iron works and, in 1877,

WHITE HORSES

Pen-y-Craig, Saundersfoot,
Pembrokeshire SA69 9NR
Tel/Fax: 01834 814835
e-mail: whitehorses@lineone.net
website: www.whitehorses-countryhouse.com

A private lane leads to **White Horses**, which enjoys a peaceful, secluded setting in grounds that include mature trees and shrubs.

The W.T.B. '5 Star' Victorian property has three guest rooms for bed and breakfast, decorated to a high standard. All rooms with unrivalled sea-views.

Guests at White Horses have the best of land and sea, Pembrokeshire National Park Coast Park is minutes away and steps from the garden lead to wonderful sandy beaches.

CWMWENNOL COUNTRY HOUSE

Swallowtree Woods, Saundersfoot,
Pembrokeshire SA69 9DE
Tel: 01834 813430
website: www.cwmwennol.co.uk

A drive through beautiful Swallowtree Woods
leads to **Cwmwennol Country House**, which was
built in 1870 for the manager of the Vickerman
Estate. The present owners are Vicki and Roy Meacher, who escaped from the stresses of corporate
business careers to enjoy the superior quality of life in this lovely tranquil spot and to share it with
their guests. The recently refurbished accommodation is a mixture of singles, twins and doubles; all
the rooms have en suite facilities, tv, radio alarm clocks, tea/coffee trays and beach or woodland views.

Top of the range is a glamorous four-poster room with a jacuzzi and a private balcony. A log fire in
a copper-hooded hearth keeps things cosy in the comfortably furnished lounge, and the patio is an
attractive alternative in the summer months. The restaurant provides a warm and relaxing atmosphere
for enjoying a leisurely meal featuring local produce. Guests
walking in the sunken rose garden might spot badgers or
foxes feeding, and a boat trip round nearby Caldey Island
could well be rewarded with the sight of puffins and seals.
A long, sandy beach is a very short walk from the hotel,
and other outdoor attractions in the vicinity include fishing,
golf, riding and the largest theme park in Wales.
Saundersfoot itself is a very picturesque village whose
fishing industry has largely given way to sailing and water
sports.

the village school opened to provide
education for the workers' children.
Finally closing in 1992, the school has
been reopened as the **Victorian School
Museum** and provides today's visitors
with the chance to taste 19th century
school days. Sitting at 100-year-old
desks with slates and pencils, visitors can
relive the austere school world of over a
century ago; but the life of a Victorian
school child was not only work and,
outside, the playground has been
recreated to match the environment
where Victorian children would let off
steam. Also at the museum is a display
that brings the mining history of the
village back to life and, along with the
reconstructed mine shaft, visitors can see
the hardships of the children as young as
six who worked at the colliery until the
school opened.

CALDEY ISLAND
2½ miles S of Tenby off the A4139

This peaceful and tranquil island, which
along with its sister island of St
Margaret's lies just a short distance off
the coast from Tenby, has been the home
of monks for some 1,500 years. As well
as the modern working monastery that is
home to a community of 20 monks of
the Reformed Cistercian Order, there are
the remains of a 13th century monastery
which was also founded by the
Cistercians. St Illtud's Church, along
with the old priory ruins, can be visited,
and a small museum on the island tells
the history of this beautiful island.

Today's monks live their lives
according to the austere Rule of St
Benedict which necessitates them
attending seven services a day - the first
beginning at 3.15 am.

A county of contrasts, Carmarthenshire has a wealth of interesting places and superb countryside to enchant the visitor. There are coastal strongholds at Laugharne and Kidwelly, abbey ruins at Talley and Whitland and the famous rugby and industrial centre of Llanelli. Covering some 1,000 square miles, the county also has beautiful clean beaches, seaside towns and villages and rural idylls. A place of myths and legends, Carmarthenshire has remained essentially Welsh in most aspects.

The coastline, which is over 50 miles long, includes the award-winning Pembrey Country Park and beach, once the site of a munitions factory, and Pendine, whose long stretch of sand saw many land speed world records made and broken. Of the seaside villages, Laugharne is certainly the most famous, due mainly to the fact that it is the place where Dylan Thomas lived for the last years of his short life. But the village does not rely solely on its literary links, as it also has one of the country's most handsome castles and offers wonderful views over the estuary of the River Taf.

Inland lies Carmarthen, the county town, whose origins lie back in the time of the Romans. The town is a centre for the agricultural communities of West Wales, and to the east is an area associated with the legends and

Llyn Brianne

mysteries of Merlin the magician. Also in this part of Carmarthenshire is one the country's most recent important projects - the National Botanic Garden of Wales. Dedicated to conservation, horticulture, science and education and boasting the largest single-span glasshouse in the world, this is one of the country's newest gardens, while close by lies Aberglasney, one of the oldest, first mentioned in 1477. Evidence of the Roman occupation of Carmarthenshire is most striking at the Dolaucothi Gold Mines, to the northwest of Llandovery. At Cenarth, visitors can see salmon fishermen on the River Teifi still using the coracle, a tiny round boat whose origins are lost in the mists of time. A fascinating museum tells the story of these distinctive little craft.

Aberglasney Gardens

ADVERTISERS AND PLACES OF INTEREST

LOCATOR MAP

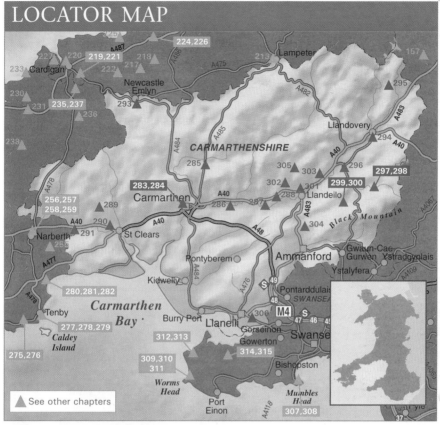

© MAPS IN MINUTES ™ 2002   © Crown Copyright, Ordnance Survey 2002

CARMARTHEN

One of the oldest Roman towns in Wales, Carmarthen (or Caerfyrddin in Welsh) is now the county town of Carmarthenshire and lies at the centre of the West Wales agricultural community. At the site of **Caer Maridunum**, the most westerly Roman fort in Britain, the remains of the amphitheatre can still be seen and the Roman town walls were known to have been visible in the 12th century. However, the historic old part of Carmarthen grew up around **Carmarthen Castle**, which was originally built in around 1109 by Henry I. Overlooking the River Tywi, little remains of the castle today except the early 15th century gatehouse. The **Guildhall**, which was built in 1767 to replace the hall of 1583, is in Nott Square - named after Major General Sir William Nott, victor of the First Afghan War in the 1840s and a native of Carmarthen. The town's Victorian Old Art College has, since 1991, been the home of **Oriel Myrddin**, a contemporary craft gallery and regional art venue. Focusing on the present and the future, the work of some of the most innovative and interesting craftspeople in Wales is displayed here and, in the retail area, there is a wide range of crafts for purchase. By contrast, housed in a new development on the banks of the River Tywi is the **Carmarthen Heritage Centre** which, through displays, multi-media and video presentations, tells the story of the town from the time of the Roman occupation in AD 75 through to the present day.

If legend is to be believed, Carmarthen was Merlin's city and one particular story associated with the town has, thankfully,

KING STREET GALLERY & ALEXANDER DESIGN

30 King Street, Carmarthen, Carmarthenshire SA31 1BS
Tel: 01267 267652
e-mail: dianaheeks@headweb.co.uk

A 17th century building next to the Carmarthen Library is home to **King Street Gallery**, the first private gallery in Carmarthen. Opened in October 2001, it is run by a cooperative of six artists: the works of Janet Bligh, Diana Heeks, Charlotte Leadbeater, Ann Morgan, Paul Stokle and Dorothy Morris are on show in a light, well-planned gallery, and visitors have the chance to watch the artists at work, to discuss their work and perhaps even to commission a work for themselves. These six established artists also encourage younger local talent, offering a part of the gallery for exhibitions, one-person shows and community-based projects.

The building has been splendidly adapted for its new role, and there's plenty of natural light, particularly on the lofty, oak-beamed top floor where the six are based. Tim Haycock and his Danish-born mother Marianne Thune-Haycock use gallery space to display his furniture and her paintings. They occupy the first floor of Alexander Design (Rosa Danica), which displays "Three Generations" of artists. There are not only lively, original paintings, prints and cards, but also traditional and colourful Danish-style hand-painted furniture and contemporary design by Tim Haycock. Also on display are Gwili pottery and delightful Danish decorative mobiles. Alexander Design: Tel 01994 231178, website www.rosadanica.co.uk. The Gallery is open Monday to Saturday from 10 to 4.

AUDREY BULL ANTIQUES

2 Jacksons Lane, Carmarthen,
Carmarthenshire SA31 1QD
Tel: 01267 222655

Audrey Bull Antiques was established in 1946
and is still in the same family. Jane and
Jonathan Bull are assisted by their daughter
Anita, while their son Matthew manages the
restoration workshop.

They are general antique dealers,
specialising in 19th and 20th century furniture,
Welsh oak pieces, pictures, silver, porcelain and
jewellery. The jewellery they buy and sell ranges
from antique and secondhand to gem-set and

modern designer creations. The restoration workshop
prides itself on repairing and polishing so that the
original patination is preserved: they do not follow the
fashion of making the furniture match the repair - they
make the repair match the furniture.

Behind the green-shuttered frontage in a
pedestrianised shopping street there's always a good
selection of stock on display, and the shop is open from
10 to 5 Monday to Saturday. The other Audrey Bull
Antiques is in Tenby (see entry on page 284).

so far turned out not to be true.
Carmarthen's inhabitants are eternally
grateful that, when Merlin's Oak was
removed during a road widening scheme,
the town remained unharmed and the
prophecy, "When Merlin's Oak shall
tumble down, then shall fall Carmarthen
town" was not realised. According to
another tradition, the magician is said
still to live in a cave on Merlin's Hill
(Bryn Myrddin) just outside Carmarthen
where he is kept in perpetual
enchantment by Vivien, the lady to
whom he taught all his spells. The Ivy
Bush Royal Hotel in Carmarthen has
notable literary connections. A stained
glass window and stone circle
commemorate the 1819 Eisteddfod,
when Iolo Morganwg introduced the
Gorsedd (society of bards) to the
Eisteddfod (see also St David's). The
essayist and dramatist Sir Richard Steele

stayed at the Ivy Bush in the later years
of his life. Steele is best known for his
periodical essays and for his
collaboration with Joseph Addison.
Educated, like Addison, at Charterhouse
and Oxford, Steele published his first
work in 1701, when he was 28. It had
the far from catchy title of *The Christian
Hero: An argument proving that no
principles but those of religion are sufficient
to make a great man*. Steele had two
wealthy wives and several children. Bad
health and pressing debts forced him to
move to Wales, and he died in
Carmarthen in 1729. Notable sons of
Carmarthen include Brindley Richards,
who wrote *God Bless the Prince of Wales*.

Carmarthen has a thriving food
market, where one of the local
specialities on sale is Carmarthen ham,
which is air-dried, sliced and eaten raw,
like the Spanish Serrano ham.

AROUND
CARMARTHEN

BRONWYDD ARMS
2 miles N of Carmarthen on the A484

From Bronwydd Arms Station the **Gwili Railway** offers visitors the opportunity to step back in time and take a short steam train journey through the Gwili Valley on part of the old Great Western Railway line.

Gwili Railway

This line originally opened in 1860 and, although it finally closed in 1973, it has, since the late 1970s, been run by volunteers. Visitors can enjoy the train journey, and the other end of the line, Llwyfan Cerrig, is the perfect place for a picnic.

PONTARSAIS
5 miles N of Carmarthen on the A485

The village is best known as the home of **Gwili Pottery**. To the west of the village lies **Llanpumpsaint**, the Church of the Five Saints - Ceitho, Celynen, Gwyn,

GWILI POTTERY

Bronwydd Road, Pontarsais, Carmarthenshire SA32 7DU
Tel: 01267 253449
e-mail: gwilipottery@aol.com
website: www.gwili.co.uk

A team of highly skilled craftswomen runs **Gwili Pottery**, which is located close to the A485 five miles north of Carmarthen. Finely made hand-thrown and hand-decorated ceramics have been produced here for 25 years, and the pottery, set in a converted barn on a hillside overlooking the Gwili Valley, has built up a far-reaching reputation for the range, quality and beauty of its output.

One end of the building is a studio/pottery where the pieces are thrown and turned, decorated and fired, while at the other end is a gallery where the range of these beautiful and highly desirable pots, jugs, mugs and bowls is on display. The view from the pottery is of unspoilt rural beauty, with swans gliding across the lake and kites flying overhead, and among the nearby attractions are Llanpumpsaint, the church dedicated to five 6th century saints, and the Gwili Railway, which puffs through the valley on part of the old Great Western Railway line.

Gwyno and Grynnaro. Living in the 6th century, the saints were all brothers and members of the semi-royal Cunedda family, which goes some way to explain this mass sanctification.

ABERGWILI

1½ miles E of Carmarthen off the A40

The **Carmarthenshire County Museum** occupies a lovely old house that was previously a palace of the bishop of St David's and visitors to the museum can still see the bishop's peaceful private chapel. Concentrating on Carmarthenshire's past, the museum's displays range from Roman gold through to Welsh furniture and there is also a reconstruction of a school room. The palace's grounds, too, are open to the public, and the delightful parkland is ideal for a stroll and a picnic.

Found on land that has been farmed for over 2,000 years, the **Merlin's Hill Centre**, at Alltyfyrddin farm, explains the history and legends of the surrounding area and its connections with Merlin the magician. As well as listening out for the wizard's wailings - he is supposed to be imprisoned in the hill - visitors can also explore this dairy farm and learn about farming, past and present. From Alltyfyrddin there is an ancient path which leads up to the site of an Iron Age hill fort.

LLANARTHNE

7½ miles E of Carmarthen on the B4300

To the southwest of the village lies **Paxton's Tower**, designed by SP Cockerell and built in the early 19th century on the Middleton estate for William Paxton; it was dedicated to Lord Nelson. Constructed so that this Gothic eyecatcher could be seen from the main house, it affords panoramic views from the tower over the estate and Tywi valley.

CAPEL DEWI UCHAF COUNTRY HOUSE

Capel Dewi, Carmarthenshire SA32 8AY
Tel: 01267 290799 Fax: 01267 290003
e-mail: uchaffarm@aol.com
website: www.walescottageholidays.uk.com

Approached by a long, leafy lane, a distinguished old property has been saved from neglect by Fredena (Freddie) Burns, whose expertise in home-making and gardening has brought **Capel Dewi Uchaf Country House** triumphantly back to life. The premises date back at least 500 years and lie in an area of Special Scientific Interest, skirted by a Roman road and bordered on one side by the delightful River Twyi.

The bedrooms are in traditional country style, with beams, brass beds, chintz and patchwork; they comprise two double rooms, a twin-bedded room and a two-room family suite, all with en suite facilities. Self-catering accommodation is also available in converted stables. The garden is a lovely quiet spot for taking afternoon tea, and the vegetable and soft fruit area supplies the house, where the day starts with a wholesome farmhouse breakfast that has won Best Breakfast in Wales awards. Fishing is available on a private stretch of water, and beyond the grounds there are superb walks, terrific views and a large number of places of interest to the visitor.

To the south of
Llanarthne, and set in the
18th century parkland of
Middleton Hall (which no
longer exists), is the
**National Botanic Garden of
Wales** - a Millennium project
that covers an amazing 568
acres on the edge of the
beautiful Towy Valley.
Dedicated to conservation,
horticulture, science and
education, this national
botanic garden, the first to
be constructed in Britain for

National Botanic Garden of Wales

over 200 years, is centred around a great
glasshouse that is the largest single span
house of its kind in the world. Among
the many delights to be found within
this old parkland are one of Europe's
longest herbaceous borders, a double
walled garden, a Japanese garden,
lakeside walks and the Physicians of

Myddfai, an exhibition that pays tribute
to the legendary Welsh healers of the
Middle Ages (see under Llandovery).
Tribute is also paid to the Welsh botanist
Alfred Russel Wallace, whose theories of
natural selection paralleled those of
Charles Darwin. However, this is also
very much a garden of the future and, in

RO-FAWR FARM

Golden Grove, Dryslwyn, Carmarthenshire SA32 8RP
Tel: 01558 668505 Fax: 01558 669067
website:www.rofawrfarm.com
e-mail: ann@rofawrfarm.co.uk

The centrepiece of **Ro-Fawr Farm** is an old stone-built
farmhouse dating back to 1802 and set in pretty gardens
in the beautiful Towy Valley in West Wales. The setting
and the scenery are among the loveliest in the whole of
Wales, and the owner Ann Maclean shares the wonderful
location with guests who come here for a holiday for walking, fishing, bird-watching and the amazing
wildlife or simply taking a well-earned break. The Dairy, The Cottage and the Victorian Barn have
been converted to the highest standards to offer supremely luxurious and comfortable self-catering
accommodation in which period charm combined with up-to-date amenities earns the maximum
rating from the Wales Tourist Board.

Relaxed comfort is the order of the day, and guests have the
added bonus of not just enjoying the beautiful surroundings, but
also the heated indoor swimming pool and the all-weather tennis
court. The splendid riverside location makes the farm an ideal
base from which to embark on birdwatching outings, picnic walks
and visits to the many local places of interest, including the
historical castles of Dinefwr,Dryslwyn and Carreg Cenen. Ro-
Fawr is situated between the two coastal areas of Pembrokeshire
and Gower and is very near to the National Botanic Garden of
Wales and the enchanting lost garden of Aberglasney.

the Energy Zone, there is a biomass furnace using salvaged or coppiced wood for heating the site, and the Living Machine sewage treatment system.

DRYSLWYN

8½ miles E of Carmarthen on the B4300

By the side of the River Tywi lie the remains of **Dryslwyn Castle** built on the hill by one of Lord Rhys' descendants in the mid-13th century. An ideal location for a stronghold, the castle throughout its life suffered several savage attacks that no doubt contributed to its present ruined condition.

LLANGATHEN

11 miles E of Carmarthen off the A40

The village is home to **Aberglasney** (see panel below), one of the oldest and most interesting gardens in the country. The first recorded description of Aberglasney house and gardens was made by the bard Lewis Glyn Cothi in 1477 when he wrote of "a white painted court, built of dressed stone, surrounded by nine gardens of orchards, vineyards and large oak trees." At a later date, at the beginning of the 17th century, the estate was sold to the Bishop of St David's and it was Bishop Anthony Rudd, whose grand tomb can be found in the village

church, who improved both the house and gardens in a manner befitting a bishop's palace.

GOLDEN GROVE

11 miles E of Carmarthen off the B4300

To the east of the village lies **Gelli Aur Country Park** on part of the estate of the ancestral home of the Vaughan family. Containing remnants of a 17th century deerpark, the landscaped parkland was laid out in the 18th century and the country park also includes a Victorian arboretum planted by Lord Cawdor. The original mansion, now part of an agricultural college, was the work of the architect Joseph Wyatville.

LLANSTEFFAN

7 miles SW of Carmarthen on the B4312

This village, near the mouth of the River Tywi, is dominated by the ruins of **Llansteffan Castle** on a headland above the estuary. The successor to an earlier defensive earthwork, the castle dates from the 12th century and the main remaining feature is the impressive gateway dating from 1280. To the southwest of the castle lies **St Anthony's Well**, the waters of which were thought to have medicinal properties.

Llansteffan, along with Ferryside, its

ABERGLASNEY GARDENS

Llangathen, Carmarthenshire SA32 8QH
Tel/Fax: 01558 668998
e-mail: info@aberglasney.org.uk
website: www.aberglasney.org.uk

Aberglasney is one of the country's most exciting garden restoration projects, and the gardens are well on the way to becoming one of the leading garden attractions in the UK. The recovery and restoration are taking place under the aegis of the Aberglasney Restoration Trust, set up in 1995, and the nine acres contain six different garden spaces including three walled gardens. At the heart is a unique, fully-restored Elizabethan/Jacobean cloister and parapet walk giving wonderful views over the site. The gardens have already won many awards from the Wales Tourist Board and other prestigious bodies. There's a café in the gardens.

neighbour across the river mouth, is a paradise for walkers as well as sailors and the waymarked walks around the estuary take in some truly breathtaking coastal scenery. The promontory of Wharley Point, in particular, affords stunning views across the Taf and Tywi estuaries to Carmarthen Bay.

LAUGHARNE
9 miles SW of Carmarthen on the A4066

This pretty rural town of Georgian houses on the estuary of the River Taf is home to one of the country's most handsome castles. Originally an earth and timber fortress, **Laugharne Castle** was built in stone around the 13th century and although much of the fortification still remains, it is the transformations undertaken by Sir John Perrot in the 16th century that make this a particularly special site. Granted Laugharne by Queen Elizabeth

Laugharne

I, Perrot, an illegitimate son of Henry VIII, turned the castle into a comfortable mansion that after seeing action in the Civil War declined into the ruins seen today.

However, romantic though the castle ruins are, this is not all Laugharne Castle has to offer as the Victorian garden has been splendidly restored. Both the castle ruins and the superb surroundings have provided inspiration for artists over the centuries and, in particular, they are the subject of a dramatic watercolour by JMW Turner. Writers, too, have found this an inspiring place and both Dylan Thomas, who wrote in a gazebo in the grounds, and Richard Hughes, author of *A High Wind in Jamaica*, are associated with Laugharne Castle. This coastal town is today a shrine to its most famous resident, Dylan Thomas, who spent the last four years of his life living at **The Boathouse** set in a cliff overlooking the Taf estuary. Discovering this small out-of-the-way place in the 1940s, Thomas famously "got off the bus and forgot to get on again", and it was while in Laugharne that he wrote some of his best works, including *Under Milk Wood*, a day in the life of his imaginary village of Llareggub (read the name backwards to find why it has this odd name). Thomas,

Dylan Thomas Boathouse

notoriously prone to destructive drinking sprees, died in The White Horse Bar in New York in 1953, at only 39 years of age. The parish church of St Martin, where he is buried, contains a replica of the plaque to his memory which can be seen in Poets' Corner, Westminster Abbey. The Boathouse is now a heritage centre dedicated to the writer and, as well as the fascinating memorabilia on display here, there is also an interpretation centre, bookshop and tea room.

PENDINE

13½ miles SW of Carmarthen on the A4066

The vast expanse of sand which makes Pendine a popular place with families for a day out by the sea was used in the 1920s by Sir Malcolm Campbell and others for attempting land speed records. In 1924, Sir Malcolm broke the World Motor Flying Kilometre Record here by averaging 146 miles per hour. He later raised that to 174 mph, and went on to achieve speeds in excess of 300 mph on the salt flats at Bonneville, Utah. In 1927, while attempting to beat Sir Malcolm's record, Welshman JG Parry Thomas was decapitated in an accident on the beach and his car, Babs, lay buried in the sand for some 44 years before being unearthed and restored. Babs can now be seen in all its gleaming glory at the **Museum of Speed**, which explores the history of this stretch of sand where so many records were broken. However, not all the speed attempts involved land vehicles as it was from these sands in 1933 that the intrepid aviatrix Amy Johnson set off on her solo flight across the Atlantic.

ST CLEARS

8½ miles SW of Carmarthen on the A40

This small market town, which still has remnants of a Norman motte, was the

COEDLLYS COUNTRY HOUSE

Llangynin, St Clears, Carmarthenshire SA33 4JY
Tel: 01994 231455 Fax: 01994 231441
e-mail: keith@harber.fsworld.co.uk
website: www.coedllyscountryhouse.co.uk

Tucked away in a tranquil spot in the heart of Carmarthenshire, **Coedllys Country House** provides the perfect country hideaway. It overlooks its own wooded valley and rolling green fields, and owners Keith and Valerie Harber make no compromises in giving their guests the very best - "quality, comfort, peace and a warm welcome". The bedrooms are notably airy and spacious, furnished with antiques and equipped with tv, clock radio, hairdryer and a host of extras, from a comfortable sofa to bathrobes and slippers, teas and coffees, fresh fruit and flowers, bottled water and magazines. "Robin" has an en suite shower and antique double bed; "Chaffinch" has bath and shower en suite and twin antique beds; "Swallow" has an en suite shower room and a wonderfully comfortable double antique bed.

Rooms are let on a bed and breakfast basis, with evening meals available by prior notice. Non-smokers only. Coedllys Country House has another attraction in the shape of a small sanctuary of rescued animals, who enjoy a chat over the fence, with children eight years and over only. Tucked away it may be, but the house is certainly not remote, as the main A40 is only three miles away. Pembrokeshire's resorts and beaches, Cardigan Bay, the beautiful Teifi Valley and Dylan Thomas's Laugharne are all within easy reach.

GLYN-COCH STUDIOS

Ffynnongain Lane, Pwll Trap, St Clears,
Carmarthenshire SA33 4AR
Tel: 01994 231867
e-mail: huwandthelma@compuserve.com
website: www.glyn-coch.com

The Jones family took over **Glyn-Coch Studios** in 2000 and
now the shop offers a wide range of locally made crafts,
including the exquisite floral patterned Glyn-Coch Design
China decorated by the firm founded there in 1980. Robert
Paul Stokle paints historic seascapes and impressionist pictures in his studio, and you can see pottery
being made. A tearoom serves light snacks and from April to October you can stay on a small camping
and caravan site. From the woodland walk you can see rare Norfolk Horn Sheep. The craft centre is
open Tuesday to Sunday and on bank holidays all year round.

site of the defeat of Owain Glyndwr by
Pembrokeshire's army in 1406. Later, in
the 1840s, St Clears was the home to
more trouble when it featured in the
Rebecca Riots, during which the rioters
destroyed toll gates.

WHITLAND

13 miles W of Carmarthen on the B4328

This small market town and centre of the

dairy industry is historically important
as the meeting place of the assembly
convened by Hywel Dda in the 10th
century. Born towards the end of the
9th century, Dda made a pilgrimage to
Rome in AD 928 and, some 14 years
later, he was ruler of most of Wales.
Summoning representatives from each
part of Wales to Whitland, Dda laid
down a legal system that became known

IVYDENE GARDEN CENTRE & FLORISTS

Abbey Road, Whitland, Carmarthenshire SA34 0GR
Tel: 01994 240453 Fax: 01994 241193

Ivydene Garden Centre & Florists is located eight
miles from the coast in a setting that shows Wales in
all its rural splendour. The Abbot family, headed by
son of the family Craig, took over the business in May
2001 and later moved it across the road - the A40
Carmarthen-Haverfordwest road. The whole family
has put a great deal of effort and expertise into

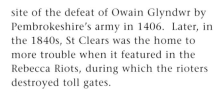

Ivydene, and under their ownership it should be
assured of continuing success.

The site is neat, attractive and well-ordered,
with bedding and garden plants outside in great
variety, and a well-stocked shop with cut flowers
and garden products next to the glasshouse.
Wreaths and bouquets, wedding displays, pot
plants, hanging baskets for summer and winter,
shrubs, trees, feed, compost, "beauty products" for
the garden, cut flowers, bedding plants.......
everything is clearly labelled, making buying and
browsing a real pleasure that is enhanced by the
friendly, helpful owners and staff.

for its wisdom and justice and which remained in force in Wales up until the Act of Union with England in 1536. This system and its instigator are remembered at the Prince of Wales Design award winning building the **Hywel Dda Centre**; here, too, is a **Memorial** in the form of six gardens representing the six separate divisions of the Law: Society and Status, Crime and Tort, Women, Contract, the King, and Property.

Just north of the town lie the remains of the once great **Whitland Abbey**, which was founded in 1140 by Bernard, the first Norman Bishop of St David's.

LLANBOIDY

12 miles NW of Carmarthen off the A40

In old stone farm buildings to the north of the village is a chocoholic's dream - the **Welsh Chocolate Farm**, where chocolates of all shapes, sizes and flavours are made. As well as watching chocolate making demonstrations and

touring the factory to see just how the chocolate is produced, visitors can buy gifts and treats for family and friends (and selves) at the farm shop, which has the largest selection of chocolates in Wales. And as this is rich dairy country there are also farmhouse cheeses and other dairy delights at the shop (don't even try to resist the homemade fudge!), along with a wide range of hand roasted coffee beans prepared daily.

NEWCASTLE EMLYN

14 miles NW of Carmarthen on the A484

In Newcastle Emlyn the first printing press in Wales was set up by Isaac Carter in 1718. The town grew up around **Newcastle Emlyn Castle**, which was built in 1240 by Maredudd ap Rhys beside the River Teifi. Like that of many other castles in Wales, Newcastle Emlyn's turbulent history is in some ways confirmed by the present condition of this now ruined fortress, as it changed

THE OLD SADDLERS ANTIQUES

Bridge Street, Newcastle Emlyn,
Carmarthenshire SA38 9DU
Tel: 01239 711615

Antiques, collectables and bric-a-brac of all kinds fill the display areas in the **Old Saddlers Antiques**, a business built on quality, taste and the experience of owner Elisabeth Coomber.

Behind a traditional shopfront on a prominent site in the centre of Newcastle Emlyn, visitors will discover a fascinating collection of

items spread over several rooms, from porcelain and china to copper kettles, brasses, pictures, toys, garments, mirrors, clocks, cushions and one-off items: a man trap, a Welsh dresser, an old wooden cheese press, a toy traveller's caravan.

Everything in this splendid place is interesting, nothing ordinary, and with a constant turnover of the stock every visit will produce a different selection of things to browse and to buy.

Salmon Leap Waterfalls

harbouring Royalist
sympathisers. On the B4571
a mile north of Newcastle
Emlyn lie **Old Cilgwyn
Gardens**. This is a 14-acre
mixed garden set in 900 acres
of parkland that includes a
53-acre Site of Special
Scientific Interest. The
garden, which was the site of
the last duel to be fought in
Wales, has ornamental pools
and a cast concrete bridge.
Open all year by appoint-
ment. Tel: 01239 710244.

hands several times until it was
destroyed during the Glyndwr rebellion
in the early 1400s. Having fallen into
disrepair, the castle was granted to Sir
Rhys ap Thomas by Henry VII in the late
15th century and became a country
residence before being, once again, all
but demolished during the Civil War for

CENARTH

16 miles NW of Carmarthen on the A484

This ancient village, which was first
mentioned by Geraldus Cambrensis in
the late 12th century when he passed
through on his journey with Archbishop
Baldwin, has for centuries been a centre

THE NATIONAL CORACLE CENTRE & 17TH CENTURY FLOUR MILL

Cenarth Falls, Carmarthenshire SA38 9JL
Tel/Fax: 01239 710980
e-mail: martinfowler@coraclecentre.fsnet.co.uk
website: www.coraclecentre.co.uk

Martin Fowler, who developed the **National Coracle Centre**
from a virtually derelict property, owns and runs one of the
most fascinating museums in Wales. The Centre, which is set
in the grounds of a 17th century flour mill, was the site of the
inaugural meeting of the Coracle Society in 1990, and the
building was officially opened by Earl Lloyd George of Dwyfor
in June 1991. The exhibits on view include coracles from
around the world, from tiny local one-man fishing boats to a bamboo parisal from India, and a large
and heavy guffa, a cargo and passenger carrying craft from Iraq.

Fibreglass is increasingly used in the manufacture of
modern coracles, but some are still made with willow,
hazelwood, hot pitch and linseed oil. Cenarth was once an
important coracle fishing village, but since the early 1970s
coracles have been used mainly for taking children for rides
or for demonstration purposes. Visitors to this unique
attraction can see a coracle being made, and a demonstration
on the river can be arranged with notice. At the back of the
Centre the mill and wheel can be visited, and also within
the grounds are walks with views overlooking the famous
Cenarth Falls and the salmon leap.

for coracle fishermen. Situated on the banks of the River Teifi, famous for its **Salmon Leap Waterfalls**, the conservation village is home to **Cenarth Mill**. Dating from the 18th century the watermill, which has two pairs of stones (one for barley, the other for oats) is powered by the river close to the salmon leap. Now restored and producing wholemeal flour, the mill complex also houses the **National Coracle Centre** (see panel opposite), where visitors can see a unique collection of these ancient boats from around the world. Dating back to the Ice Age, these little round boats, once covered in skins, are still used for salmon fishing and at the Centre visitors can see demonstrations of coracles at work.

DREFACH

12 miles NW of Carmarthen off the A484

Many of the water driven mills of this area still continue to produce flour and distinctive woollen goods, and this important part of the region's industrial heritage is explored in the **Museum of the Welsh Woollen Industry**. One of the most traditional and rural industries, the processes involved in the spinning, weaving and dyeing of wool are explained here, and there are also demonstrations of cloth making and dyeing carried out on 19th century machinery. As well as trying their hand at spinning, visitors can stroll around the sites of the old woollen mills in the village, which still produce flannel cloth and tweeds, and follow all or part of the Woollen Mill Trail through the scenic Teifi Valley. There are 24 miles of waymarked trails from the Museum, the longer ones taking in the seven so-called flannel villages.

LLANDOVERY

As it is situated at the confluence of the Rivers Bran, Gwennol and Tywi, Llandovery's Welsh name, Llanymddyfri (meaning the church amid the waters), seems particularly apt. Evidence suggests that the area around Llandovery has been important since Roman times, and the church contains Roman tiles within its fabric. Rhys Pritchard, known as a preacher and as the author of the collection of verses *The Welshman's Candle*, lived here in the 17th century, as did the renowned Methodist poet and hymn writer William Williams in the 18th century.

Llandovery Castle, the remains of which overlook the cattle market, was the most easterly Norman castle within Carmarthenshire, constructed in 1116 by Richard Fitzpons only to be captured and destroyed some 42 years later. Although it was repaired in the late 12th century by Henry II, the castle was left to decay after 1403 and only the tumbledown remains

Llandovery Town Centre

CWM RHUDDAN MANSION

Llandovery, Carmarthenshire SA20 0DX
Tel/Fax: 01550 721414

Five star WTB bed and breakfast accommodation is provided at **Cwm Rhuddan**, a superb Victorian mansion in French chateau style set in beautiful landscaped gardens with glorious views. Three en suite bedrooms offer space and splendour, all king size beds including a four-poster , central heating, open fires,tv, hospitality tray and tea/ coffee making facilities. A sumptuous breakfast is served in the elegant dining room, and guests can relax in style in the sitting room, which boasts original features and antique furnishings; there is also a large recreation room with table tennis. Children and pets are welcome. Garaging available.

are visible today. Visiting in the 19th century, the author George Borrow called Llandovery "the pleasantest little town in which I have halted". The history of this town, which has pleased many before and since George Borrow, is told at the **Llandovery Heritage Centre** where the legends surrounding the hero Twm Sion Cati - the Welsh Robin Hood - and the local **Physicians of Myddfai** are also explored. The legend concerning the physicians is that a lady appeared one day from a lake in the Black Mountain. A local farmer's son fell in love with her and she agreed to marry him on condition that he did not hit her three times without cause. Over the years he had given her three light taps for what he thought was poor behaviour and sure enough she returned to the lake. But before disappearing she passed on her herbal healing secrets to her three sons, who became the first of the famous

Physicians of Myddfai, a line of healers who practised from the 12th to the 18th centuries. A new venture among a group of farmers in Myddfai (a short drive south of Llandovery) is bringing together this age-old legend and the growing modern interest in the properties of herbs. They hope to establish a centre where visitors can learn more about the legend and modern practices and where the farmers would sell their own brand of herbal products. The Church of St Mary on the Hill was built within the ramparts of a Roman fort that once stood in the town, and some Roman tiles can be seen in the walls of the church; also of note are the barrel-vaulted chancel and tie-beam roof.

CILYCWM

3½ miles N of Llandovery off the A483

The attractive **Dolauhirion Bridge**, spanning the River Tywi, was built in 1173 by William Edwards, and the

TOWY BRIDGE INN

Rhandirmwyn, Nr Llandovery, Carmarthenshire SA20 0PE
Tel: 01550 760370

The Dancyger family realised a lifetime's ambition when they bought the **Towy Bridge Inn**, with Mum, Fran and daughter Abi being joint licensees, Abi being one of the youngest in the country. The 200-year-old building enjoys a wonderful riverside setting with the Cambrian Mountains making an imposing backdrop. When the sun shines, it's lovely to sit at a bench by the river, but the bar is equally delightful, with old oak beams and an open wood-burning fire. Inside or out, this is a super little place for enjoying a glass or two of real ale and some good Welsh cooking. Children are welcome, and there's a separate family room.

village's chapel is said to have been the first meeting place of Methodists in Wales. Close by lies **Twm Sion Cati's Cave**, the hideout of the 16th century "Robin Hood of Wales". A poet whose youthful escapades earned him his title, Twm Sion (who died in 1620) curtailed his activities and settled down after marrying the heiress of Ystradffin and he even became a magistrate.

LLANGADOG

5 miles SW of Llandovery on the A4069

This small town in the Vale of Towy once boasted a castle, although all that remains today is a mound, as the castle was destroyed by its owners in 1277 rather than letting it fall into the hands of the English.

To the southwest of Llangadog lies

THE CASTLE HOTEL

Queen Square, Llangadog, Carmarthenshire SA19 9BW
Tel: 01550 777377 e-mail: castlellangadog@yahoo.co.uk
website: www.castlellangadog.co.uk

The Castle Hotel is a traditional Georgian coaching inn in the centre of this pretty village. Smartly refurbished by owners Steve and Mary Bevan, it has a warm, friendly atmosphere and is visited by guests from all over the world. Bed & Breakfast accommodation is available all year round in five pleasantly appointed bedrooms. The bar has an old-world look with beams and an open fire, while outside the sheltered beer garden supports upwards of 30 different herbs, many of which are used in the excellent dishes served in the à la carte restaurant.

CROSS INN

Llanddeusant, Llangadog, Carmarthenshire SA19 9YG
Tel: 01550 740617 Fax: 01550 740684
website: www.cross-inn.co.uk

Peter and Rosalyn Faulkner stepped off the treadmill of city life to take over the **Cross Inn**, which enjoys a tranquil location in the Brecon Beacons National Park. They have renovated the upstairs for bed and breakfast accommodation and confirmed the inn's place at the centre of village life with well-kept real ales and good food based on prime local produce including Welsh Black Beef steaks. Wonderful walks, with sightings of red kites almost guaranteed, start and finish at the inn, and guests making a day of it can set out with a packed lunch provided by the hosts. Private fishing and bicycle hire can also be arranged.

BLACK MOUNTAIN CARAVAN & CAMPING PARK

Llanddeusant, Llangadog, Carmarthenshire SA19 9YG
Tel/Fax: 01550 740217
website: www.breconbeacon-holidays.com

Black Mountain Caravan & Camping Park is surrounded by a particularly wild and unspoilt area of the Brecon Beacons National Park, with stunning views towards the 2,630' Fan Brycheiniog. David and Sharon Rainsley's site is a mixture of caravans and camping, with six-berth static caravans for hire and ample room for private vans. The site is very well-equipped, with hard standings, electrical hook-ups, toilets, showers, a laundrette, a pub and a well-stocked shop. Walking, fishing, pony trekking, caving and exploring sites of historic interest are activities within easy reach, and the owners organise guided walking holidays on routes convenient for the Caravan Park.

BLAENLLYNNANT

Gwynfe, Llangadog, Carmarthenshire SA19 9SB
Tel: 01550 740376 e-mail: info@cennencottages.co.uk
Fax: 01550 740364 website: www.cennencottages.co.uk

Blaenllynnant self-catering cottages are situated at the southwest edge of the Brecon National Park in a setting of peace, seclusion and spectacular views and excellent walking country. All are five star rated by the Welsh Tourist Board. The cottages, recently converted from 19th century barns and architect-designed to the highest standards, are set around the former farmyard and ponds, as is the farmhouse. Stone-walled and slate-roofed, each cottage has its own lawns and car parking.

Ysgubor Fawr (Big Barn) is a large cottage in grand style and sleeps eight. The living room has an open stone-built log fire, with a gallery, a tv area and door opening on to a terrace and lawn. The spacious dining room, also with log fire and can seat 20, has a lofty beamed ceiling, overlooked by a bay window with painted screen depicting saints, which can be opened to accommodate a string quartet for dining entertainment. A door opens to an evening terrace. Both rooms have slate floors. The fully fitted kitchen enables caterers to serve a large party. There are two twin bedded rooms on the

ground floor and two double bedded rooms on the first floor with high ceilings, all with en suite fully tiled bathrooms and boarded floors.

Ty Nant (Cottage by the Stream) is a smaller building sleeping four plus two. The living/dining room has a wood-burning stove and doors opening on to the terrace and lawn, the kitchen is fully fitted and a single bedroom has an adjoining bathroom. All have slate floors. The first floor has one single and one double bedroom, each with en-suite tiled bathrooms, all single bedrooms have double beds. First floors are boarded.

Y Bwthyn (The Cottage) is single storey with lounge/dining room, opening on to the terrace, wood burning stove and fully fitted kitchen all with slate floors, a twin bedded room with boarded floor and en suite fully tiled bathroom.

Rhyblid Fach (Little Rhyblid) is about ten miles away and sleeps six. It is on a quiet lane and has spectacular views of the valley below. The ground floor has a living/dining room, wood burning stove and gallery over, opening on to a terrace, a fully fitted kitchen, fully tiled bathroom and a twin bedded room. On the first floor are two double bedded rooms with fitted carpets, one with a fully tiled en-suite bathroom. There is oil fired central heating and the ground floors are quarry tiled. The terrace, with mature trees overlooks the view and there is private car parking.

All the cottages are fully equipped with new or antique furntiure, have full oil fired central heating, tv with videos, radios, telephones, patio furnitue, portable barbecue and welcome pack. Logs are included. They can be occupied separately or as a group, Ysgubor Fawr catering for all. No pets or smokers please and no children under 12 unless part of a group occupying all cottages.

Blaenllynnant was home to Sir John Williams, physician to Queen Victoria and founder and first president of the National Library of Wales in Aberystwyth. Within four miles are Carreg Cennen Castle, Wales' most dramatic castle and Garn Goch, the largest Iron Age Fort in Wales, as well as a golf course. Within 15 miles are the National Botanic Gardens of Wales, the Aberglasney Lost in Time Gardens, and another two castles - the 16th century National trust Newton House and the 13th century Castle of Dinefwr. Rhyblid Fach is two miles from Myddfai and its legend of the Meddygon of Myddfai (the Doctors of Myddfai) medieval herbalists whose recipes are still used today. This is good walking country with the mountains and the Llynfan Fach volcanic lake close by.

Carn Coch, the largest hill fort in Wales, whose earthworks and stone ramparts cover some 15 acres.

BRYNAMMAN

13½ miles SW of Llandovery on the A4069

Brynamman means "hill by the River Amman" and the village lies on the southeastern edge of the Brecon Beacons in the foothills of the Black Mountains. However, 200 years ago there was no village, just a scattering of farms within easy reach of the water. As coal began to be extracted here from the 17th century the village grew in importance. It was not until 1831 that the first shop opened in the new settlement and in 1840 a contract was drawn up between the Llanelli Railway and Dock Company and John Jones. Nicknamed the architect of Brynamman, Jones was responsible for building the mountain road that enabled the mined coal to reach the market place

and the limekilns. Commercial mining began here in 1810 and by 1860 the local a ironworks employed most of the 1,000 inhabitants of Brynamman; but by 1889 these works had gone. With its economy relying on coal mining, Brynamman was badly hit during the coal strikes of the 1920s that were to mark the end of Brynamman as an industrial village. Today, a few shops and businesses survive but the railway has gone.

TRAPP

12 miles SW of Llandovery off the A483

Situated on the top of a precipitous limestone crag on the Black Mountain and with a vertical drop to the River Cennen below, **Carreg Cennen Castle**, to the east of Trapp, enjoys one of the most spectacular locations of any Welsh castle. Although the present castle dates from the late 13th or early 14th century, there was undoubtedly a fortress here

Continued on page 310

PENCRUG FARM

Gwynfe, Llangadog, Carmarthenshire SA19 9RP
Tel/Fax: 01550 740686

In 1986, after many years living and working in London, George and Olwen Fleming found the perfect antidote to the stresses of city life when they bought **Pencrug Farm**. In an area renowned for its scenic beauty, this isolated hill farmhouse was originally a traditional longhouse, expanded down the years with the incorporation of barns at either end to produce a dwelling full of character and old-world charm, with a rendered stone facade, a slate roof and masses of oak beams and uprights. In this delightful setting, as far as can be from the urban rush, the owners welcome guests for short or long stays in three quiet, comfortable bedrooms reached by a spiral staircase, with handbasins, tea-makers and a shared bathroom.

An excellent breakfast, with free-range eggs, is served in the spacious kitchen, and evening meals are available by prior arrangement; all the meat served at Pencrug is home-reared. The splendours of the Brecon Beacons National Park are on the doorstep, and the brooding presence of the Black Mountain beckons serious walkers. Fishing, riding and golf can all be arranged nearby, and the area is the best one in Wales for spotting the red kite. Among the many man-made attractions are the romantic remains of Carreg Cennen Castle on the Black Mountain and Carn Coch, the largest hill fort in Wales.

Carreg Cennen Castle

Start	Carreg Cennen Castle
Distance	4 miles (6.4km)
Approximate time	2 hours
Parking	Car park at Carreg Cennen Castle
Refreshments	Farm café next to car park
Ordnance Survey maps	Landranger 159 (Swansea, Gower & surrounding area), Outdoor Leisure 12 (Brecon Beacons National Park – Western & Central areas)

The major attraction of this popular and well-waymarked walk in the western foothills of the Black Mountain is the ever-changing views of Carreg Cennen Castle, perched on its precipitous rock, from many different angles. The finale is superb – a steady ascent through woodland to the castle entrance.

One of the most dramatically sited castles in Britain, Carreg Cennen occupies a 300ft-high (91m) exposed vertical limestone outcrop above the Cennen valley. It is everyone's idea of what a ruined castle should be like; it is even complete with an underground passage, hewn from the rock, which leads down into a cave. Originally a Welsh fortress, stronghold of the Lords Rhys, it was taken by the English and rebuilt and strengthened in the late 13th and early 14th centuries. Most of its extensive remains belong to that period. Despite its apparent impregnability, it was besieged and captured on a number of occasions and passed through several hands until it was largely demolished to prevent its use by brigands after the War of the Roses.

At the far end of the car park go through a gate into the farmyard of Castle Farm. Do not continue ahead between the farm buildings towards the castle, but turn right and go through another gate adjacent to a barn. Head downhill across a field, making for a stile and footpath sign in the bottom left-hand corner – like most of the signs on

this walk it has a castle symbol on it. Climb the stile and turn left along a narrow lane.

Ignore the first stile on the right and follow the lane downhill, curving left to a second stile just before a cottage, at a public footpath sign to Llwyn-bedw Ⓐ. Turn right over the stile, head downhill across a field, bearing slightly right to climb a stile in the field corner, and continue along a steep downhill path to climb another stile at the bottom. Go across the next field, cross a footbridge over the River Cennen and bear slightly left to head uphill to a stile. Climb it and continue steeply uphill, keeping parallel with a wire fence and line of trees on the left, towards a farm. In front of the buildings turn right to walk along a track, initially across sloping fields and later continuing through an area of scattered trees. After fording a stream the track bends to the right and then curves left to reach a footpath sign a few yards ahead.

Turn left here over a stile and walk along a track, by a hedge-bank on the right, bearing slightly left to cross a footbridge over a narrow stream and continuing to a stile. Climb it and bear slightly right along an enclosed track; this later emerges briefly into a more open area before continuing as a tree-lined route by the infant River Loughor on the right, a most attractive part of the walk. Climb a stile and if you want to see the source of the Loughor which issues from a cave here, another stile immediately to the right gives access.

Continue along the track, which curves slightly left and winds gently uphill, by a wire fence on the right. It then turns left to continue initially by a hedge-bank on the right, and later veers left away from it to a stile. Climb the stile, bear right to pass between two hollows and head across to climb a stile on to a lane **B** .

Turn left, climb a stile beside a cattle-grid and continue along the lane as far as a right-hand bend **C** . Here keep ahead along a track, by a wire fence and hedge-bank on the right. To the right are the Pillow Mounds, long grassy mounds that look like burial chambers but which were artificial rabbit warrens made by local people in the 19th century to ensure a regular supply of fresh meat. The track curves left to a stile; climb it, keep ahead to climb another and continue straight across the middle of a field, bearing slightly left to a gate.

Go through, continue along the left-hand edge of a field, by a wire fence on the left, climb a stile in the field corner by gorse bushes and keep ahead along a sunken grassy track above the Cennen valley, now heading downhill. At a fork take the left-hand, lower track which bends sharply left at a footpath sign and continues down to a crossroads of tracks and paths. Climb the stile straight ahead, descend steps and continue down along the stony, tree- and hedge-lined path, climbing another stile and keeping by a

stream on the right. Turn right to cross a footbridge over the stream, turn left along the other bank, climb a stile and keep ahead to cross another footbridge over the River Cennen **D** .

Turn right and almost immediately turn sharp left, at a footpath sign to Carreg Cennen, on to an attractive path which heads steadily uphill through the lovely, sloping Coed y Castell (Castle Wood) towards the castle, a grand finale to the walk. Continue past the castle entrance at the top and follow the path as it descends, turning right through a kissing-gate, on through another one and down through Castle Farm to return to the start. ●

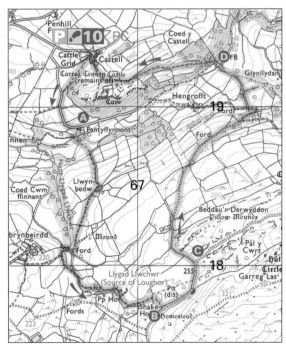

Carreg Cennen Castle

Taken on behalf of the Yorkists in 1462, the fortress was dismantled on the orders of Edward IV, leaving the romantic ruins seen today. A visit here is well worth the effort to enjoy the impressive views and to appreciate what a daunting task attacking the castle must have been. There is only one way up: a steep, grassy hill protected by a complicated system of defences.

before that; some attribute a castle here to Urien, a knight of Arthur's Round Table. Despite its origins being shrouded in obscurity, the castle is known to have been hotly fought over. Carreg Cennen fell to Owain Glyndwr's Welsh insurgents and, during the War of the Roses, it became a base for bandit Lancastrians.

One local legend tells of a narrow underground tunnel which leads from the castle to a wishing well where visitors used to throw corks into the water to make their dreams come true. The well's waters were also thought to have special powers, particularly in curing eye and ear complaints.

Trapp itself has a connection with

THE WELSH DRESSER MAN

1 Quay Street, Llandeilo, Carmarthenshire SA19 6BL
Tel: 01558 822748

On the old road into the hilltop town of Llandeilo, lives the **Welsh Dresser Man** who's name is synonymous with the handsome and distinctive piece of furniture that has been a unique expression of Welsh craftsmanship since medieval times.

That man is Leslie Jones, who after 30 years as a craft lecturer "retired" to his workshop in Quay Street, where his creations continue the centuries-old tradition and are destined to become family heirlooms of future generations.

The Welsh Dresser has always been known for its individuality of design, construction and decoration, which has enabled experts to pinpoint the exact place of origin of a piece and even the craftsman himself, whose "artist's signature" is plain to see in the minute detail of each creation.

Leslie's dressers are individually crafted by hand

from prime Welsh oak. Customers can opt for a copy of a particular dresser or specify variations in height, width, depth and colour. Apart from the dressers, a wide range of traditional and contemporary furniture can be made to specification. You'll get a welcome in the hillside but a prior phone call will be appreciated.

water as the village is the source of Brecon Carreg mineral water. In the converted barns of Llwyndewi Farm is **Trapp Arts and Crafts Centre**, which specialises in crafts from Wales. The shop stocks an interesting range of quality items including stained glass, lovespoons, pottery and jewellery, and the Art Gallery, on the first floor, is devoted to showing the work of local artists. Demonstrations and exhibitions run throughout the summer months and the centre has a coffee shop.

LLANDEILO

11½ miles SW of Llandovery on the A483

The former ancient capital of West Wales, Llandeilo's hilltop position shows off to best advantage this pretty little market town. Pastel coloured Georgian houses line the main road, which curves elegantly up from the **Tywi Bridge** (its

central span is said to be the longest in Wales) to the Church of St Teilo, dedicated to the 6th century saint who gave the town its name. Serving the rich agricultural land which surrounds it, Llandeilo was also one of the original founders of the Welsh Rugby Union, and the so-called Lichfield Gospels, the most perfect Welsh Christian manuscripts, were written here.

To the west of the town lies **Dinefwr Castle**, the ancient seat of the Princes of Deheubarth, one of the three ancient kingdoms of Wales. The fortress was built on the site of an Iron Age fort and legend has it that Merlin's grave is in the area. Overlooking the River Tywi, the first stone castle here is believed to have been built by Rhys ap Gryffydd in the 12th century and, seen as an important target, it was dismantled by Rhys Grug in 1220 to prevent Llywelyn from taking

COTTAGE INN

Pentrefelin, Nr Llandeilo, Carmarthenshire SA19 6SD
Tel: 01558 822890 Fax: 01558 823309

The Cottage Inn has been a hostelry for several centuries and in the old days served as a welcome place of refreshment for drovers and as an overnight stop for passengers on the coaching route. The tradition of hospitality is now being maintained by Kevin and Cindy Skone. Kevin has been in the licensed trade for 25 years, and he and his Australian-born wife offer today's visitors a warm country welcome. Black oak beams and highly polished darkwood furnishings add to the period feel in the bar, where the wall behind the serving area features some eye-catching work in carved oak. Real ales are kept in tip-top condition, and the wines are carefully selected from both Old and New Worlds to enjoy on their own or to accompany the food for which the inn has established a fine reputation.

The best local produce, including fish and seasonal game, is put to fine use by the talented chef, and the menu is always supplemented by daily blackboard specials. With a location right on the A40, convenient yet secluded, the Cottage Inn is a perfect place to pause, and for tourists to the area around Llandeilo, the ancient capital of West Wales, it offers an ideal base for a holiday. The five en suite bedrooms, with traditional decor and pretty embroidered bed linen, look out on to delightful views of rural Wales, and there's easy access not only to lovely unspoilt countryside but to many places of interest, including Dryswyn and Carreg Cennen Castles and the gardens at Middleton Hall and Aberglasney.

THE MAERDY

Dan y Cefn, Manordello, Llandeilo, Dyfed SA19 7BD
Tel: 01550 777448 Fax: 01550 777067
e-mail: maerdycottages@btopenworld.com
website: www.walescottages.org.uk/maerdy
    or www.ukworld.net/maerdy

2001 saw the completion of an ambitious restoration and
conversion programme in which a derelict 300-year-old
farmhouse and its original stone outbuildings have been
turned into a group of cottages offering top-class self-
catering accommodation. Margaret Jones, who masterminded the transformation, has furnished the
seven cottages in traditional style, including many antiques, and all are fully equipped to provide
peace, privacy and everything needed for a real home from home experience. The largest of the cottages
can comfortably sleep up to ten, and two of them are suitable for wheelchair users, with WTB Access
Grade 2. All the cottages have central heating and log or log effect fires.

Margaret is a renowned cook and offers a catering service of home-baked pies and cakes and full
evening meals including soups, casseroles, sauced main courses,
curries and lovely puddings. Pets are welcome at the **Maerdy**,
which lies just off the B4302 Talley-Llandeilo road. Six of the
cottages are here, while the seventh, Dan y Cefn, is situated on
the other side of the valley a short drive away. The grounds at
Maerdy offer plenty of space for children to play in safety, and
walks straight from the cottage doors promise abundant delights
for country lovers, birdwatchers, casual strollers and serious hikers.
A true rural retreat. WTB four and five star rating. Visa accepted.

THE GLYNHIR ESTATE

Glynhir Mansion, Glynhir Road, Llandybie,
Carmarthenshire SA18 2TD
Tel: 01269 850438 e-mail: glynhir@glynhirestate.com
Fax: 01269 851275 website: www.theglynhirestate.com

Owned and run since the 1960s by the Jenkins family, the **Glynhir
Estate** lies in an area of outstanding natural beauty at the foot of
the Black Mountain. At the heart of the estate, through a courtyard
with a clock tower, Glynhir Mansion has four spacious bedrooms
for bed and breakfast, all with hot and cold water, one en suite and three sharing two bathrooms. The
large, comfortable sitting room boasts a welcoming log fire, a baby grand piano, tv, video and music
centre. Meals are taken in the dining room, one of the oldest parts of the mansion, and tea and coffee
are available throughout the day.

Close to the mansion are six sympathetically restored cottages providing fully equipped self-catering
accommodation, sleeping from five to seven guests. This is no longer a working farm, but the old

central farmyard is home to free-roaming ducks, chickens, pigeons,
peacocks and peahens; there are also several horses, flocks of sheep
and two wild boar cross pot-bellied pigs. The five-acre grounds
include a huge walled garden where vegetables, soft fruit and herbs
are grown for the house. The River Loughor runs through unspoilt
woodland, and paths lead up to a vantage point above a spectacular
30 foot waterfall. Carole Jenkins runs a pottery at Glynhir, and
painting courses are held regularly throughout the year. Close to
the estate, rambling, riding, fishing, golf and birdwatching are
among the activities that can be arranged.

313

CARMARTHENSHIRE

THE ANGEL INN

Salem, Nr Llandeilo, Carmarthenshire
Tel: 01558 823394

The Angel Inn is the focal point of a pretty hamlet set in the countryside close to Llandeilo, once the capital of West Wales. Rod Peterson, a former Welsh Chef of the Year, bought the Angel in 2002 with his partner Elizabeth Smith, and already his superior cooking is attracting custom from all over South Wales. Excellent local suppliers provide the raw materials for the imaginative dishes served in the spacious restaurant, where preparation and presentation are both taken very seriously. The inn has a bar lounge and a locals bar with games room, and plans for 2003 include the provision of two letting bedrooms.

this strategic position. The castle ruins are surrounded by **Dinefwr Park**. Extensive areas of parkland were landscaped by Capability Brown in 1775 and incorporated the medieval castle, house, gardens and ancient deer park into one breathtaking panorama. Footpaths through the parkland lead to the castle, bog wood and beech clumps and offer outstanding views of the Tywi valley. The site is one of international importance for wintering birds, including white-fronted geese, shovelers, curlews and lapwings.

TALLEY

8½ miles W of Llandovery on the B4302

This village, with its backdrop of rolling hills, takes its name from Tal-y-llychau, meaning Head of the Lakes. Between two lakes lies **Talley Abbey**, founded in the late 12th century by Rhys ap Gryffyd, and the only Welsh outpost of the austere Premonstratensian canons who, ejected by the Cistercians in the early 13th century, had appealed to the Archbishop of Canterbury and were granted their own religious rights in 1208. Of the few remains to have survived, an immense tower still overshadows the peaceful abbey lawns. The nearby 18th century Church of St Michael is something of an oddity: it was built with no aisle and its interior was entirely taken up with box pews.

CRUGYBAR

7 miles NW of Llandovery on the B4302

Just to the northeast of the village, and nestling in the beautiful foothills of the Cambrian Mountains, lies **Felin Newydd**, a 200-year-old working watermill believed to have been constructed on the site of a grist mill used by Roman soldiers working on the nearby gold mines. Restored in the 1980s, when fascinating graffiti on the mill walls linked the building with 19th century Welsh colonists of South America, the mill is now capable of grinding flour once more.

The land around the mill is quiet, unspoiled and ideal for discovering all manner of wild plant and animal life. Lucky visitors have been known to see red kite circling overhead although there are also more friendly ducks and chickens to amuse young children. A renovated byre has been converted into a cosy tearoom that also includes an interesting selection of local crafts for sale.

PUMPSAINT

8 miles NW of Llandovery on the A482

Near this hamlet, whose names means Five Saints, is the **Dolaucothi Gold Mines**, which date back some 2,000 years to a time when the open-cast gold workings were secured by the Roman army. Once a likely source of gold bullion for the Imperial mints of Lyons

LLWYN HALL

Llwynhendy, Nr Llanelli,
Carmarthenshire SA14 9LJ
Tel: 01554 777754 Fax: 01554 744146
e-mail: llwynhall@btinternet.com
website: www.llwynhall.com

On the eastern fringes of Llanelli lies
Llwyn Hall, a handsome country house
set in its own grounds overlooking
Loughor Estuary. Llwyn Hall offers
superior bed and breakfast accommodation in six guest bedrooms, five en suite,
one with private adjacent bathroom, all
with tv and beverage tray.

Accommodation includes a garden suite for up to two adults and two small children. Colours in
the rooms are beautifully co-ordinated and much of the furniture is antique, both in the bedrooms

and in the two very roomy and
comfortable lounges. Llwyn Hall has
quite a reputation for its food, which
includes lunches, à la carte and table
d'hote dinners and special occasion
meals. Afternoon tea is also available,
and packed lunches can be made up for
guests planning a day out.

Llwyn Hall was built in the mid-19th
century and was enlarged by John
Humphreys, a local entrepreneur and
tea-blender who lived here with his wife
and eight children until the late 1930s.
The workshop at the rear of the house
used to be the blending room. After a
period of severe neglect the house was

bought by the current owner, who undertook extensive renovation and restoration work to restore
the Hall to its former glory. Though elegant and sumptuously appointed, Llwyn Hall is also a very
relaxed and informal place, and a stay here is guaranteed to recharge batteries worn low by the hustle

and bustle of city life. The views
alone are sure to lift the spirits,
and the numerous local
attractions include, almost on
the doorstep, a Wildfowl and
Wetland Centre, the National
Botanical Gardens which are
only a 20 minute drive away, as
are the Gardens at Aberglasney.
The great outdoors beckons all
around, and the Hall has drying
facilities for walkers, ramblers
and cyclists. Llwyn Hall also
boasts a four bedroom country
cottage, "Han-y-Bont", which
may be rented in its entirety by
larger groups, or is also offered
as bed and breakfast rooms.

and Rome, the mines are still in a remarkable state of preservation despite being abandoned by the Romans in AD 140; they were reopened for a short time between 1888 and the late 1930s. Visitors to this National Trust site can see both the ancient and modern mine workings, including a number of audits - the horizontal tunnels dug into the hillside for drainage and access. There is also the opportunity to try gold panning, to see an exhibition of vintage mining machinery and to tour the surrounding woodland on a waymarked trail. The tea room at the Mine is well worth a visit to sample the excellent home baking of farmer's wife Irene Williams.

Wildfowl and Wetlands Centre

LLANELLI

Essentially an industrial town with tinplating, steel, chemical and engineering works, Llanelli was named after the Celt St Elli, to whom the parish church is dedicated. While heavy industry certainly put the town on the map, Llanelli is perhaps more famous as the home of the Scarlets, one of the most famous rugby teams in Wales; the saucepan tipped rugby posts at Stradey Park and the Scarlets' anthem, *Sospan Fach*, are both reminders of Llanelli's industrial heritage. In Stepney Street, the Stepney Wheel was made in the early 20th century; this was an inflated spare tyre on a spokeless rim, to be fixed over a punctured wheel. In India, the term Stepney Wheel is still sometimes applied to any spare tyre. Housed in a former mansion set in a large civic park, **Parc Howard Museum and Art Gallery** has a collection of local paintings and 19th century Llanelli pottery as well as displays on the history of the town.

However, Llanelli is not all industry and rugby as the town is home to one of the country's newest attractions, the **Millennium Coastal Park and Cycleway**. Providing all manner of leisure activities and peaceful wildlife havens, the park incorporates wetlands, gardens, woodlands, a golf course and both sailing and watersports.

To the east of Llanelli lies the **Wildfowl and Wetlands Trust** bird sanctuary, which is one of the eight centres established by the Trust founded by Sir Peter Scott at Slimbridge in 1946. Also a haven for wild plant and animal life throughout the year, the centre's 200 acre saltmarsh is home to flocks of curlew, lapwing and redshank, which visitors can observe from secluded hides. The Discovery Centre has hands-on activities to help visitors find out about conservation.

GORSLAS

9 miles NE of Llanelli on the A476

On **Mynydd Mawr**, a mountain to the north of the village, there was a well that, centuries ago, so legend says, was looked after by a man called Owain. After watering his horses one day, Owain forgot to replace the slab of stone which covered the well and a torrent of water poured down the mountainside. The great rush of water would have drowned the whole area if Owain had not galloped his horse around it and used magic to check the flood. The lake of water which was left is known as Llyn Llech Owain - the lake of Owain's stone slab.

Today, **Llyn Llech Owain Country Park** includes the lake, as well as the peat bog which surrounds it, an area of largely coniferous woodland and dry heath. The lake and peat bog, designated a Site of Special Scientific Interest, are home to a variety of rare plants such as Bogbean, Round Leafed Sundew and Royal Fern. The park's visitor centre has an exhibition that describes both the history and the natural history of the park.

PEMBREY

5 miles W of Llanelli on the A484

This village lies on the flat lands which border Carmarthen Bay and during World War II a Royal Ordnance Factory produced munitions for the Allied Forces. At the factory's peak, in 1942, it covered some 500 acres and employed 3,000 people; it ceased production in 1965. Since then the land has been landscaped, and as **Pembrey Country Park** it offers visitors an unusual mix of pine forests, sand dunes, beaches and such attractions as a dry ski slope, a toboggan run, a miniature railway and an adventure playground. Pembrey Pines Trail is a four-mile walk through dunes and woodland, with splendid views. There's also a visitor centre, and to the east lies Pembrey Saltmarsh, a local nature reserve and a Site of Special Scientific Interest. The park also includes **Cefn Sidan**, one of Europe's best and safest beaches, from which there are glorious views over the Gower coastline.

KIDWELLY

7½ miles NW of Llanelli on the B4308

This historic town, whose charter was granted by Henry I in the 12th century, boasts an ancient church and a 14th century bridge over the River Gwendreath. However, the most interesting and impressive building is undoubtedly the remarkably well preserved Norman **Kidwelly Castle**, which stands on a steep bluff overlooking the river. The castle spans four centuries but most of what remains today is attributed to a Bishop of Salisbury who endeavoured to build a home-from-home from Sherbourne Abbey in Dorset. One of Wales' best kept secrets, Kidwelly Castle gives a fascinating insight into the evolution of a medieval castle into a domestic dwelling of more settled times.

For hundreds of years, the ghost of Gwenllian, daughter of the King of Gwynedd and the wife of the Prince of South Wales, was said to haunt the countryside around the castle. During an attack on the Norman castle in 1136 which Gwenllian led, she was decapitated and legend has it that her headless ghost was unable to find rest until a man searched the battlefield and returned her skull to her. Princess Gwenllian was certainly a warrior, and she was perhaps also a writer. Some have attributed parts of *The Mabinogion* to her, and if the attribution is correct, she would be Britain's earliest known woman writer.

On the outskirts of the town, marked by its 164ft redbrick chimney, lies the **Kidwelly Industrial Museum** - housed in an original tinplate works. Here visitors have a unique opportunity to see how the plate was made as well as learning something of the county's industrial past. The Museum contains Britain's sole surviving pack mill.

...INSULA AND THE
...OAST

...a marks the gateway to the southernmost bulge
...eninsula, a region designated an Area of
...Much of it is owned by the National Trust. The
...made up of a succession of sandy, sheltered
...tline it is dotted with charming and relaxed
...e resorts.

This is also an area rich in natural beauty, with a long history that can be explored not only at the Gower Heritage Centre but also through its various castles, religious sites and ancient monuments. The area has many small family farms that yield some of the finest produce in South Wales; Gower is known in particular for its cockles and its laverbread (edible seaweed). The peninsula

Three Cliffs Bay, Parkmill

was once the haunt of elephants and bears and rhinoceros and other large beasts whose bones have been found in the many caves on the shoreline.

The Vale of Glamorgan is characterised by gentle rolling hills, genteel towns, pretty villages and a splendid natural coastline. An area of rich farmland, the Vale of Glamorgan stands at the foot of the spectacular valleys of south Wales and offers visitors an enticing heritage coastline. This is another area rich in history, where Norman warlords built their castles and where one of the oldest seats of learning was founded at Llantwit Major.

Treorchy

Behind the coastal region lie the valleys of southwest Wales which are known the world over for their coal mining and heavy industry heritage. The best known is the Rhondda Valley, where only one mine survives from the numerous collieries that once powered not just this country but many parts of the world. Though mining has all but gone from the valleys the heritage remains: the towns and villages with their rows of cottages where life revolved around the colliery, the chapel and the music, especially male voice choirs. These famous choirs were formed mainly by communities working in the coalmines and ironworks of the south Wales valleys and in the quarries of north Wales; most of them welcome visitors dropping in on rehearsals as well as attending concerts.

In many cases, nature has reclaimed the hills and vales once scarred by the mining industry and, while the legacy of pride in the industry remains, the various new country parks and nature reserves developed on the sites of the old mines are giving the area a new appeal.

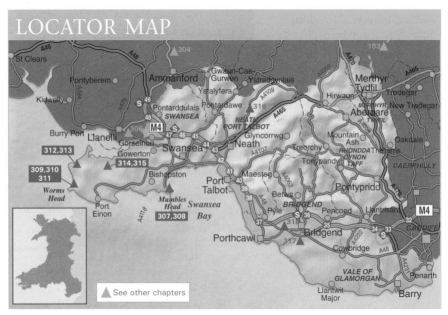

LOCATOR MAP

© MAPS IN MINUTES ™ 2002   © Crown Copyright, Ordnance Survey 2002

ADVERTISERS AND PLACES OF INTEREST

SWANSEA

Swansea, the second city of Wales, is an attractive and welcoming place with an appealing blend of traditional and modern. It was founded in the late 10th century by Sweyne Forkbeard, King of Denmark. Its English name means "Sweyne's Ey" - ey being an inlet. **Swansea Castle**, which gained notoriety in the 18th century when the northern block became a debtors' prison, was first built by the Norman Henry de Newburgh in the late 11th century. However, it was all but destroyed by Owain Glyndwr in the early 1400s when he ransacked the town that had grown up around the fortification.

As early as the 14th century, shipbuilding and coalmining were important industries in the area and by 1700 Swansea was the largest port in Wales. Smelters from Cornwall arrived here, attracted by the plentiful supply of coal, and copper works also flourished; Nelson's ships were covered in Swansea copper. At one time 90% of the country's copper was smelted here and, in the heyday of the industry, other metals such as tin, lead, nickel and zinc were imported to the town for smelting and refining. In the 19th century Swansea porcelain was another famous

Swansea City Centre

local product. Much of the traditional industry has disappeared and the old dock area has been transformed into a marina surrounded by stylish waterfront buildings. This **Maritime Quarter** is arguably the most impressive part of the town and is alive with cafés, pubs and restaurants. Here, in a former warehouse, is the **Swansea Maritime and Industrial Museum**, where the town's industrial heritage is explored. From the early days of the port right through to the devastating bombing raids of World War II, there is plenty to see and learn at the museum. Here, too, is Abbey Woollen Mill, where visitors can see woollen goods produced by traditional means on machinery that dates mainly from before 1900.

The town is also home to the

Swansea Marina

oldest museum in Wales, the **Swansea Museum**, which contains a fascinating range of permanent displays ranging from ancient Egyptian Mummies to Swansea and Nantgarw porcelain and pottery. More artefacts from Egypt can be seen at the **Egyptian Centre**, where over 1,000 objects, from impressive painted coffins to everyday household items, can be seen which date back as far as 3500 BC.

However, Swansea does not dwell in the past and at the **Glynn Vivian Art Gallery** a broad spectrum of the visual arts is on display. Based on the bequest of Richard Glynn Vivian, the gallery houses an international collection of Swansea porcelain and various Old Masters as well as numerous paintings and sculptures by 20th century artists including Hepworth, Nicholas, Nash, Ceri Richards and Augustus John.

Swansea has its own Botanical Garden, housed in the walled garden of **Singleton Park**, and at **Plantasia**, visitors can wander around a giant hot house and discover a wide range of colourful exotic plants. The hot house is also home to numerous exotic insects, fish and reptiles, such as leaf cutting ants, and there is a butterfly house where the various colourful species fly freely. **Clyne Gardens**, at Blackpill off the A4067 Mumbles road, are known in particular for their marvellous rhododendrons, including National Collections, their imposing magnolias and an extensive bog garden. In 2001 the rhododendrons captured 23 awards from the Royal Horticultural Society. These 19th century landscaped gardens were laid out by the Vivian family, who were also responsible for nearby Sketty Hall, a 19th century version of an Italian parterre garden. No mention of Swansea would be complete without referring to the town's most famous son, Dylan

Thomas, who described the town as viewed from his hillside home:

Ugly, lovely town crawling, sprawling, slummed, unplanned, jerry-villa'd, and smug-suburbed by the side of a long and splendid curving shore......

His former home on steep Cwmdonkin Drive displays a blue plaque with the simple inscription, "Dylan Thomas, Poet, 1914-53. Born in this house". Cwmdonkin Park, close to his home, was much loved by Thomas, whose poem *The Hunchback in the Park* was set there. In the **Dylan Thomas Centre**, dedicated to the poet's life and works, the exhibitions feature some of his original manuscripts, letters to friends and family and a moving American documentary about him. There are numerous Dylan Thomas Trails to follow, and the annual Dylan Thomas Celebration (27th October to 9th November in 2002) attracts visitors from around the world. If Dylan Thomas was Swansea's most famous son, its most famous dog was Jack, a retriever who lived in the city during the 1940s. He was reputed to have saved 27 humans and two dogs from drowning and was awarded the canine Victoria Cross.

GOWER PENINSULA

BISHOPSTON
1 mile SW of Swansea off the A4118

The sheltered Bishopston Valley contains an extensive area of ancient woodland tha supports a wide variety of plants and birds. A 2-mile footpath leads along the valley from Kittle to Pwll Du.

MUMBLES
4½ miles SW of Swansea on the A4067

This charming Victorian resort grew up around the old fishing village of Oystermouth, which has its roots in

Roman times and where the Normans built a castle to defend their land. Now in ruins, **Oystermouth Castle** was the home of the de Breos family and the gatehouse, chapel and great hall all date from around the 13th to 14th centuries. Surrounded by small but beautiful grounds overlooking the bay, the ruins are now the scene of re-enactments which chart the history of the castle and, in particular, the siege of the fortress by Owain Glyndwr. It is now a popular sailing centre, with numerous pubs, a restored late-Victorian pier and, on the headland, a lighthouse guarding the entrance into Swansea harbour. The churchyard of All Saints Church at Oystermouth contains the grave of Thomas Bowdler, the literary censor, who published an expurgated

The Mumbles

edition of Shakespeare in 1818 that put the term "bowdlerise" into the language. His *Family Shakespeare* omitted words

and expressions which he considered could not with propriety be read aloud by a father to his family. Sex was out, but cruelty and violence remained largely unexpurgated. Bowdler died at Rhydding, near Swansea, in 1825, leaving a "bowdlerised" version of Gibbon's *Decline and Fall of the Roman Empire*. An unusual attraction in Mumbles is the **Lovespoon Gallery**, where visitors will find an amazing variety of these unique love tokens. Lovespoons were traditionally carved from wood by young men and presented to their sweethearts as a token of their devotion. The custom dates back many centuries, but in these less romantic days the spoons are often bought simply as souvenirs of Wales. The Gallery is open from 10 to 5.30 Monday to Saturday.

The **Mumbles Passenger Railway** was the world's first, and from 1807 to its closure in 1960 the five-mile line used horse, sail, steam, battery, petrol, diesel and electricity. On Bank Holidays in the mid-Victorian period it was known to carry up to 40,000 passengers.

Beyond The Mumbles - the unusual name is derived from the French *mamelles* meaning *breasts* and is a reference to the two islets of the promontory beyond Oystermouth - lies the lovely **Gower Peninsula**, designated an Area of Outstanding Natural Beauty. Gower's southern coast is made up of a succession of sandy, sheltered bays and the first of these, **Langland Bay**, is just around the headland from the village.

PARKMILL

8 miles SW of Swansea on the A4118

This village is home to the **Gower Heritage Centre** which is itself centred around a historic water mill built in the 12th century by the powerful le Breos family, the Norman rulers of Gower.

CLAUDES RESTAURANT

93 Newton Road, Mumbles, Swansea SA3 4BN
Tel: 01792 366006 Fax: 01792 368931
website: www.claudes.org.uk

Andrew and Penny Lauder bring skill, experience and enthusiasm to their restaurant in the centre of Mumbles. **Claudes** is a prettily appointed licensed restaurant that's open for lunch and dinner Tuesday to Saturday and for Sunday lunch. Andrew's cooking is fresh, light and imaginative, with local produce featuring prominently. His lunchtime set menu of one, two or three courses proposes delightful dishes like pan-fried chicken livers with red onions and aged balsamic vinegar sauce, or risotto of poached fish and herbs.

The longer evening à la carte choice continues in the same

appetising modern vein with the likes of thyme-coated salmon pavé with cauliflower purée and a green pea cordon, or stir-fried Welsh Black beef strips with chilli and lemon grass jam and coriander cream. Desserts are equally tempting, and the cheeseboard includes several of the best Welsh varieties. The upper floor of Claudes is reserved for private parties. Claudes offers a bespoke outside catering service for special events in the home or office, and gift vouchers are available.

Originally constructed to supply flour for nearby Pennard Castle, this water mill is a rare survivor in Wales of a rural complex that would once have been found in most villages and hamlets. The Heritage Centre has displays on the history of this beautiful region along with a farming museum. Visitors can also tour the mill, where the restored machinery grinds flour on most days. Younger visitors to the centre can make friends with the farm animals and everyone will enjoy wandering around the craft units and workshops where a wheelwright, a potter, a blacksmith and a mason can be seen plying their trades.

PENMAEN

7 miles SW of Swansea off the A4118

Tradition has it that a village is buried here beneath the sand dunes. The National Trust owns an area that includes High Pennard, topped by a prehistoric hill fort, and Three Cliffs Bay, where there are old lime kilns, an ancient burial chamber and a pillow mound - an artificial warren used to farm rabbits. Cut into the rocks is Minchin Hole, a geological Site of Scientific Interest where evidence has been found of mammals and early man.

OXWICH

11 miles SW of Swansea off the A4118

One of Gower's prettiest villages, Oxwich lies huddled along a lane at the western end of a superb three mile long beach. Once a small port exporting limestone and also a haven for smugglers, Oxwich is today a marvellous holiday area with safe bathing, clean beaches, wind surfing and water skiing. The village has some picturesque cottages of the traditional Gower style which include one that was once occupied by John Wesley. The village **Church of St Illtud**, half hidden

by trees, is well worth seeking out as its ancient font is believed to have been brought here by St Illtud himself.

Just to the south of the village lies **Oxwich Castle**, a grand Tudor manor house built around a courtyard. Although this was probably the site of an earlier fortification, the splendid house was established by Sir Rice Mansel in the 1520s and added to by his son, Sir Edward Mansel, whose building work includes the Elizabethan long gallery. The Mansel family's time at this lavish mansion was short lived, and after they left in the 1630s the house fell into disrepair, although the southern wing was used as a farmhouse and the southeast tower still survives to its full height of six storeys.

For walkers there are plenty of footpaths to explore and the walk to **Oxwich Point**, in particular, provides some magnificent views of the Gower Peninsula. Close to the beach lies part of the **Oxwich Nature Reserve**, home to many rare species of orchid as well as other plant life and a variety of birds.

KNELSTON

12½ miles SW of Swansea on the A4118

To the north of this attractive village lies **Arthur's Stone**, a large burial chamber capstone. Traditionally, this is said to be the pebble which King Arthur removed from his shoe while on his way to the Battle of Camlann in the 6th century. According to legend, Arthur threw the stone over his shoulder and the stone lies exactly where it landed. Up until the 19th century, local girls would enact a ritual here to discover whether their lovers were true or not. At midnight and with a full moon, the girls would place a honey cake soaked in milk on the stone and then crawl under it three times. At this point, if their lovers were true, they would join them.

Continued on page 326

WALK **11**

Oxwich, Port-Eynon Bay and Oxwich Point

Start	Oxwich
Distance	6 miles (9.7km)
Approximate time	3 hours
Parking	Oxwich
Refreshments	Hotel and beach kiosk at Oxwich
Ordnance Survey maps	Landranger 159 (Swansea & Gower), Explorer 10 (Gower)

After an initial inland section along farm tracks and field paths this route includes a magnificent stretch of coastal walking along Port-Eynon Bay to Oxwich Point. From here it follows an up-and-down route through the beautiful woodlands that clothe the point, finally passing by a delightful secluded church, half-hidden among the trees, to return to Oxwich.

From the car park, head across the beach towards Oxwich Bay Hotel and turn right along the lane into Oxwich village. At a crossroads, turn left along a lane that heads uphill and, where it bears slightly right just before the top, turn sharp left **A** on to a track to see the ruins of Oxwich Castle. The track bears right to pass through a metal gate and keeps to the right of the castle, an early 16th century fortified manor-house (now reopened to the public by CADW). Opposite the castle, turn right off the track, go through a metal gate and walk straight across a field to climb a stone stile on to a lane in front of a caravan site.

Turn half right (not fully right to head downhill) along a narrow, hedge-lined lane, keeping by the caravan site

on the left, and where the lane bends right turn left **B** along a track, passing to the right of farm buildings. This hedge-lined track heads gently uphill and later levels off to continue to a T-junction. Turn right for a few yards and then turn left through a metal gate to walk along the left-hand edge of a field, by a hedge on the left. At the end of the field, turn left through a metal gate and head downhill, between a wire fence on the left and a hedge on the right, towards a farm. Go through a metal gate into the farmyard, turn left and then curve to the right to reach a T-junction **C**.

Turn right along a tarmac lane and at a junction keep ahead along a track signposted "Western Slade Farm, Footpath Only". Where the track peters out just after passing through the farm, keep ahead along the left-hand edge of a field, by a hedge on the left. Climb a stile at the end of the field, immediately turn left **D** over another stile and follow a narrow, enclosed, downhill path – initially it is overgrown but it soon improves – to climb another stile. Continue gently downhill through a wooded valley, eventually climbing a stile onto a tarmac track by houses on the edge of Horton **E**.

Ahead is a public footpath sign to Oxwich; here turn left onto a narrow, enclosed path and after climbing a stile continue along a path that keeps below the line of limestone cliffs on the left and above a glorious, rocky, sandy beach on the right. The next 2½ miles (4km) of the walk is along this magnificent stretch of coast, with superb views across Port-Eynon Bay, to Oxwich Point. After rounding the point the long, sandy curve of Oxwich Bay comes into sight, backed by Cefn Bryn.

Soon after rounding Oxwich Point you enter Oxwich Wood, which is part of Oxwich National Nature Reserve, to follow a winding and undulating path through these superb coastal woodlands. This is a delightful section of the walk.

Approaching Oxwich, the path turns left inland and heads steeply uphill via a long flight of steps, bearing right to continue along the top edge of the woods. On reaching another long flight of steps, turn right to descend them, bearing left at the bottom **F** to reach the 13th century Church of St Illtyd in its beautiful secluded setting above the bay and surrounded by trees.

Continue past the church, following the path leading down into Oxwich. Turn right along the beach to return to the car park at the starting point. ●

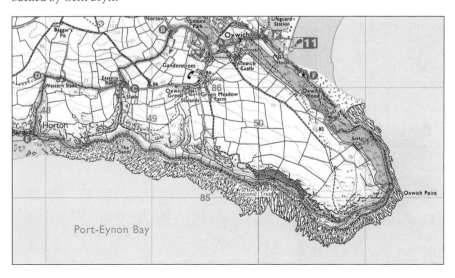

RHOSSILI

16 miles SW of Swansea on the B4247

This village, on the westernmost area of the Gower Peninsula, is thought to have been named after St Fili, who is said to have been the son of St Cenydd. Inside the small church is a memorial plaque to a Gower man, Edgar Evans, who is perhaps better known as Petty Officer Evans, who died in the ill-fated expedition to the Antarctic led by Captain Scott in 1912.

To the west of Rhossili lies **Worm's Head**, an island which is a National Nature Reserve. Reached by a causeway at low tide, there is public access to the

Rhossili Beach

island, but those making the crossing should take great care not to be cut off by the tide. Worm's Head marks the southern edge of Rhossili Bay, whose beach can be reached by a steep downhill climb. At low tide, the remains of several wrecks can be seen, most notably the

CAFÉ RENDEZVOUS BED & BREAKFAST

New Park Cottage, Rhossili, Gower, Swansea SA3 1PL
Tel: 01792 390645

Rhossili Bay Beach and the National Trust's Worm's Head Nature Reserve are among the most picturesque and most photographed spots in the whole of this part of Wales, and both are within very easy reach of **Café Rendezvous**. David and Honor Crawford have recently acquired the premises, which they have developed into a bed and breakfast establishment and a delightful bistro. The accommodation in the attractive white-painted building comprises two luxurious beamed cottage-style bedrooms, both with private entrances, en suite facilities, traditional furnishings and stunning sea views. Rhossili is a favourite place for open-air activity; the bay for surfing and windsurfing, the Downs for walking and paragliding.

CAFÉ RENDEZVOUS LICENSED BISTRO & TEA ROOM

New Park Cottage, Rhossili, Gower, Swansea SA3 1PL
Tel: 01792 390645

One part of **Café Rendezvous** is a bed and breakfast establishment, the other a licensed bistro offering quality eating for all the family at very reasonable prices. A constantly changing, freshly prepared variety of fish, meat and poultry dishes, often with interesting and original sauces, is served in a relaxing candlelit ambience overlooking Rhossili Bay. The chef is happy to prepare vegetarian dishes, and the bistro also serves bar meals and children's meals. The bistro opens at 6.30, and booking is advisable. It also operates as a tea room and tea garden, with stunning views across the water to Devon.

WORM'S HEAD HOTEL

Rhossili, Gower, Swansea SA2 8PP
Tel: 01792 390512 Fax: 01792 391115
e-mail: info@the wormshead.co.uk website: www.thewormshead.co.uk

The **Worm's Head Hotel** is located in an Area of Outstanding Natural
Beauty at the western tip of the Gower Peninsula and takes its name
from the famous Worm's Head, a nearby island. All 19 bedrooms at the
Short family's hotel have en suite or private bathroom, tv, telephone
and tea/coffee facilities, and all take advantage of the views of the
surrounding countryside. Welsh bacon, local farm eggs and laverbread are among the breakfast
offerings, and in the restaurant, Gower lobster and crab, Towy salmon and fish from Carmarthen Bay.
Meals are also served in the bars and cream teas are a daily afternoon treat.

Worm's Head

Helvetia, which was wrecked in 1887. The
area is very popular with fishermen,
surfers abd bathers, and behind **Rhossili
Beach** lies **The Warren**, under the sands
of which are the remains of old Rhossili
village and church.

LLANGENNITH

15 miles W of Swansea off the B4271

This quiet village is home to
the largest church on the
Gower peninsula. It was built
in the 12th century on the
site of a priory founded six
centuries earlier by St Cenydd
and was destroyed some 400
years later by Viking raiders.
Inside, there is a curious
gravestone thought to mark
the resting place of St
Cenydd. To the west of the
village and marking the
northern edge of Rhossili Bay lies **Burry
Holms**, another small island which can
be reached via a causeway at low tide.
On the island are the remains of an Iron
Age earthwork and also a monastic
chapel dating from the Middle Ages.

BRYN Y MOR COTTAGE

Cock Street, Llangennith, Gower, West Glamorgan SA3 1JE
Tel: 01792 386259

Bryn Y Mor is a converted semi-detached cottage in an elevated
position that commands magnificent views over Llangennith
beach. Ann Bevan's sympathetically modernised cottage provides
everything needed for a relaxing, independent self-catering
holiday: sunny lounge, fully fitted new kitchen/diner, two
bedrooms with sea views, bathroom and storage or convector heaters in all rooms. An enclosed garden
with barbecue and patio area completes the picture. The beach is only a few minutes away, the nearby
village has a pub, post office/shop and church, and the area is blessed with miles of beautiful walks.

KING'S HEAD HOTEL

Llangennith, Gower, Swansea SA3 1HU
Tel: 01792 386212 Fax: 01792 386355

A row of three 17th century buildings behind a splendid rough-stone wall make up the **King's Head Hotel**, which stands in the coastal village of Llangennith opposite the largest church on the Gower Peninsula. The village attracts holiday-makers, car tourers and lovers of the great outdoors. The King's Head, owned and managed by the Stevens family since the 1980s, is well able to cater for the healthy appetites that they bring.

In the characterful bars, with beams and exposed stone, an impressive variety of food is served, nearly all of it home made and most of it based on Welsh produce: beef, milk, butter - even the custard is Welsh. Thai food is something of a speciality, and the Indian dishes and the pizzas are also very popular, but old-fashioned British cooking is also well represented with some excellent pies such as steak and kidney; chicken, leek and asparagus; and venison with mushrooms and blueberries (Welsh venison, of course!). The King's Head is just as good at quenching thirsts, and one of the real ales on tap is called Butch's Brew after the pub's Jack Russell. The Stevens family also own the Greyhound Inn at Llanrhidian (see below).

THE GREYHOUND INN

Old Walls, Llanrhidian, Swansea SA31
Tel: 01792 391027

The Stevens family, who own and run the very successful King's Head Hotel in Llangennith (see above), are finding equal success at their more recent acquisition, the **Greyhound Inn**. This grand old coaching inn enjoys a rural setting 12 miles from Swansea on the B4295 Gower Peninsula road and is an excellent place for refreshment. The Greyhound's bars are very traditional and welcoming, with plenty of chairs

set at neatly laid tables, and outside is a large garden with a children's play area.

Nearly all the food served is home made, with Thai and Indian specialities as well as traditional pub dishes. The fresh fish dishes are outstanding, and the extensive carvery in the function room is a popular Sunday event. The King's Head has its Jack Russell, and the Greyhound has a dog who one day decided to take up residence - a greyhound, of course, and his name is Skinny. The pub is close to some of the finest beaches in the country, and other local attractions include the atmospheric Weobley Castle.

LLANRHIDIAN

10½ miles W of Swansea on the B4295

Close to the wild and lonely north coast of the Gower Peninsula, where some of the finest beaches in the country can be found, this village is also close to **Weobley Castle**. Dating from the early 14th century and built by the de Bere family, Weobley is more a fortified manor house than a castle and stands today as one of the few surviving such houses in Wales. On an isolated site overlooking the eerie expanse of Llanrhidian Marsh, this house has been remarkably well preserved and visitors can gain a real insight into the domestic arrangements of those days and, in particular, the owners' desire for comfort. In the late 15th century the house came into the hands of Sir Rhys ap Thomas, an ally of Henry VII, and

further improvements were made including the addition of a new porch and an upgrade of the accommodation in the private apartments. As well as seeing the interior of this impressive house, visitors can also view an exhibition on the Gower Peninsula - its history and other ancient monuments.

LOUGHOR

6½ miles NW of Swansea on the A484

A strategic location on the mouth of the River Loughor gave this village prominence and importance down the centuries. The Romans built their station of Leucarum here in the 1st century and, in the early 12th century, the Norman, Henry de Newburgh, built **Loughor Castle** on the edge of the Roman site. Unfortunately, all that is left of the stronghold, which protected the

WELCOME TO TOWN COUNTRY BISTRO

Llanrhidian, Gower, Swansea SDA3 1EH
Tel: 01792 390015
website: www.thewelcometotown.co.uk

An attractive whitewashed 17th century building that was once a court of justice now summons lovers of good food from near and far. Ian and Jay Bennett's **Welcome to Town Country Bistro** has a lovely traditional look, with roundback wooden chairs set at neatly laid, white-clothed tables, black beams, white-panelled walls and a feature stone hearth. Ian, a critically acclaimed Master Chef of Great Britain, opened the bistro with is wife in the summer of 2001. They offer friendly service in a relaxed atmosphere, and visitors (booking strongly advised) can look forward to a superb meal prepared to the highest standards. Sewin on a pea pancake with sorrel sauce; best end of Welsh lamb with saffron sauce, grilled aubergine and pesto; sea bass with olive crust, buttered spinach and gazpacho sauce - these and similar terrific dishes highlight the best local produce prepared in a fresh, imaginative modern style.

Vegetarian selections are available on a daily basis - the main course choice might be baked goat's cheese on sweet pepper relish with a rocket salad. Desserts are as mouthwatering as the rest of the menu, with a selection of Welsh cheeses (perhaps Llan Boidy, Perl Wen and Caerfilli) as an alternative. Excellent wines complement the outstanding food, and there's an excellent choice of coffees and speciality teas. The Bistro is a short walk from the coast and an RSPB reserve, and walkers who have worked up a thirst can quench it with a glass of two of real ale at the bar before their meal. The Bistro is open Tuesday to Sunday for lunch, Tuesday to Saturday for dinner, and also Bank Holidays.

confluence of the Burry Inlet and the River Loughor, is the ruined 13th century square tower.

PORT TALBOT

Well known for its steel industry, Port Talbot was named after the Talbot family, who were responsible for the development of the town's docks in the 19th century. Now called the Old Docks, this area saw significant expansion again in the 20th century when a new deep water harbour was opened by the Queen in 1970. Today Port Talbot is home to factories and processing plants, and also to the solar centre of **Baglan Bay Energy Park**, which explains the history of the area and its power generating potential.

Coal mining has taken place in the area around Port Talbot for centuries and during this time many superstitions have grown up. In 1890, the miners at Morfa Colliery reported seeing ghostly images in and around the colliery. They were said to be fierce hounds, which became known as the "Red Dogs of Morfa", and they would run through the streets with their appearance being accompanied by a sweet, rose-like scent which filled the mine shaft. Such were the number of eerie manifestations that on the morning of 10th March 1890, nearly half the morning shift failed to report for work. Later which same day, there was an explosion at the colliery - 87 miners died in the disaster.

AROUND PORT TALBOT

NEATH

4 miles N of Port Talbot on the A465

While Neath's industrial history dates back to the late 16th century, when the first copper smelter in South Wales was built here by Cornishmen, the town has

its origins in Roman times. Remains of Roman Nidum can still be seen close to the ruins of **Neath Abbey**, which was founded in the 13th century by Richard de Granville on land seized from the Welsh in around 1130. The abbey buildings were converted into a mansion for Sir John Herbert in the 16th century and it was later used to house copper smelters. It was also de Granville who built **Neath Castle**, in the mid 12th century, around which the town grew and whose scant remains can be found near a town centre car park.

Housed in the Old Mechanics Institute, the **Neath Museum and Art Gallery** has permanent displays on the history of the town, including finds from the time of the Roman occupation, as well as regularly changing art and photographic exhibitions. The Museum has many hands-on activities, including grinding corn, using a Celtic loom and making a wattle fence.

Held each September, **Neath Fair** is the oldest such event in Wales, founded by Gilbert de Clare in 1280.

ABERDULAIS

6 miles NE of Port Talbot off the A4109

From as early as 1584 the power generated by the magnificent National Trust owned **Aberdulais Falls** has been harnessed for a number of industries, including copper smelting and tin plating. Today, the waterwheel, the largest currently in use for the generation of electricity, makes the Falls self-sufficient in enviromentally friendly energy. The Turbine House provides access to a unique fish pass.

CRYNANT

9 miles NE of Port Talbot on the A4109

In one of the most beautiful and unspoilt valleys of the South Wales coalfield, **Cefn Coed Colliery Museum** (see panel) provides a wonderful opportunity for visitors to discover what life was like for the miners who worked underground in some of the most difficult conditions experienced anywhere in the world. Through photographs, maps and other exhibits, the tradition and legacy of mining are brought to life. The museum also has a well-stocked souvenir and gift shop, with one of the best selections of genuine and reproduction miner's lamps in the region. It is ideal for finding a special present from Wales.

CYNONVILLE

6 miles NE of Port Talbot on the A4107

Virtually surrounding the village (to the north, west and south) lies the **Afan Forest Park**, a large area of woodland where there are trails for cycling, walking and pony trekking. At the Park's **Countryside Centre** an exhibition explains, with the aid of hands-on displays, the landscape and history of the Afan Valley. The **South Wales Miners' Museum**, also at the centre, illustrates the social history of the valleys' mining communities.

PONT-RHYD-Y-FEN

3½ miles NE of Port Talbot on the B4287

This village was the birthplace of the actor Richard Burton.

MARGAM

3 miles SE of Port Talbot on the A48

To the southeast of the town lies **Margam Country Park** surrounding a mansion built in the 1840s by the Talbot family. The land once belonged to **Margam Abbey**, a Cistercian house which was founded in 1147 by Robert, Earl of Gloucester. Following a violent revolt by the lay brothers, the abbey went on to become one of the wealthiest in Wales but, at the time of the Dissolution of the Monasteries, the estate passed on to Sir Rice Mansel, who built the first mansion on the estate in 1537.

The park today boasts several buildings left by previous owners including **Margam**

CEFN COED COLLIERY MUSEUM

Crynant, Neath SA10 8SN
Tel: 01639 750556 Fax: 01639 750556

Cefn Coed Colliery museum is situated in the heart of the picturesque Dulais Valley and tells the story of the life of the Victorians to the 1950s and how important the coal industry was to the local community. This unique museum is housed in its existing building, which closed in 1968, and is one out of four collieries in Wales with headframes still in existence.

Experience the harsh, damp and dark conditions that the colliers went through in the very authentic simulated underground gallery, which is equipped with various aspects of mining, such as the stalls, pit props, tramways and other equipment used underground. Or visit one of the many highlights of the museum, such as the distinctive boiler house with its suite of six Lancashire steam boilers or see the magnificent 1927 Worsley Mesne Steam winding engine which is now electrically driven.

As well as exhibiting many fascinating artefacts from the coal industry of mining tools and equipment, the museum also houses a restored and unique gas tram, which ran in Neath until 1920 and the model of which can be seen in Neath Museum. The gift shop sells a wide selection of coal figures, Welsh souvenirs and a vast selection of books based on the coal industry, as well as some of the best selection of genuine and reproduction mining lamps in South Wales.

Abbey Church (all that remains of the abbey), a classical 18th century orangery and a restored Japanese garden from the 1920s. This huge recreational area - the park covers some 800 acres - also includes a visitor centre, waymarked trails, a deer park, bird of prey centre and the **Margam Stones Museum**, where visitors can see a collection of early Christian memorials dating from Roman times through to the 10th and 11th centuries. The finest examples are the great Cross of Conbelin, the 9th century Cross of Einion and a 6th century memorial with Irish Ogham and Latin inscriptions.

PONTYPRIDD

This friendly valley town is justly proud of its past, which is revealed in the **Pontypridd Museum** housed in an old chapel close to Pontypridd's historic stone bridge over the River Taff. As well as its industrial heritage, the town has a long tradition of music and in the main park are two statues commemorating Evan and James James, a father and son songwriting team who were responsible for composing the words and music for the Welsh National Anthem, *Land of my Fathers* (*Hen Wlad fy Nhadau*).

Perhaps better known to today's visitors, however, are the two opera stars Sir Geraint Evans and Stewart Burrows, who were born in the same street in nearby Clifynydd, and the durable, ever-popular Tom Jones. Just outside Pontypridd, at Fforest Uchaf Farm, Penycoedcae, is the **Pit Pony Sanctuary**, where visitors can meet more than 25 horses and ponies, including several retired pit ponies. Also here are pit pony memorabilia and a reconstruction of a typical pony-powered Welsh drift coalmine.

AROUND PONTYPRIDD

LLANTRISANT
4 miles SW of Pontypridd on the B4595

This old town takes its name, Three Saints, from Saints Illtud, Gwyno and Dyfod, to whom the parish church is dedicated. All that remains of 13th century **Llantrisant Castle** is part of a round tower; it was probably to this castle, in 1326, that Edward II and Hugh Despenser were brought after falling into the hands of Queen Isabella.

Though some of the traditional heavy industry still remains, Llantrisant is best known nowadays for being the home of **The Royal Mint**, which transferred here from Tower Hill, London in 1967. At the **Model Centre**, a craft and design gallery, there is a permanent Royal Mint display

The Royal Mint

along with a shop, café and a programme of events and exhibitions.

Standing in the town centre is a statue of a figure dressed in a fox skin head-dress. This is the town's memorial to Dr William Price, an amazing and eccentric character who lived from 1800 to 1893. Espousing many causes, some of which scandalised straight-laced Victorian Britain, Price was a vegetarian who believed in free love, nudism and radical politics. His most famous deed, considered infamous at the time, was his attempt in 1884 to be allowed to cremate his illegitimate son Iesu Grist (Jesus Christ) who had died in infancy. As a result of the controversy, and the ensuing court case, cremation became legal in Britain.

TREHAFOD
1½ miles NW of Pontypridd off the A4058

While this area was associated with heavy industry and, in particular, coal mining, the Rhondda and Cynon valleys of today are very different and the only working deep mine left in South Wales is **Tower Colliery**. In the Rhondda Valley alone there were once 53 working mines in just 16 square miles but, although they have now gone, the traditions of the colliery still live on.

When the Lewis Merthyr Colliery closed in 1983, it re-opened as the **Rhondda Heritage Park**, a fascinating place where former miners guide visitors around the restored mining buildings. As well as seeing the conditions in which the miners worked and hearing stories from miners whose families worked in the mines for generations, visitors can also see exhibitions on the role of the women in a mining village, the dramatic history of the 1920s strikes for a minimum wage and the tragedy of mining disasters. Between 1868 and

1919 in Rhondda one miner was killed every six hours and one injured every two minutes. The cultural and social history of a mining community, through brass bands, choirs and the chapel, is explored and visitors also have the opportunity to put on a hard hat and travel down the mine shaft in a cage.

ABERDARE
9 miles NW of Pontypridd on the A4233

Situated at the northern end of the Cynon valley, Aberdare, like other valley towns, is famous for its strong music tradition - particularly male voice choirs. In **Victoria Square** is a statue of the baton waving choir conductor, Griffith Rhys Jones (1834-97).

The landscape of Aberdare was once shaped by coal mines and heavy industry, but with the closure of the mines the countryside is, through ambitious land reclamation and environmental improvement schemes, returning to its pre-industrial green and lush natural state. Just a short distance from the busy town centre is **Dare Valley Country Park**, which was created on former colliery land and where trails tell of the natural and industrial history of the area.

MERTHYR TYDFIL

The main road in this area of Wales, the A645, acts as a dividing line: to the south are the historic valleys once dominated by coal mining and the iron and steel industries, while, to the north, lie the unspoilt southern uplands of the Brecon Beacons National Park. This rigidly observed divide is explained by geology, as the coal bearing rocks of the valleys end here and give way to the limestone and old red sandstone rocks of the Brecon Beacons. The close proximity of the two different types of rock also explains the nature and growth of industry in this particular area of South Wales as the iron smelting process required not just coal but also limestone. The iron ore was locally available too. These ingredients all came together in the most productive way at Merthyr Tydfil and this former iron and steel capital of the world was once the largest town in Wales. It took its name from the martyr St Tydfil,

Cyfarthfa Castle

the daughter of the Welsh chieftain Brychan (after whom Brecon is named). She was martyred by the Irish for her Christian beliefs in AD 480.

Described as "the most impressive monument of the Industrial Iron Age in Southern Wales", **Cyfarthfa Castle** is a grand mansion situated in beautiful and well laid out parkland. Built in the 1820s, this was the home of the Crawshay family, who constructed their grand house to overlook their ironworks, which at the time were the largest in the world. Today, this mansion is home to a **Museum and Art Gallery** which not only covers the social and industrial history of Merthyr Tydfil and the surrounding area but also has an extensive collection of fine and decorative art. The parkland, too, is well worth exploring and, at the Visitor Centre, information on the park's amenities and natural history can be found.

Joseph Parry's Ironworker's Cottage, in Chapel Row, provides a contrasting view of life in Merthyr Tydfil during its heyday. A superb example of a skilled

ironworker's home, the cottage gives an interesting insight into the living conditions of those days. It was here that Joseph Parry, the 19th century composer famous for writing the haunting hymn *Myfanwy*, was born and on the first floor is an exhibition of his life and work.

Another of the town's claims to fame lies in the political sphere: it was the first constituency in Britain to return a socialist Member of Parliament when, in 1900, Kier Hardie was elected to Westminster.

AROUND MERTHYR TYDFIL

PONTSTICILL

3 miles N of Merthyr Tydfil off the A465

From here the **Brecon Mountain Railway** travels a short yet very scenic route up to Pontsticill Reservoir in the Brecon Beacons National Park. The charming vintage steam trains follow the tracks of the old Merthyr Tydfil to Brecon line, which has been re-opened by railway enthusiasts.

BRIDGEND

Known in Welsh as Pen-y-Bont Ar Ogwr (meaning "the crossing of the River Ogmore"), this bustling market town lies at the confluence of the Rivers Ogmore, Garw and Llynfi and it was once regarded as so vital a route that it had two castles, one on either side of the River Ogmore. The remains of 12th century **Newcastle Castle** lie on the west riverside while the more extensive ruins of 14th century **Coity Castle** stand guard on the other. Originally built by the Norman Payn de Turberville and strengthened over the following three centuries, Coity Castle was finally abandoned in the late-16th century, having withstood a siege by Owain Glyndwr 150 years earlier.

Bridgend's distinction as a market town dates back as far as the early 16th century and down the ages there have been tanneries, a woollen factory and local potteries in the area. However, for the last 250 years or so, Bridgend has been an agricultural market centre to support the industrial towns of the valleys.

AROUND BRIDGEND

TONDU

3½ miles N of Bridgend on the A4063

The nationally important Tondu Ironworks have now been incorporated into the **Tondu Heritage Park**, while the site of an old colliery and open cast coal workings has been developed into the **Parc Slip Nature Reserve**. The reserve's network of paths lead visitors through the various different wildlife habitats, such as grassland, woodland and wetland, where a wide variety of plants, birds and animals have made their homes.

EWENNY POTTERY

Ewenny, Nr Bridgend, South Wales CF35 5AP
Tel: 01656 653020
website: www.ewennypottery.com

Alun and Jayne Jenkins are carrying on a long local and family tradition at **Ewenny Pottery**, which prides itself on being the oldest family pottery in Wales. On the outskirts of Ewenny village near the town of Bridgend, the Pottery has been owned continuously by the Jenkins family, and the present incumbents are continuing the tradition by making a range of beautiful glazed earthenware for ornamental and domestic use.

Visitors are welcome to watch the pots being made, either on commission or for stock, and to view the full range of the finished ware in the showroom. The pottery industry has existed in the area since medieval times due to the ready availability of materials: local red earthenware clay to form the pots, glaze materials to give a finish, stone to build the kilns and coal to fire the pots in the kilns. Ewenny Pottery is open Monday to Saturday, and also Sunday afternoon in the summer.

BRASERIA EL PRADO

High Street, Laleston, Bridgend,
South Wales CF32 0LD
Tel: 01656 649972
Fax: 01656 668377

Braseria El Prado is a long, low, white-painted building by the main roundabout in Laleston, a couple of miles west of Bridgend. The style throughout is Spanish/Mediterranean, and the Spanish owner Jesus de Celis worked in some of the best Mediterranean establishments in the country before opening his own restaurant, El Prado, which he now runs with his daughter Natalia.

The L-shaped bar serves an impressive range of drinks, and in the restaurant diners can choose from an excellent selection of starters and meat, poultry and fish main courses. The long list of starters includes stuffed or garlic mushrooms, fish soup, paté and spicy chicken wings as well as small portions of some of the main courses. Mains include a wide variety of seafood, from trout and cod to sole and sea bass, crayfish tails and lobster, while meat-eaters might opt for a quail or two, lamb kebab, steak, spare ribs or duck breast in an orange and Cointreau sauce.

BETWS

5 miles N of Bridgend off the A4063

Just south of the village lies **Bryngarw Country Park**, which throughout the year presents a variety of enchanting landscapes including woodland, grassland, water features and formal gardens. A visitor centre provides information on the country park and on the many species of plants and birds to be found here. Perhaps the most interesting feature of the park is the exotic Japanese Garden, which was laid out in 1910 and where there are not only a series of interlinked ponds and an oriental tea garden pavilion, but also superb azaleas, rhododendrons, magnolias and cherry trees.

The house at the centre of the estate, **Bryngarw House**, was built in 1834 by Morgan Popkin Treherne as a "small but elegant dwelling". Now a conference and function centre, the house has undergone a major restoration programme which has, fortunately, left its original character and atmosphere intact.

MAESTEG

8 miles N of Bridgend on the A4063

This ancient market town was the centre of iron making in the 1820s, but the last great furnace was 'blown out' in 1886; one of the ironworks is now a sports centre. Maesteg was once linked to the coast at Porthcawl by a tramway, traces of which can be seen at Porthcawl. The Tabor chapel in Maesteg was where *Land of My Fathers* was first sung in public in 1856. The Welsh words were written by Evan James, the music by his son James James. For 112 years, Talbot Street was the only alcohol-free high street in Britain, so covenanted in the will of the teetotal spinster after whom the street was named. In the summer of 2002, a restaurant challenged the covenant, and the magistrates ruled in his favour.

LLANGEINOR

5 miles N of Bridgend on the A4064

This pretty village is home to a historic church on a mountainside whose Norman tower was built over the foundations of a religious site dating back to the 6th century. The church, which is dedicated to St Ceinwyr, was restored in the late 19th century.

HOEL-Y-CYW

4 miles NE of Bridgend off the B4280

To the northeast of the village lies **Mynydd y Gaer**, a wonderful local landmark which, from its near 1,000 foot summit, provides spectacular views across the valleys to the north and the Bristol Channel to the south.

MERTHYR MAWR

2 miles SW of Bridgend off the A48

Situated down river from Bridgend, this delightful village of thatched cottages bordered by meadows and woodland lies on the edge of **Merthyr Mawr Warren**, one of the largest areas of sand dunes in Europe. Now a Site of Special Scientific Interest, the dunes offer the perfect habitat for a wide variety of plants and animals.

Surrounded by the dune system are the remains of **Candleston Castle**, a 15th century fortified manor house that was, until the 19th century, the home of the powerful Cantelupe family. Local children believe the house to be haunted but the biggest mystery of Candleston is the fate of the village of Treganllaw (meaning "the town of a hundred hands") which is thought to have been engulfed by the dunes.

On the road approaching the village is the 15th century New Inn Bridge which

has some interesting holes in its parapet through which in the old days sheep were pushed into the river for their annual dip!

NEWTON

4½ miles W of Bridgend off the A4106

Dating back to the 12th century, the village was founded as a "new town" and by the 17th century was a thriving port from where grain and knitted stockings were exported.

The imposing limestone church was originally built as a fortress by the Knights of the Order of St John of Jerusalem in the late 12th or early 13th century.

PORTHCAWL

6 miles W of Bridgend on the A4229

One of South Wales' most popular resorts, Porthcawl has much to attract the traditional British seaside holidaymaker. There are award winning clean sandy beaches at Sandy Bay, Trecco Bay and the quieter Rest Bay, along with an amusement park that provides a wide variety of rides, from white knuckle roller coasters to more gentle carousels. This is also a haven for surfers, sailors and fishing enthusiasts, while the headlands above Rest Bay are the site of the famous Royal Porthcawl Golf Club.

As well as the kiss-me-quick hats, there is a more dignified side of Porthcawl that centres around the Edwardian promenade, a legacy of the prosperous days when this was a port exporting coal and iron. The history of the town can be discovered at **Porthcawl Museum**, where there is a fascinating collection of artefacts, costumes and memorabilia on display, while at **Porthcawl Harbour** there are still several historic buildings which date from the heyday of this busy port. During the summer, two veteran steamships leave the harbour for trips along the Bristol Channel and across to Lundy Island.

KENFIG

6½ miles W of Bridgend off the B4283

This village was originally founded in the 12th century by Robert, Earl of Gloucester, who also built **Kenfig Castle** here. However, just some 300 years later the sands of Kenfig Burrows had swamped the settlement and the medieval town lies buried in the dunes although the remains of the castle keep are still visible. The legend of Kenfig Pool has it that on a quiet day when the water is clear, the houses of the buried town can be seen at the bottom of the lake and the bells of the old church can be heard ringing before a storm.

Today, this marvellous area of dunes to the northwest of the present village is the **Kenfig National Nature Reserve**. With over 600 species of flowering plants, including orchids, a freshwater lake and numerous birds, this is a haven for all naturalists as well as ramblers.

Penarth Medieval Village

PENARTH AND THE VALE OF GLAMORGAN

Often described as the "garden by the sea", Penarth (the name means "bear's head" in Welsh) is a popular and unspoilt seaside resort which developed in Victorian and Edwardian times. Built for the wealthy industrialists of Cardiff's shipyards, this once fashionable town has lost none of its late 19th and early 20th century elegance and style typified by the splendidly restored pier, the promenade and the formal seaview gardens. If the town seems to have been lost in a time warp, a visit to the **Washington Gallery**, housed in an old cinema, will dispel this view through its exciting collection of modern and comtemporary art.

To the south of Penarth lies a **Medieval Village** which is slowly being uncovered by archaeologists. The village originally grew up around a manor house belonging to the Constantin family (some of the first Norman invaders in Wales) in the 12th century and, by 1320, it was ruled by William de Caversham. However, in the mid 14th century the Black Death reached Cosmeston village, killing around one third of the population, and following a period of decline it was left to decay. Today, several of the village's buildings have been reconstructed, allowing visitors, with the help of costumed characters, to gain a real insight into life in a medieval village.

The Medieval Village is in **Cosmeston Country Park**, an area of lakes, woodlands and meadows created from a disused limestone quarry. A peaceful and tranquil habitat for many birds and animals, with a wide range of plant life, the country park has a visitor centre, picnic areas and a café.

In 1897, **Lavernock Point**, to the southeast of the country park, was the site of Marconi's early experiments in radio transmission and the scene of the historic reception of the words "Are you ready?", which were transmitted to **Flat Holm**, an island some three miles away. A tiny island with a wealth of wildlife, Flat Holm also has a history that dates back to the Dark Ages, when it was used by monks as a retreat. Vikings, Anglo Saxons, smugglers and cholera victims are known to have sought refuge on the island, which was also fortified twice, once by the Victorians and again in World War II. Today, it is a Site of Special Scientific Interest, with a local nature reserve that is home to, among other wildlife, slow worms, shelducks and the largest colony of gulls in Wales.

AROUND PENARTH

BARRY ISLAND
5 miles SW of Penarth on the A4055

Barry Island is not an island but a peninsula, facing Barry, whose natural, sheltered harbour has been used since Roman times; **Cold Knap Roman Buildings**, to the west of this seaside resort, are all that remains from those days. A popular place for holidaymakers for generations, Barry Island offers its visitors all the traditional seaside resort trappings, from sandy beaches to a funfair, as well as views across the Bristol Channel to the Devon coast. The latest all-weather attraction is the **Barry Island Railway Heritage Centre**, which has opened its extended line from Barry Island into the neighbouring Waterfront Dock Development. To the north of the

resort is the **Welsh Hawking Centre**, where 200 birds of prey have their homes and there are regular flying demonstrations.

LLANTWIT MAJOR
14 miles W of Penarth off the B4265

This delightful town is perhaps the Vale of Glamorgan's most historic settlement and it was here, in AD 500, that St Illtud founded a church and school. One of the great Celtic saints who travelled in Britain, Ireland and Brittany, St Illtud was a contemporary of both St David and St Patrick. Although little is known of St Illtud, he does feature in the book *The Life of St Samson of Dol*, which was written around 100 years after his death. The church and school he founded here are believed to be the oldest learning centres in the country. The only remains of his original church to have survived are the dedication stones, but the imposing **Church of St Illtud** seen today is a combination of two buildings, one an early Norman structure and the other dating from the late 13th century. Inside can be seen a fine collection of Celtic crosses which includes St Illtud's or St Samson's cross, which was found buried in the church grounds on top of two skeletons.

ST DONAT'S
15 miles W of Penarth off the B4265

Close to the village lies **St Donat's Castle**, which dates from around 1300 and was once owned by the American newspaper magnate William Randolph Hearst. Hearst, whose life was fictionalised in the classic Orson Welles film *Citizen Kane*, spent huge sums of money restoring and furnishing this historic building, where he entertained film stars and world figures. To the west of the village lies **Nash Point**, a

Continued on page 342

Ogmore Castle and Merthyr Mawr

Start	Ogmore Castle
Distance	5 miles (8km). 4 miles (6.4km) if stepping-stones are used
Approximate time	2½ hours (2 hours if using stepping-stones)
Parking	Car park at Ogmore Castle
Refreshments	Pub and farm café at Ogmore Castle, snacks at Ton Farm near Merthyr Mawr
Ordnance Survey maps	Landranger 170 (Vale of Glamorgan & Rhondda area), Pathfinder 1163, SS 87/96/97 (Bridgend (South) & Porthcawl)

From the picturesque ruins of Ogmore Castle the route crosses meadows lying between the Ewenny and Ogmore rivers to the equally picturesque village of Merthyr Mawr. Then a gentle climb across fields is followed by a descent through woodland on the edge of high dunes to the scanty remains of Candleston Castle. Finally there is a relaxing stroll along a lane to Merthyr Mawr before crossing the meadows again back to the start. This is an easy walk but expect some overgrown and indistinct paths north of Merthyr Mawr.

Ogmore Castle was built by the Normans to guard an important river crossing as they consolidated their control of the Vale of Glamorgan. The 12th century castle ruins, comprising parts of the outer walls and the keep, occupy a delightful position above the River Ewenny not far from the coast.

There is a choice of routes from Ogmore Castle to Merthyr Mawr depending on whether you cross the River Ewenny by the stepping stones or the footbridge. Using the footbridge route both ways adds about 1 mile (1.6km) to the walk, or ½ mile (800m) if using it in only one direction.

Either cross the stepping stones over the River Ewenny and take the path ahead across meadow land, joining and keeping by a wall on the right, to reach a

suspension footbridge over the River Ogmore. Or walk back up to the road, turn left, after ¼ mile (400m) turn left beside a bus shelter, at a public footpath sign saying "Merthyr Mawr Coastal Path" go through a metal-kissing gate, keep ahead to cross a footbridge over the River Ewenny and continue across meadows to climb a stone stile beside the suspension bridge.

Cross the bridge **A** and follow the road ahead into the idyllic village of Merthyr Mawr with its collection of widely spaced thatched cottages. At a T-junction turn right **B** , then take the first turning on the left and walk along a lane for ¼ mile (400m), heading uphill. Where the lane bends to the right **C** , keep ahead along a gently ascending track to Whitney Farm. Go through two metal gates to the

WALK 12

left of the farm and continue along a hedge-lined track. Where the track turns left to a gate, keep ahead along a grassy path partially enclosed by trees and hedges. The route now becomes more difficult to follow and the path may be muddy and overgrown in places. Later bear slightly right to continue along the left-hand edge of a field and by the right-hand edge of woodland, go through a metal gate, turn left to pass through a gap in a hedge-bank and turn right to head diagonally across a field – there is no visible path – making for a stile at the corner of a wood.

Climb the stile, bear right along the bottom right-hand edge of a field, by a line of trees and a wire fence on the right, and go through a gap in a wall into the next field. A few yards ahead, where the field edge turns right, turn sharp left **D** and head back to pass through another gap in the wall only a few yards above the previous one. Continue uphill across the field – again there is no visible path – making for the right-hand corner of a wood. Keep along the right-hand edge of the woodland as far as Candleston Farm, passing through two gates and finally turning left through a metal gate in a field corner.

Walk along a track, turning right towards the farm, turn left through a metal gate and turn right again to pass to the left of the farm buildings. At a left-hand bend ahead **E**, turn sharply left along the lower of the two paths that bend left at this point. Follow the path downhill through trees,

at a fork take the right-hand path and continue downhill, below the dunes of Merthyr Mawr Warren on the right, to reach Candleston Castle car park **F**. Turn left to pass through the main entrance to the car park; the meagre ruins of what was a 15th-century fortified manor house lie just to the left on the edge of the dunes.

Keep ahead along a tree-lined lane for just under 1 mile (1.6km) into Merthyr Mawr, passing the 19th century church. In the village turn right **B** and retrace your steps to the start, via either the footbridge or the stepping-stones.

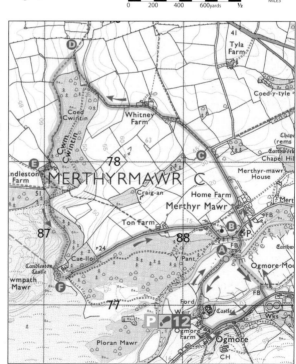

headland with two lighthouses and the remnants of an Iron Age fort. This area of the coast is overlooked by limestone cliffs which, through wind erosion, have begun to resemble giant building blocks.

SOUTHERNDOWN

19 miles W of Penarth on the B4265

This popular holiday centre, overlooking Dunraven Bay, is home to the **Glamorgan Heritage Coast Centre**, which has displays and information about the 14 mile long stretch of wild and beautiful coastline, which begins in the west at Newton.

OGMORE

19 miles W of Penarth on the B4265

Lying at the mouth of the River Ogmore, this pretty village is also close to a ford across the River Ewenny where the ruins of **Ogmore Castle** can be seen. Built in the early 12th century by William de Londres, this was once the foremost stronghold in the area although all that can be seen today are the remains of a three storey keep and the dry moat. The castle grounds are said to be haunted by a ghost known as Y Ladi Wen (The White Lady) who guards the treasure thought to be buried here. For its part, the River Ogmore is supposed to be haunted by the tormented spirits of misers who died without disclosing where they had hidden their riches. Legend has it that these spirits will be released from their misery only when their hoards are found and thrown into the river, downstream of the castle.

EWENNY

17½ miles W of Penarth on the B4265

This charming rural village is home to **Ewenny Priory**, which was founded in 1141 by Maurice de Londres, the son of William de Londres of Ogmore Castle.

This is one of the finest fortified religious houses in Britain and, while its precinct walls, towers and gateways give the priory a military air, it is believed that they were built for reasons of prestige rather than defence.

Close by lies 400-year-old **Ewenny Pottery**, said to be the oldest working pottery in Wales.

COWBRIDGE

12½ miles W of Penarth off the A48

This handsome and prosperous town has been the principal market town of the Vale of Glamorgan since medieval times and today it is noted for its quality shops, crafts and restaurants. The original Norman grid layout of the town is visible to this day, particularly in the mile long main street, and Cowbridge's 14th century town walls and gatehouse still stand.

ST NICHOLAS

6 miles NW of Penarth on the A48

To the south of the village lie **Dyffryn Gardens** which, as part of the Dyffryn estate, were landscaped in the 19th century. One of the finest surviving Thomas Mawson gardens in Britain, Dyffryn offers a series of broad sweeping lawns, Italianite terraces, a paved court, a physick garden and a rose garden as well as a vine walk and arboretum. Perhaps the most impressive features are the Pompeian Garden and the Theatre Garden where open air plays and concerts are held.

History, ancient and modern, abounds in this region of South Wales, with the distinguished ruins of Norman fortifications and the remains of the industrial past of the valleys. An area of contrasts, like much of Wales, it would be easy to pass through this region on a journey to the Gower Peninsula or Pembrokeshire, but that would be to miss out on much of the Welsh heritage.

The valleys of the Wye and Usk offer some truly glorious scenery as well as the equally breathtaking sight of Tintern Abbey. An inspiration for both poets and artists, this abbey was at one time one of the richest in the country and the magnificent ruins beside the River Wye are still a stirring sight. This area, too, is one that saw much contest between the Welsh and the English, so not surprisingly there are numerous fortifications to be seen and explored. The Three Castles - White, Skenfrith and Grosmont - provided a valuable defence from their strong yet isolated positions while most towns of note also had their own fortress.

Along this stretch of coastline lies Cardiff, the capital city of Wales and a place which is successfully blending the ancient with the modern. The Romans occupied various sites in this area, but it was heavy industry and the

Wye Valley

influence of the Bute family that made Cardiff such a powerful port. The home of Welsh rugby, the superb Millennium Stadium and a recently rejuvenated waterfront, Cardiff is a city that vibrates with life, energy and enthusiasm.

To the north lie the valleys that provided so much wealth until the decline of coal mining and the iron industry. Much of the land that was once an industrial wasteland has been reclaimed by nature, with the help of sensitive human intervention, but there are still some monuments to the great industrial age remaining, chiefly at the Big Pit Mine and Blaenavon Ironworks.

Cardiff Bay

ADVERTISERS AND PLACES OF INTEREST

LOCATOR MAP

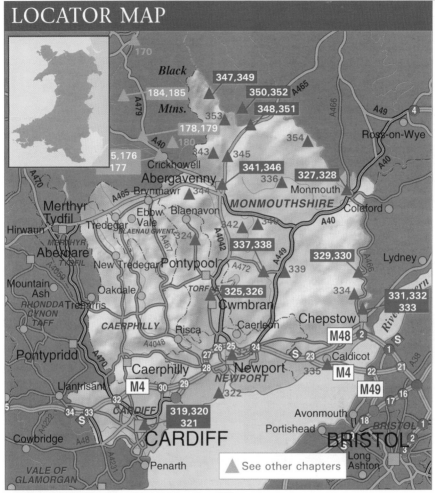

SEDUTI

8-10 High Street Arcade, Cardiff CF1 1BB
Tel: 029 2037 2523 Fax: 029 2037 6250
e-mail: info@seduti.com
website: www.seduti.com

In one of the many modern shopping arcades in the centre of Cardiff, **Seduti** is a smart, stylish showcase for top-quality Italian designer furniture. Seduti - "sit down" in Italian - is spread over three floors, allowing plenty of space for visitors to see the pieces in what is

effectively a home environment. The cool, contemporary showrooms also feature some very stylish artwork, soft furnishings and home decorations. Young, enthusiastic owner Lorna Oakley's business also offers a design

consultancy (both domestic and commercial) and accepts commissions for made-to-order furniture. Seduti is open from 10 to 6 Monday to Saturday and at other times by appointment.

NICE

12 High Street Arcade, Cardiff CF10 2BB
Tel: 029 2064 5481 Fax: 029 2064 1847
e-mail: tracy@nicespace.co.uk
website: www.nicespace.co.uk

Tracy Lucas, who trained at art college, possesses abundant imagination and a keen eye for design, both of which are reflected in the unique collection of gifts and design-led items that fill her shop **Nice**. Set within a bright, stylish, glass-roofed shopping arcade in the

centre of the city, the space is filled with a treasure trove of unusual gifts and items for the home; there's nothing, absolutely nothing, that's boring or ordinary, and the shop is the perfect place to find a fun wedding present.

The stock ranges from eye-catching nick-nacks to rugs and chairs by way of handmade greetings cards and wacky things like an inflatable monitor cover or a bar of chocolate flavoured soap. Other stylish items guaranteed to "funk up" a home include Alessi gear, fabulous bathroom goodies and design icons by the likes of Ron Arad and Philippe Starck.

CARDIFF

The capital city of Wales is a delightful place with an unexpected beauty, a long history, a sporting tradition and an exciting rejuvenated waterfront that is attracting visitors in their thousands. The Cardiff area was first settled by the Romans in the 1st century, but from their departure a few centuries later to the arrival of the Normans in the 11th century little was recorded of life around what is now Cardiff. In 1091, Robert FitzHamon built a primitive fortress on what remained of the Roman fortification and this was, over the years, upgraded to a stone castle around which the town began to develop. Overrun by Owain Glyndwr in the early 15th century, the town and its castle came into the hands first of the Tudors and then of the Herbert family and their descendants the Marquesses of Bute.

However, Cardiff is very much a product of the Industrial Revolution and its story is intertwined with that of the Marquesses of Bute. They controlled the docklands and, as the town began to thrive as a coal exporting port, the family made a vast fortune. Some of this wealth was poured back into the rebuilding, in the 19th century, of **Cardiff Castle** on the site of the previous fortification. A no-expense-spared project initiated by the 3rd Marquess, the Castle is an extravagant and opulent Victorian version of a castle of the Middle Ages, designed by the eccentric architect William Burges. With his flamboyant imagination allowed to run riot, Burges created magnificent rooms rich in murals, stained glass and marble which really do have to be seen to be believed. However, while the building is very much a flight of wealthy Victorian fancy, outside in the grounds can be seen the well preserved medieval castle keep and stonework dating from Roman times. Visitors to the castle today also have the opportunity to look around the **Welsh Regiment Museum** and look out over Cardiff from the top of the Norman keep. Also planned for 2002 is a special exhibition on the Castle's major conservation project.

Cardiff Castle

As might be expected in a capital city, Cardiff is home to many of the national treasures of Wales and at the superb **National Museum and Gallery of Wales** there is a vast collection of archaeology, natural history and ceramics as well as permanent exhibitions on the Evolution of Wales and Man and the Environment. The art gallery is home to a fine collection that includes some superb Impressionist and Post-Impressionist works. The museum and gallery, along with the City Hall, are located in **Cathays Park**, where there are other civic buildings and also various departments of the University of Wales.

The area once known as Tiger Bay - Cardiff's historic dockland and the birthplace of Shirley Bassey - is one of the country's most exciting and imaginative regeneration developments. Now called **Cardiff Bay**, this revived waterfront is home to the new **National Assembly**, the impressive **Pierhead Building** which was built in 1896 for the Bute Docks Company and the **Cardiff Bay Visitor Centre**. At this award winning tubular building, visitors can see a futuristic exhibition which lays out the full vision of the complete development which, among other aims, is reuniting the city with its dockland. The single most important part in the revival of the Bay is the massive Cardiff Bay Barrage, a barrier that stretches for a kilometre across the mouth of the Bay. Of particular interest to children at Cardiff Bay is **Techniquest**, the country's leading science discovery centre, where visitors can explore many aspects of science and technology through a range of interactive exhibits. The former church for Norwegian sailors, which is where the

author Roald Dahl was baptised, is now the **Norwegian Church Arts Centre** which maintains the links which have grown up over the years between the two nations. Deconsecrated in the 1970s, the church also has a coffee shop.

Although Cardiff's famous Arms Park, the home of rugby football for so many years, has gone, its replacement, the **Millennium Stadium**, which hosted the last great sporting event of the 20th century, the Rugby World Cup Final in November 1999, is set to become an equally revered shrine to the Welsh national game and is already proving a highly successful replacement for Wembley. Visitors to the stadium can not only see the hallowed turf but also learn how the pitch was laid, find out how the 8,000 ton steep roof opens and closes, and walk from the Welsh players' dressing room, through the tunnel and on to the pitch.

GIFT HORSE

204 Whitchurch Road, Cardiff CF14 3NB
Tel/Fax: 029 2061 9358
e-mail: peter@gift-horse.co.uk
website: www.gift-horse.co.uk

Gift Horse is a smart double-fronted shop in an exclusive shopping area in the northwest suburbs of Cardiff. Opened in 1992, it is owned and managed by Penny Gregson and her son Peter, and the spacious, well laid-out interior is filled with attractive gift ideas on tables, racks, shelves and walls and in display cabinets. Gift Horse specialises in silkscreen

prints, etchings and engravings by artists such as Gaveau, Richard Spare and G Ferrari.

Glass and ceramics also feature prominently in the shop, most of the pieces coming from small studios in the UK and Europe. Greetings cards, jewellery, necklaces, paperweights, bronze and silver miniatures and larger bronze sculptures - these are just some of the other items on show at this excellent shop away from the bustling city centre. Gift Horse is definitely well worth a visit to find a special gift or something attractive for the house.

Cardiff City Hall

A mile or so from the city centre stands **Llandaff Cathedral**, a beautiful building set in a grassy hollow beside the River Taff. The cathedral suffered severe bomb damage during World War II and part of its restoration programme included a controversial Epstein sculpture, *Christ in Majesty*, which dominates the interior. Inside, visitors will also find some delightful medieval masonry, a marvellous modern timber roof and some works of art by members of the Pre-Raphaelite movement.

Two miles north of the city centre, **Roath Park** is a 19th century urban park with handsome trees, formal flower beds, a wild area and a memorial to Scott of the Antarctic.

ST FAGANS

3 miles W of Cardiff off the A48

On the outskirts of Cardiff, this picturesque village is home to the **Museum of Welsh Life** in the large grounds of St Fagans Castle, a splendid Elizabethan mansion. Founded in 1948, this is a museum unlike most other museums as it contains an assortment of buildings, collected from all over Wales, which have been re-erected in these glorious surroundings. Ranging from a

Celtic village and farmhouses to a Victorian schoolroom, a farmyard complete with animals, a pre-war grocery, a miner's institute, a toll keeper's cottage and a House for the Future, each of the 40 or so buildings has been furnished to reflect a period in its history. As well as this superb collection, the museum holds demonstrations on traditional craft skills, and visitors can enjoy a delightful stroll round the formal gardens, the Italian Garden, the modern knot garden and the terraces that descend to a series of fishponds.

TONGWYNLAIS

3 miles NW of Cardiff on the A470

Situated in the Taff Valley and hidden by trees, **Castell Coch** appears to be a fairytale castle of the Middle Ages, yet it only dates from the 19th century. Built on the site of a 13th century castle, Castell Coch was designed by the eccentric architect William Burges for the 3rd Marquess of Bute as a companion piece to Cardiff Castle. As the Marquess was reputed to be the wealthiest man in the world - the family owned the thriving Cardiff docks - money was no object and so this elaborate castle was constructed. While the medieval illusion of the place is maintained by the working portcullis and drawbridge, the interior decoration is perhaps even more astonishing. All perfectly preserved, each room is a masterpiece, with eye-catching details such as paintings of butterflies on the domed ceiling of the drawing room, scenes from Aesop's Fables and Greek mythology on the walls, and bird and animal mouldings around the doors. The Marquess planted a vineyard in the castle grounds which, it is said, produced the only commercially made wine in Britain between 1875 and 1914. There are now more than a dozen commercial vineyards in Wales alone.

NEWPORT

14 miles NE of Cardiff on the A48

There is more to this large conurbation than first meets the eye and, despite the reminders to the town's history as a port and its links with industry, Newport is, perhaps surprisingly, an ancient place. The Romans certainly settled in the area in the 1st century and the town's **St Woolos Cathedral Church**, splendidly situated on the hilltop, is just the latest building on a site which has been a place of worship since the 6th century. The church was founded by St Gwynllyw (Woolos is the English version of his name), who was, before his conversion, a cruel and wicked man. He is said to have had a dream one night that he would go to a hill and find there a white ox with a black spot. This Gwynllyw did the next day and, finding the said ox, saw it as a sign from God and became a devout Christian.

The history of Newport's docks is explored at the **Pillgwenlly Heritage Community Project**, while at the **Newport Museum and Art Gallery** there is a range of displays on the town's origins, including a Roman mosaic floor which was excavated close by. Not to be missed here are the John Wait teapot display and the Fox collection of decorative art. An impressive reminder of Newport's more recent past is the massive **Transporter Bridge** across the River Usk. Specially designed in 1906 by Ferdinand Arnodin to allow traffic to cross the river without disrupting the movement of shipping, the bridge is one of very few of its kind: one is in Middlesbrough, two others are in France. Newport was the home of the poet WH Davies, who penned the famous lines:

What is this life if, full of care,
We have no time to stand and stare...

To the west of the town lies **Tredegar House and Park** (see panel opposite), the home of the influential Morgan family for more than 500 years. The present dignified red brick house dates from the 17th century and is one of Wales' architectural wonders. Visitors can tour the rooms and discover just what life was like here, both above and below stairs, as well as finding out something of this great Welsh family. Its more colourful and famous members include Sir Henry Morgan, the notorious pirate, Godfrey, the 2nd Lord Tredegar, who survived the Charge of the Light Brigade and whose horse is buried in the grounds, and Viscount Evan, whose menagerie included a boxing kangaroo. The park that surrounds the house is

CHURCH HOUSE INN

Church Road, St Brides Wentlooge, Newport NP10 8SN
Tel: 01633 680807 Fax: 01638 681289
e-mail: kitandhuw@tesco.net

After years of experience in the licensed trade, Huw and Kita Williams realised a long-cherished ambition when they took over the **Church House Inn**. It's a really nice traditional old pub, first recorded as a seller of ale in 1815, with flagstone floors, wooden tables and a cheerful fire blazing in winter in the bar. The inn has a separate lounge and a restaurant serving classic Welsh dishes; snacks and light meals are served in the bar. Outside are picnic tables, a large car park and slides, swings, a climbing frame and - in summer - a bouncy castle to keep the children happy and the parents relaxed.

TREDEGAR HOUSE

Newport, South Wales NP10 8YW
Tel: 01633 815880

Situated just two miles outside Newport, M4 junction 28, and set in 90 acres of award winning gardens and parkland, **Tredegar House** is one of the finest examples of Restoration architecture in Wales, and was the ancestral home of the Morgans for over 500 years.

Visitors, today, can discover what life was like for those who lived "above and below" stairs. A stunning sequence of staterooms, elaborately decorated with carvings, gilding, and fine paintings contrast with the fascinating and extensive domestic quarters. Lakeside walks, beautful walled gardens, orangery and spectacular stable block complete the "country house" picture. There are a gift shop, tea room and craft workshops together with special events in the house and park throughout the year.

equally impressive, with early 18th century walled formal gardens, an orangery with restored parterres, and craft workshops; visitors can take a carriage drive through the parkland and children have their own adventure playground. There's a tea room and a gift shop, and a suite of rooms is available for corporate events.

CAERLEON

2½ miles NE of Newport on the B4236

Despite its close proximity to Newport, Caerleon has managed to maintain the air of a rural town, but its chief attraction is the remarkable Roman remains. Caerleon is one of the largest and most significant surviving Roman military sites in Europe, set up in AD 75 by the 2nd Augustinian Legion and originally called Isca. A substantial Roman town grew up around the military base and among the remains to be seen at **Caerleon Roman Fortress and Baths** are a large amphitheatre where thousands watched the gladiators, the only surviving barracks to be seen in Europe and a complex system of Roman baths which were the equivalent of

today's sports and leisure centres. Finds excavated from the remains are on show at the **Legionary Museum**, where, along with the weapons, mosaics and models, visitors can see one of the largest collections of engraved gem stones. Caerleon has more to offer than Roman remains - impressive though they are - and the town has some fine examples of timbered buildings. It also has links with King Arthur: one local legend suggests that the Roman amphitheatre was the site of King Arthur's Round Table. Caerleon's most famous son was the novelist Arthur Machen, who wrote this fond tribute to his birthplace:

I shall always esteem it as the greatest piece of fortune that has fallen to me, that I was born in that noble, fallen Caerleon-on-Usk, in the heart of Gwent....

Alfred, Lord Tennyson, visited Caerleon, staying at the riverside Hanbury Arms while seeking inspiration for his *Idylls of the King*.

PENHOW

7 miles E of Newport off the A48

This hamlet is home to Wales' oldest lived-in fortress, **Penhow Castle**, which still has its stout Norman keep and an impressive 15th century Great Hall complete with minstrels' gallery. Visitors to the castle are invited to guide themselves through the various rooms using a recorded commentary, heard through a personal stereo, which tells of the 850-year history of the building. The castle was at one time owned by the family of Jane Seymour, Henry VIII's third wife, who died soon after giving birth to a son, who became Edward VI.

CAERPHILLY

8 miles N of Cardiff on the A469

Famous for its distinctive white crumbly cheese which is sadly no longer made here, Caerphilly was the birthplace of the much-loved comedian Tommy Cooper. The town's **Visitor Centre**, as well as providing tourist information, has an exhibition on local history and culture, a display of Welsh crafts and a fine Welsh food shop. The town is dominated by the massive **Caerphilly Castle**, which is not only one of Britain's

Caerphilly Castle

largest castles (only Windsor and Dover are its equal) but is also one of the finest surviving examples of medieval military architecture in Europe. This great fortress was built largely in the late 13th century by the Norman Lord Gilbert de Clare. Along with the "wall within walls" defence system, he also employed a

mighty water defensive arrangement which included lakes and three artificial islands. The castle was restored in the 19th century by the Marquess of Bute, but nothing seems to be able to restore the castle's famous leaning tower, which manages to out-lean the leaning tower of Pisa. Today the castle is home to an intriguing display of full size working replica siege engines.

DERI

9 miles N of Caerphilly off the A469

To the north of Deri, in beautiful Darran Valley, lies **Parc Cwm Darran**, a glorious country park which, along with the adventure playground and informative Visitor Centre, also has a six-acre coarse fishery.

PONTLLANFRAITH

6 miles NE of Caerphilly on the A4048

Close to this town lies **Gelligroes Mill**, a 17th century water mill restored to full working order. In the early 20th century the mill was owned by Arthur Moore, a radio enthusiast, who, on the night of 11th April 1912, claimed to have heard distress signals from the sinking *Titanic*. No one believed Arthur until two days later, when the news reached England of the disaster.

CWMFELINFACH

3½ miles NE of Caerphilly on the A4048

Covering some 1,000 acres of both woodland and farmland, the **Sirhowy Valley Country Park** provides the ideal opportunity to walk, cycle or ride along the park's numerous trails. The Full

Moon Visitor Centre has all the details of the park's natural history and of other activities here while in the heart of the country park is **Ynys Hywel Centre**, a converted 17th century farmhouse which has conference facilities and a weekend coffee shop.

CWMCARN
6 miles NE of Caerphilly on the B4591

Just to the west of the town lies **Cwmcarn Forest Drive**, a seven mile stretch of high forest road that provides some of the most magnificent panoramic views of the south wales countryside and, beyond, to the Bristol Channel. Another attraction is the **Mabinogion Sculpture Trail**, which depicts characters from the Celtic folklore tales of the *Mabinogion*. The drive's visitor centre has details of the route and what can be seen

Llancaiach Fawr Manor

at various points and also a coffee shop and a gift shop which is well stocked with local handicrafts.

RISCA
5½ miles NE of Caerphilly on the B4591

To the south of Risca, at High Cross on the Monmouthshire Canal, is the **Fourteen Locks Canal Centre**, where this complicated systems of locks was constructed to raise and lower barges some 168 feet in just half a mile with only the minimal wastage of water. There are several walks from the centre, which take in the locks, ponds, channels, tunnels and weirs, as well as the countryside in which the centre is sited. Open from Easter to September, the visitor centre has a display that follows the growth and the heyday of the Monmouthshire Canal and the decline that started when the railways began to take trade off the water.

NELSON
5½ miles NW of Caerphilly on the A472

As well as being home to an open air handball court dating from the 1860s and still in use, this village is home to **Llancaiach Fawr Manor**, a handsome Elizabethan manor house which has been lovingly restored to the year 1645 and the time of the Civil War.

During this turbulent time, the Pritchard family lived here and visitors to this living history museum can meet both members of the family and their servants, all in authentic costumes, as they carry on with their daily lives. As well as preparing meals, gardening and exchanging gossip of the day, a number of events from that time, such as archery and falconry, are staged.

This is a wonderfully entertaining and informative museum where visitors also get the chance to meet some of the house's eight ghosts on the special ghost tours.

PONTYPOOL

Known to have been in existence before the time of the Normans, Pontypool is credited with being the home of the Welsh iron industry. The first forge here is believed to have been in operation as early as 1425, and the first ironworks opened in 1577. It is said which the first iron working forge in America was started by emigrants from Pontypool in around the mid-17th century. This valley also prides itself on being the earliest place in Britain to have successfully produced tin plate, in 1720, and today the town's industrial heritage can be explored at the **Pontypool Valley Inheritance Centre** where both the industrial and social history of the town and surrounding Torfaen valley is detailed. The museum is located in the late-Georgian stables of Pontypool Park,

once the home of the Hanbury family, who were, appropriately, owners of a local ironworks. **Pontypool Park** is a 19th century landscaped park whose main attractions include a shell grotto and a unique double-chambered ice house. The formal Italian gardens have recently been restored with the help of Heritage Lottery funding.

The canals, too, have played an important part in the development of Pontypool and this particular legacy is recalled at **Junction Cottage**, a tollkeeper's cottage of 1814 lying at the junction of the Monmouthshire and Brecon Canal and the River Lwyd. Industry seems worlds away at **Llandegfedd Reservoir**, to the east of Pontypool, where the lake and surrounding countryside provide numerous opportunities for fishing, sailing, walking and bird watching.

MILL FARM

Cwmafon, Nr Pontypool, Gwent NP4 8XJ
Tel/Fax: 01495 774588

Caroline and Clive Jayne extend a very warm welcome to **Mill Farm**, where they offer bed and breakfast accommodation in an idyllic countryside setting. The farm, once the home of the local miller, has its origins in medieval times but the main part is early Tudor. The old-world charm of inglenooks, beams, oak panelling and spiral stone staircases survives intact, but visitors will find nothing lacking in the way of modern amenities.
The antique-furnished en suite bedrooms - one with a four-poster bed - ensure a peaceful, comfortable night's sleep, and in the lounge guests can relax and enjoy a glass of Welsh wine by the indoor heated pool, for which robes and towels are provided. In the summer a relaxing hour or two can be passed on the terrace, or enjoying a leisurely game of boules or croquet in the garden, exploring the mountainside or wandering in the ancient woodlands.

A generous Welsh breakfast is served until midday in the beautiful dining room. Nearby, pubs and a Bistro serve excellent local produce, and the adjacent village of Abersychan is building a reputation for antiques and collectables. Although set in quiet rural surroundings, the farm is close to many of the region's leading attractions: among these are the World Heritage Site of Blaenavon, the cradle of the Industrial Revolution, the ironworks and Big Pit Museum. Finally for complete tranquillity - adults only! AA four diamonds.

CWMBRAN

3 miles SW of Pontypool on the A4051

This new town in the old industrial valleys of South Wales was founded in 1949 and was once dominated by heavy industry itself. Today, the mines and large works have gone and major environmental improvement schemes, including planting forests, have taken away many of the old eyesores. Not far from the town are some interesting and historic places including the **Llanyrafon Mill and Farm Museum** and the **Llamtarnam Grange Arts Centre**. **Greenmeadow Community Farm**, set within the town's planned green belt, is home to all manner of farm animals, and farm trails, a children's adventure playground and an unusual dragon sculpture are among the other attractions which go to provide a popular and entertaining day out.

LLANTARNAM GRANGE ARTS CENTRE

St David's Road, Cwmbran, Gwent NP44 1PD
Tel: 01633 483321 Fax: 01633 860584
e-mail: art@llantarnamgrange.fsnet.co.uk

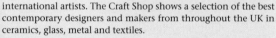

Brown tourists signs with the symbol of a pot lead visitors to **Llantarnam Grange Arts Centre** located in a large Victorian house in the centre of Cwmbran. The Centre's four art galleries show a changing programme of contemporary exhibitions of paintings and craft by local, national and

international artists. The Craft Shop shows a selection of the best contemporary designers and makers from throughout the UK in ceramics, glass, metal and textiles.

Also on sale are prints and paintings by local artists, cards and gift wrap. The café serves morning coffee, snacks, lunches and afternoon tea with home-baked cakes. The Centre is open from 10 to 5 Monday to Saturday (closed Bank Holidays). Admission is free, as is parking in the adjacent Glyndwr car park. The main galleries, craft shop and café are all on the ground floor and wheelchair accessible. Education and seminar rooms are available to hire for meetings, classes, etc.

Key personnel at the Centre:

Hywel Pontin, Director; Louise Jones-Williams, Administrator; Charlotte Kingston, Education Officer.

MOUNT PLEASANT INN

Wesley Street, Old Cwmbran, Gwent NP44 3LX
Tel/Fax: 01633 484289

Mount Pleasant Inn is a traditional family-run pub just off the busy main street of Old Cwmbran and 50 yards from the banks of the Monmouthshire and Brecon Canal. Neat and bright, with a tiled floor and wooden bar counter, this purpose-built pub is in the capable hands of John and Diane Brain, who took over in 1999. Diane does all the cooking, and many of her dishes, including the Sunday roast, use meat supplied by an excellent local butcher. The Mount Pleasant is open from 4 to 11 Monday to Friday, all day Saturday and lunchtime and evening on Sunday.

BLAENAVON

6 miles NW of Pontypool on the B4246

Despite once having been associated with the heavy industries of coal mining and iron working, Blaenavon is set in surprisingly pleasant countryside which can be further explored by taking the **Pontypool and Blaenavon Railway**, the highest standard gauge track to have survived in Wales. Half the site lies within the Brecon Beacons National Park. The oldest colliery in Wales, **Big Pit Mine**, closed in 1980, but has been reopened as a monument to the past, with former miners and engineers from the site giving guided tours accompanied by plenty of anecdotes. Visitors, armed with helmet, lamp and battery pack, can travel down a 90 metre shaft in a pit cage and walk through the underground roadways, air doors, stables and engine houses which were built by past generations of mineworkers and where thousands of miners, some of them children, laboured in arduous conditions. On the surface at this site, designated Britain's 18th World Heritage Site by UNESCO, there are more buildings to explore, including the winding engine-house, the blacksmith's workshop and the pithead baths. The other side of the town's industry, iron working, can be discovered at the **Blaenavon Ironworks**, a marvellous site that not only represents an important aspect of the Industrial Revolution but is also one of Europe's best preserved 18th century ironworks. Built against a cliff-face in the 1780s and then at the cutting edge of technology, the ironworks,

whose power came from a steam engine, became the second largest in Wales. Visitors to the ironworks can see the whole process of production, including the row of blast furnaces and ingenious water balance tower by which the material was transported. Here, too, the human element of the vast ironworks is covered, as a small terrace of workers' cottages, built between 1789 and 1792, has been preserved.

EBBW VALE

15 miles NW of Pontypool on the A4048

This old steelmaking town, whose member of Parliament was once the formidable orator and social reformer Aneurin Bevan, was transformed by the 1992 Garden Festival. Following the festival, the site was developed into **Festival Park** with houses, shops and a range of leisure activities.

A monument to Aneurin Bevan stands on the outskirts of the town, which still

Ebbw Vale Festival Park

has a number of fine houses which were built by the wealthy steel and coal magnates of the area.

TREDEGAR
1½ miles W of Ebbw Vale on the B4256

This pretty town was the birthplace of Aneurin Bevan, founder of the National Health Service and Member of Parliament for Ebbw Vale. The ashes of Bevan, in 1960, and of his wife Jennie Lee, in 1988, were scattered in the hills above Tredegar. It was in Tredegar that the novelist AJ Cronin worked as a doctor and where he collected information for his book, *The Citadel*, which was later made into a film starring Robert Donat and a television series with Ben Cross. Brown tourist signs lead to the **Elliot Colliery Winding House**, now a museum of a colliery that once employed more than 2,000 people.

Close by lies **Bryn Bach Country Park**, a 600-acre area of grass and woodland, with a man-made lake, an abundance of wildlife, a visitor centre and opportunities for walking and fishing.

MONMOUTH

This prosperous and charming old market town grew up at the confluence of three rivers - the Wye, Monnow and Trothy - which are all noted for their fishing. The River Wye is crossed by a five arched bridge built in 1617 but the Monnow boasts the most impressive of the town's bridges. **Monnow Bridge** is one of Monmouth's real gems, and its sturdy fortified gatehouse, dating from the 13th century, is the only one of its kind in Britain. Long before the bridge was constructed, the Normans built **Monmouth Castle** here in around 1068. Later rebuilt by John of Gaunt in the late

SMITHS ANTIQUES

1 Agincourt Square, Monmouth NP25 3BT
Tel: 01600 772644
e-mail: john@monmouthantiques.co.uk
website: www.monmouthantiques.co.uk

The Smith family has 40 years' experience in the antiques trade, and their marvellous shop, **Smiths Antiques**, in the centre of Monmouth, is run by father and son partners Edward and John. John's wide-ranging interests and taste are reflected in a truly remarkable floor-to-ceiling stock of antiques, collectables and curiosities, from silver and brass to shipwreck Ming

china, books, paintings, clocks, rings, old gramophone records, cigarette cards, Persian rugs, pianos and all kinds of musical instruments, furniture, stuffed animals - even an elephant's skeleton.

With the goods spilling out on to the pavement like an exotic bazaar, Smiths Antiques has become something of a landmark in the town, and there's no more fascinating way of passing an hour or two than a browse into the depths of the shop. On the same site, Bonita stocks modern china and wrought-iron furnishings for home and garden. Both businesses are open seven days a week.

1300s, the castle was the birthplace of his grandson, later Henry V, in 1387. Much later, in the 17th century, **Great Castle House** was built by the 3rd Marquess of Worcester from the ruins of the castle and he lived here while his other homes, Badminton and Troy House, were being rebuilt. Today, the castle houses both the **Castle Museum** and the **Regimental Museum** where the histories of the castle and the Royal Monmouthshire Royal Engineers are explored. The **King's Garden** is a recreation of a small medieval courtyard garden, planted with herbs that would have been common around the time of Henry V.

Another interesting building in the town is the 14th century **St Mary's Church** whose eight bells are said to have been recast from a peal which Henry V brought back from France after his victory at Agincourt. The story goes that as Henry was leaving Calais, the ringing of bells was heard and he was told that the French were celebrating his departure. He immediately turned back and took the bells to give as a present to

Monnow Bridge, Monmouth

his native town. One of the graves in the churchyard is that of an obscure house-painter called John Renie, who died in 1832 at the age of 33. His headstone is an acrostic of 285 letters that reads "Here lies John Renie". This epitaph can be read over and over again, upwards, downwards, backwards and forwards, and if doglegs and zigzags are also included, it is apparently possible to read "Here lies John Renie" in 45,760 different ways. The memorial also records the deaths of his two sons, one at the age of one year and nine months, the other at the age of 83. An earlier Monmouth man, Geoffrey of Monmouth, was the Prior at St Mary's before becoming Bishop of St Asaph in

North Wales. It was probably in Monmouth that Geoffrey wrote his massive work, *A History of the Kings of Britain*, with its legends of King Arthur and Merlin.

Also in the town is the **Nelson Museum**, where a fascinating collection of material and artefacts about the great Admiral can be seen. This interesting collection of memorabilia was accumulated by Lady Llangattock, the mother of Charles Stuart Rolls, and generously donated to Monmouth. The history of the town is illustrated in displays in the same building as the Nelson Museum. The exploits of the Hon Charles Rolls in cars, balloons and aeroplanes are featured here; one of the most evocative pictures is of Rolls in the basket of his "Midget" balloon at Monmouth Gasworks in about 1908. Some five miles from the town is the Rolls estate where Charles grew up and developed an early interest in engineering and motoring that led to his forming the Rolls-Royce company. Charles died in an air accident in 1910 and his statue, along with a monument to Henry V, can be seen in the town's main Agincourt Square. He is buried in the churchyard of St Cadoc's, at Llangattock-vibon-Avel, not far from Monmouth.

Just to the west of the town, and practically on the border with England, lies **The Kymin**, a National Trust owned hill overlooking the River Wye. From here there are spectacular views across the picturesque landscape and the **Round House**, also found here, was erected by the Kymin Club in 1794. The members of this club were local worthies who liked to hold open-air lunch parties on the Kymin. They decided to construct a building so that they could picnic inside in bad weather, and the result is the Round House - round so that the

views could be enjoyed from every part of the house. The National Trust have restored the property, which can be visited on Sundays and Mondays. Offa's Dyke footpath runs through the land. Nearby is the **Naval Temple**, built to commemorate the Battle of the Nile and opened in the early 19th century.

TRELLECK

4½ miles S of Monmouth on the B4293

This village's name means "Three Stones" and these large prehistoric monoliths can be found to the southwest of Trelleck. For reasons unknown they are called **Harold's Stones**; they do not represent all the historical interest here as, close to the Church of St Nicholas, is a mound known as the **Tump**, which is all that remains of a Norman motte and bailey. The church was built in the 13th century on the site of much older Christian buildings.

TINTERN PARVA

7½ miles S of Monmouth off the A466

This riverside village, which nestles among the wooded slopes of the lovely Wye Valley, is a most beautiful place and the whole of the valley, between Monmouth and Chepstow, is designated an Area of Outstanding Natural Beauty. Here are found the enchanting ruins of **Tintern Abbey**, which lie beside the river. The abbey was founded by Cistercian monks in 1131 and largely rebuilt in the 13th century by Roger Bigod, the Lord of Chepstow Castle. The monks farmed the rich agricultural land as well as remaining dedicated to their rigorous regime of religious devotions right up until the time of the Dissolution. A rich and powerful abbey in its day, Tintern is now a majestic ruin with much delicate tracery and great soaring archways still intact, in a glorious setting that has inspired

Tintern Abbey

painters and poets such as Turner and Wordsworth.

A mile from the abbey, along the A466 Chepstow-Monmouth road, is the Victorian **Old Station** which now acts as a visitor centre for the Wye Valley. Here, too, are a countryside exhibition, a collection of signal boxes, a gift shop and a model railway.

CHEPSTOW

12½ miles S of Monmouth on the A48

This splendid old market town, which lies on the border with England, takes its name from the Old English "chepe stow", meaning "market place". It occupies a strategic crossing on the River Wye - an important crossing between England and Wales. Situated on a crag overlooking the river are the well-preserved ruins of **Chepstow Castle**, which William Fitzosbern began building in 1067 as a base for the Norman

TINTERN ANTIQUES

The Old Bakehouse, Tintern, Monmouthshire NP16 6SE
Tel/Fax: 01291 689705

In a lovely old greystone building that was a bakehouse from the 17th century right up to the 1950s, Dawn Floyd has assembled a wide range of antiques and collectables that reflect her interests and the experience gained from 25 years in the trade. The bright, well-kept display space houses a fascinating collection of desirable objects, from jewellery, silver and toys to planters, jugs, vases, tea services, pictures, mirrors and small items of furniture.

PARVA FARM VINEYARD

Parva Farm, Tintern, Monmouthshire NP16 6SQ
Tel: 01291 689636

It is thought that the Romans planted a vineyard here, but today's Parva Farm Vineyard was planted in 1979. Judith and Colin Dudley have developed and extended the business, producing still and sparkling Welsh wines, mead and country wines. Visitors can stroll among the vines and admire the Wye Valley views before sampling the wine and browsing in the gift shops and the plant sales area that is a second string to their bow: Colin is a trained horticulturist, and Judith makes lovely floral displays for all occasions.

conquest of south east Wales. Its importance can be judged from the fact that it was built of stone; most Norman fortresses of the time were in motte and bailey form, built of earth and wood. Chepstow Castle began life as a keep, and towers, walls, fortifications and gatehouses were added to prepare it for the Welsh wars, in which, as it happened, it played no part. The Castle is open

Chepstow Castle

for visits throughout the year. A major exhibition "A Castle at War" relates the history of the castle. A group of local people have come together to form the Chepstow Garrison; dressing up and re-enacting scenes from Chepstow's past,

they have become a popular attraction for both local residents and tourists. Built at the same time as the castle keep, and by the same William Fitzosbern, is the Parish and Priory Church of St Mary, which suffered considerable damage after

THE WORKSHOP GALLERY

13 Lower Church Street, Chepstow, Monmouthshire NP16 5HJ
Tel/Fax: 01291 624836
e-mail: ned@nedheywood.com
website: www.nedheywood.com

Behind a modestly sized frontage on Lower Church Street, the **Workshop**

Gallery has a spacious interior with four rooms devoted to the display of ceramics and pottery from around the United Kingdom.

Ned Heywood has been potting for over 30 years, producing an astonishing variety of pottery, stoneware and sculpture including commissions for individuals, local organisations and national and international companies.

Works by Ned and assistant Julia Land are on sale in the Workshop and in the Gallery, which also shows works by important British potters such as Walter Keeler and Michael Casson.

ARTISTS CORNER LTD

6-7 Beaufort Square, Chepstow, Monmouthshire NP16 5EP
21 Bridge Street, Chepstow, Monmouthshire NP16 5EP
Tel: 01291 627393/628098
e-mail: artistscorner@btopenworld.com
website: www.artistscorner.co.uk

Steve and Jacqui Sullivan established **Artists Corner** in 1999 to sell their own artwork. Their speciality is pastel landscapes that are full of vibrant colour, and Jacqui has a range of over 60 pen and ink drawings of local landmarks which she markets as signed limited edition prints. Shortly after opening they approached a number of local artists and offered to exhibit their works, and at the same time they began to stock art materials. The business grew rapidly and they moved to a second location two blocks down the hill; one is in busy Beaufort Square in Chepstow's main shopping area, the other next to the museum and directly opposite the castle.

Their Aladdin's Cave stocks a huge range of art and craft materials - paints, brushes, pencils, easels, inks - as well as educational toys, kits, greetings cards, handmade ceramics, china and models, including Warhammer models. The Sullivans' in-house framing department is able to offer both bespoke and contact picture framing, and in the well-lit gallery original works and limited edition prints are displayed.

FOXGLOVES ANTIQUES

20 St Mary Street, Chepstow,
Monmouthshire NP16 5EW
Tel: 01291 622386
website: www.foxglovesantiques.co.uk

Antiques and fine furniture, china, small collectables and jewellery are the main stock in trade at Foxgloves, which is centrally located in a cobbled pedestrian walkway. Lesley Brain opened **Foxgloves** in 1994 and has built up a fine reputation throughout the region. The items are displayed on two floors of an 18th century building, and every piece is of the finest quality. One of the most popular ranges is reproduction Victorian and Edwardian jewellery designed and made by a craftswoman with detailed historical knowledge.

Mrs Brain is always pleased to consider purchasing small single objects of virtue, individual items of furniture, collections or accumulations of interest or entire house contents. She also offers a house clearance service, written valuations for insurance and full probate valuations for solicitors. Foxgloves also undertakes bespoke renovation and restoration work and French polishing by Adrian Poole, who works on pieces for the shop or customers' own pieces.

the suppression of the Priory in 1536. The vast three-storey original nave gives some idea of the grand scale on which it was built. The church contains some imposing and interesting monuments, including the Jacobean tomb of Margaret Cleyton with her two husbands and 12 children. This lady paid for the town's gatehouse to be rebuilt in 1609. Also entombed here is Henry Marten, friend of Oliver Cromwell and signatory to the death warrant of Charles I. Marten spent many years imprisoned in Chepstow Castle, in the tower that now bears his name. William Fitzosbern also founded the Abbey at Cormeilles in Normandy, with which Chepstow is twinned.

Opposite the castle is **Chepstow Museum**, where the rich and varied history of this border town is revealed. Housed in an elegant 18th century building that once belonged to a wealthy Chepstow merchant family, the museum has displays on the town's many industries, including shipbuilding, fishing and the wine trade. Chepstow was at one time an important centre for shipbuilding, and one of the many photographs in the exhibition shows the closing stages in the building of *War Genius* in National Shipyard No1 in 1920. Ships were built here well into the 1920s, and the tradition was revived during World War II with the construction of tank landing craft. A great deal of interest has recently been created by a project to restore one of the ferries that used to carry cars over the River Severn from Aust to Beachley before the Severn Bridge opened in 1966. (Aust and Beachley are both in England, but the ferry crew came from Chepstow, and the project was conceived in Chepstow.) The *Severn Princess* was

MADY GERRARD

Grove Cottage, St Arvans,
Monmouthshire NP16 6EU
Tel: 01291 625764 Fax: 01291 621890
e-mail: gerrard@mady.fslife.co.uk

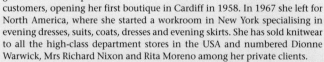

Born and educated in Budapest, **Mady Gerrard** trained as a knitwear designer and worked on exclusive knitted garments for export. She came to the UK in 1956 and began to make bespoke knitted garments for private customers, opening her first boutique in Cardiff in 1958. In 1967 she left for North America, where she started a workroom in New York specialising in evening dresses, suits, coats, dresses and evening skirts. She has sold knitwear to all the high-class department stores in the USA and numbered Dionne Warwick, Mrs Richard Nixon and Rita Moreno among her private clients.

Mady won the American Knitwear Design Award in 1974. Back in the UK, her latest project is painting silks and velvets in beautiful colours. These fabrics are made into scarves, shawls, tunics, kaftans, evening skirts, cushions and waistcoats with bow ties for men. Each item is a one-off and never repeated. There is always a big selection in stock at the cottage, and special orders are welcome. Visits by appointment.

discovered in a very sad state by a Chepstow resident while holidaying in Ireland. The ferry had found a second career as a coastal freighter but was, when discovered, laid up neglected in Kilkieran harbour. It was decided that an attempt should be made to rescue her and sail her back to Chepstow for restoration. The Severn Princess Preservation Group was formed, the ferry bought for one guinea, and the salvage attempt was under way. The *Severn Princess* was towed back to Chepstow and restoration work began. The plan as we went to press was to move her to Beachley, from where she plied across the Severn, to continue restoration work. The full story of the project can be found on the preservation group website: www.severnprincess.co.uk

Throughout the town itself, the

medieval street pattern is still much in evidence, along with surviving sections of the town wall, called the Port Wall, and the impressive **Town Gate**. But Chepstow is also a thriving modern town, and its attractions include an excellent racecourse offering both Flat and National Hunt racing; the highlight of the jumping season is the valuable and prestigious Welsh Grand National. The racecourse lies within the grounds of historic Piercefield Park. Piercefield Picturesque Walk was created in the 1750s by Valentine Morris the Younger and follows the Wye river cliff up to the Eagle's Nest. Chepstow is at one end of **Offa's Dyke**, the 8th century defensive ditch and bank built by the King of Mercia. It is also the starting point for the long-distance Wye Valley and Gloucestershire Way walks.

CALDICOT CASTLE

Church Road, Caldicot NP26 4HU
Tel: 01291 420241 Fax: 01291 435094
e-mail: caldicotcastle@monmouthshire.gov.uk website: www.caldicotcastle.co.uk

Visit **Caldicot Castle** in its beautiful setting of tranquil gardens and a wooded country park. Founded by the Normans, developed in royal hands as a stronghold in the Middle Ages and restored as a Victorian family home, the castle has a romantic and colourful history. Find out more with an audio tour, explore the medieval towers and take in the breathtaking views of the parklands and surrounding area from the battlements. Enjoy a leisurely game of chess or drafts, using giant playing pieces, visit the Children's Activity Station or relax in the gardens and grounds. Events take place throughout the season. Open Daily March to October 11 am to 5pm. Take junction 23a from M4 and B4245 to Caldicot.

CALDICOT

15 miles S of Monmouth on the B4245

Caldicot Castle (see panel opposite) dates from Norman times and was restored for use as a family house in the 1880s. Of particular note here is the sturdy round keep and the gatehouse dating from the 14th century. The castle, which is set within a wooded country park, hosts occasional medieval banquets.

CAERWENT

14 miles SW of Monmouth off the A48

Close to the Wentwood Forest, this town - which is now more of a village - was the site of **Venta Silurum**, a walled Roman town built by the invaders for the local Celtic Silures tribe. Sections of the Roman defences still remain and are some of the best preserved in Britain,

while inside the walls can be seen the remains of the forum basilica and the Romano-Celtic temple. Venta Silurum is thought to have been the largest centre of civilian population in Roman occupied Wales.

RAGLAN

6½ miles SW of Monmouth off the A40

To the north of this pretty village of shops and inns lies **Raglan Castle**, one of the finest late medieval fortresses in Britain. Built towards the end of the Middle Ages, and thus in relatively peaceful times, the castle was also constructed with comfort in mind and it represents wealth and social aspirations as much as military might. Started by Sir William ap Thomas in 1435, the castle was continued, in the same lavish manner, by his son William Herbert, who

CRETA COTTA

Jubilee Cottage, Penrhos, Nr Raglan, Monmouthshire NP15 2LE
Tel: 01600 780416 Fax: 01600 780586
e-mail: cretacotta@waitrose.com
website: www.cretacotta.co.uk

A long-standing love affair with Crete persuaded Sue Oswell to open **Creta Cotta** which specialises in Cretan terracotta. That was in 1993, and on setting up the business Sue travelled to Crete and visited a number of producers of terracotta pots and pithoi. She settled on sourcing a supply from a small family, which takes great pride in the quality of its products. Since then Creta Cotta has gone from strength to strength and Jubilee Cottage, set in rural Monmouthshire, is a place well worth seeking out for its wide selection of attractive terracotta pots.

Each pot is hand-made using traditional techniques, and firing at over 1,100°c makes them frostproof. Sizes range from a few centimetres high to a full metre. The collection includes stunning feature pithoi, large and small planters, and a variety of pots suitable for water features. A variety of plants are usually available to purchase too. For anyone who can't get along to Jubilee Cottage a mail order service is available, and delivery can be arranged nationwide.

Creta Cotta is close to the Offa's Dyke footpath and the three Castles walk and is open weekends and Bank Holidays from 10.00 am to 6.00 pm. All other times by arrangement.

was responsible for the addition of the formal state apartments and the magnificent gatehouse. Despite being more a palace than a fortress, Raglan Castle withstood one of the longest sieges of the Civil War.

To the west lies **Clytha Castle**, a folly designed by John Nash for an owner of the Clytha Park estate in memory of his wife.

USK
11½ miles SW of Monmouth on the A472

This delightful small town, which takes its name from the river on which it sits, was founded by the Romans in AD 75. Well known for its excellent local fishing - the River Usk is a fine salmon river - the town attracts fishermen from far and wide. Also noted for its floral displays and historic buildings, Usk is home to the **Gwent Rural Life Museum**, housed in several historic buildings, which tells

Clytha Castle

Continued on page 371

CROSS KEYS INN

24 Bridge Street, Usk, Monmouthshire
Tel: 01291 672535/ 673794 Fax: 01291 672535
e-mail: pentre@barbox.net
website: www.crosskeys.usk.barbox.net

The Cross Keys is a handsome slate-roofed pub on the busy main street of Usk. Hanging baskets and window boxes make a colourful seasonal show at the front, and the interior is equally appealing and full of character, with a log fire, lots of polished wood and gnarled beams made from ship's timbers. The little bar servery was once a large fireplace, and the smaller of the two dining areas was converted from outbuildings. Upstairs, the ceiling in the lounge boasts some fine Cornish plasterwork of Tudor roses and cherubs.

Owned and run by Geraldine Griffiths, the inn serves a good selection of real ales and excellent home cooking by Geraldine spans bar snacks and full meals. The family also owns a farm, which supplies the beef for some of the favourite dishes. Usk is a delightful little town well worth taking time to explore, and here, too, the Cross Keys comes into its own with comfortable, characterful accommodation in traditionally furnished bedrooms , some with characteristic beams - and if there's no room at the inn, Geraldine's parents have a new guest house within walking distance.

THE CASTLE INN

Twyn Square, Usk,
Monmouthshire NP15 1BH
Tel: 01291 673037
Fax: 01291 673615

The Castle Inn has been dispensing hospitality in its town centre location for at least 400 years. For the last seven it has been in the capable hands of Lee Evans and his mother Dawn, who offer the friendly ambience of a traditional pub combined with excellent food and a comfortable bed for the night (or, indeed, many nights). Usk is renowned for its floral displays, and the white-painted, slate-roofed Castle adds its own splashes of colour with cheerful hanging baskets and window boxes.

Oak beams, open fires, polished wooden furniture and brass ornaments paint an equally attractive picture in the bar, and the award-winning chef prepares first-class dishes to be enjoyed in the restaurant. Fish is something of a speciality (the River Usk is famous for its salmon), and Sunday lunch is always a very popular time of the week. Snacks are served all day in the tea room. Guests staying overnight have the choice of eight en suite bedrooms - singles, doubles and family rooms. The town has much to offer the visitor, including antique shops, historic houses, a splendid Rural Life Museum and excellent fishing.

THE RAT TRAP

Old Chepstow Road, Llangeview, Nr Usk, Monmouthshire NP15 1EY
Tel: 01291 673288 Fax: 01291 673305
e-mail: info@rattraphotel.com website: www.rattraphotel.com

John Collingbourne brings years of experience to the Rat Trap, a cheerful, welcoming hotel and restaurant. The Rat Trap offers bed and breakfast or full-board accommodation in 15 en suite bedrooms, including a four poster room, all furnished and maintained to a high standard, with tv, direct-dial phone and tea/coffee-making facilities. There is a well-stocked bar with beams, antiques and open fire, and an extensive and imaginative menu in the restaurant. A vegetarian selection is always available, and other special requests will be catered for wherever possible. Children and pets are welcome in the hotel.

THE CLYTHA ARMS

Clytha, Nr Abergavenny, Monmouthshire NP7 9BW
Tel: 01873 840206 Fax: 01873 840209
e-mail: one.bev@lineone.net website: www.lineone.net/~one.bev/

The Clytha Arms is a splendid free house set in its own grounds six miles from Abergavenny, and Andrew and Beverley Canning have been in this handsome converted dower house since 1992. With six real ales and snacks in the public bar, it is also building a reputation for the quality of the food served in the restaurant with dishes such as sea bass with Thai herbs, the local favourite of bacon with laverbread and cockles, and stuffed fillet steak with Carmarthen ham and wild mushrooms. Comfortable overnight accommodation comprises four en suite rooms (one with a four-poster bed) with tv and tea/coffee facilities.

The Monmouthshire and Brecon Canal

Start	Abergavenny
Distance	5½ miles (8.9km)
Approximate time	2½ hours
Parking	Off Castle Street, Abergavenny
Refreshments	Pubs and cafés at Abergavenny
Ordnance Survey maps	Landranger 161 (Abergavenny & The Black Mountains), Outdoor Leisure 13 (Brecon Beacons National Park – Eastern area)

As most of this walk is either across riverside meadows, along a canal towpath or along the track of a disused railway, it is bound to be easy and relaxing. The sections along the banks of the River Usk and the towpath of the Monmouthshire and Brecon Canal are especially attractive and there are some fine views over the Usk valley to the Sugar Loaf and Ysgyryd Fawr. In addition both the canal and the disused railway are of interest to those keen on industrial history.

Encircled by the outlying hills of the Black Mountains and situated where the River Usk has made a gap in the mountains, Abergavenny guards one of the main routes into the heart of South Wales, a position appreciated by the Norman conquerors, who built the castle. In the Middle Ages Abergavenny Castle was one of the main border strongholds, the scene of a massacre of Welsh chiefs in 1175, but nowadays little remains and the "keep" is a 19th-century imitation, built as a hunting lodge and now a museum. More impressive is the large medieval church, originally the chapel of a Benedictine priory. Abergavenny lies on the eastern edge of the National Park and makes an excellent walking centre.

The walk begins at the entrance to the castle grounds. Facing the entrance, turn right and head down the lane beside the castle walls. After about 100 yds (91m) the lane ends and ahead are two paths; take the right-hand, lower, one which descends by a wall on the right, and turn right at the bottom on to a paved path. Pass through a metal barrier and continue across a meadow to reach the bank of the River Usk. Ahead is a grand view of Blorenge.

Turn right on to another paved path that follows the river along to Usk Bridge Ⓐ , turn left over the bridge and immediately turn right, at a footpath sign to the cemetery, along a lane. The lane passes to the right of the cemetery and heads gently uphill. At a public footpath sign by a junction of paths and tracks turn left Ⓑ , in the Llanfoist direction, along a tarmac track – part of the Usk Valley Walk – that heads downhill to pass under a road bridge. Continue along the pleasant hedge- and tree-lined track into Llanfoist Ⓒ .

WALK **13**

Cross a road and continue along the track ahead, which is signposted "Blorenge and Usk Valley Walk", passing to the right of Llanfoist church and heading steadily uphill between trees. At a fork bear right to an aqueduct but just before reaching it turn right up steps to join the canal towpath **D**. Turn right to follow the towpath for 1½ miles (2.5km) by the tree-fringed, tranquil waters of the canal, high above the Usk valley with fine views to the right over Abergavenny and the Sugar Loaf, and below the steep, thickly wooded lower slopes of Blorenge on the left. The canal was built between 1797 and 1812 to provide a link between Brecon and the Bristol Channel and carried coal, iron, lime and agricultural produce. After the inevitable decline and fall into disuse, it was restored and reopened in 1970 as a recreational waterway.

At the first bridge turn left over the canal and turn right to walk along the other bank, passing under a second bridge and continuing past a marina by Govilon Boat Club. At a third bridge **E** climb steps to leave the canal and turn right along the track of a disused railway, part of a line

built in the 1860s to link the coal mines around Merthyr Tydfil, Tredegar and Ebbw Vale to the Monmouthshire and Brecon Canal. Follow the track for just under 1½ miles (2.4km); it is lined most of the way with attractive willows and silver birches and there are more fine views of Blorenge and the Usk valley. On reaching a T-junction of tracks, pass through a wooden barrier and turn left **C** to retrace part of the outward route to the Usk Bridge on the edge of Abergavenny.

Cross the bridge and for the final section you can either continue along the outward route by taking the paved path beside the river, or alternatively head diagonally across the meadows, along a faint but discernible path from which there is a fine view of the castle ruins backed by the distinctive profile of Ysgyryd Fawr. Go through a kissing-gate in the far corner of the meadows and continue to the car parks adjoining Castle Street to return to the start. ●

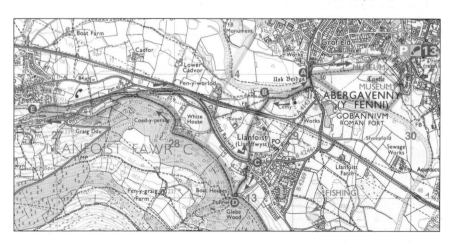

THE COURT CUPBOARD CRAFT CENTRE

New Court Farm, Llantilio Pertholey,
Abergavenny, Monmouthshire NP7 8AU
Tel: 01873 852011
e-mail: bmc@craftinwales.com

The Court Cupboard Craft Centre enjoys a picturesque period setting in a converted stone barn on the western slopes of the Skirrid Mountain north of Abergavenny. The centre was set up exclusively for the members of the Black Mountains Circle, a group of local people involved in traditional occupations, whose products and skills have been chosen for their quality and variety. The Circle takes its name and much of its inspiration from the Black Mountains in the Brecon Beacons National Park and is run by the members themselves.

A comprehensive selection of most of the members' work is on sale in the Centre. The arts and crafts featured cover an enormous range, from studio ceramics, porcelain and smoke-fired pottery to glass design, jewellery, original paintings, beeswax pictures, hand-made photographic cards, hand-made furniture, turnery and pyrography, metal sculpture, blacksmiths and calligraphy; woven rugs, wools and fleeces, canvaswork and designer cushions, quilts, knitting, children's wear, samplers, basket making......the list goes on, and some members welcome visitors to their workshops in the vicinity. These include Keith Foster (original paintings, Tel: 01495 756718), Catrin Petts (lettering, Tel: 01873 858827) and the Black Mountains Pottery (Tel: 01874 711518).

The Centre has a varied programme of workshops and also changing exhibitions of work by other artists and craftspeople. From the A465 Abergavenny bypass follow the brown signs from the junction with the B4521 to find the Court Cupboard Craft Centre, which is open from 10.30 to 5 every day throughout the year.

A comfortable coffee shop offers a selection of coffees, teas and locally made cakes; there's ample free parking and wheelchair access to the toilets.

the story of life in this Welsh border region from Victorian times up until the end of World War II. Among the many themes covered here are domestic and agricultural life and exhibits ranging from hand tool crafts to mechanisation.

ABERGAVENNY

12½ miles W of Monmouth on the A465

A particularly pleasant and thriving market town, Abergavenny dates back to Roman times when the modest fort of Gobannium was established. Here, too, is the Norman **Abergavenny Castle**, where in 1175 the fearsome Norman lord, William de Braose, invited the Welsh lords to dine and then murdered the lot while they were disarmed at his table. Today, the restored keep and hunting lodge of the castle are home to the **Abergavenny Museum** (see panel on page 373), where exhibits from

NANTYDERRY NURSERIES

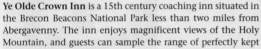

Nantyderry, Nr Abergavenny, Monmouthshire NP7 9DW
Tel: 01873 880377 e-mail: info@nantyderrynurseries.co.uk
Fax: 01873 881076 website: nantyderrynurseries.co.uk

Nantyderry Nurseries were established over 30 years ago and have been in the Robinson family ever since. Many of the plants sold are home-grown, the speciality being seasonal bedding plants. Quality and value for money are watchwords throughout all the products on sale, from the seasonal plants to shrubs and conifers, herbs and alpines, cut flowers, seeds and bulbs, stoneware and garden ornaments, pots, paving and edging stones, tools and garden sundries, peats and compost and wild bird care. Open seven days a week - summer 10 to 6, winter 10 to 5 - Nantyderry has ample free parking and good wheelchair access.

YE OLDE CROWN INN

Old Hereford Road, Pant-y-Gelli, Nr Abergavenny,
Monmouthshire NP7 7HR
Tel/Fax: 01873 853314
e-mail: yeoldcrown@aol.com

Ye Olde Crown Inn is a 15th century coaching inn situated in the Brecon Beacons National Park less than two miles from Abergavenny. The inn enjoys magnificent views of the Holy Mountain, and guests can sample the range of perfectly kept real ales (the inn has been a CAMRA Guide entry for several years) or try one of the exceptional choice of malts. Mel and Rosemary Mitchell propose a particularly varied selection of dishes on lite bite, specials and restaurant menus. The light bite menu alone is very extensive, with sandwiches and baguettes, jacket potatoes, ploughman's platters and salads both simple and a bit out of the ordinary (warm bacon and prawn; hot chicken with Seville orange dressing and deep-fried pasta).

Hot snacks run from scampi and super home-made fish cakes to lasagne, gammon steaks, meat pies, lamb's liver, chilli con carne, garlic chicken breast and sausages and mash with onion gravy. Traditional Sunday lunch, with a choice of starters, main course and desserts, is a very popular occasion, and for all meals parties can be catered for. Ye Olde Crown makes an excellent base for touring a very attractive part of Wales, and offers comfortable bed and breakfast accommodation in four bedrooms - a double, two twins and a single - with private bathroom. The bedrooms have tea/coffee making facilities and enjoy splendid views.

MONMOUTHSHIRE FARM HOLIDAYS

c/o Hopyard Farm, Glanbaiden, Govilon, Abergavenny,
Monmouthshire NP7 9SE
Tel/Fax: 01873 830219 Freephone: 0800 0935 156
website: www.downourlane.co.uk

Monmouthshire Farm Holidays offers a selection of bed and
breakfast and self-catering accommodation throughout the
county, providing excellent bases from which to explore its
many scenic and historic treasures. All the properties have been inspected by the Wales Tourist Board,
and the main aim of the group is to ensure a warm welcome to their homes and a high level of services
and facilities. There is a variety of accommodation available ranging from Welsh brig houses to 16th
century converted barns, some on working farms, others not. The properties themselves offer a variety
of facilities such as home cooked evening meals, four poster beds, indoor and outdoor swimming

pools, flexible arrival and departure times and may include a castle on the
land, a river at the end of the garden or spectacular views across the Brecon
Beacons. You can be sure that they will be all appointed to a high standard
and be situated in a superb location to relax and unwind.

The owners of these properties have an extensive knowledge of the area
and can guide and assist any guest to get the best from their holiday. There
are five self-catering establishments in the Monmouthshire Farm Holiday
Group, four of them located around Abergavenny, the fifth near Chepstow.
The Group also offers eight farm properties for bed and breakfast
accommodation in locations ranging from Grosmont in the north of the
county to just outside Chepstow and Newport. Call the Freephone number
or visit the website for further details.

MINOLA SMOKED PRODUCTS

Triley Mill Shop, Abergavenny, Monmouthshire NP7 8DE
Tel: 01873 736900 e-mail: mailorder@minola-smokery.com
Fax: 01873 736909 website: www.minola-smokery.com

Minola Smoked Products enjoys an international reputation
for quality and reliability. The range of products includes
salmon, trout, haddock, mackerel and kippers, meat, poultry
and cheese, and a very unusual smoked unsalted butter.
Minola's customers span the world, from small delicatessens
and wine bars to renowned restaurants and hotels as far a field
as Bahrain and the Far East. Their mail order customer list runs
into thousands of discerning food lovers who know that Minola always produces the very best.

In their premises just outside Abergavenny they use whole and split Welsh logs fired in iron
smoke pots in ten smoke houses to produce the unique flavours and textures of
their multi-award winning products. Minola uses only natural convection - no
humidifiers or electric or gas equipment - and once the products leave the
smokers they move into a state-of-the-art temperature-controlled environment.

Minola Smoked Products was formed in 1984 by Hugh and Jane Forestier-
Walker, who previously farmed rainbow trout and Scottish salmon. For 16 years
their smokery operated from Filkins near the source of the Thames in the
Cotswolds, but to meet increasing demand for it's fine products, they developed
a former game factory in May 2000. The smokery is now located a short distance
north of Abergabenny; from the centre take the road out through Mardy, go
under the railway bridge and immediately turn left into Triley Mill. The factory
shop is open seven days a week.

ABERGAVENNY MUSEUM

The Castle, Castle Street, Abergavenny, Monmouthshire
Tel: 01873 854282

Abergavenny Museum is set in the grounds of a "ruined" Norman Castle, where you can enjoy a picnic during the summer and a brisk walk on colder days. The museum building was formerly a hunting lodge built by the Earl of Abergavenny.

The displays tell the story of this historic market town from prehistory through to the present day - they are on several levels and with some help most areas are accessible to wheelchair users.

Features include: regular programme of temporary exhibitions, reconstruction of Basil Jones' Grocery Shop, a well known local store, and an activity Room for children, where there is the opportunity to colour, cut and stick.

prehistoric times to the present day detail the history of the town and surrounding area. Displays include recreations of a Victorian kitchen and a saddler's workshop. The castle and its

grounds have been open to the public since 1881. Just down the road lies another interesting place to visit - the **Childhood Museum**. Notable treasures in St Mary's Church include medieval choir stalls, fine altar tombs and an imposing wooden figure of Jesse. The church originally belonged to the 11th century Benedictine priory. One of the most accessible gateways to the Brecon Beacons National Park, Abergavenny is a popular place during the summer. Surrounded by glorious countryside, it is a place from where all manner of activities, including walking, pony trekking and canal cruising, can be enjoyed. A little way south of town, the 1,834ft Blorenge is a popular tourist spot. One of the car parks at its base is called Foxhunter; it was presented by Colonel Sir Harry Llewelyn in memory of his wonderful show jumper, who died in 1959 and is buried nearby.

LLANTHONY

10 miles S of Hay off the B4423

In the beautiful Vale of Ewyas, also known as Llanthony Valley, **Llanthony Priory** was built on a spot which has links with the beginnings of Christianity in Wales, and in the 6th century was

THE SMITHY

Llanthony, Nr Abergavenny, Gwent NP7 7NW
Tel: 01873 890781

The Smithy is a beautiful secluded cottage which Gaynor and Jim Elliott have lovingly restored to offer characterful self-catering accommodation in three attractively furnished bedrooms. Beamed pitched ceilings, antique polished floors, open hearths and comfortable sofas enhance the period appeal of the cottage, which in earlier times was a weaver's and dyer's

mill and a blacksmith's forge. Entrance is into a well-equipped country kitchen, and the sitting room is a delightful place to relax. The wild garden has several sitting areas, and trout fishing is available on a stretch of the River Honddu that flows through the grounds.

PENYCLAWDD COURT

Llanfihangel Crucorney, Abergavenny,
Monmouthshire NP7 7LB
Tel: 01873 890719 Fax: 01873 890848
e-mail: pyccourt@hotmail.com
website: www.1stmanorhouse.com

Penyclawdd Court is a Grade One listed, medieval manor house with 17th Century additions. It's a unique house which has been lovingly restored by historical food specialist Julia Horton McNichol, over the past 20 years.

Lying within the Brecon Beacons National Park, there are dramatic mountain views from each of the bedrooms and every effort has been made to combine authenticity with complete comfort. The grand 17th Century Courtroom boasts a four poster bed (one of several in the house) and has its own sitting room, whilst the

Tudor cosiness of the Oak Room leads to its outrageously decadent bathroom.

The Dining Hall has a vast stone fireplace where they smoke their own local salmon and have demonstrated Tudor cookery for countless TV and radio programmes. All meals from Tudor feasts to the famous Welsh breakfasts are taken here by candle and firelight only. Suppers can be provided for resident guests in parties of six or over and set menus can be arranged from Tudor, traditional medieval fare.

The grounds contain a scheduled ancient monument; with motte and bailey remains, complete with dry moat and a wet moat where you can test your skills with a coracle. For the landlubbers there are herb gardens, a "mystic" knot garden and a yew maze.

Penyclawdd Court lies off the A465 Hereford road, 4.9 miles north of Abergavenny, at the foot of the Black Mountains. The environs abound with hospitable inns, quality restaurants and sporting opportunities; there's pony trekking, fly fishing, golf and, of course, the whole of the Black Mountains to assault.

For further information contact Julia Horton-McNichol on the above numbers or e-mail address or visit the website.

TREVELOG PONY TREKKING CENTRE

Llanthony, Nr Abergavenny, Monmouthshire NP7 7NW
Tel: 01873 890216 e-mail: vicky@llanthony.net website: www.ponytrekking.net

Set in the glorious Llanthony Valley, **Trevelog Pony Trekking Centre** welcomes visitors of all ages and abilities. Friendly, experienced guides who know the surrounding area take all treks from the Centre, which opened in 1955 and is now run by Vicki Jones. The ponies are Cross Cobs, ranging from 12 hands to 16 hands, all sturdy, surefooted and suitable for both beginners and more experienced riders. Basic tuition is given to beginner riders before the treks. They can accommodate hourly, half day or full day treks all year round. If accommodation is required, the Centre can provide telephone numbers for local B&Bs; camping is also available.

chosen by St David for a cell. The Priory was founded by the Norman William de Lacy in the 11th century when he established a hermitage that evolved into the priory whose wonderful ruins can be seen today.

The beauty and tranquillity of the location have inspired many: Eric Gill and Walter Savage Landor are among those who made their homes here. For many years the site was in a state of near decay, but the Welsh Office graded it as an Ancient Monument and it is being restored.

LLANVETHERINE

9 miles NW of Monmouth on the B4521

To the south of the village lies one of the Three Castles, **White Castle**, which is so called because when it was built the masonry was rendered with gleaming white plaster, patches of which can still

ALLT-YR-YNYS HOTEL

Walterstone, Nr Abergavenny, Herefordshire HR2 0DU
Tel: 01873 890307 Fax: 01873 890539
e-mail: allthotel@compuserve.com
website: www.allthotel.co.uk

Nestling in the foothills of the Black Mountains, on the fringes of Brecon Beacons National Park, **Allt-yr-Ynys** is an imposing Gade II listed 16th century manor house. The house was once the home of the Cecil family, whose ancestry traces back to Rhodri Mawr, King of Wales in the 8th century; a later distinguished member of the family was Lord Burleigh, Chief Minister to Elizabeth I.

Features of the past are numerous, including moulded ceilings, oak panelling and beams, but Allt-yr-Ynys also offers all the comforts expected of a modern hotel.

Outbuildings have been transformed into spacious, well-appointed guest bedrooms, and top of the range is the splendid Jacobean suite with a 16th century four-poster bed. Fine dining is offered in the award-winning restaurant, and the hotel is an excellent venue for a conference or function, with space for up to 100 in a private room. Among the amenities are a heated pool, jacuzzi, clay pigeon shooting and private fishing. The hotel lies five miles north of Abergavenny off the A465 and is close to many scenic, historic and tourist attractions.

THE SKIRRID INN

Llanfihangel Crucorney,
Nr Abergavenny, Gwent NP7 8DH
Tel: 01873 890258

Signposted off the A465 north of Abergavenny, **The Skirrid Inn** is the oldest public house within the borders of the Principality of Wales, with a history that can be traced back beyond the Norman Conquest. It is recorded that in 1110 in this alehouse below the Skirrid Mountain, a court was convened to try two brothers, James Crowther for robbery with violence, John for sheep-stealing. James was sentenced to nine months in prison, and John was hanged from a beam at the inn. Many years later, Owain Glyndwr is said to have marshalled his troops in the cobbled courtyard before his march on Pontrilas.

The mounting stone on to which he climbed is thought to have been used subsequently by many of the succeeding Princes of Wales and Kings of England; it can still be seen in the courtyard. The stone structure of the inn is believed to be original, while the main doorway and many of the windows are medieval. The oak beams, made from ship's timbers, are particularly fine, and the wooden panelling in the dining room is said to be from a British man o' war. For many centuries the inn was a public meeting house as well as an alehouse and courts were held from the 12th to the 17th centuries.

A hanging beam, with scorch and drag marks still visible, is a chilling reminder of the harshness of medieval justice. The lofty bar retains original Welsh slate, some ancient oak settles and a collection of beaten copper pans and salvers. The inn, whose sign depicts Skirrid Mountain, has two bedrooms for overnight guests, both en suite, one with a four-poster. The Skirrid has only a handful of rivals for the title of Oldest Inn in Great Britain: among them are the Trip to Jerusalem in Nottingham, the Fighting Cocks in St Albans, the God Begot in Winchester and Ye Old Ferry Boat Inn at Holywell in Cambridgeshire.

be seen. Starting life as a simple earthwork not long after the Norman Conquest, White Castle was rebuilt in stone during the late 12th and 13th centuries to provide, along with Skenfrith and Grosmont castles, a triangle of fortresses to control this strategic entry point into Wales. Situated in a beautiful and isolated place, the ruins are still able to conjure up the romance of the Middle Ages. Much later, during World War II, Hitler's deputy, Rudolf Hess, fed the swans on the castle's moat while held at a local mental hospital following his mysterious flight from Nazi Germany.

GROSMONT
9½ miles NW of Monmouth on the B4347

This village takes its name from the French, "gros mont", meaning "big hill"; it is the site of **Grosmont Castle**, the most northerly of the Three Castles.

Now in ruins, Grosmont started life as a steep earthen mound but, after having been replaced by a stone fortification, it was unsuccessfully besieged by both Llywelyn the Great and Owain Glyndwr.

GALLERIES IN THE BLACK MOUNTAINS

CELLAR GALLERY

Grove Farm, Walterstone, Herefordshire HR2 0DX
Tel: 01873 890293
e-mail: christine.hunt@virgin.net
website: www.artcellar.co.uk

A converted cider cellar in the heart of the countryside is home to a permanent exhibition of paintings and prints for sale by Christine Hunt. Her work incorporates the use of many different mediums, from realistic pastels to more expressionistic compositions in oil and acrylics, often relating to her experiences in running this small hill farm overlooking the Black Mountains. Open most days but please telephone before making a special journey. The Gallery is sign posted from Pandy off the A465 Hereford to Abergavenny road.

DOWNEY BARN GALLERY

The Coach House, Cwmyoy, Nr Abergavenny, Monmouthshire NP7 7NT
Tel: 01873 890993

Situated by the famous crooked Church of Cwmyoy in the dramatic Black Mountains countryside, Downey Barn Gallery houses the unusual collection of work by Artist Caroline Downey. It includes her uniquely styled "Sculptured Board" paintings-winner of worldwide Jubilee Competition 2002. Also prints, rustic metal sculptures and other work on sale. Enjoy a visit, meet the artist, and capture the rural atmosphere of this charming "traditional barn" gallery perched on the hillside amid landscaped gardens featuring decorative ironwork gates. Open most days-best to phone if making a special journey. Follow signs from main A465 Abergavenny/Hereford at Pandy.

THE BELL AT SKENFRITH

Skenfrith, Monmouthshire NP7 8UH
Tel: 01600 750235 Fax: 01600 750525
e-mail: enquiries@skenfrith.com
website: www.skenfrith.com

On the banks of the River Monnow in the beautiful village of Skenfrith,
the 17th century **Bell** has been restored to its former glory by owners
William and Janet Hutchings. Log fires, flagstone floors, oak beams
and antique furniture reinforce the coaching inn pedigree, and the eight
bedrooms are individually appointed in an elegantly simple, unfussy
style that combines a traditional look with up-to-the-minute amenities.
All the bedrooms have en suite bathrooms, widescreen tv, DVD players
(a small selection of DVDs available at reception), direct-dial phone
and ISDN connection for laptops. Some rooms have four-posters; two
are beamed attic suites.

The spacious bar, with wooden tables and chairs, roomy sofas,
newspapers and magazines, has the relaxed atmosphere of a bistro
and a terrific bar menu offering such dishes as peppers piedmontese,
a terrine of pheasant with Puy lentils and pancetta, roast cod with
fennel herb butter and Usk Valley rack of lamb with roast parsnips
and walnut garlic pickle. Desserts keep up the good work with such
temptations as chocolate blueberry torte with rhubarb syrup. Chef
Leigh Say and his team swear by seasonal locally sourced ingredients
on the menus for both the bar and for the non-smoking restaurant,
where a really superb two or three course dinner is served. The wine
list features wines from around the world, and guest ales add to the
permanent choice of beers.

During exploration of the ruins, an
Arabic "faience jar" was found here -
undoubtedly a relic from the Crusades.

SKENFRITH

5½ miles NW of Monmouth on the B4521

At this point the Monnow Valley forms
something of a gap in the natural
defences of the Welsh Marches and its
was here that the Normans built

Skenfrith Castle, the last of the Three
Castles - the others being White and
Grosmont. Situated beside the river,
Skenfrith Castle was built in the 13th
century by Hubert de Burgh and is noted
for its fine round tower keep and its well
preserved curtain wall. Once the
troubled domain of medieval warlords,
this border region today is peaceful and
undisturbed.

TOURIST INFORMATION CENTRES

ABERAERON

The Quay
Aberaeron
SA46 0BT

Tel : 01545 570602
Fax: 01970 626566
e-mail: aberaerontic@ceredigion.gov.uk

ABERDYFI

The Wharf Gardens
Aberdyfi
LL35 0ED

Tel : 01654 767321
Fax: 01654 767321

Seasonal

ABERGAVENNY

Swan Meadow
Monmouth Road
Abergavenny
NP7 5HH

Tel : 01873 857588
Fax: 01873 850217
e-mail:
abergavenny-tic@tsww.com

ABERYSTWYTH

Terrace Road
Aberystwyth
SY23 2AG

Tel : 01970 612125
Fax: 01970 626566
e-mail: aberystwythtic@ceredigion.gov.uk

BALA

Penllyn
Pensarn Road
Bala
LL23 7SR

Tel : 01678 521021
Fax: 01678 521021

BARRY ISLAND

The Promenade
Paget Road
Barry Island
CF62 5TQ

Tel : 01446 747171
e-mail: tourism@valeofglamorgan.gov.uk

Seasonal

BLAENAU FFESTINIOG

Unit 3
High Street
Blaenau Ffestiniog
LL41 3HS

Tel : 01766 830360
Fax: 01766 830360

Seasonal

BLAENAVON

Blaenavon Ironworks
Stack Square
Blaenavon
NP4 9RQ

Tel : 01495 792615
Fax: 01495 792615
website: www.blaenavontic.com
e-mail: blaenavon.ironworks@btopenworld.com

Seasonal

BORTH

Cambrian Terrace
Borth
SY24 5HU

Tel : 01970 871174
Fax: 01970 626566
e-mail: borthtic@ceredigion.gov.uk

Seasonal

BRECON

Cattle Market Car Park
Brecon
LD3 9DA

Tel : 01874 622485
Fax: 01874 625256
e-mail: brectic@powys.gov.uk

BRIDGEND

McArthurGlen Designer Village
Junction 36/M4
Bridgend
CF32 9SU

Tel : 01656 654906
Fax: 01656 646523
e-mail: bridgend-tic@tsww.com

BUILTH WELLS

The Groe Car Park
Builth Wells
LD2 3BT

Tel : 01982 553307
Fax: 01982 553841
e-mail: builtic@powys.gov.uk

Seasonal

CAERLEON

5 High Street
Caerleon
NP18 1AE

Tel : 01633 422656
Fax: 01633 422656
e-mail: caerleon-tic@tsww.com

CAERNARFON

Oriel Pendeitsh
Castle Street
Caernarfon
LL55 1ES

Tel : 01286 672232
Fax: 01286 678209
e-mail: caernarfon.tic@gwynedd.gov.uk

CAERPHILLY

Lower Twyn Square
Caerphilly CF83 1JL

Tel : 029 2088 0011
Fax: 029 2086 0811
e-mail: tic@caerphilly.gov.uk

CARDIFF

Cardiff Visitor Centre
16 Wood Street, Cardiff
CF10 1ES

Tel : 029 2022 7281
Fax: 029 2023 9162
e-mail: enquiries@cardifftic.co.uk

CHEPSTOW

Castle Car Park, Bridge Street
Chepstow
NP16 5EY

Tel : 01291 623772
Fax: 01291 628004
e-mail: chepstow-tic@tsww.com

COLWYN BAY

Imperial Buildings
Station Square, Princes Drive
Colwyn Bay
LL29 8LF

Tel : 01492 530478
Fax: 01492 534789
e-mail: colwynbay.tic@virgin.net

CONWY

Conwy Castle Visitor Centre
Conwy
LL32 8LD

Tel : 01492 592248
Fax: 01492 573545
e-mail: conwy.tic@virgin.net

Seasonal

CORRIS

Corris Craft Centre
Corris
SY20 9SP

Tel : 01654 761244
Fax: 01654 761244
e-mail: corris.tic@gwynedd.gov.uk

Seasonal

CRICKHOWELL

Beaufort Chambers, Beaufort Street
Crickhowell
NP8 1AA

Tel : 01873 812105

Seasonal

DOLGELLAU

Ty Meirion, Eldon Square
Dolgellau
LL40 1PU

Tel : 01341 422888
Fax: 01341 422576
e-mail: ticdolgellau@hotmail.com

HARLECH

Gwyddfor House
High Street
Harlech
LL46 2YA

Tel : 01766 780658
Fax: 01766 780658

HOLYHEAD

Penrhos Beach Road
Holyhead
LL65 2QB

Tel : 01407 762622
Fax: 01407 761462
e-mail: holyhead.tic@virgin.net

KNIGHTON

Offas Dyke Centre
West Street
Knighton
LD7 1EN

Tel : 01547 529424
e-mail: oda@offasdyke.demon.co.uk

LAKE VYRNWY

Unit 2 Vyrnwy Craft Workshops
Lake Vyrnwy
SY10 0LY

Tel : 01691 870346
Fax: 01691 870346
e-mail: laktic@powys.gov.uk

Seasonal

LLANBERIS

41b High Street
Llanberis
LL55 4EU

Tel : 01286 870765
Fax: 01286 871924
e-mail: llanberis.tic@gwynedd.gov.uk

Seasonal

LLANDEILO

Car Park Crescent Road
Llandeilo
SA19 6HN

Tel : 01558 824226
Fax: 01558 824226
e-mail: carmarthentic@carmarthenshire.gov.uk

Seasonal

LLANDOVERY

Heritage Centre, Kings Road
Llandovery
SA20 0AW

Tel : 01550 720693
Fax: 01550 720693

LLANDRINDOD WELLS

Old Town Hall
Memorial Gardens
Llandrindod Wells
LD1 5DL

Tel : 01597 822600
Fax: 01597 829164
e-mail: llandtic@mail.powys.gov.uk

LLANDUDNO

1-2 Chapel Street
Llandudno
LL30 2YU

Tel : 01492 876413
Fax: 01492 872722
e-mail:llandudno.tic@virgin.net

LLANELLI

Public Library
Vaughan Street
Llanelli
SA15 3AS

Tel : 01554 772020
Fax: 01554 750125

Seasonal

LLANFAIRPWLL

Station Site
Llanfairpwll
LL61 5UJ

Tel : 01248 713177
Fax: 01248 715711
e-mail:llanfairpwll.tic@virgin.net

LLANGOLLEN

Town Hall, Castle Street
Llangollen
LL20 5PD

Tel : 01978 860828
Fax: 01978 861563
e-mail: llangollen.tic@virgin.net

LLANIDLOES

54 Longbridge Street
Llanidloes
SY18 6EF

Tel : 01686 412605
Fax: 01686 413884
e-mail: llantic@powys.gov.uk

MACHYNLLETH

Canolfan Owain Glyndwr
Machynlleth
SY20 8EE

Tel : 01654 702401
Fax: 01654 703675
e-mail: mactic@mail.powys.gov.uk

MAGOR

First Services & Lodge
Jct 32a/M4 Magor
NP6 3YL

Tel : 01633 881122
Fax: 01633 881985
e-mail: magor-tic@tsww.com

MERTHYR TYDFIL

14a Glebeland Street
Merthyr Tydfil
CF47 8AU

Tel : 01685 379884
Fax: 01685 350043
e-mail: merthyr-tic@tsww.com

MOLD

Library, Museum & Art Gallery
Earl Road, Mold
CH7 1AP

Tel : 01352 759331
Fax: 01352 759331
e-mail: mold.tic@virgin.net

Seasonal

MONMOUTH

Shire Hall
Agincourt Square
Monmouth
NP5 3DY

Tel : 01600 713899
Fax: 01600 772794
e-mail: monmouth-tic@tsww.com

MUMBLES

The Portacabin
Oystermouth Square
Mumbles
SA3 4DQ

Tel : 01792 361302
Fax: 01792 363392

Seasonal

NEW QUAY

Church Street
New Quay
SA45 9NZ

Tel : 01545 560865
Fax: 01970 626566
e-mail: newquaytic@ceredigion.gov.uk

Seasonal

NEWPORT

Museum & Art Gallery
John Frost Square
Newport
NP20 1PA

Tel : 01633 842962
Fax: 01633 222615
e-mail: newport-tic@tsww.com

NEWTOWN

The Park
Back Lane
Newtown
SY16 2PW

Tel : 01686 625580
Fax: 01686 610065
e-mail: newtic@powys.gov.uk

OSWESTRY (MILE END)

Mile End Services
Oswestry
SY11 4JA

Tel : 01691 662488
Fax: 01691 662883
e-mail: oswestry.tourism@btconnect.com

OSWESTRY (TOWN)

The Heritage Centre, 2 Church Terrace
Oswestry
SY11 2TE

Tel : 01691 662753
Fax: 01691 657811
e-mail: owbta@micro-plus-web.net

PENARTH

The Esplanade
Penarth Pier
Penarth
CF64 3AU

Tel : 020 2070 8849
e-mail: tourism@valeofglamorgan.gov.uk

Seasonal

PONT NEDD

Fechan
Nr Glynneath
SA11 5NR

Tel : 01639 721795
Fax: 01639 722061
e-mail: pontneddfechan-tic@tsww.com

Seasonal

PORTHMADOG

Y Ganolfan, High Street
Porthmadog
LL49 9LD

Tel : 01766 512981
Fax: 01766 515312
e-mail: porthmadog.tic@gwynedd.gov.uk

PRESTATYN

Offa's Dyke Centre
Central Beach
Prestatyn
LL19 7EY

Tel : 01745 889092

Seasonal

PRESTEIGNE

The Judge's Lodging
Broad Street
Presteigne
LD8 2AD

Tel : 01544 260650
Fax: 01544 260652

Seasonal

PWLLHELI

Min y Don
Station Square
Pwllheli
LL53 5HG

Tel : 01758 613000
Fax: 01758 701651
e-mail: pwllheli.tic@gwynedd.gov.uk

RHAYADER

The Leisure Centre
North Street
Rhayader
LD6 5BU

Tel : 01597 810591
e-mail: rhayader.tic@powys.gov.uk

RHOS ON SEA

The Promenade
Rhos on Sea
LL28 4EP

Tel : 01492 548778
Fax: 01492 548778

Seasonal

RHYL

Rhyl Childrens Village
West Parade
Rhyl
LL18 1HZ

Tel : 01745 355068
Fax: 01745 342255

RUTHIN

Ruthin Craft Centre
Park Road
Ruthin
LL15 1BB

Tel : 01824 703992

ST DAVIDS

National Park Visitor Centre
The Grove
St Davids
SA62 6NW

Tel : 01437 720392
Fax: 01437 720099
e-mail:
enquiries@stdavids.pembrokeshirecoast.org.uk

SWANSEA

Plymouth Street
Swansea
SA1 3QG

Tel : 01792 468321
Fax: 01792 464602
e-mail: tourism@swansea.gov.uk

TYWYN

High Street
Tywyn
LL36 9AD

Tel : 01654 710070
Fax: 01654 710070
e-mail: tywyn.tic@gwynedd.gov.uk

Seasonal

WELSHPOOL

Vicarage Garden
Church Street
Welshpool
SY21 7DD

Tel : 01938 552043
Fax: 01938 554038
e-mail: weltic@powys.gov.uk

WREXHAM

Lambpit Street
Wrexham
LL11 1WN

Tel : 01978 292015
Fax: 01978 292467
e-mail: tic@wrexham.gov.uk

INDEX OF ADVERTISERS

INDEX OF WALKS

Jarrold
Pathfinder Guides

- Ordnance Survey mapping

- 28 walk routes, graded easy, moderate and challenging

- Introduces you to the area and highlights the most scenic routes

- Details useful organisations, refreshment stops and places to leave your car

- Series covers all of the UK

Take the fuss out of planning a walk!

Available at tourist outlets, bookshops and specialist walking outlets

Jarrold
Short Walks

- 20 easy-to-follow walks for the whole family
- Ordnance Survey mapping and colour photography
- Handy pocket-sized format
- Points of interest for children
- Information on refreshment stops, public facilities and transport

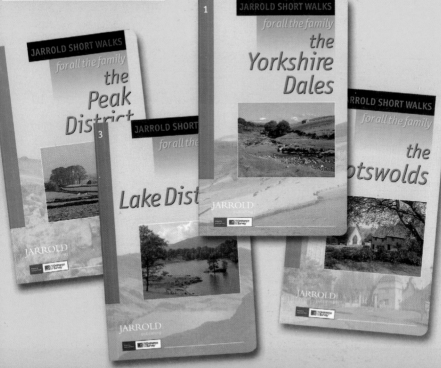

Travel Publishing

The Hidden Places

Regional and National guides to the less well-known places of interest and places to eat, stay and drink

Regional guides to traditional pubs and inns throughout the United Kingdom

Regional and National guides to 18 hole golf courses and local places to stay, eat and drink

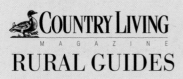
RURAL GUIDES

Regional and National guides to the traditional countryside of Britain and Ireland with easy to read facts on places to visit, stay, eat, drink and shop

For more information:

Phone: 0118 981 7777   **Fax:** 0118 982 0077
e-mail: travel_publishing@msn.com   **website:** www.travelpublishing.co.uk

ORDER FORM

To order any of our publications just fill in the payment details below and complete the order form. For orders of less than 4 copies please add £1 per book for postage and packing. Orders over 4 copies are P & P free.

Please Complete Either:

I enclose a cheque for £ [   ] made payable to Travel Publishing Ltd

Or:

Card No: [   ]   Expiry Date: [   ]

Signature: [   ]

NAME: [   ]

ADDRESS: [   ]

TEL NO: [   ]

Please either send, telephone, fax or e-mail your order to:
Travel Publishing Ltd, 7a Apollo House, Calleva Park, Aldermaston, Berkshire RG7 8TN
Tel: 0118 981 7777   Fax: 0118 982 0077 e-mail: karen@travelpublishing.co.uk

	Price	Quantity		Price	Quantity
Hidden Places Regional Titles			**Hidden Inns Titles**		
Cambs & Lincolnshire	£7.99	....	East Anglia	£5.99	....
Chilterns	£8.99	....	Heart of England	£5.99	....
Cornwall	£8.99	....	Lancashire & Cheshire	£5.99	....
Derbyshire	£7.99	....	North of England	£5.99	....
Devon	£8.99	....	South	£5.99	....
Dorset, Hants & Isle of Wight	£8.99	....	South East	£5.99	....
East Anglia	£8.99	....	South and Central Scotland	£5.99	....
Gloucs, Wiltshire & Somerset	£8.99	....	Wales	£5.99	....
Heart of England	£7.99	....	Welsh Borders	£5.99	....
Hereford, Worcs & Shropshire	£7.99	....	West Country	£5.99	....
Highlands & Islands	£7.99	....	**Country Living Rural Guides**		
Kent	£8.99	....			
Lake District & Cumbria	£8.99	....	East Anglia	£9.99	....
Lancashire & Cheshire	£8.99	....	Heart of England	£9.99	....
Lincolnshire & Nottinghamshire	£8.99	....	Ireland	£10.99	....
Northumberland & Durham	£8.99	....	Scotland	£10.99	....
Somerset	£7.99	....	South of England	£9.99	....
Sussex	£7.99	....	South East of England	£9.99	....
Thames Valley	£7.99	....	Wales	£10.99	....
Yorkshire	£8.99	....	West Country	£9.99	....
Hidden Places National Titles					
England	£10.99	....			
Ireland	£10.99	....	**Total Quantity**	[ ]	
Scotland	£10.99	....			
Wales	£9.99	....	**Total Value**	[ ]	

READER REACTION FORM

The *Travel Publishing* research team would like to receive reader's comments on any visitor attractions or places reviewed in the book and also recommendations for suitable entries to be included in the next edition. This will help ensure that the *Country Living series of Rural Guides* continues to provide its readers with useful information on the more interesting, unusual or unique features of each attraction or place ensuring that their visit to the local area is an enjoyable and stimulating experience. To provide your comments or recommendations would you please complete the forms below and overleaf as indicated and send to:

The Research Department, Travel Publishing Ltd,

7a Apollo House, Calleva Park, Aldermaston, Reading, RG7 8TN.

Your Name:

Your Address:

Your Telephone Number:

Please tick as appropriate: Comments ☐ Recommendation ☐

Name of Establishment:

Address:

Telephone Number:

Name of Contact:

READER REACTION FORM

Comment or Reason for Recommendation:

....

....

....

....

....

....

....

....

....

....

....

READER REACTION FORM

The *Travel Publishing* research team would like to receive reader's comments on any visitor attractions or places reviewed in the book and also recommendations for suitable entries to be included in the next edition. This will help ensure that the *Country Living series of Rural Guides* continues to provide its readers with useful information on the more interesting, unusual or unique features of each attraction or place ensuring that their visit to the local area is an enjoyable and stimulating experience. To provide your comments or recommendations would you please complete the forms below and overleaf as indicated and send to:

The Research Department, Travel Publishing Ltd,

7a Apollo House, Calleva Park, Aldermaston, Reading, RG7 8TN.

Your Name:

Your Address:

Your Telephone Number:

Please tick as appropriate: Comments ☐ Recommendation ☐

Name of Establishment:

Address:

Telephone Number:

Name of Contact:

READER REACTION FORM

Comment or Reason for Recommendation:

....

....

....

....

....

....

....

....

....

....

INDEX TO TOWNS & PLACES OF INTEREST